The Governance of Global Competition

The Governance of Global Competition

Competence Allocation in International Competition Policy

Oliver Budzinski

Associate Professor of Economics, Philipps-University of Marburg, Germany

Edward Elgar

Cheltenham, UK • Northampton, MA, USA

Published by
Edward Elgar Publishing Limited
Glensanda House
Montpellier Parade
Cheltenham
Glos GL50 1UA
UK

Edward Elgar Publishing, Inc.
William Pratt House
9 Dewey Court
Northampton
Massachusetts 01060
USA

A catalogue record for this book
is available from the British Library

Library of Congress Cataloging in Publication Data
Budzinski, Oliver, 1970–
The governance of global competition : competence allocation in international competition policy / by Oliver Budzinski.
p. cm.
Includes bibliographical references and index.
1. Competition, International. 2. International economic relations. 3. Antitrust law—Economic aspects. I. Title.

HF1414.B83 2008
382′.3—dc22 2007039432

ISBN 978 1 84720 630 5

Typeset by Cambrian Typesetters, Camberley, Surrey
Printed and bound in Great Britain by MPG Books Ltd, Bodmin, Cornwall

Contents

Figures

Tables

Abbreviations

AMC	Antitrust Modernization Commission
DIAC	Draft International Antitrust Code
ECJ	European Court of Justice
ECMR	European Community Merger Regulation
ECN	European Competition Network
ECSC	European Coal and Steel Community
EU	European Union
FCC	Federal Communication Commission
FDI	foreign direct investment
FERC	Federal Energy Regulatory Commission
FTC	Federal Trade Commission
GATT	General Agreement on Tariffs and Trade
GCI	Global Competition Initiative
ICN	International Competition Network
ICP	International Competition Panel
ICPAC	International Competition Policy Advisory Committee
IMF	International Monetary Fund
ITO	International Trade Organization
NAAG	National Association of Attorneys General
NAAT	not appreciably affecting trade
NCA	National competition Authority
PD	Prisoners' Dilemma
R&D	research and development
SEC	Securities and Exchange Commission
SIEC	substantial impediment of effective competition
SLC	substantial lessening of competition
UEMOA	Union Economique et Monétaire Ouest Africaine
UN	United Nations
UNCTAD	United Nations Conference on Trade and Development
WBG	World Bank Group
WG	WTO Working Group on the Interaction of Trade and Competition
WGDP	world gross domestic product
WTO	World Trade Organization

Foreword

This monograph was accepted as an habilitation thesis by the Department of Economics of the Philipps-University of Marburg. It presents the results of a refereed scientific research project funded by the Volkswagen Foundation within its Priority Area 'Global Structures and Governance'. I am very grateful for the noble financial support of the Volkswagen Foundation between October 2001 and February 2005. Additional research was financially supported by the FAZIT Foundation between March and August 2005. Without the generous and non-partisan support of these two scientific foundations, this book would not have been possible.

During my research at the Philipps-University of Marburg and the New York University, Professors Eleanor M. Fox, Lars P. Feld, Harry First and, in particular, Wolfgang Kerber supervised the project and injected important ideas and valuable comments. I am very grateful for their continuous support and perpetual willingness for helpful discussions. Their input has clearly influenced this book! I am particularly indebted to Wolfgang Kerber and Lars P. Feld who willingly took the burden to act as referees during the habilitation procedure.

My deep thanks go to all my colleagues at Wolfgang Kerber's Chair of Economic Policy at the Philipps-University of Marburg during these years, who created a great atmosphere and constituted a wonderful team to work with. Many thanks to my scientific colleagues Friedrich Gröteke, Klaus Heine, Gisela Linge (thank you also for your editorial assistance!), Karsten Mause, Claudia Schmidt and, in particular, Arndt Christiansen with whom I intensively discussed several parts of the manuscript. Also many thanks to Annette Heberle and to all the student assistants, in particular Thomas Augsten, who worked with me on the project between 2002 and 2004, Margot Lörcher, Katharina Schlake and Christian Steuer. Furthermore, I am deeply indebted to Barbara Güldenring (Bachelor of Arts in English Language and Literature Studies, Messiah College, Grantham, PA, United States) for continuous and extremely valuable editorial assistance.

Parts of this book have been presented to several conferences around the world. I am very grateful to all discussants and participants who critically reviewed my ideas and, thus, helped me to improve them. I am also grateful for valuable comments by an anonymous referee in the course of the Elgar review procedure.

Finally, neither the research project nor this book could have been done without the support of my wife, Daniela Budzinski. I definitely did not spend enough time with you, my love, during recent years! And thank you for your editorial assistance with tables, figures, and so on.

Oliver Budzinski

1. Introduction

The governance of global competition represents a highly topical issue. It is connected to the more general debate about globalisation although, in times like these, an ubiquitous meaning is ascribed to this term. Depending on one's perspective, globalisation either fuels a beneficial process towards more world welfare or destroys local welfare and social relations. Concerning economic policy, however, globalisation is often discussed in terms of the loss of national and regional governance capacity. This book addresses the effects of globalisation on the governance of a particular field of economic policy: competition policy. The globalisation of markets and competition belongs to the major trends within the more general phenomenon of overall globalisation. According to consensual economic insight, competitive markets generally represent the best available coordination mechanism for economic activities. More precisely, workable competitive markets contribute to optimal allocation, innovation dynamics, consumer sovereignty, economic freedom, and flexibility and responsiveness of the economy. In doing so, material welfare becomes maximised compared to other available coordination mechanisms. In this context, the international spread of competitive markets implies a higher welfare potential for the world economy. Or, in other words, the advantages of market economy and the division of labour do not cease at historically and politically defined borders.

However, competitive markets need an accompanying governance in order to prevent the self-destruction of competition. Competition puts pressure on the participating actors, in particular on enterprises, and it is this pressure which is predominantly responsible for the efficiency and welfare gains due to competitive markets. The market participants are forced to search continuously for and create superior solutions to economic problems. However, there exists an alternative strategy to respond to competitive pressure. Instead of improving one's own performance in competition, the market participants can attempt to protect themselves against the forces of competition, for example, by building coalitions between competitors, by monopolisation or by other anticompetitive arrangements and practices. If market participants engage in such anticompetitive strategies, overall welfare losses result, with consumers and non-participating competitors particularly suffering. Moreover, companies, which are protected from the disciplining forces of competition, become powerful in economic and non-economic terms – to the disadvantage of society. Therefore, any market economy requires a competition policy, which prevents market competition from self-destruction.[1]

Historically, this competition policy was – and to a significant extent still is – located at the nation-state level. For a considerable time in modern history, this coincided with public protective instruments, which artificially (and incompletely/imperfectly) separated markets according to national borders. However, due to the lowering of trade barriers and technological developments, markets and competition have become more and more internationalised in the last few decades and this development is likely to continue. This creates the core problem with which this book deals: what are the adequate governance structures to protect competition in international and global markets?

Imaginable solutions for the problem of the governance of global competition embrace a broad field and a lively academic discussion, covering, at one extreme 'national competition policies suffice to provide an effective governance of global competition' (radical decentralism), to the other extreme of 'a centralised global authority, enforcing original global laws is necessary to govern global competition' (radical centralism). In between, a large number of – more or less complex – intermediate solutions can be constructed and discussed. I argue in this book that these intermediate solutions between decentralism and centralism are particularly worth analysing. The pivotal goal of this study is twofold:

- I provide a theoretical framework, based on economic theory, for analysing complex institutional governance arrangements between centralism and decentralism. It consists of a theory of competence allocation in multilevel systems of institutions. This analytical framework serves to derive the conclusions of this study in regard to the international competition policy system. However, it furthermore represents a general economic framework, which can be applied to any field in which complex institutional arrangements between centralism and decentralism are necessary for adequate governance structures.
- I suggest a design of an international multilevel competition policy system, which represents an example of an adequate governance of global competition from a broad economic point of view, that is, the integrative consideration of different approaches of economics, basic legal implications, and related political insights.[2]

---

1 However, in the economic literature, a number of different opinions on the adequate design of competition policy exist. See, for example, Budzinski (2007) and Kerber and Schwalbe (2007).

2 Competition policy represents an inherently interdisciplinary task including (at the least) economics, legal sciences and politics.

Each of the two interrelated aspects departs from the existing literature, which lacks a systematic and analytical approach towards complex institutional arrangements for international competition policy (although examples of such arrangements are frequently designed and discussed). Consequently, my design suggestion is different from the existing concepts with regard to several elements. The following paragraphs present the structure of the study and report the respective basic results.

CHAPTER 2: GLOBALISATION OF COMPETITION AND BUSINESS STRUCTURES

The analysis begins with a description of the environment in which international competition policy takes place. In doing so, section 1 of Chapter 2, 'The internationalisation of business activity and competitive markets' describes how business has expanded into the international sphere and, thus, both driven and responded to the globalisation of markets. As the driving forces of this development: (1) the market-enhancing and competition-intensifying role of liberalisation of foreign trade and deregulation of services and network industries, as well as (2) innovations in communication and transportation technologies are identified.

As a consequence, business patterns have, accordingly, evolved towards new forms of interfirm arrangements (often informal in character) and international corporate structures (for example, through M&A strategies). More often than not, they represent (pro-)competitive responses to the evolution of the business environment. However, with the globalisation of business behaviour, the occurrence of anticompetitive strategies has also expanded to the global level. Section 2 of Chapter 2, 'The corresponding globalisation of anticompetitive practices and structures', describes in terms of aggregate numbers, anecdotal evidence, and outstanding examples, how international cartels (section 2.1), abuse of global market power including unfair and predatory strategies (section 2.2), and cross-border mergers (section 2.3) are playing an increasing role in international competition.

CHAPTER 3: INTERNATIONAL COMPETITION POLICY BETWEEN DECENTRALISM AND CENTRALISM

After Chapter 2 has demonstrated that cross-border anticompetitive practices empirically do represent a virulent problem, Chapter 3 analyses why neither purely national competition policy (radical decentralism), nor monolithic global competition policy (radical centralism) represents a sufficient solution.

Section 1 of Chapter 3, 'The limits of national competition policy regimes in globalised markets', addresses the first part of the problem – the limits of radical decentralism. National competition policy regimes cannot provide sufficient protection for competition in internationalising markets and, moreover, generate frictions themselves. This assessment rests on a number of aspects:

- The procompetitive forces of trade liberalisation do not represent a complete substitute for an international competition policy (section 1.1). Instead, an internationally effective competition policy regime is necessary to permanently secure the advantages of trade liberalisation. Otherwise, public restrictions of competition (trade barriers) become substituted by private restrictions of competition (cartels, incontestable monopolies, and so on). This insight advocates the necessity of an international regime.
- National competition policy regimes must rely on extraterritorial antitrust enforcement in order to cope with inbound anticompetitive arrangements and practices from abroad (or with participants from abroad). Although regimes with important domestic markets can exercise non-negligible power on foreign enterprises, extraterritorial competition policy enforcement entails considerable loopholes, generates jurisdictional conflicts, and produces significant inefficiencies due to multiple procedures (section 1.2). An important reason for these deficiencies is the inability of national regimes to tackle competition concerns in international markets directly and with a view to world welfare. Instead, these regimes are forced to take an inbound view of domestic competitive impact only. Competitive concerns of global markets enter the national jurisdictional sphere only if they also affect the national sub-segments of the affected markets. Consequently, only the inbound-related features of comprehensive international anticompetitive arrangements and practices are addressed, ignoring outside and outbound effects.
- Moreover, national competition policy regimes may develop an interest in profitably restricting international competition at the expense of foreign countries. With such strategic competition policies (section 1.3), national regimes actively distort and deter global competition instead of protecting it.

However, as section 2 of Chapter 3, 'The limits of a uniform worldwide competition policy regime', argues, the complete transfer of competition policy competences to supranational authorities, enforcing supranational laws, is also insufficient. The main problems are:

- national sovereignty (section 2.1);
- public choice problems of centralised governance (section 2.2); and
- the overall adequacy of centralised supranational governance as a replacement for national competition policies in the face of the onward co-existence of regional/local and international markets (section 2.3).

Section 3 of Chapter 3 discusses the prospects of having a 'competition of competition policy regimes'. However, a second-order competitive solution – detecting rules for competitive markets by institutional competition – experiences severe limitations if one undertakes an innovative, differentiated analysis. Although 'competitive antitrust' does not represent an overall solution, it entails elements that can play useful roles in an international competition policy system – namely, a variant of yardstick or benchmark competition.

Thus, neither radical decentralism nor radical centralism provides sufficient or adequate solutions to the governance problem of global competition. Consequently, section 4 of Chapter 3, 'Concluding remarks: competence allocation as a problem', calls for a differentiated analysis and promotes more complex 'intermediate' institutional arrangements, which combine the advantages of decentralism and centralism.

CHAPTER 4: TOWARDS AN INTERNATIONAL MULTILEVEL SYSTEM OF COMPETITION POLICIES

Chapter 4 develops the theoretical framework for the analysis of complex institutional arrangements, creating and shaping an international competition policy system between centralism and decentralism. In doing so, section 1 of Chapter 4, 'The concept of multilevel systems of institutions – general idea and working properties', presents a theory of competence allocation in multilevel systems of institutions. It consists of ingredients from modern governance theories (section 1.1), the general theory of institutional multilevel systems (interrelated governance on global, national, local, and so on, levels), and the economics of federalism (section 1.2). In multilevel systems of institutions, the allocation and delimitation of competences both within a governance level (horizontal allocation) and between governance levels (vertical allocation) become decisive for the overall performance of the system. The economics of federalism plays an important role because it provides criteria for the centralisation or decentralisation of government competences. Reformulating and re-interpreting these criteria in the specific context of competition policy allow for an economic analysis of competence allocation and its effects in a multilevel system of competition policies (section 1.3). The relevant categories are:

- externalities and spillovers;
- efficiencies in terms of production, transaction, and administrative costs;
- preference orientation;
- agency problems and lobbyism; and
- institutional evolution and adaptability.

This theory-driven analysis subsequently allows for the derivation of a number of evaluation criteria with which different competence allocations can be comparatively assessed regarding the resulting economic performance of the overall system (section 1.4).

Having made this claim, the capacity of the presented analytical framework is outlined by analysing existing multilevel systems of competition policies from that perspective (section 2 of Chapter 4; 'Existing multilevel competition policy regimes – an analytical overview'). The relevant examples include 'The US antitrust system: ongoing discussion about federalism?' (section 2.1), 'The EU competition policy system and its reform dynamics' (section 2.2), 'The WTO competition regime: creating an additional level of antitrust jurisdiction?' (section 2.3), 'The international competition network: a virtual global level?' (section 2.4). All of these regimes are analysed along similar lines. First, the respective regimes are described in the language of multilevel systems. Secondly, the state of competence allocation and delimitation is identified. Thirdly, the previous evolution, current problems, and future challenges of competence allocation within those systems are analysed. The common result, explored in 'Concluding Remarks' (section 3 of Chapter 4), is that competence allocation problems are at the heart of these acting and emerging multilevel competition policy systems. An analytical approach towards these problems, therefore, benefits the related discussions and reform debates.

CHAPTER 5: A COMPARATIVE ANALYSIS OF DIFFERENT RULES FOR THE ALLOCATION AND DELIMITATION OF COMPETENCES

Real-world competition policy regimes always consist of a more or less complex mixture of institutions. In order to identify which concrete institutions are responsible for the success or failure of an antitrust regime, a disaggregated approach is necessary. Thereby, a systematic analysis of the responsible system elements, which determine competence allocation and delimitation, becomes possible and subsequently enables a more differentiated line of argument about an adequate design of an international competition policy system. Chapter 5 contributes to this task by identifying 'stylised competence allocation rules' and comparatively analysing them according to the theoretical framework developed in Chapter 4.

Section 1 of Chapter 5, 'Design options for rules for the allocation of competences', presents and defines a selection of stylised competence allocation rules. This section is split into institutional solutions stemming from existing antitrust regimes (section 1.1) and those that are additionally suggested by the academic literature (section 1.2). Since the options available for constructed competence allocation rules are infinite, this selection cannot be complete. However, it includes both the most important practical solutions and their prominent academic alternatives. In particular, the following stylised rules for the allocation and delimitation of competences are analysed:

- effects doctrine;
- turnover thresholds;
- nondiscrimination rule;
- best practice recommendations and peer pressure;
- location doctrine;
- relevant markets rule;
- X-plus rule;
- voluntary lead jurisdiction (advanced comity principle); and
- mandatory lead jurisdiction.

In section 2 of Chapter 5, 'An institutional-economic analysis of competence-allocating rules', the actual analysis of these institutional solutions according to the derived criteria is exercised. The results are comparatively concluded in section 3 of Chapter 5 ('A comparative conclusion'). Comparatively superior performances can be expected from the mandatory lead jurisdiction model, which performs particularly well regarding efficiency and adaptability, and the nondiscrimination rule, which shows specific advantages regarding lobbyism control as well as preference conformity and adaptability. A combination of these two rules is particularly promising because, on the one hand, they complement each other well (apart from room for improvement regarding externalities) and, on the other hand, all the other analysed rules perform significantly worse. For instance, the X-plus rule has a significant weak point regarding preference conformity, the relevant markets rule regarding efficiency, and both the location doctrine and the effects doctrine regarding externalities, efficiency and lobbyism.

CHAPTER 6: ON THE APPROPRIATE DESIGN OF AN INTERNATIONAL MULTILEVEL SYSTEM OF COMPETITION POLICIES

Chapter 6, the final chapter, presents the policy conclusions. After reintroducing 'Elementary features of an international multilevel system of competition policies' (section 1 of Chapter 6), the relatively superior competence allocation rules from the preceding analysis, mandatory lead jurisdiction model and nondiscrimination rule are scrutinised regarding their combination potentials as well as concerning amendments to the stylised variants that further improve their performance (section 2 of Chapter 6, 'The fundamental principles of competence allocation'). Against this background, section 3 of Chapter 6, 'The levels and their interrelations', presents a design example of an international multilevel system of competition policies that, as expected, fulfils the economic requirements outlined in the submitted study. The following is a very brief overview of the main results.

In this concept, the global level (section 3.1) is responsible for appointing a lead jurisdiction for a given cross-border competition case. It selects lead jurisdictions according the following criteria: (1) regional gravity of the aggregate turnover of the participating enterprises; (2) the absence of discriminatory provisions in the potentially competent competition policy regime; and (3) willingness and experience of the potentially competent antitrust authorities to employ a world welfare standard. Furthermore, the global level is competent to supervise the competition rules of the potentially competent jurisdictions in regard to discriminating provisions and practices. Thirdly, the global level deals with complaints from other jurisdictions about the appointed lead jurisdiction. However, the global level does not possess substantive competition rules and does not decide antitrust cases itself. It 'merely' has jurisdictional and supervision competences.

The national level as well as existing regionally limited supranational regimes, like the European Union (EU), is the place where concrete antitrust cases with cross-border effects are decided (sections 3.2 and 3.3). The competition policy regimes at these levels can qualify for lead jurisdiction and, then, are responsible for reviewing and deciding a given case in view of the interests of all affected countries. Additionally, these regimes stay autonomous regarding purely domestic cases. There remains scope for subnational competition policy (section 3.4) since specific markets will remain localised.

The suggested concept combines the advantages of decentralism and centralism. It presents a regime in which decentralised substantive competences are complemented by centralised jurisdictional competences – supplemented by supervision and revision elements. Thereby, the advantages of decentralised governance (flexibility, preference orientation, marketability, and so on) can be realised without suffering from its major disadvantage regarding international antitrust: the incoherence of the overall system and the resulting negative efficiency implications, as well as loopholes in the protection of competition.

Finally, section 4 of Chapter 6, 'Concluding remarks', presents the overall conclusion of the book. It summarises the main goals and the respective results. After this introductory overview, Chapter 2 starts with the actual analysis.

2. Globalisation of competition and business structures

1. THE INTERNATIONALISATION OF BUSINESS ACTIVITY AND COMPETITIVE MARKETS

In the context of this book, only the economic dimension of the otherwise (ostensibly) ubiquitous process commonly called 'globalisation' is of interest. Speaking very generally, economic globalisation means the integration of formerly separated markets across national borders. Thus, the emergence of international and global markets is addressed. Although it does not represent an inevitable ingredient of globalisation as such, more often than not an increasing speed of the globalisation of markets and economic activities is also connected.

Globalisation in terms of worldwide economic integration is not a unique phenomenon of the last few decades. There have been eras of economic internationalisation and globalisation before, for instance through the period of the Gold Standard from the 1880s until the outbreak of the First World War. However, what is in the focus of this book is the process of international economic integration in the last two or three decades. It seems to be beyond controversy that an internationalisation of economic activities has occurred in these times. Therefore, or nonetheless, it suffices to point towards the development of few particularly important economic figures, namely the development of foreign direct investment (FDI), which include both greenfield investments and mergers and acquisitions, and the development of trade flows (here: exports of goods), compared to the development of overall economic activity (world gross domestic product (WGDP)) (Klodt 2005: 9–15). Table 2.1 shows that international trade and, in particular, FDI have grown at higher rates than the WGDP. Obviously, this can be interpreted as evidence of an increasing weight of cross-border economic activities.

The modern process of market globalisation is predominantly driven by two factors.[1]

[1] There is a huge amount of literature on the causes and the extent of economic globalisation. See, for example, Dunning (1997), Stierle (1999), Erb et al. (2000: 13–34), Budzinski and Kerber (2003), Klodt (2005), Voigt and Schmidt (2005: 39–51), and the chapters in Weinstein (2005).

Table 2.1 Indicators of the globalisation of the world economy

	1982	1990	2000	2003
World gross domestic product (billion US$)	10 805	21 672	31 895	36 214
1982 = 100	100	201	295	335
Export of goods and services (billion US$)	2 053	4 300	7 036	8 025*
1982 = 100	100	209	343	391*
FDI (capital outflows, billion US$)	28	242	1150	611
1982 = 100	100	864	4 107	2 182

Notes:
* 2002
All data in standardised real terms.

Source: Klodt (2005: 10), expanded with data from www.unctad.org.

- Liberalisation and deregulation: the liberalisation of trade in goods and services in the context of the General Agreement on Tariffs and Trade (GATT, leading into the creation of the World Trade Organization (WTO) in 1995), which eroded the largest part of the harmful and protectionist practices of most countries in order to protect national industries and their supracompetitive profits against foreign competitors. The liberalisation of foreign trade was reinforced by internal deregulation in many countries. Since the 1980s, a number of traditionally regulated industries – like energy, transportation, postal services, banking, insurance, and so on – have been deregulated in many countries in order to create consumer surplus through breaking up the sclerotic and deficient structures, which had developed as a consequence of overregulation. The liberalisation and deregulation of capital and money flows is likely to represent the most important factor.
- Technology and innovation: innovative information and transportation technologies have significantly reduced the costs of both financial transfers and export–import activities (in goods and services) while, simultaneously, increasing their speed (see Table 2.2). In this context, computer technology and the Internet belong to the most important innovations.

These two driving forces of economic globalisation have often interacted in order to reinforce each other. For instance, the liberalisation of financial capital flows worked together with the development of a technology that allows

Table 2.2 Development of transport and communication costs

Year	Ocean freight (1920 = 100)	Average air transportation revenue per passenger mile (in 1990 US$)	Cost of a 3-minute telephone call, New York–London (in 2000 US$)	Price of computers (relative to GDP deflator; 2000 = 1000)
1920	100			
1930	65	0.68		
1940	67	0.46		
1950	38	0.30		
1960	28	0.24	60.42	1 869 004
1970	29	0.16	41.61	199 983
1980	25	0.10	6.32	27 938
1990	30	0.11	4.37	7 275
2000			0.40	1 000

Source: Masson (2001: 5–6)

the transfer of money around the world in seconds by a mouse click. Similarly, the new transportation technologies developed their force only subsequent to the liberalisation and deregulation of postal services in many countries.

However, these trends in liberalisation and deregulation do not completely cover the world economy. Nations that adhere to concepts of economic order and organisation other than concepts of competitive market economies usually do not participate in the integration process. Although non-market economies have become the exception in the aftermath of the end of the Cold War and the breakdown of the Soviet Union, some still exist (for example, Cuba, North Korea) and others are only on their way towards stable market economies.[2] Nevertheless, 'non-developing developing countries' currently seem to represent the more important phenomenon. These countries often do not possess adequate internal institutions to allow them a beneficial participation in international economic interrelations. Africa, for instance, currently represents the least globalised continent. In summary, it may be somewhat more adequate to use the term 'internationalisation' instead of globalisation. However, since globalisation has become the common denominator for these processes, this term is synonymously employed in this book.

2 Note, for example, that China has introduced comprehensive features of a market economy almost exclusively in specific (and comparatively small) areas of its territory, leaving the large rest of the country under socialist economic structures.

Internationalisation and globalisation of markets do not imply that each market becomes an international one in the course of time. Within traditional countries, a coexistence of national and more regional or local markets can be observed, depending – among other things – on the characteristics of the respective goods and services as well as on the preferences of consumers. It is difficult to identify reasons why this would be different even in a fully integrated world economy.

Regarding competition, globalisation along the lines of liberalisation and internationalisation of markets represents a generally procompetitive process. A market enlargement effect occurs, which intensifies competition in that market because new competitors emerge. This is particularly beneficial if the formerly national market was characterised by an anticompetitive situation. Both an industry-wide cartel or a market dominating enterprise regarding the national dimension become challenged by outside competition if the market internationalises. Along this avenue, sclerotic market structures and powerful national monopolies can be turned into competitive markets again.

The market enlargement effect implies a changing situation for incumbent enterprises. They face new challenges and chances and, hence, are driven by globalisation and driving forces of globalisation at the same time. On one hand, enterprises lose the market positions, which they have achieved on national markets, because their importance threatens to diminish in a larger market. What has been a market leader in the national context may well become a small competitor on a worldwide scale. On the other hand, the globalisation of markets offers opportunities for enterprises to internationalise their activities and, thereby, improve their business and their (competitive) profits.[3]

Irrespective of its defensive (regain incumbent market positions) or offensive (gain new market positions) character, the internationalisation of business activities represents a logical and inevitable response to globalisation – and reinforces it. Enterprises adjust their strategies according to the larger geographical reach of their activities, competing with enterprises from other countries in similar situations. Along with the procompetitive modes of business behaviour and interfirm arrangements and alliances, which now also reach an international dimension, the internationalisation of business activities also entails potentially anticompetitive arrangements and practices. The following section explores these issues because they represent a challenge for the governance of competition. Nevertheless, it must be emphasised that the internationalisation of business activities generates procompetitive effects in the first place.

[3] See on business responses to globalisation also Safarian (1997), Weizsäcker (1998), Erb et al. (2000: 34–59), and García-Canal et al. (2002).

2. THE CORRESPONDING GLOBALISATION OF ANTICOMPETITIVE PRACTICES AND STRUCTURES

If the internationalisation of markets creates additional competitive pressure, then business strategies to escape this pressure and gain protection from competitive forces are as likely as procompetitive responses. Consequently, it should be no surprise that all kinds of anticompetitive business arrangements and practices can be observed in international markets. Furthermore, the occurrence of international: (1) cartels and surrogates; (2) predatory practices; and (3) mergers have become more frequent during the last two decades.

2.1 Anticompetitive Arrangements

The problem of international cartels, which had been widespread in the nineteenth as well as in the first part of the twentieth century, diminished following the spreading of anticartel laws and policies around the major trading nations in the aftermath of the Second World War.[4] Cross-border cartels and cartel surrogates became rare exceptions until they reappeared in the course of market globalisation. For instance, the 1990s were characterised by a significant increase in the number and anticompetitive impact of international cartels. Empirical studies identify more than 150 international cartels from 1990 to 2003,[5] among them about 40 cross-border hardcore cartels[6] with private enterprises from more than 30 nations involved (see Table 2.3). Moreover, price-fixing has become the most frequent type of arrangement and, hence, the type of cartel, which generates the most severe harm to consumers, has developed to be the dominating one in the international sphere. In the late 1990s, over 90 per cent of the overall criminal fines collected by US antitrust authorities derived from the prosecution of international cartels.[7] Obviously, there is an additional number of unknown cases, which is difficult to estimate.

[4] See on the history of cartelisation and anticartel policy, Schröter (1996), Gerber (1998a), Peritz (2000), and Wells (2002).

[5] Note that the interwar period between the First and Second World Wars entailed about 179 international cartels (Connor 2004: 242). This means that in terms of international cartels the almost 15 years since 1990 match the two interwar decades, which are sometimes called the time of cartelisation. Moreover, the number of unknown cases should be smaller regarding the historical period compared to nowadays because: (1) cartel prosecution has intensified since then, and (2) knowledge about illegal arrangements in the past (when they were not illegal throughout the trading nations) should generally be more comprehensive than knowledge about ongoing ones.

[6] According to the OECD (2002), hardcore cartels include price-fixing, output- and quota-cartels, market division arrangements, and boycott cartels.

[7] See on the whole paragraph, ICPAC (2000: 171), Tarullo (2000), Evenett et al. (2001), Hüschelrath (2002), Levenstein and Suslow (2002, 2004), OECD (2002), and Connor (2004).

Table 2.3 Recent international hardcore cartels: an exemplary overview

Industry	Time	Country of origin of indicted firms
Aluminium phosphide	Jan 1990–Nov 1990	Brazil, Germany, India, US
Beer	1993–1998	Belgium, France
Bromine products	Jul 1995–Apr 1998	Israel, US
Cable-stayed bridges	Sep 1996–Dec 1997	France, US
Carbon cathode block	Feb 1996–Dec 1997	Germany, Japan, US
Carbonless paper	1992–1995	France, Germany, Spain, South Africa, UK
Cartonboard	1986–1991	Austria, Canada, Finland, France, Germany, Italy, Netherlands, Norway, Spain, Sweden, UK, US
Cement	1983–Aug 1994	33 European firms, eight national cement trade associations, and the European Cement Association
Citric acid	1991–1995	Austria, France, Germany, Netherlands, Switzerland, US
Explosives	1988–1992	Norway, UK, US
Ferrosilicon	Oct 1989–Jun 1991	Germany, Norway, US
Ferry operators (Adriatic Sea)	1987–1994	Greece, Italy
Ferry operators (cross-Channel freight)	Oct 1992–Dec 1992	France, Netherlands, Sweden, UK
Fine arts	Apr 1993–Dec 1999	UK, US
Graphite electrodes	Jul 1992–Jun 1997	Germany, Japan, US
Isostatic graphite	Jul 1993–Feb 1998	Japan, US
Laminated plastic tubes	1987–1996	Switzerland, US
Lysine	Jun 1992–Jun 1995	Germany, Japan, South Korea, US
Maltol	Dec 1989–Dec 1995	US plus unnamed firms
Marine construction services (heavy-lift)	1993–1997	Netherlands, US
Marine transportation services (heavy-lift)	1990–1995	Belgium, US
Monochloroacetic acid	Sep 1995–Aug 1999	France, Germany, Netherlands
Nucleotides	Jul 1992–Aug 1996	Japan, South Korea
Organic peroxides	1997–1998	France, Netherlands, Spain, UK
Plastic dinnerware	Nov 1991–Apr 1992	Canada, US
Shipping (Central West Africa)	1972–1992	Zaire, Angola, Northern Part of Continental Europe

(*continued*)

Table 2.3 continued

Industry	Time	Country of origin of indicted firms
Shipping (Far East)	1991–1994	30 countries
Shipping (French-African)	1975–1992	12 countries
Shipping (North-Atlantic)	1994–1996	11 countries (including Poland)
Sodium erythorbate	Jul 1992–Dec 1994	US plus unnamed firms
Sodium gluconate	Aug 1993–Jun 1995	France, Japan, Netherlands, Switzerland, US
Sorbates	1979–1996	Germany, Japan, US
Stainless steel	Jan 1994–Mar 1995	Belgium, France, Germany, Italy, Spain, Sweden, UK
Steel beam	1988–1994	Belgium, France, Germany, Luxembourg, Spain, UK
Steel-heating pipe (pre-insulated pipe)	Late 1990–1996	Austria, Denmark, Finland, Germany, Italy, Sweden, Switzerland
Steel tube, seamless	1990–1995	France, Germany, Italy, Japan, UK
Sugar	Jun 1996–Jul 1990	Denmark, Ireland, UK
Tampico fibre	Jan 1990–Apr 1995	Mexico, Netherlands, US
Thermal fax paper	1991–1992	Japan, US
Vitamins	Jan 1990–Feb 1999	Canada, Germany, Japan, Switzerland, US
Wastewater construction	Jun 1988–Jan 1995	Germany, Switzerland, US
Zinc phosphate	Mar 1994–May 1998	France, Germany, Norway, UK

Source: Levenstein and Suslow (2004: 807–811).

Several frequent features of international cartels, like a strong regional specialisation and extensive multimarket contacts, allow for suspicions that they dispose of advanced coordination opportunities and, thus, possess superior stability (Worm 2004: 53–57). Even after the cartels are forced to break up, non-competitive structures and cartel-created trade barriers tend to prevail, for instance in the shape of post-cartel joint ventures or implicit cooperative pricing arrangements. While the initial harm by the explicit cartels occurs in all types of countries, developing countries with their consumers and producers are particularly harmed by the prolonged anticompetitive effects (Levenstein and Suslow 2004: 824–826).

The trend towards an internationalisation of hardcore cartels is also somewhat documented in the volume of fines imposed by the European

Commission on cross-border cartels. The all-time record peak of €1.84 billion of 2001 was outdone as soon as 2006 with a new record volume of €1.85 billion, but only until April 2007, when the fine volume reached €2 billion. Among the largest cross-border cartels, the so-called vitamins cartel – according to the European Commission the hardcore cartel with the most damaging impact on competition ever in the common market – consisting of eight interdependent price-fixing and market-sharing cartels among 13 enterprises from Switzerland, Japan, and from within the EU stands out. About a decade long, they restricted worldwide competition on 12 singular vitamin markets with effects on a wide range of such different consumer markets as cereals, biscuits, drinks, animal feed, pharmaceuticals, cosmetics, and so on.[8] Although being exceptional regarding size and duration, the vitamins cartels are typical examples in terms of participation from Asia and Europe as well as their truly global scope (Connor 2004: 242–243). Another typical example is represented by the graphite electrodes cartel, a horizontal, combined price-fixing, quota, and market division cartel in which the participating firms from the US, Japan and Germany agreed to: (1) increase and maintain prices worldwide; (2) eliminate price discounts; (3) allocate volume among conspirators; (4) divide the world market among themselves and designate price leaders in each region; (5) reduce or eliminate exports to members' home markets; (6) restrict capacity; (7) restrict non-conspirator companies' access to certain technologies; (8) exchange sales and customer information in order to monitor and enforce the cartel agreement; and (9) issue price announcements and price quotations in accordance with the agreement. The cartel lasted, at least, between 1992 and 1997 and included virtually each important competitor on this market (Levenstein and Suslow 2004: 826–836). In 2007, the elevators and escalators cartel topped the all-time chart of cross-border cartel fines in the EU (more than €900 million).[9]

In summary, cartel activity remains high on international markets and no major decline can be expected (Hüschelrath 2002; Guersent 2004; Bond 2005). Furthermore, widespread modern (non-hardcore cartel) cooperative business arrangements – including, for instance, strategic alliances, research and development (R&D) cooperations, and networks of all kind (many of which are cross-border) – have the potential for informal cartelisation (apart from being follow-ups to diminished cartels from time to time). Although they

---

8 See on the US case against the vitamins cartels as well as on their international implications First (2001a) and on the respective EU case Peiró (2002).

9 See press release IP/07/209 dated 21 February, 2007 by the European Commission 'Competition: Commission fines members of lifts and escalators cartels over €990 million'.

are, more often than not, initially procompetitive, they generate cooperation structures, which eventually facilitate future anticompetitive collusion (Pryor 2001a).

2.2 Predatory Practices and Abuse of Market Power

Dominant enterprises could attempt to conquer the increasing competitive pressure through market globalisation and liberalisation by engaging in predatory and deterring practices, thus, abusing their powerful market positions. Temporarily, dominant market positions probably more often than not refer to (the private protection of) national markets and abusive strategies tend to target entry deterrence in order to avoid challenges to dominant incumbents because of the liberalisation of market access. In particular, this refers to vertical practices like barriers to resources or distribution systems, and so on (Worm 2004: 61–72). Starting market globalisation, dominance on international or even global markets seems to be less likely in the initial period of dynamically increasing markets (in a geographic sense). However, in the long run, dominant market positions with the inherent potential for abusive business behaviour are likely to re-emerge on the international level.

Anecdotal evidence indicates that anticompetitive modes of behaviour on international markets based on predation and abuse of market power have also become more frequent in recent decades. One of the most outstanding examples is provided by the Microsoft case (for example, Fisher and Rubinfeld 2001; Gilbert and Katz 2001; Grimes 2003). As the world's leading software company and dominating supplier of operating systems (with a world market share of more than 90 per cent), Microsoft was accused in a number of lawsuits of having deliberately raised rivals' costs and suppressed competition to illegally maintain its monopoly and to monopolise further software markets. American and European antitrust authorities believe they have identified anticompetitive conduct such as unfair and restrictive contracting as well as anticompetitive exclusionary arrangements with PC manufacturers and distributors and bundling of middleware and application software with its dominating operating system software with the intention to drive (actual and potential) competitors out of the market. Pepsico's complaint in several countries about unfair business practices in abuse of a dominant market position by the Coca-Cola Company is an additional example (Hamilton and Flecher 2004).

Although no comprehensive data are available, there is plausible indication that international abuse of market power and international predation are and will be among the strategies with which business both responds to and uses to drive globalisation (Worm 2004: 61–72).

2.3 International Merger Activity

Cross-border mergers are a natural business response to geographically growing markets. First, in internationalised and, thus, larger markets, the optimal firm size should be different from smaller national markets. Secondly, internationalisation strategies of formerly domestic enterprises can be realised faster and with fewer costs through acquisitions of foreign companies. In particular, the purchase of knowledge about local characteristics (in terms of consumer preferences, supply and sales chains, institutional arrangements, cultural conventions, traditions, legal and administrative issues, and so on) and of a locally well-known brand represent important advantages of the acquisition strategy compared to internal, organic growth. Consequently, market globalisation is likely to generate cross-border mergers.[10] The term 'cross-border merger' denotes each merger that affects markets in more than one country (that is, the pro-/anticompetitive impact of the merger occurs in more than one country), irrespective of whether the merging enterprises originate from different countries or not. This definition ensures that the two motives described above are both represented.

Merger activity has always occurred in waves (see Figure 2.1 and Table 2.4),[11] starting with the great merger wave at the end of the nineteenth century, predominantly in the US. With respect to the internationalisation of markets and business activities, the most recent merger wave is particularly interesting. The second half of the 1990s was strongly characterised by a massive wave of cross-border mergers, which caused an intensive academic and political discussion.[12] This can be traced back to a number of distinctive characteristics:

- With its peak in 2000, the 1990s' merger wave exceeded the last wave by approximately five times (see Figure 2.2).
- Different from all the historic merger waves, it consisted of a unique amount of cross-border mergers (see Table 2.5). This is not only true regarding the origin of the merging companies, but even more so when concerning the regional distribution of the affected markets.

[10] The term 'merger', as it is employed in this book, comprises all types of 'mergers and acquisitions activity' irrespective of technical differences (merger to trusts versus building of a group or concern, and so on).

[11] See also Lamoureaux (1985), O'Brien (1988), Müller (1998: 66–76), Kleinert and Klodt (2000a: 17–20, 2002), and Carroll (2002).

[12] See Black (2000), Hansen (2000), Kleinert and Klodt (2000a, 2000b, 2002), Andrade et al. (2001), Pryor (2001a, 2001b), Karpoff and Wessels (2002), Budzinski and Kerber (2003), Evenett (2003), and Budzinski (2004b: 64–69).

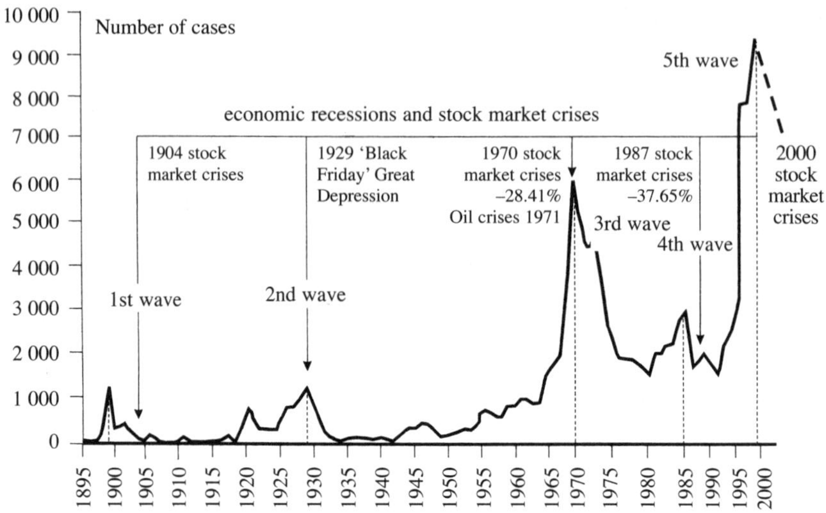

Source: This diagram draws on Jansen and Müller-Stewens (2001: 3–4) and has formerly been used in Budzinski (2004b: 65)

Figure 2.1 Historical merger waves

- Not only did the total value of mergers reach an all-time peak, but the average transaction volume also significantly exceeded previous mergers. For instance, the transaction values of Vodafone Airtouch–Mannesmann (US$190 billion in 2000) and AOL–Time Warner (US$106 billion in 2000) more than doubled the biggest merger[13] so far and outperformed the GDP of middle-sized industrial countries like Portugal (in 2001 about US$110 billion).
- While mergers traditionally are characterised by the acquisition of a smaller company by a bigger one, the 1990s' merger wave consisted to a significant extent of mergers between equally sized companies.
- This megamerger wave encompasses virtually every industry and, contrary to the other merger waves, especially service and technology industries (Andrade et al. 2001; Evenett 2003).

Following recessive tendencies of the relevant stock markets as well as the cooling of the world economy, cross-border merger activity has been signifi-

[13] Exxon/Mobil (US$86.4 billion in 1998). At the beginning of the fifth merger wave, the Time Warner merger with a transaction volume of US$14 billion was the all-time leader.

Table 2.4 The five merger waves

Period	Special features
1897–1904 1st wave	'Industrialisation' and cartel prohibitions (US, Canada) induce massive horizontal integration; mergers to monopolies and trusts with the intention of market dominance; high percentage of market-wide mergers including five or more companies
1916–1929 2nd wave	Predominantly vertical integration; striving for the control over the whole production chain; reaction to new antitrust laws that hamper horizontal mergers (US)
1965–1969 3rd wave	The 'conglomerate era', but also horizontal and vertical integration; diversification and portfolio theory as dominant strategies (predominantly US); economies of scale and industrial mass production
1984–1990 4th wave	Strategic mergers to gain short-run profits; development of M&A markets and specialised M&A enterprises ('merger-mania'); in the beginning many conglomerate mergers (economies of scope, especially Europe), later increasingly horizontal and vertical integration; other driving forces: liberalisation and deregulation of markets, globalisation of business and especially financial markets.
1993–2000 5th wave	High percentage of cross-border mergers; increasing transaction volumes (megamergers); mergers of equals; predominantly horizontal integration due to core-competence strategy and shareholder value orientation; other driving forces: globalisation of business, European market integration, trade liberalisation, deregulation of network industries, 'new economy'.

Source: Budzinski (2004b: 66).

cantly lower in the period 2001–2003. However, since 2004 a new merger boom is accelerating, leading to a new all-time record-breaking transaction volume of US$3900 billion in 2006 (see Figure 2.2) – an impressive figure that was reached without any single transaction approaching the 100 billion dimension. Moreover, with several new megamergers announced during the first quarter (see Table 2.5), 2007 looks promising for yet another record-breaking year.

From a competition economics perspective, the cross-border megamerger wave entails procompetitive and anticompetitive effects and cannot a priori be

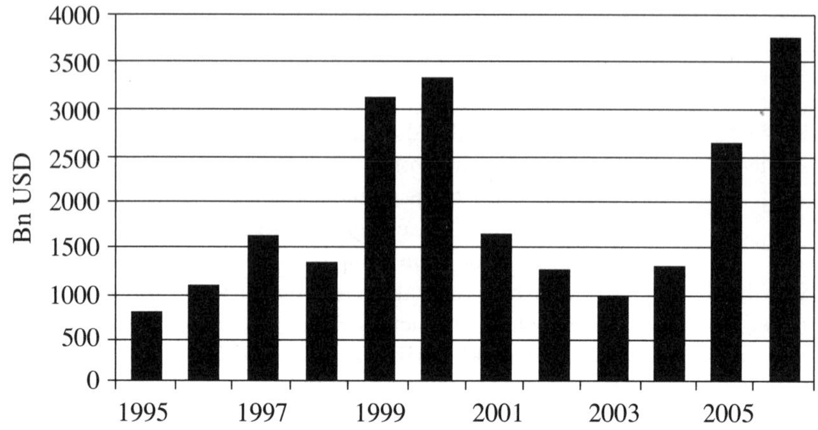

Sources: www.m-and-a.de and www.thomson.com

Figure 2.2 Total value of announced worldwide transactions

classified as an antitrust concern. On one hand, the processes of liberalisation and deregulation increase competition by the enlargement of markets, opening up sclerotic national market structures. Although the mergers of the 1990s were gigantic and more is still to come, they did not necessarily imply the emergence of market dominance or anticompetitive oligopoly effects. On the other hand, however, ongoing merger dynamics can overcompensate market enlargement and cause market dominance on a global scale in the course of time. Such a development would be particularly severe if markets were fully globalised. There could be no further liberalisation any more, bringing (experienced) horizontal competitors from abroad into over-concentrated markets. Consequently, the disciplining threat of easy market entry would not be available any more to break up sclerotic world markets.[14] The Boeing–Airbus duopoly on the world market for large jet aircraft, a consequence of the 1997 Boeing–McDonnell Douglas merger (and many other mergers in the past five decades) is a striking example.

The domination of the core-competence approach (Prahalad and Hamel

[14] Helfat and Lieberman (2002) argue against the background of empirical evidence that companies, which produce similar products in different geographical markets and/or use similar resources and modes of production compared to the ones within the respective industry, have a significantly higher likelihood of entering the respective market than other companies.

Table 2.5 Cross-border mergers in the last decade

Volume in billion USD	Merging companies (country of origin)		Industry	Year
190	Vodafone Airtouch (GB)	Mannesmann (D)	Telecommunications	2000
106	AOL (US)	Time Warner (US)	Internet media	2000
91	Barclays (GB)	ABN-Amro (NL) (pending)	Financial institutions	2007
73	AT&T (USA)	BellSouth (USA)	Telecommunications	2006
71	Pfizer (US)	Warner-Lambert (US)	Pharma	2000
67	Sanofi Synthélabo (F)	Aventis (D, F)	Pharma	2004
62	Exxon (US)	Mobil Oil (US)	Oil	1998
59	JP Morgan Chase (USA)	BankOne (USA)	Financial institutions	2007
58	Glaxo Welcome (GB)	Smithkline (GB)	Pharma	2000
57	Travelers (Citigroup) (US)	Citicorp (US)	Financial institutions	1998
54	Procter & Gamble (US)	Gilette (US)	Consumer goods	2005
50	Nations Bank (US)	Bank America (US)	Financial institutions	2005
49	SBC Communications (US)	Ameritech (US)	Telecommunications	1998
49	Vodafone Group (GB)	Air Touch Communications (US)	Telecommunications	1999
47	Pfizer (US)	Pharmacia (US)	Pharma	2002
47	J.P. Morgan Chase (US)	Bank One (US)	Financial institutions	2004
46	AT&T (US)	MediaOne (US)	Telecommunications	1999
43	AT&T (US)	Tele-Communications (US)	Telecommunications	1998
42	Total Fina (F)	Elf Aquitaine (F)	Oil	1999
42	Bell Atlantic (US)	GTE (US)	Telecommunications	1998
41	Daimler-Benz (D)	Chrysler (US)	Automobiles	1998

Table 2.5 *continued*

Volume in billion USD	Merging companies (country of origin)		Industry	Year
40	Deutsche Telekom (D)	Voicestream Wireless (US)	Telecommunications	2000
40	Vivendi (F)	Seagram (CDN)	Water supply, media	2000
40	France Telecom (F)	Orange (GB)	Telecommunications	2000
40	Suez (F)	Gaz de France (F)	Energy	2006
39	BP (GB)	Amoco (US)	Oil	2000
37	Zürich Vers. (CH)	BAT (GB)	Tabacco, finance	1997
35	Sprint (US)	Nextel (US)	Telecommunications	2005
32	Mittal Steel (NL)	Arcelor (LUX)	Steel	2006
29	Global-Crossing (Bermuda)	US West (US)	Telecommunications	1999
13	Repsol (E)	YPF (ARG)	Energy	1999
13	Citigroup (US)	Benacci (MEX)	Financial institutions	2001
12	BHP (AUS)	Billiton (GB)	Steel, metals	2001

Sources: compiled from www.m-and-a.de, www.dealogic.de, www.manda-institute.org

1990)[15] raises additional problems. Following the switch of the dominant business strategy from diversification (until the 1980s) to the strengthening of core competences, the 1990s wave focused on horizontal mergers instead of conglomerate mergers. This fuelled cross-border mergers because companies with similar core competences in foreign countries represent particularly 'fitting' targets for acquisitions. However, horizontal mergers are much more critical from a competition policy point of view than vertical or even conglomerate mergers.

In summary, and in spite of the procompetitive effects of market globalisation, there is a case for an anticompetitive impact caused by ongoing cross-border merger dynamics. International merger dynamics are speeding up again and new records can be expected. The reason is that the process of the adjustment of the business structures to international markets is definitely far from being completed. This process, however, comprises both procompetitive adjustment strategies and anticompetitive ones.

2.4 Co-Evolution of Anticompetitive Practices and Competition Policy?

The globalisation of pro- and anticompetitive business behaviour along with the internationalisation of competition obviously entails the question whether competition policy or antitrust policy[16] must co-internationalise in order to maintain effective governance of anticompetitive business conduct and protect competition on cross-border markets. Thus, the question at hand is whether a corresponding globalisation of competition policy is necessary. The fact that anticompetitive effects of market globalisation exist, however, does not preclude the necessity of a supranational competition policy response. It must be analysed whether the currently predominating competition policy regimes – mainly on a national basis – suffice to cope with cross-border anticompetitive arrangements and practices. Furthermore, an important issue addresses whether decentralised (non-supranational) competition policy regimes might even play a beneficial role in international antitrust. These questions are analysed in the following chapter by pointing to the shortcomings of both a waiver of international competition policy and a complete replacement of the existing antitrust forces.

---

15 For empirical evidence on the role and impact of the core competences approach as a driving-force for mergers and acquisitions, see Hussinger (2005).

16 Competition policy and antitrust policy are treated as synonyms in this book. The first expression is more popular in Europe, whereas the latter is traditionally favoured by US authors.

3. International competition policy between decentralism and centralism

In this chapter, I contrast the two extreme views, namely 'there is no need for an international competition policy at all' (section 1) and 'we need an uniform global competition law, enforced by a single world authority' (section 2). In doing so, it becomes clear that any real-world international competition policy regime is, and will be, set somewhere in between those extremes (section 4). Neither of the simple but extreme solutions is suitable for addressing the internationalisation of business activities adequately. This provides the grounds for a more differentiated discussion of this issue in Chapters 4 to 6.[1]

An excursus complements this chapter. It addresses a specifically academic discussion of the necessity of an internationalisation of antitrust, which deserves special treatment. Section 3 deals with a second-order problem: does competition itself provide an instrument to derive or generate an international competition policy regime? This points towards the role of institutional or regulatory competition of competition rules.

1. THE LIMITS OF NATIONAL COMPETITION POLICY REGIMES IN GLOBALISED MARKETS

To internationalise competition policy, at first glance, seems to be a highly logical consequence of the internationalisation of competition. Globalising markets imply that the objective of regulation geographically exceeds the regulating jurisdiction. The resulting incongruence of the borders of competitive interaction and competition control is intuitively problematic. This is embedded in the more general issue of global governance, that is, the generally upheld fear that the nation state loses its regulatory power in the face of

[1] Since many of the arguments used to promote the extreme solutions can also be applied in a more pronounced way to discuss more complex designs of an adequate international regime, some of the arguments in the following section are addressed again in the following chapters. As the rationale of this chapter is to demonstrate the insufficiency of the extreme solutions, the discussion of these arguments is more brief in this chapter and more elaborate in the following chapters.

globalisation and, in particular, in relation to multinational, globally acting business. Market globalisation is – in the minds of the people – often strongly connected to the increasing power of giant enterprises and the spreading of an unregulated and uncontrolled (as well as uncontrollable) capitalism. Even among informed economists, the belief is widespread that those 'shadows' of globalisation provide a strong case for international economic regulation through competent international organisations like the WTO, the World Bank Group (WBG) or the International Monetary Fund (IMF) in order to regain governance capabilities (which the nation states are believed to have inevitably and irreversibly lost).[2] In this context, an international competition policy regime represents something like a missing link to the comprehensiveness of the world economic order.

However, in order to provide a case for an internationalisation of competition policy, it does not suffice to refer to widespread beliefs or fears. This is particularly true since, in the academic discourse on international competition policy, a number of arguments have been raised, which cast doubt on the merits of any international competition policy regime.[3] Therefore, the following sections present the limits of national competition policies in globalising markets. The line of argument is threefold. First, I discuss whether the globalisation of competition and free trade erodes the need for competition policy altogether (section 1.1). Secondly, I demonstrate why national agencies, enforcing national laws, can neither effectively nor efficiently deal with anticompetitive business behaviour on international markets (section 1.2). And, thirdly, I argue that national competition policies themselves can be the source of restrictions of international competition (section 1.3).

1.1 Does Worldwide Competition Erode the Scope for Competition Policy?

The globalisation of markets and business activities, which was described in Chapter 2, is basically a process of enhancing competition and not one of restricting it. During the last few decades, significant waves of trade liberalisation and industry deregulation have occurred, directed for instance at telecommunica-

---

[2] See Nobel laureate Stiglitz (2002). This type of globalisation critique – calling for more effective international governance structures – has very little in common with the 'anti-capitalistic' branch of globalisation opponents – despite the fact that both address the same fears of the people. The market economic globalisation critique is ordoliberal in the sense that it is not against maximum market globalisation but demands a corresponding globalisation of the institutional framework of the world economy.

[3] However, fundamental opposition is relatively seldom encountered. For exceptions see Meessen (1989, 2000), De Léon (1997) and Stephan (2004).

tions, transportation services, banking and finance, insurance services, energy, and so on, all industries, which were traditionally either monopolised by state-owned or state-protected companies or tightly regulated. This was complemented by the emergence of new communication technologies, in particular in the context of the Internet, which allows for additional commercialisation channels (for example, in regard to the distribution of books, music, pharmaceuticals, and so on). The interplay of these developments has a number of significant procompetitive effects:

- former state-protected market positions become challenged by the entry of new competitors following deregulation;
- domestic enterprises with dominant positions face new competitive pressure by foreign enterprises following the opening of formerly protected domestic markets by trade liberalisation;
- traditional non-tradable goods and, in particular, services become tradable due to technological progress, creating new competitive pressure on the related industries.

In summary, market globalisation, trade liberalisation and industry deregulation all represent a challenge for sclerotic national market structures. In these markets, the degree of both actual and potential competition has been low; contestability has been eroded by decades of trade protection, over-regulation and state intervention. Only the opening of these markets for actual or potential entries from the 'outside'[4] can effectively re-establish competition by creating a new contestability. National competition policy without trade liberalisation has – for several reasons – not been able to achieve this.

Highlighting the procompetitive effects of market enlargement and deregulation, some have argued that trade liberalisation might in fact be the better competition policy. If the enlargement of markets through trade liberalisation generates contestability by providing additional, actual and potential competitors, competition policy becomes superfluous in a world of free market entry across borders.[5] In this regard, trade liberalisation and competition policy can be viewed as being substitutes. The removal of cross-border trade restrictions challenges existing anticompetitive arrangements and

[4] May it be from abroad (trade liberalisation), from other industries (deregulation), or from innovative start-ups for example, Doc Morris's Internet-distribution challenge to the German pharmacy market).

[5] See for – radical or qualified – protagonists of this line of argument Hazledine (1992), Hauser and Schoene (1994), De Léon (1997), Neven and Seabright (1997), Rosenthal and Nicolaides (1997), Freytag and Zimmermann (1998), and Kee and Hoekman (2003).

structures in the domestic markets and, consequently, erodes the scope and necessity for an active competition policy against those types of restrictions on competition.

In their comprehensive analysis, Neven and Seabright (1997: 382–389) identify three areas in which trade liberalisation and competition policy are good substitutes (see also Hazledine 1992; Cadot et al. 2000: 3–6):

- competition policy against barriers to entry, which is highly obvious since trade liberalisation is immediately directed towards the removal of artificial public barriers to foreign entry;
- competition policy towards mergers since, with larger markets, the optimal extent of competitive enterprises increases while market shares decrease (Safarian 1997; Weizsäcker 1998; Kleinert and Klodt 2000a, 2000b). Altogether, while efficient mergers may be promoted, output-decreasing (anticompetitive) mergers are discouraged;
- competition policy against collusive arrangements because trade liberalisation destabilises incumbent cartels by increasing the number of outsiders and (thereby) aggravating the detection and sanctioning of defecting cartel members (Feinberg 1989).

However, according to Neven and Seabright (1997), trade liberalisation and competition policy are only imperfect substitutes since specific types of predatory strategies might be encouraged in the face of freer trade.

So, the question is at hand whether even national competition policy becomes superfluous in the face of market globalisation, not to mention an international competition policy? There are a number of arguments, which cast doubts on the substitutes hypotheses.

First of all, trade liberalisation only challenges existing national anticompetitive arrangements and market structures, which previously emerged and persisted only because of public protection. As the empirical overview in section 2 of Chapter 2 clearly demonstrates, the globalisation of business leads to a parallel emergence of international anticompetitive arrangements and market structures. The market enlargement effect of globalisation – which is the essential content of the substitutes hypotheses – fairly decreases the anticompetitive impacts of such restrictions to competition which were created for smaller markets. Moreover, due the significant increase in market extent, it is probable that it will take the market agents some time to compensate and recreate anticompetitive arrangements and structures. However, the substitutional effect of trade liberalisation is only a temporary one since – in principle – international markets can be subject to the same anticompetitive business strategies as national markets once the participating enterprises have internationalised themselves.[6] The significant increase in international cartels, the ability of enterprises like Microsoft to exert (and abuse) world market power, and the examples of world markets, which have developed to be tight oligopolies (or even duopolies like Boeing-Airbus), hint at the possibility that the time gained by trade liberalisation to create an accompanying effective international competition policy regime might be less than expected.[7]

In accordance with this, theoretical findings suggest that the consideration of anticompetitive arrangements across jurisdictions significantly matters. Apart from the market enlargement argument, which can be applied to argue that creating restrictions to competition is more difficult and, thus – at least temporarily – more unlikely in international markets,[8] trade liberalisation generally provides incentives to create cross-border private restrictions to competition. For instance, Ross (1988: 244) derives that while trade liberalisation discourages mergers for market power between domestic firms, it encourages mergers for market power between domestic and foreign enterprises.[9]

Additionally, the existence of private barriers to entry must be considered, for example, like vertical arrangements to exclude potential foreign entries from domestic distribution channels (more elaborately: Cadot et al. 2000; Hamilton and Stiegert 2000). On the one hand, trade liberalisation does not tackle such private barriers, and on the other hand, the removal of public protection can motivate business to replace public market barriers with private ones. This hints at arguments for a different hypothesis. Competition policy and trade liberalisation can be viewed as being complements instead of substitutes. The procompetitive effects of trade liberalisation may be eroded if the decreasing public restrictions on competition are only replaced by private

---

6 Nobody has yet put forward a sound argument why a worldwide market should be different in nature from any national market (which can be pretty large, for example, US or Russian markets) so that it becomes an impossibility to restrict its competitive character.

7 It belongs to the most essential features of any realistic notion of competition that the competing enterprises have stronger incentives to escape the competitive pressure the stronger the latter gets.

8 See Neven and Seabright (1997: 389–396). However, 'unlikely' does not mean 'impossible' wherefore scope for (international) competition policy is maintained.

9 See also, Cadot et al. (2000). Moreover, Gaudet and Kanouni (2004) show that even anticompetitive mergers between domestic enterprises need not be frustrated if trade barriers have not been prohibitive before the liberalisation occurred. According to Collie (2003), the intensification of protectionist trade policies represents an optimal policy response in the face of anticompetitive foreign mergers, implying that the creation of countervailing anticompetitive market power is more effective to cope with foreign private anticompetitive market power than trade liberalisation.

ones.[10] According to this view, an international competition policy is not becoming superfluous by trade liberalisation but instead represents a necessary ingredient in order to materialise the potential gains from trade liberalisation and maintain them in the long run.[11]

This is reinforced if one reviews the contestability argument more deeply. Globalisation appears to be a 'paradise for contestability' only at first sight. At a second glance, one can identify a trade-off between an increased difficulty to limit contestability on the one hand and an increased persistence of limited contestability on the other. The second effect is closely related to the reason why trade liberalisation is so successful in breaking up sclerotic structures on domestic markets. After trade liberalisation, foreign companies, which produce similar goods for their markets, can easily enter the market. In most industries, market entry requires industry-specific sunk costs, which can be significant (or even prohibitive). Such entry costs, however, are significantly lower for enterprises, which have a history of producing the respective good (although they supplied different geographic markets). According to the theoretical and empirical insights of Helfat and Lieberman (2002), companies with similar pre-entry production structures have a significant higher probability to enter markets. In sclerotic markets with high entry costs, newcomers from other industries or newly created enterprises are unlikely. Therefore, all hope to challenge the incumbents and revive competition lies in allowing foreign enterprises of similar industries to compete (trade liberalisation). However, the crucial point is that this opportunity no longer exists in fully globalised markets.[12] Such markets may be more difficult to dominate, but once sclerotic world markets have developed, potential competition plays a significant smaller role. No potential competitors are available, which can easily enter the market because they are producing similar products in different geographical markets (and, thus, face lower industry-specific sunk costs). Instead, only companies that are completely new and inexperienced in the respective industries serve as potential competitors – however, with a much lower entrance probability than industry-experienced companies from abroad. Losing the opportunity of breaking up sclerotic markets by competition from the 'outside'

---

10 See Feinberg (1991), Scherer (1994), Jacquemin (1995), Fox (1997), Iacobucci (1997), Meiklejohn (1999), Cadot et al. (2000), Hamilton and Stiegert (2000), Wins (2000: 97–103), and Klodt (2001). For instance, the completion of the integrated single market within the EU is considerably co-credited to the European competition policy activities. See Ehlermann (1992) and Gerber (1998a).

11 Nicolaides (1996) even reverses the argument and identifies effective competition policy to be an important facilitator of trade liberalisation.

12 '[F]ree trade is a once-for-all event. Once it is fully implemented, tendencies towards monopolisation will no longer be constrained by added import competition'. Hazledine (1992: 57).

means that the prevention of such market situations becomes even more important on a global scale. This provides a strong argument for an international competition policy (Budzinski 2002b).

Eventually, even though market globalisation is a powerful process, it seems rather unrealistic that we should end up with all markets fully globalised. Due to the characteristics of the products, transportation costs, and preferences, there will remain a scope for national, regional and local markets. This supports the view that trade liberalisation is not a good substitute for national competition policy.[13]

Altogether, trade liberalisation and competition policy represent to a large extent complementary tasks. While trade liberalisation tackles public restrictions of global competition, competition policy addresses private ones. Depending on the ideological background, one may give one more weight than the other. However, in regard to the governance of global competition, both an international trade regime and an international competition regime contribute to the completion of an effective world economic order.

1.2 Can National Competition Policy Cope with Worldwide Competition?

1.2.1 The inbound focus of national competition policies

However, an international competition policy regime would be dispensable if the existing national competition policy regimes, by protecting competition within their border, were able to sufficiently protect worldwide competition. An important aspect is that national competition policies, in doing so, usually focus on national welfare instead of world welfare. In general, the existing competition authorities in the world are legally bound to pursue a jurisdictional[14] welfare standard, that is, they are focused to improve the welfare of the inhabitants of their jurisdictions instead of improving world welfare.[15] As

---

[13] However, it does not provide an argument for an international competition policy. Instead, the prevalence of local and regional markets backs the future role of national competition policy. This aspect will be discussed again in section 2 of this chapter.

[14] In some cases, I use the terms 'jurisdiction'/'jurisdictional' instead of 'nation'/'national' in order to include the EU competition policy which is clearly supranational but comprises a specific region (as opposed to an international regime for the world economy). Synonymously, the term 'regional and national' is meant to include EU competition policy.

[15] See on the national-versus-global-welfare discussion, for example, Fox and Ordover (1995), Fox (1997, 1998a, 2000a, 2000b), Guzman (1998, 2004), Neven and Röller (2000), Grewlich (2001), and Durand et al. (2004). A different line of argument is represented by the controversial consumers-versus-total-welfare-standard discussion.

soon as competition extends the geographical scope of the existing antitrust jurisdictions, that is, there is an incongruence of the territorial scopes of the (larger) markets and (smaller) jurisdictions, one and the same interfirm arrangement or anticompetitive practice can have effects in more than one jurisdiction. This points to the jurisdictional interface, that is, how exactly the unilateral and non-coordinated jurisdiction of many national antitrust policies work over antitrust cases with cross-border effects. This is thoroughly explored below.

1.2.2 Extraterritorial application of competition rules

In the absence of an effective international competition policy regime, the national competition authorities are left to deal with international anticompetitive arrangements and behaviours. The best they can do is attempt to apply their domestic competition laws to both foreign and international arrangements. If, in doing so, every country manages to protect its domestic markets against inbound restraints of competition, the remaining scope for a worldwide competition policy might be negligible. The benefits, prospects, limits, and deficiencies of such an extraterritorial proliferation and enforcement of national competition laws have been subject to the most elaborate discussion among legal, economic and political experts on competition.[16] By drawing on

---

This one aims at the economic assessment standard of distinguishing between procompetitive and anticompetitive practices. The question is to what extent increases in producer surplus can compensate or even outweigh decreases in consumer surplus. Using economically precise connotations, a consumer welfare standard focuses on changes in consumer surplus only, whereas a total welfare standard concentrates on the sum of the changes of consumer and producer rents. In the latter concept, the welfare redistribution between consumers and producers is not of relevance. See, for example, Chang et al. (2002), Lyons (2003), Neven and Röller (2005), Salop (2005), Farrell and Katz (2006), Haucap et al. (2006), and Heyer (2006) on the pros and cons of the two concepts. In the competition policy literature, however, these two distinct concepts are often confused. In particular, the total welfare standard is sometimes denoted as 'consumer welfare standard' by arguing that, in the end, private households are the owners of the producing enterprises (an assumption, which obviously needs some qualifications in regard to state ownership, retained profits, and international asset distribution) and, thus, increasing firm profits (increasing producers' rents) serve them (as consumers). However, the changing distribution of rents between producers and consumers has its economic meaning, for instance in terms of allocative efficiency, income distribution and so on, wherefore analytical clearness is beneficial.

[16] In my opinion, the most comprehensive analysis is Basedow (1998). Additionally, the following paragraphs draw on Castel (1984), Rishikesh (1991), Immenga (1994), Torremans (1996), Fox (1997, 1999a, 2000b, 2003a), Grimes (1998), Guzman (1998), Falvey and Lloyd (1999), Griffin (1999), Kerber (1999), Lloyd and Vautier (1999: 13–32), Wins (2000: 75–84), Kennedy (2001: 22–40), Pavic (2001), Adam (2002: 113–122, 168–171), Zanettin (2002: 7–52), Dabbah (2003: 159–205), Hovenkamp (2003), Podszun (2003: 12–49, 55–61), and Basedow (2004).

this abundance of literature, I briefly review the effectiveness as well as the shortcomings of national competition policy in international markets.

Due to the increasing internationalisation of competition and enterprise activities, anticompetitive arrangements and behaviours often affect markets in more than one jurisdiction. Consequently, next to domestic markets, competition in markets in jurisdictions outside the home countries of the colluding enterprises can be restricted. While the competition agencies of the jurisdictions in which the colluding enterprises are located will generally address any competitive concerns within their markets, they are generally not interested in competitive concerns abroad. If the other affected jurisdictions respond by applying their domestic laws to those arrangements (irrespective of whether they are located within their territories), those jurisdictions act extraterritorially in an attempt to unilaterally internalise the negative external effects.

The major instrument of extraterritorial competition policy is the effects doctrine,[17] which was invented in 1945 by the US courts in the Alcoa case,[18] kicking off the currently widespread extraterritorial application of jurisdictional competition laws. According to the effects doctrine, anticompetitive business practices that affect domestic markets are subject to the domestic competition law, irrespective of the location of the arrangements/practices and the participating enterprises. Thus, business practices between non-US enterprises, taking place off-shore, are nonetheless subject to US antitrust laws as soon as US markets are affected. In the following decades, the effects doctrine was applied to a large number of anticompetitive arrangements and conducts. Initially, the focus was on cartels and cartel surrogates as well as on predatory strategies with mergers being addressed under the effects doctrine some decades later.[19]

---

[17] However, though dominating in antitrust practice nowadays, it does not represent the only design option for an extraterritorial application of competition rules. See Basedow (2004: 322–325). The implications of the effects doctrine as a competence allocation rule as well as some stylised alternatives are analysed in depth in Chapter 5, sections 1–2.

[18] The originally US company Aluminium Co. of America (Alcoa) was taken over by the Canadian-incorporated Aluminium Limited (1928). The Canadian enterprise, then, engaged in a Swiss quota cartel ('Alliance', 1931 and 1936) together with several European aluminum companies. Although the cartel was established outside the US and no indication was given that significant planning took place within the US, the US courts claimed jurisdiction over this case, establishing the effects doctrine. According to Podszun (2003: 20), the basic idea had been discussed before, for example, in the *Strassheim v Daily* (1911) and *Sisal Sales Corp.* (1927; Mexican export cartel) cases.

[19] In the *CIBA* case (1970), the US authorities permitted a merger of two foreign enterprises only on the condition of several divestments with regard to US subsidiaries. As the first full prohibition of a foreign merger, generally the French-Canadian

Furthermore, a significant extension of the extraterritorial application of US antitrust laws has been under controversial discussion most recently. Empagran, an association of non-US companies, which were hurt outside the US by the worldwide vitamins cartels, tried to sue Hoffmann-La Roche, one of the cartel leaders, in a private lawsuit for treble damages. The Court of Appeal for the District of Columbia confirmed the US jurisdiction, although neither the parties nor the affected markets, where the companies had been injured, were located inside the US. According to the court, the mere possibility that US citizens could also have been damaged by the cartel (that is, the cartel, in general, also affected US markets) constitutes jurisdiction for US antitrust laws and courts even if the actual plaintiffs consist only of non-US companies/citizens and the actual damage occurred abroad. However, in June 2004, the US Supreme Court overruled the DC Court of Appeal, claiming that a reasonable relation to US markets remains necessary condition and highlighting comity to other country's sovereignty regarding inbound antitrust.[20] An 'independent foreign harm' cannot constitute US jurisdiction. Although some ambivalence in regard to possible interpretations of this decision by lower courts still remains, the imminent extension of the extraterritorial reach of US antitrust laws and courts towards an almost unlimited worldwide ('imperial') application has, for now, been prevented.[21]

The innovation of the US antitrust policy has been imitated by most of the other competition policy jurisdictions in the world until now. Consequently, extraterritorial competition policy based on the effects doctrine or similar doctrines is widespread today. The EU, for instance, started to assert jurisdictions over anticompetitive arrangements abroad in the 1960s.[22] Starting with a somewhat limited effects principle, which required the existence of a subsidiary within the EU (for example, in the ICI judgment of 1972),[23] the extraterritorial reach of EU competition rules has been extended towards a fully fledged effects doctrine. The latter has been in force at the latest since the

---

Connaught–Institut Mérrieux merger (1990) is cited. For US effects doctrine cases in regard to all types of anticompetitive practices see Grimes (1998: 220–231), Griffin (1999: 160–163, 169–170) and Fox (2003a: 370, n. 36).

[20] In terms of conflict law, this represents some kind of combination between an effects principle and the balancing approach (that is, balancing foreign and domestic interests). See – without reference to Empagran – Basedow (2004: 324).

[21] On controversial perspectives and opinions on the Empagran case see Baudenbacher and Behn (2004), Bernheim et al. (2004), Bush et al. (2004), Buxbaum (2004), First and Fox (2004), Körber (2004), and Stiglitz and Orszag (2004).

[22] See for EU cases Basedow (1998: 19–23), Griffin (1999: 173–174, 178–179) and Zanettin (2002: 17–22).

[23] Basedow (2004: 323) calls this a pseudo-territorial principle since it relies on considerations of territoriality, which represent a precondition of extraterritorial jurisdiction.

1988 Wood Pulp judgment by the European Court of Justice. In 1996, the European Commission prohibited the joint acquisition of the South African enterprises Impala Platinum Holding Ltd and Lonrho LPD by Gencor Ltd (South Africa) and Lonrho plc (UK) because it would have created a duopoly in the world platinum and rhodium markets (the remaining competitor being the South African Anglo American Corporation). In doing so, the Commission (affirmed by the European Court of Justice) for the first time extended its extraterritorial competition policy enforcement to mergers.[24] Most prominent is the 2001 EU prohibition of the proposed merger of the US enterprises GE–Honeywell (European Commission 2001a).

As the examples from the US and the EU have demonstrated, extraterritorial proliferation of competition policies can be an effective tool in attacking foreign or international anticompetitive arrangements and practices – at least in individual cases. However, the governance of global competition by the unilateral application of the effects doctrine (or similar rules) through regional and national competition policies is characterised by a significant number of severe problems and shortcomings, which render the emergence of a safe-and-sound antitrust system impossible.

To claim jurisdiction over business people from other nations and over business practices taking place abroad is likely to generate opposition from the foreign countries in whose sovereignty the extraterritorial enforcement intervenes. When the US invented extraterritorial antitrust enforcement in the late 1940s, the legitimacy of such a step was controversial at best. To protect their citizens and enterprises from foreign authorities, a number of countries enacted blocking statutes.[25] They explicitly refused foreign jurisdiction over (anti-)competitive practices of their domestic enterprises and some of them prohibited any cooperation or information sharing by either their citizens/enterprises or the domestic (antitrust) authorities with the 'aggressive' extraterritorial enforcer. However, since more and more nations themselves engaged in extraterritorial competition policy enforcement, the relevance of such blocking statutes faded and is rather negligible today. Nevertheless, claiming the right to protect domestic competition by enforcing domestic

---

24 See European Commission (1996) and Fox (1999a). Even before, in 1982, the Bundeskartellamt ordered a modification of the Philip Morris (USA)/Rothmans (UK, SA) merger in the tobacco market by prohibiting the combination of their German subsidiaries. See Klodt (2001: 880), Fox (2003a: 370, n. 36), and for more German cases Podszun (2003: 21–26).

25 Starting with Ontario in 1947, antitrust-related or -motivated blocking statutes were enacted in Australia, the UK, Canada, South Africa and many more countries. See more elaborately on the development of blocking statutes in competition policy Zanettin (2002: 22–23, 34, 49–52).

antitrust laws extraterritorially and accepting foreign antitrust action against domestic enterprises are different issues for a considerable number of jurisdictions. This inconsistency even applies to the effects doctrine innovator – the US – which, from time to time, also has its problems with viewing foreign competition policy decrees against US companies as legitimate.[26]

One of the most obvious problems of extraterritorial enforcement is investigation abroad and the assertion of sanctions against foreign enterprises, in particular against powerful multinationals.[27] In order to evaluate the (anti-) competitive effect of an arrangement or business practice, the competent agency needs information from the participating enterprises. In particular, but not exclusively, in criminal cases, the enterprises can be very reluctant to offer the relevant information, wherefore competition authorities usually have a number of formal investigation rights like official requests, to search offices or headquarters of suspicious enterprises, to confiscate documents, to summon and hear witnesses or defendants, and so on. All these information-gathering instruments belong to the 'exercise of state power' which is bound to the territory of the investigating jurisdiction. If participants of anticompetitive arrangements and practices or evidence lies abroad, the investigating competition agency cannot apply these instruments. Instead, it is limited to informal requests on a voluntary basis. It is quite obvious that the investigation process is significantly hampered if the evidence for restrictive arrangements and practices lies abroad.

The problem is very similar in regard to the enforcement of decisions, sanctions and remedies. If the respective foreign enterprises refuse to obey the order of the competition agency, to pay a fine, to defy a prohibition, and so on, the domestic competition authorities cannot reasonably enforce their decisions by forcible means outside their territories.

However, although no formal power to enforce domestic competition laws against foreign enterprises exists, several jurisdictions have been successful in fighting inbound anticompetitive arrangements and practices – as reported above. One avenue to assert investigation and enforcement power over foreign enterprises is through domestic subsidiaries. For instance, the Bundeskartellamt successfully threatened to impose a fine on the German turnovers of the German subsidiaries of Philip Morris and Rothmans in order

---

[26] For instance, in the EU cases against IBM (1980s), Microsoft (1990s up to now), Boeing–McDonnell Douglas (1990s) and GE–Honeywell (2001), US press and officials (including antitrust officials) doubted the legitimacy of the EU's action. See Falvey and Lloyd (1999: 7), Fox (1998b, 2003a: 373–375) and Gerber (2003). Since conflicts between competition policy jurisdictions occur even without blocking statutes (and, therefore, represent a more severe problem), I address them in depth in a separate paragraph.

[27] See with focus only on industrial countries, for example, Zanettin (2002: 41–49).

to enforce its remedies on the South-African-British merger.[28] Even if the 'suspicious' enterprises do not have assets within the territorial reach of the regulating jurisdiction, they can be interested in unrestricted access to the domestic market. If extraterritorial application of competition rules is reasonably only practiced if domestic markets are affected, there should be a minimum commercial interest in unrestricted market access by the foreign enterprises. Thus, jurisdictions with important enough domestic markets have considerable powers to enforce their competition laws against foreign enterprises.

Typically enough, the US and the EU have always been particularly successful with regard to the extraterritorial application of their competition rules. Probably only few enterprises can afford to be sanctioned in their activities on these two crucial internal markets. With their extraordinary (extraterritorial) enforcement power, both jointly dominate the international antitrust arena, creating a duopoly of antitrust enforcement in world markets. Can this duopoly be sufficient to effectively protect worldwide competition, perhaps neglecting only a small, residual margin?[29] On the one hand, the margin is considerable – it includes markets of industrialised countries like Australia and Japan as well as emerging, big economies like China, India, Brazil, Russia, and so on. In particular, China and India have important enough domestic markets to destroy the contemporary enforcement duopoly once they are intensifying their competition policy activities.[30] On the other hand, things look different with regard to jurisdictions with small or less important domestic markets, in particular if they are developing countries. More often than not, they do not have the power to enforce their competition rules or protection-of-domestic-competition interests against foreign enterprises, especially if the latter are incorporated in big industrial countries or powerful multinational

---

[28] 'The Federal Cartel Office . . . initially earned only mild surprise by the two firms in question and by the public as well. The tobacco firms were less amused, however, when recognising that they would have to pay a considerable fine on their German sales if they ignored the decision of the Cartel Office.' Klodt (2001: 880).

[29] See for an affirmative statement Möschel (2005a: 605, 2005b).

[30] There are growing signs that both countries plan to intensify their extraterritorial antitrust activities. See generally Drexl (2005), concerning China, Owen et al. (2005) and Williams (2005), and concerning India, Singh (2003) and Bhattacharjea and Nanda (2005). On increasing extraterritorial enforcement ambitions of other (potentially) important countries see, for example, the chapters in Graham and Richardson (1997) and Basedow (2002) as well as Doern (1996a), Sanekata and Wilks (1996), Rodriguez and Williams (1998), Tavares de Araujo and Tineo (1998), Cowie and Alves de Mattos (1999), Clark (2000), First (2000), Hellmann (2001), Lee (2002), Pangestu et al. (2002), Poapongsakorn (2002), Letin (2004), Reynolds (2004), Williams (2004), First and Shiraishi (2005), and Bakhoum (2006). This will, on one hand, increase the number of jurisdictions, which are – in tendency – able to protect themselves, but, on the other hand, aggravate the other problems of extraterritorial antitrust enforcement.

global players respectively. Telling examples include the cement cartel in Egypt,[31] the international aluminium cartel,[32] the heavy electrical equipment cartel,[33] the Kimberly-Clark–Scott paper merger,[34] or the Italimpiante–Mannesmann merger.[35] The common features of these cases are that: (1) enterprises from industrial countries with a well-elaborated competition policy restricted competition on markets of less developed countries, which either lacked sufficient competition policy resources and/or important market positions to produce credible deterrence power; and (2) the competition authorities of the industrialised countries (namely the US and the EU) refused to enjoin the practices because competitive harm affected 'only' markets outside their territories.[36]

Hence, there is a significant power asymmetry in regard to the extraterritorial enforcement of domestic competition policies. Economically important jurisdictions are relatively more capable in protecting domestic competition against inbound anticompetitive arrangements and practices, whereas economically less important jurisdictions (small and/or developing countries) face severe problems in fighting restraints of competition from multinational enterprises.[37]

---

[31] Companies from Mexico and the EU allegedly engaged in a predatory pricing arrangement on the Egypt cement market in order to prevent local cement firms from exporting to the Canary Islands.

[32] The international aluminium cartel was an international price cartel between most of the important world market producers of aluminium (reportedly with the approval of a number of industrial countries' governments), which harmed consumers all around the world. However, countries in the South of Africa and in East Asia were particularly harmed because as aluminium importers only, they did not benefit in terms of producers' surplus.

[33] This cartel of international companies is of particular interest because 'first, that even though it was publicly documented, it was never prosecuted and, second, that . . . it applied worldwide except in the United States and in the European Union (which is probably the reason why it was never prosecuted in these jurisdictions).' Jenny (2003a: 613).

[34] Kimberly-Clark–Scott Paper is a US merger case with significant effects in Mexico.

[35] The Italian-German merger created a monopoly on the world market for specific specialised pipes for oil drilling operations. However, these products were exclusively sold to developing countries. Consequently, the merger was not blocked in the countries of origin of the merging enterprises.

[36] See on the whole paragraph, including the reported cases (and more examples), Jacquemin (1995), Fox (1998a, 2000a, 2003a), Jenny (2003a), and Levenstein and Suslow (2004). Some of the examples are also discussed in Stiglitz (2002).

[37] This power asymmetry even offers scope for a strategic (mis-) use of the effects doctrine. Strategic applications of competition rules are systematically analysed in section 1.3 of this chapter.

When different jurisdictions deal with one and the same alleged anticompetitive arrangement or practice independently from each other, this parallel treatment can be a source of conflict between the concurrent competent jurisdictions. A lot of contributors to the literature on international competition policy view the generation of jurisdictional conflicts as a major shortcoming of the extraterritorial application of competition laws.[38] Indeed, as Table 3.1 shows, extraterritorial competition policy has generated a number of jurisdictional conflicts with varying degrees of fierceness. It is probably no accident that most of them are related to cross-border mergers. Particularly prominent are two cases of conflict over merger control between the US and the EU.[39]

The first case is the Boeing–McDonnell Douglas merger (1996, approved 1997).[40] This merger created a duopoly on the world market of civil passenger jet aircrafts with more than 100 seats (the US company Boeing–MDD and its EU competitor Airbus).[41] It was approved without significant modifications by the US antitrust authorities. However, the European Commission expressed severe competitive concerns and a prohibition of the merger was indicated. This was furiously attacked by antitrust officials, politicians, and the media in the US. When European politicians sided with the Commission, the conflict threatened to escalate, almost leading towards a severe transatlantic trade conflict. Eventually, the Commission gave in and 'only' imposed modifica-

[38] See, for example, Behrens (1993), Campbell and Trebilcock (1993, 1997), Gerber (1999, 2003), Griffin (1999), Gifford and Sullivan (2000), Neven and Röller (2000, 2003), Grewlich (2001), Klodt (2001, 2005), Kovacic (2001), Budzinski and Kerber (2003), Hovenkamp (2003), Neugebauer (2004: 170–176), and Heyer (2005).

[39] In both cases, the EU challenged a merger which the US authorities approved. A counterexample is the Air Liquide–BOC merger which was approved (subject to substantial commitments) by the European Commission but subsequently challenged by the US authorities (wherefore, the companies abandoned the project). See for very brief analyses, Evans and Salinger (2002), Neven and Röller (2003), Neugebauer (2004: 175), and Canenbley and Rosenthal (2005: 180). Interestingly enough, this case generated significantly less interest, rage, and controversial literature than the other two cases.

[40] See Berg and Müller (1997), *European Commission* (1997), Nader (1997), Fox (1998b), Boeder (2000), Gifford and Sullivan (2000), Kovacic (2001), and Budzinski and Kerber (2003: 17–19, 93–96).

[41] Market shares before the merger were Boeing ≈ 60%, Airbus ≈ 30%, and MDD ≈ 10%. All other competitors like Tupolew or Lockheed had left the market at that point of time. Following the contemporary EC Merger Regulation, the merger was very likely to strengthen an existing dominant position of Boeing and, therefore, would have had to be prohibited. Other affected markets were military jets and rocket systems. However, the European Commission waived investigating these markets with regard to comity (US defence interests). Nonetheless, the Commission did fear cross-subsidisation from MDD's governmental aid for military research programmes to Boeing's R&D on civil aircraft.

tions on the merger, in particular the liquidation of exclusive agreements between Boeing–MDD and three big US airlines.[42]

The second case is the proposed merger between General Electric and Honeywell (2001).[43] The US antitrust authorities permitted this merger because: (1) they did not identify significant competitive concerns;[44] and (2) moreover, they believed the merger would increase efficiency. Contrarily, the European Commission decided to prohibit the merger because of the creation and strengthening of dominant positions in regard to several markets for jet aircraft engines, turbines and avionics. In particular, the Commission feared that GE–Honeywell would be able to monopolise a number of markets related to jet aircraft by: (1) bundling engine-related products with avionics (the former being GE's and the latter Honeywell's core competence) as well as products with services; and (2) predatorily exploiting its market power in financial services related to the leasing of jet aircraft.[45] The alleged foreclosure because of vertical and conglomerate effects received much attention in the literature. It is often neglected, however, that the Commission also held horizontal concerns (addition of market shares towards monopolisation) in regard to the engine markets for regional jet aircrafts[46] and business jet

---

[42] American Airlines, Delta Airlines, and Continental Airlines.

[43] See European Commission (2001a), Giotakos et al. (2001), Patterson and Shapiro (2001), Akbar (2002), Briggs and Rosenblatt (2002), Drauz (2002), Evans and Salinger (2002), Fox (2002), Giotakos (2002), Jin (2002), Kolasky (2002), Nalebuff (2002), Pflanz and Caffarra (2002), Reynolds and Ordover (2002), Schmitz (2002), Gerber (2003), Morgan and McGuire (2004), Shenefield (2004), and Veljanovski (2004). However, it is very difficult to identify interest biases of the 'academic' contributions to this highly controversial subject since most contributors are either affiliated to the European Commission (Drauz, Giotakos) or to the US antitrust authorities (Kolasky), or have served as paid experts and/or are otherwise related to GE (Caffarra, Nalebuff, Pflanz, Rey, Shapiro, and so on). Additionally, some articles are more or less exclusively based upon the possibly biased literature (in tendency: Jin, Morgan, McGuire). Since effective rules or conventions about making all relations of that kind public when publishing articles (in particular paid confidential expertise for enterprises) are lacking, this list need not be comprehensive.

[44] The notable exception was the US market for military helicopters. Here, the Department of Justice (Antitrust Division) demanded some modifications.

[45] The GE company GECAS (General Electric Capital Aviation Services) dominates the market for leasing civil passenger jets of varying classes to airlines. With a continuation of the 'GE-only strategy', which has been practised before and in combination with Honeywell's strong market position as a producer of engines for regional and business jet aircraft, the Commission feared that the remaining competitors would have been driven out of these markets.

[46] Market shares were GE ≈ 40–50%, Honeywell ≈ 40–50%, Rolls-Royce ≈ 5–10%.

aircraft[47] as well as the market for small marine gas turbines.[48] Although all relevant markets were viewed as being more or less world markets, the competent competition authorities came to incompatible assessments of the merger and, again, a transatlantic conflict occurred. This time, however, the European Commission effectively blocked the merger.

In the absence of blocking policies (that is, general acceptance of the legitimacy of mutual extraterritorial competition policy), jurisdictional conflicts can be caused by deviating competition laws. However, 'true' conflicts, that is, contradictory judgments by the competition authorities as demanded by the law, are rare.[49] Alleged anticompetitive arrangements and practices, which one jurisdiction prohibits, are most often not prescribed or dictated by the concurrent one. The 'normal' conflict arises because one jurisdiction prohibits a practice that is not prohibited under the law of the concurrent jurisdiction. Next to deviating laws, conflicting decisions can be the result of deviating fact assessments. Even with identical competition laws, two jurisdictions may come to incompatible judgments because they interpret the facts differently, delimitate markets in a deviating way, or use different competition economics (or use the same competition economics differently) to assess the anticompetitive impact. An additional driving force of conflict, in such cases, is that the conflicting jurisdictions each view their assessment as being the only right one. Things become even more complicated if non-competition interests (like industrial policy or strategic considerations) are injected into the extraterritorial governance of competition.[50] Eventually, inconsistencies can emerge because each competition agency limits itself (voluntarily or bound by law) to the assessment of competitive harm for its internal markets. One and the same arrangement or practice may cause competitive concerns in one jurisdiction and remain unproblematic in another one. However, although inconsistent decisions result, no conflict is likely to occur if all affected jurisdictions generally accept the legitimacy of extraterritorial competition policy. This is different with the other conflict sources, which may lead to conflict even if world markets are assumed.

With regard to the Boeing–MDD merger, industrial policy considerations

47 Market shares were Honeywell ≈ 50%, Pratt & Whitney ≈ 30%, GE ≈ 20%, Rolls-Royce < 10%.

48 Market shares were Honeywell ≈ 50–60%, Rolls-Royce/Allison ≈ 30–40%, GE ≈ 10%, Pratt & Whitney < 10%.

49 See nevertheless for exceptional cases Griffin (1999: 166, n. 44).

50 Since strategic competition policies are not limited to the extraterritorial application of domestic competition rules, these issues are more thoroughly discussed in section 1.3 of this chapter.

seem to be a major driving force on both sides of the Atlantic.[51] Although the US antitrust authorities referred to a failing-firm defence to justify the serious horizontal effects of the merger, important US interests to promote Boeing against its European competitor are clearly at hand. MDD was not in receivership and had even returned to profitability before the merger was announced. Therefore, the US authorities did not doubt that MDD could survive as a producer in the civil passenger jet aircraft market but, instead, argued that it was unlikely to be able to exert competitive pressure on Boeing.[52] On the other side, the EU has obvious interests in the world market position of its highly subsidised prestige object Airbus Industries, the focus of Boeing's exclusive agreements with US airlines (a market in which Airbus had significant deficits), instead of the alternative of demanding the sale of Douglas Aircraft Company (the relevant subsidiary of MDD) to an independent third party, may provide a hint for that. The suspicion that mutual industrial policy interests may have eventually resulted in a compromise at the expense of competition further proves the problem of power asymmetries in the absence of an international competition policy. Big enough jurisdictions may be able to negotiate favourable (for them) solutions at the expense of smaller countries (and global competition itself).

Concerning the proposed GE–Honeywell merger, Gerber (2003: 88–89) identifies four patterns of conflict argumentations in response to the Commission's prohibition decision. First, the legitimacy of the European Commission to deal with a merger of two US firms, in a deviating way compared to the US authorities, was called into question, particularly in the media. Since most of these commentators are not known to be prominent critics of the US extraterritorial practice, populism can be suspected to play an important role here. Second, one suspects that the European decision was guided by industrial policy considerations.[53] However, most of the benefiting enterprises are located in North America. Third, and more interesting, diverging competition rules might be the source of the conflict. Although the merger

---

[51] In the words of Eleanor M. Fox (1998b) 'The United States of Boeing versus the European Union of Airbus'. See on the effects of the subsidisation by both the US and the EU as well as of related state-aid agreements for competition in that market, Irwin and Pavcnik (2004) and the literature cited therein.

[52] However, even a study by the Chicago-owned economic consulting company Lexecon concluded that the merger was price raising. Other studies held that ongoing competition by MDD could have a price-decreasing effect of about 7%. See Fox (2003a: 374, n. 51).

[53] Gerber (2003: 88) quotes a *Business Week* article by Gary Becker as well as a statement by a US senator. Connected to this is the weaker claim that the US system is more objective and less prone to political influences. See Patterson and Shapiro (2001). See on the two systems and their differences sections 2.1–2.2 of Chapter 4.

control laws differ – the US prohibition standard 'substantial lessening of competition' (SLC) versus the (then) EU standard 'creation or strengthening of a dominant position' (market dominance) – the differing standards are viewed to be unlikely in making up for the different treatment of the GE–Honeywell case. Instead, a difference in elementary competition policy principles and objectives is frequently claimed, in particular by antitrust officials in the US, for example, the commentary of the Assistant Attorney General for Antitrust: 'Clear and longstanding US antitrust policy holds that the antitrust laws protect competition, not competitors. Today's EU decision reflects a significant point of divergence.'[54] In other words, the US antitrust policy aims to protect competition whereas the EU competition policy allegedly aims to protect competitors with the latter viewed as being inappropriate from an economic perspective.[55] Consequently, even with mutually exchanged substantive merger control laws, the outcome would probably have been equally conflicting. Fourth, eventually, the incompatible decisions of US and EU competition authorities stems from the reference to different economic theories about the anticompetitive impact of conglomerate and vertical integration, in particular of leveraging and mixed bundling. The applied theories diverge by having assumed weight either on (procompetitive) short-run price decreases or on (anticompetitive) long-run contestability problems respectively.[56]

The last aspect emphasises the elementary character of the jurisdictional conflicts problem. Whether efficiency in the sense of short-run and temporary price decreases is accepted as a defence for competitive concerns in terms of market power, increasing opportunities for foreclosure, and a long-run (persistent) decrease in contestability does not depend on the wording of the competition rules, but on the preferences of the contemporary competition authority officials for one competition theory or the other (hopefully to some extent mirroring the preferences of the respective society). Conflicts of this type can even occur if laws and objectives of national competition policies are similar. Since competition policy is directed towards future developments and effects,

---

[54] James (2001). I owe this quotation to Gerber (2003: 89).

[55] However, see the convincing discussion of Fox (2003b), demonstrating that the differentiation between 'protecting competition' and 'protecting competitors' is neither clear-cut nor unambiguous. The same is true for most general concepts in competition economics. See Burton (1994) and Budzinski (2003a, 2007) on mutually incompatible economic competition theories, efficiency definitions, and competition policy programmes. Additionally, see Heyer (2005: 403), who explicitly rejects the critique that the EU decision is not based on sound economic theory – although he argues from an economics-based US perspective.

[56] For a brief illustration see Heyer (2005: 403–406). See additionally, Reynolds and Ordover (2002).

and the future (as an indeterministic process) is not and will never be perfectly predictable, scope for deviating opinions, evaluations and conjectures about future welfare implications and appropriate policy instruments inevitably emerges and remains.[57] This is also evident with regard to the recent conflict between the US and EU authorities about the Microsoft case (2004). Although both jurisdictions principally agreed about the anticompetitive character of specific conduct of Microsoft, a conflict about the appropriate remedies to prevent such conduct in the future arose.[58]

In summary, an effective avoidance of jurisdictional conflicts mandates some kind of an international competition policy regime. Even completely harmonised national and regional competition policy regimes can – without any strategic intention – produce conflicting outcomes, generating externalities. The fact that competition policy decisions must always assess the implications of alternative paths of future development of markets[59] combined with the fact that the future is indetermined (impossible to predict perfectly) makes it impossible to avoid conflicts without implementing some type of an international regime. Only a truly international regime can overcome the inbound focus of current antitrust regimes[60] and cope with the resulting horizontal externalities.[61] An appropriate international conflict resolution seems particularly pressing in the

57 In the words of Heyer (2005: 408): '[U]nless future outcomes are perfectly predictable (which they are not), agreement on the appropriate objective function to be maximized (. . .) and the correct analytical methodology to be applied will not produce similar findings or guarantee similar decisions.' Even an ultimate and unified competition theory, which is improbable, impractical and theoretically deficient (see section 1.3.5 of Chapter 4), would not solve this problem.

58 See Heyer (2005: 407) and Müller (2005: 309), who cite sources from the US antitrust authorities and Congress publicly criticising the EU practice and questioning EU jurisdiction over the case. This stands in contrast to Monti (2004b: 497–498), who emphasises the cooperative efforts in the Microsoft case. However, more shadows are on the wall since the Korean antitrust authorities tend to impose considerably stronger and remarkably incompatible sanctions on Microsoft. See Belz (2005).

59 Will a given market perform better in the future if a proposed merger is allowed or if it is blocked? Will a reviewed business practice suspend future competition and destroy the contestability of the market or not? Will a proposed 'strategic alliance' (R&D cartel) promote innovation in the future or will it erode the incentive to engage in alternative, possibly more efficient innovation efforts? If both pro- and anticompetitive effects are a likely consequence of a specific antitrust case, which one will outweigh the other in the future? And so on.

60 To be precise, it does not overcome the inbound focus. However, the inbound focus of a global regime should produce no externalities in the foreseeable future.

61 Note that this does not imply a significantly centralised international competition policy regime. The various design options of international regimes with their varying degree of centralising and decentralising features are in the focus of Chapters 4 and 5 of this book.

face of upcoming powerful antitrust jurisdictions like China, India, Russia, and others, which enhances the potentials for new conflicts over antitrust policy – in particular against the background of significantly deviating views and theories about competition and antitrust in some of these countries.[62]

Table 3.1 Exemplary competition policy cases with jurisdictional conflicts[63]

Case	Year	Type	Conflicting jurisdictions
Alcoa (CH)	1945	Quota cartel	US/CH
Ciba (CH)/Geigy (CH)	1970	Merger	US/CH
Dyestuffs (US)	1972	Export price fixing	US/EU
Organic pigments (US)	1979	Merger	US/D
Bayer (D)/Firestone (US)	1980	Merger of French subsidiaries	F/D
Uranium cartel	1981	Price fixing	US/CDN/SA/F/UK
Philip Morris (US)/ Rothmans (SA/UK)	1983	Merger	D/UK/SA/US
IBM (US)	1985	Abuse of dominant position	US/EU
Laker Airways	1985	Predatory pricing	UK/US
Wood pulp	1988	Export price fixing	US/EU/CDN
Mérieux (F)/ Connaught (CDN)	1990	Merger	US/CDN/F
De Havilland (CDN)/Alenia-Aerospatiale (F/I)	1991	Merger	EU/F/CDN/US
Hartford Fire Insurance (UK)	1993	Market behaviour	US/UK
Japanese automakers/ United States Trade Representative	1995	Exclusive dealing, vertical foreclosure	US/JPN
British Airways (UK)/American Airlines (US)	1996	Strategic alliance	US/UK
Union Pacific (US)/ Southern Pacific (US)	1996	Merger	US/MEX

(*continued*)

[62] See Drexl (2005). The recent blocking of the Siemens–InterRos Silovyje Maschiny merger by the Russian Federal Anti-Monopoly Service (April 2005) on dubious grounds (from a competition-focused perspective) provides a foretaste.

[63] The data are predominantly taken from Klodt (2005: 45–65). See additionally Behrens (1993), Fox (1999b, 2003a), Griffin (1999), Klodt (2001), Zanettin (2002), and Neugebauer (2004).

Table 3.1 continued

Case	Year	Type	Conflicting jurisdictions
Boeing (US)/ McDonnell Douglas (US)	1997	Merger	US/EU
Fuji (JPN)/Kodak (US)	1997	Market entry deterrence	US/JPN
Air Liquide (F)/BOC (UK)	1999	Merger	US/EU
British Airways (UK)	2001	Predatory pricing	US (court decision)/EU
General Electric (US)/ Honeywell (US)	2001	Merger	US/EU
Microsoft (US)	2004	Predatory strategies	US/EU
Siemens (D)/InterRos Silovyje Maschiny (RUS)	2005	Merger	RUS/D

The multiple review of one and the same cross-border competition case by a multitude of jurisdictions and their competition authorities leads to significant inefficiencies in multidimensional ways.[64] First of all, the emergence of jurisdictional conflicts (as discussed above) can be reformulated in terms of inefficiencies, including external costs if trade or other economy and policy relations between the conflicting jurisdictions become hampered. However, even if no conflict between the reviewing jurisdictions results, considerable inefficiencies will arise both for the reviewing agencies (administrative costs) and for the reviewed enterprises (transaction costs).

If the competition authority of each jurisdiction, which is affected by an anticompetitive arrangement or practice, investigates and reviews it independent from each other, an inefficient multiplication of resource efforts is the consequence. Each authority engages in finding the same facts, scrutinises the same documents, organises hearings with more or less the same witnesses and experts, produces or orders economic analysis,[65] and so on. Even with differing competition laws, policy principles or interests, transaction costs could be significantly reduced because all the decisions will have to rely on the same

[64] See the comprehensive study in regard to multijurisdictional merger control by ICN (2002). See also, for example, Brittan and van Miert (1996), Campbell and Trebilcock (1997), Rowley et al. (2000), and Becher (2002).

[65] For instance, both the US and the EU authorities developed their own merger simulation model and their own econometric analyses during the review procedures of the Oracle–PeopleSoft merger (Budzinski and Christiansen 2007).

facts. The multiplication of administrative effort generates costs in terms of burdens for taxpayers or missing resources for other public tasks – or even for other competition policy tasks. The particularly high effort of multijurisdictional merger control may, for instance, work at the expense of criminal cartel prosecution.

Even more burdensome than the administrative costs may be the increasing transaction costs for merging or cooperating enterprises[66] facing multijurisdictional competition policy review. Among the additional costs for reviewed enterprises are, for example, the duplicate costs of multiple filings, multiple production of evidentiary documents, legal services and consulting in different jurisdictions, translations, longer time period until all procedures are closed, and increased legal uncertainty.[67] Regarding merger control for instance, considerable differences in – along with opaque provisions about – notification thresholds (based on such diverse criteria like turnover figures, market shares, combined or alternative value of the parties' assets, relation of revenues/assets/turnovers to local minimum wages, and so on – and further complicated by the fact that these criteria may relate to local, national, or worldwide figures), moment of the triggering event and timeframes, deadlines, requirements in regard to data and (confidential) information, and so on, can be catalogued along with – sometimes dubiously – high and cumulating filing fees, allowing for the suspicion that they serve as funding sources for the respecting agencies (Rowley et al. 2000: 16–22, 29). Anecdotal evidence of the extent of these inefficiencies is provided in the context of the proposed merger between Alcan (Canada), Pechinery (France), and APA Algroup (Switzerland) in the international aluminium industry (1999–2003).[68] The merger had to be notified in more than 40 jurisdictions of which 16 entered into a formal procedure, which required all documents to be translated to eight different languages.[69] During the merger control review, the services of 35 law firms and the payment of more than US$100 000 filing fees were necessary. Alcan alone produced more than 400 boxes of printed material and approximately one million pages of emails, 11 CD-ROMs worth (however, according

66 I abstract from the intentional formation of hardcore cartels because they are obviously designed to be carried out without notification to the competition authorities.

67 On the one hand, it becomes more difficult for enterprises to evaluate in advance whether they are engaging in a legal or illegal arrangement or practice. On the other hand, the probability of non-anticipatable ('surprising') outcomes increases.

68 See on the following Chenard (2002: 34–35). The 1999 attempt to merge all three companies was vetoed by the European Commission. Thus, in 1999 only Alcan–APA Algroup proceeded. A substantially modified proposal to take over Pechinery was eventually cleared in 2003. However, the exemplary numbers refer to the first trial (1999 case) only.

69 Czech, English, German, Polish, Portuguese, Russian, Spanish and Turkish.

to the report, both printed and electronic versions were requested and filed) for the US authorities only. Altogether, direct costs amounted to more than US$10 million.

Furthermore, cumulating or contradictory sanctions,[70] remedies, modification orders, and so on, generate additional burden on cooperating or merging enterprises. It must be emphasised that the bureaucratic burden of multijurisdictional competition policy eventually hits procompetitive arrangements as well as anticompetitive ones. Empirical evidence suggests that regulatory transaction costs of multijurisdictional reviews reduce cross-border merger activity significantly so that it forms a barrier against efficient combinations of assets.[71] Although I am not aware of empirical evidence, the same is most likely true for cross-border enterprise cooperation. In other words, multiple compliance costs work as a (distortionary) 'tax' (similarly, Trebilcock and Iacobucci 2004: 153) on international business activities and the competitive search for efficient business structures in international markets.

1.2.3 Discretionary bilateral cooperation as an insufficient supplement

In the previous section, it was assumed that competition authorities apply their competition rules extraterritorially in a completely autonomous way, that is, without cooperating with each other. However, discretionary bilateral cooperation can supplement extraterritorial competition policy and, thereby, perhaps serve to reduce some of its problems. As long as interagency cooperation remains bilateral and discretionary (that is, the decision whether to cooperate is made on a case-by-case basis), one cannot call this an effectively international competition policy.[72]

In the absence of an international regime, bilateral cooperation agreements between competition policy jurisdictions began to spread starting in the mid-

---

70 See as an example, regarding the Pepsico–Coca-Cola case (abusive behaviour), Hamilton and Flecher (2004).

71 See Evenett (2002), deriving that 'in many jurisdictions the effects . . . are to cut the amount of cross-border M&A in half, suggesting that [multiple] merger notification regimes are a substantial impediment on the international trade in corporate assets' (p. 55). Unfortunately, the study does not distinguish between procompetitive and anticompetitive mergers.

72 The interface between a regime of uncoordinated regional and national competition policies and an international competition policy regime is rather fuzzy. For the purpose of this analysis, a multilateral agreement – even if its content is rather informal – is viewed to constitute an international regime. This represents a simplification because, on the one hand, no requirement as to the minimum number of participating jurisdictions is explicated. On the other hand, systematic bilateral cooperation can be very far-reaching and if this occurs between the two dominant jurisdictions and their dominance is significant enough, it could effectively work as an international regime.

1970s.[73] Figure 3.1 provides an overview on the spreading and development of such bilateral agreements. Most of the cooperation agreements are restricted to mutual notification and consultation. These information-sharing processes, which most often have strict limits with regard to confidential business information, are, nevertheless, very helpful to reduce administrative costs. Even though parallel investigation and review procedures remain, the doubling of efforts at the very least becomes reduced to a certain degree. However, the consideration of the results of the consulting process most generally remains within the discretion of the participating agencies. This kind of cooperation is particularly beneficial with regard to cartel prosecution, which, consequently, is the field where those agreements are predominantly applied.

More elaborated agreements (which emerged in the 1990s) refer to comity principles to reduce jurisdictional conflicts and make decisions more coherently. Again, the fight against international hardcore cartels lies in the centre of the cooperation. Merger control issues, in which national interests (including industrial policy interests) play a more important role, are often exempted from the more far-reaching parts of the agreements. The basic idea of comity principles is to take the interests of the foreign authority into account. Negative comity means not to interfere with foreign interests if no explicit domestic interests are touched, for example, to waive 'hostile' extraterritorial enforcement against the resistance of the other jurisdiction. The positive comity principle further enhances the depth of the cooperation. A jurisdiction, which is affected by an anticompetitive arrangement or practice from abroad, waives its own procedure and, instead, leaves it to the respective foreign jurisdiction to control and sanction the arrangement or practice. The acting jurisdiction is obliged to handle the case in the interest of the demanding jurisdiction.

For the first time, positive comity was integrated into a cooperation agreement in the 1991 EU–US agreement (further enhanced with the 1998 agreement). However, merger control issues were excluded from positive comity and even regarding other cases, this instrument has been widely neglected since. Until now, the only formal application was the Amadeus case (1997), in

---

[73] See among the vast literature on bilateral competition policy cooperation agreements, for example, Whish and Wood (1994), Cocuzza and Montini (1998), Zäch (1998), Lampert (1999), Parisi (1999), Pons (1999), Janow (2000), Fullerton and Mazard (2001), Kennedy (2001: 40–67), Budzinski (2002a: 241–245), First (2003), Jenny (2003b), Podszun (2003: 72–117), Wilson (2003: 199–212), Aigner (2004), Shenefield (2004: 393–400), Wood (2004), Worm (2004: 153–167), and Canenbley and Rosenthal (2005). The focus of the literature is predominantly descriptive and comparative in regard to the different existing agreements. To my opinion the most elaborate and analytical discussion is Zanettin (2002: 53–227).

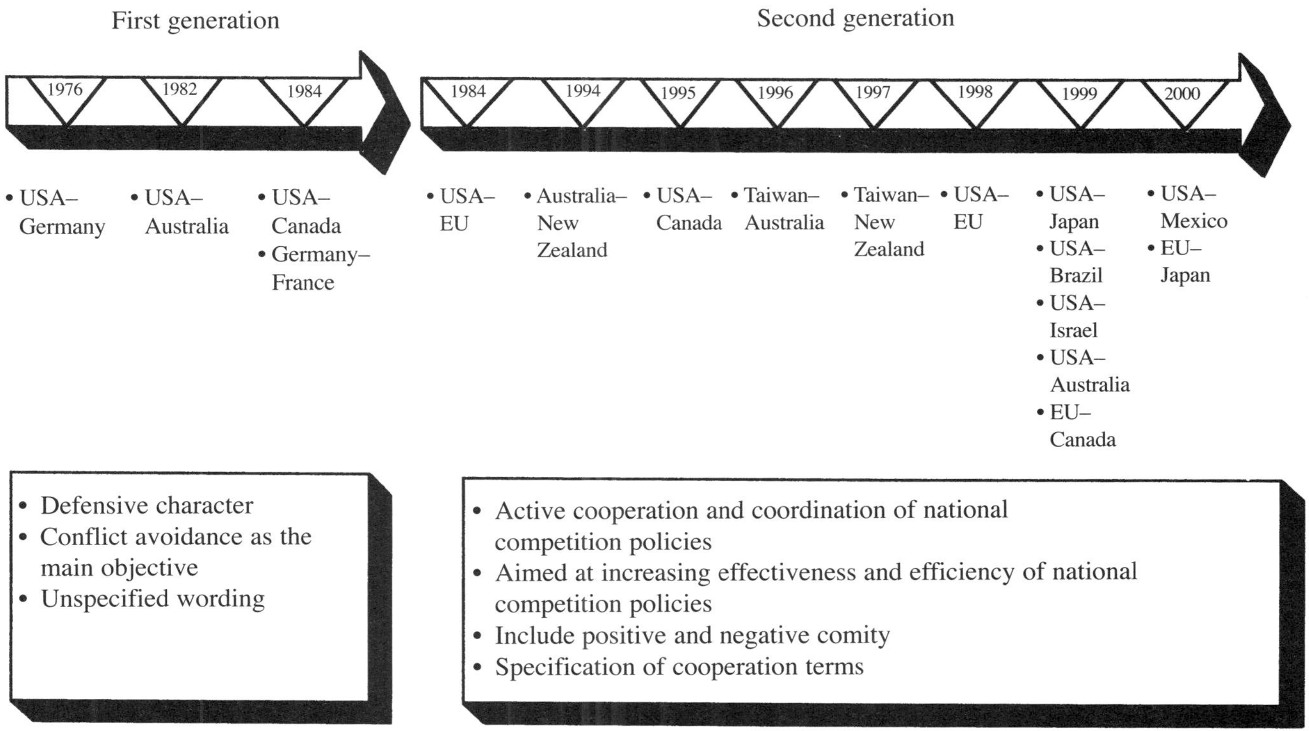

Source: Translated from Budzinski and Aigner (2004)

Figure 3.1 Development of bilateral cooperation agreements on competition policy

which the US Department of Justice formally requested the European Commission to investigate allegedly anticompetitive practices by European airlines, discriminating against US enterprises. The EU computer reservation system Amadeus was said to be acting in an exclusionary way, thus deterring the concurrent US system SABRE. However, the procedure seemed to proceed rather sluggishly and was hampered by deviating investigation techniques and evidentiary standards between the US and the EU. The case was eventually settled in 2000 by private agreements between the airlines and their reservation system companies.[74] In the context of the US–EU conflict over Microsoft, US officials accused the EU of a violation of the positive comity clause, a claim that is difficult to evaluate in the face of the voluntary character of that type of interagency cooperation.[75]

For several reasons, discretionary bilateral interagency cooperation represents an insufficient supplement to extraterritorial competition policy in a world economy. Although it does improve the governance of international competition in comparison to effects-doctrine-based competition policy only, significant shortcomings point towards the necessity of multilateral approaches and, thus, towards the superiority of an original international competition policy regime:

- Jurisdictional conflicts are not tackled effectively because genuine/serious conflicts of interests cannot be solved by mutual consideration of these conflicting interests.[76] However, conflicts due to misunderstandings can be avoided.
- Problems of multijurisdictional merger control cannot be adequately solved because of: (1) the higher importance of serious national interests; and (2) practical reasons inherent to the comity principles (Zanettin 2002: 186–187). However, the prosecution of hardcore cartels seems to represent a more beneficial field for interagency cooperation since there is a widespread consensus about the necessity to fight them.[77]

---

[74] See on this case Griffin (1999: 184–185), ICPAC (2000: 232–234), Rill et al. (2000), and Zanettin (2002: 188–189). The latter (2002, pp. 189–190) additionally views the IRI and AC Nielsen case to be an informal positive comity case. See for the facts of the case also Rill and Wilson (2000).

[75] See the detailed discussion by Müller (2005).

[76] For instance, both the Boeing–MDD and the GE–Honeywell mergers generated conflicts in the face of elaborated competition authority cooperation. With regard to the limits of comity considerations, see Griffin (1999: 167–168).

[77] The outstanding successful example is the prosecution of the international vitamins cartels. See First (2001a) and section 2.1 of Chapter 2. However, industrial policy interests may also disturb this antitrust field. 'Where no industrial policy at the source is concerned, cartel enforcement at the national level with deep cooperation of

- The asymmetry of power is not resolved. On one hand, developing countries are under-represented in existing bilateral cooperation agreements, on the other hand, the bargaining power of big industrialised jurisdictions would allow for discriminating agreements or the discriminating use of it (Fox 2000a, 2003a; Jenny 2003a, 2003b).
- Differences and incompatibilities in national competition laws, principles, policy goals, and procedures in practice impede deep and systematic cooperation.
- Even if there was an overall kaleidoscope of bilateral cooperation agreements, involving every antitrust jurisdiction, this network would most probably be characterised by significant incoherence. In multi-jurisdictional cases, each jurisdiction would have to handle a multitude of bilateral duties, probably not consistent with each other.

Altogether, a cacophony of bilateral agreements cannot adequately replace an original international competition policy. 'It seems over-optimistic to imagine that a world-wide framework for competition policy could be built up piecemeal from a network of bilateral agreements. . . . [I]t would be virtually impossible to ensure that all the agreements were compatible with each other.'[78]

1.3 The Role of Strategic Competition Policies

The previous section demonstrated that competition policy at national or regional levels produces inefficiencies, conflict potentials, and loopholes with regard to the governance of global competition, and the line of argument now takes a further step. National competition policies in internationalised markets can cause significant restrictions of international competition and, thus, can have an anticompetitive effect. Of course, competition policy represents a policy to protect competition. However, if the regulating jurisdiction is geographically incongruent with the regulated market, competition policy can be (mis-) used strategically to shift rents between jurisdictions. A strategic competition policy is an analogue to the well-known phenomenon 'strategic trade policy' and means the drafting and/or (more often) application of competition rules in a discriminatory way, thereby causing an anticompetitive impact on international markets. Strategic competition policies are jurisdictional

---

sister agencies is the success story (in progress) of international antitrust. Where industrial policy intervenes, however, the gap is great, as in the case of OPEC, marketing boards and commodity cartels.' Fox (2003a: 373).

78 Meiklejohn (1999: 1247). Such 'over'-optimism is, however, advocated by Swaine (2001: 725–741).

competition policies, which: (1) favour domestic welfare at the expense of foreign and/or international welfare (beggar-thy-neighbour competition policies); or (2) favour the welfare of domestic lobby groups at the expense of both domestic and foreign/international welfare (lobbyism-biased competition policies). In the absence of an international competition policy regime, the case for (mis-) using competition policies for strategic purposes is likely to become strengthened if trade policy instruments are increasingly not available at national and regional levels because of international trade governance in the WTO context.[79]

1.3.1 Instruments of strategic competition policies

Strategic competition policy can employ a large variety of instruments.[80] A popular strategy is to allow domestic enterprises to restrict competition (by collusion, deterrence/predation, or concentration) either within the domestic borders or on outbound markets. Exemplary instruments include the allowance or even promotion of export cartels, that is, cartels or surrogates directed exclusively towards foreign markets.[81] Typically enough, only few national and regional competition laws prohibit export cartels.[82] Alternatively, jurisdictions can run a cartel haven to allow domestic enterprises to reap supracompetitive profits at home in order to cross-subsidise their outbound activities. The same effects can be achieved by a discriminatory employment of merger control. A creation and promotion of 'national champions' or

[79] 'In other words, trade liberalization may create a "policy vacuum" fitted by strategically complacent competition policy' Cadot et al. (2000: 7). See on the interplay of strategic competition and trade policies also Schoenbaum (1994), Cadot et al. (2000: 7–12), Markl and Meissner (2000), Budzinski (2002b, 2002c), Kerber and Budzinski (2003, 2004), and De Stefano and Rysman (2004). However, Horn and Levinsohn (2001) emphasise that trade liberalisation does not promote strategic competition policies by itself (implying an increased importance of basic strategic policy incentives for politicians and for lobbyism). Greaney (1999) views strategic competition policy (in terms of allowing collusion between domestic enterprises) to be the less distortionary instrument in comparison to strategic trade policies (in terms of tariffs). Under certain (more or less strict) conditions, she even identifies an increase in global welfare!

[80] See for comprehensive overviews Gröner and Knorr (1996), Guzman (1998, 2004), Fox (2000a, esp. pp. 1795–1797) and Kerber and Budzinski (2003, 2004).

[81] For analysis of the anticompetitive and distortionary effects of export cartels see, for example, Hoppmann (1961), Victor (1992), Scherer (1994: 43–54), Schoenbaum (1994), Schultz (2002), Fox (2003a: 365–369), and Durand et al. (2004: 5–9).

[82] One of the rare exceptions – at least in regard to substantive provisions – is the EU. Contrarily, the US rather explicitly exempts purely export oriented cartels from its antitrust laws in the context of the Webb–Pomerene Act (adopted 1918), the Foreign Trade Antitrust Improvements Act (adopted 1982), and other related Acts. See, for example, Durand et al. (2004: 6) and Guzman (2004: 121).

'domestic global players' can be assisted by lax laws against purely domestic mergers. With such strategies, market power on domestic markets is tolerated (or even welcomed) in order to improve the competitiveness of newly created giant firms on outbound or international markets. An 'international competitiveness defence' in national merger control exists e.g. in the otherwise comparatively strict German merger laws in the context of the ministerial exemption ('*Ministererlaubnis*') (Kühn 1997: 133–135). A recent example of its strategic application is represented by the E.ON–Ruhrgas merger, which almost creates a monopoly on the German gas market (Roth and Voigtländer 2002; Hüschelrath and Rommel 2004). Therefore, the *Bundeskartellamt* (German Federal Cartel Office) has initially prohibited the merger. However, the German Ministry of Economics overruled the Bundeskartellamt against the most explicit advice of the German Monopolies Commission (2002a, 2002b).[83] The Ministry allowed the merger with the most probable strategic intention to create a national champion in the emerging international (European) energy markets. Very conclusive is the statement of Alfred Tacke (Administrative State Secretary in the German Federal Ministry of Economics) arguing that the merger is cleared because it 'strengthens the international competitiveness of Ruhrgas on international gas markets.'[84]

Discriminatory competition policy can be rooted in the laws themselves

---

[83] The German Monopolies Commission ('*Monopolkommission*') is an advisory council of economic and legal academic experts. Its statements are non-binding but publication of its opinion is mandatory. According to § 42 of the GWB (German law against restrictions of competition), a ministerial exemption of otherwise anticompetitive mergers is solely possible on the cumulative grounds of overwhelming public interest, international competitiveness, and absence of endangering the market economic order as a whole. Concerning E.ON–Ruhrgas, the Monopolies Commission denied the fulfilment of these conditions whereas the ministry answered in the affirmative.

[84] See Tacke (2002, my translation). He was responsible for the decision since the acting Minister Müller was a former leading director of the E.ON predecessor VEBA and, even as a minister, received a pension from E.ON – a constellation which allowed for a multitude of speculations. In the meantime, both Müller and Tacke have left the policy sphere and obtained leading positions in the companies RAG Ruhrkohle AG (which is a one-third subsidiary of E.ON) and SteAG (which is a subsidiary of RAG) respectively. See Wurmnest (2005: 113), and as an example from much press information, Dohmen (2005). The acting chairman of the German Monopolies Commission, Basedow, commented upon this development: 'When the concerned officials later change into the board of directors of companies, who are under the influence of the enterprises participating in the merger, then the press, not without cause, asks the question how far away are we really from a Banana Republic. The dignity of public institutions and proceedings deserves in any case greater respect from the officials as well as from participating business.' Basedow, cited in Wurmnest (2005: 113; translated by Barbara Majireck).

like in the case of export cartel exemptions. Additionally, competition agencies always have – to a cross-nationally differing extent – a minimum scope for discretion,[85] in particular in regard to rule-of-reason-styled antitrust policy areas. For instance, during merger control procedures, both the processes of fact finding (intensity and direction of research) and evaluation of the anticompetitive impact including possible (efficiency) defences (hypotheses about future prices, the probability of future market entries, future behaviour of competitors, estimation of efficiency potentials, probability of/incentives for, the realisation of such potentials, innovation, and so on) offer considerable scope for the informal injection of strategically biased interpretations even if the laws do not require such considerations. Moreover, selective nonenforcement of explicit competition rules represents an additional practice to produce strategic outcomes, for example, to hamper inward market access.[86] A selective enforcement strategy can, for example, be connected to the strategic employment of antidumping rules, in particular alleged social and environmental dumping by developing countries. In this context, many academic commentators identify considerable anticompetitive scope in the trade-related antidumping rules within the WTO framework and argue in favour of an inclusion of dumping and predatory pricing issues in an international competition policy context.[87]

A second way of employing competition policy strategically is to prevent foreign enterprises from doing business efficiently. By strategically misusing the effects doctrine to disadvantage procompetitive inbound conduct from foreign enterprises, domestic competitors can be protected from more efficient foreign rivals. While the above examples indicate an inwardly directed lenient competition policy, this strategy implies an outwardly directed strict (overregulating) competition policy.[88] For instance, in the conflict concerning the Boeing–McDonnell Douglas merger, the US side attacked the EU side for allegedly only striving to protect Airbus from a more efficient Boeing (overly

[85] This is even true for the US antitrust system with its strong focus on courts' decisions. For instance, the US agencies (FTC, Antitrust Division, see section 2.1 of Chapter 4) can waive bringing a domestic merger whose anticompetitive effects are exclusively outbound to the court by clearing it, for example, on vague and unproven efficiency grounds. No falsifiable demonstration of the reasoning is required since – apart from lawsuits by competitors – only merger prohibitions (and mandatory modifications) go to the courts.

[86] One example is the Kodak–Fuji case which is discussed in more depth in section 1.3.4 of this chapter.

[87] See exemplary for the large and controversial literature on this issue Messerlin (1995), Lipstein (1997), Freytag and Zimmermann (1998), Tharakan et al. (1998), Knorr (1999), Pierce (2000), and Conrad (2005: 33–56).

[88] This line of argument is, for example, stressed by Guzman (2004) and Stephan (2004).

strict outbound merger control). Vice versa, the EU side suspected an industrial policy motivation by the US side to secure Boeing an edge over Airbus towards a US world market dominance (lenient inward merger control).[89] A variant of this strategy is to employ a permissive national merger control in order to (politically) promote a national merger solution to prevent takeovers by foreign companies. This more defensive strategy can be very popular if catching phrases like 'the imminent sellout' of national assets or interests come into play.

1.3.2 The economics of the strategic competition policy dilemma

The rationale for the strategic employment of national or regional competition policies lies in the temptation to increase national (or regional respectively) welfare at the expense of foreign welfare, combined with a strategic interdependence between the (domestic and foreign) competition policy regimes. Thus, there is a scope for beggar-thy-neighbour strategies, that is, improving national welfare at the expense of global and/or foreign welfare. Such strategic competition policies are economically rational from an individualistic point of view.

Most generally, the strategic allowance or promotion of anticompetitive arrangements or practices reduces global welfare. However, it can increase national (regional) welfare if the supracompetitive gains are reaped within the borders of the strategically acting jurisdiction, whereas the (comparatively larger) burden falls completely or to a sufficient extent to producers and consumers in foreign jurisdictions. Such discriminatory strategies can obviously be economically rational from the viewpoint of a single jurisdiction, focused on its national welfare only. For instance, jurisdictions with more producers than consumers (net exporters) experience an incentive to engage in inwardly lenient competition policies to promote their domestic producers at the expense of foreign consumers. Vice versa, jurisdictions with a higher weight on consumers compared to producers (net importers) rationally tend to engage in (or attempt to) over-regulating foreign enterprise conduct because they do not gain from (for example, efficiency-related) increasing profits abroad.[90] Whenever specific cartels or mergers have cross-border effects, the

---

[89] Since both sides additionally subsidise 'their' company (in one or the other way), it is not too speculative to assume that strategic issues played a role in the clearance of the merger by the US authorities (in spite of a significant increase in horizontal concentration) as well as in the design of the remedies imposed by the EU authorities. Of course, each side views strategic considerations exclusively with respect to the other one. See section 1.2.2 of this chapter and the literature quoted there, especially Fox (1998b).

[90] See, for more elaboration, Guzman (1998: 1512–1524, 2004: 101–108).

related gains and the burdens can be distributed asymmetrically between the affected jurisdictions, opening up scope for strategic considerations either to promote a global welfare reducing arrangement or to spoil a global welfare increasing arrangement. Theoretically, this can even happen with completely harmonised competition laws (for example, Barros and Cabral 1994; Head and Ries 1997; Neven and Röller 2000).

Discriminatory strategies restrict international competition and are (economically and/or politically) mutually rational from the perspective of individual jurisdictions (or its authorities respectively). In regard to world welfare, the emerging problem can be described in terms of game theory as a Prisoners' Dilemma (PD) situation since the optimal situation is not achievable by isolated rational individual behaviour but only through an arrangement between the 'players'. Non-coordinated jurisdictional competition policy (opening up scope for strategic considerations), thus, is likely to lead to an inferior equilibrium on the world level. Table 3.2 presents a rather simple one-shot-PD for international competition policy.[91]

Obviously, the highest level of world-welfare (W) would result if both country A and B performed a competition policy, which disclaimed national-strategic elements and focused on the maximisation of international welfare instead (cooperative strategy). Following this line of thought, it is not prescribed whether such an 'international competition policy' is a national

Table 3.2 One-shot Prisoner's Dilemma of international competition policy

Country A / Country B	Strategic competition policy (non-cooperative strategy)	International competition policy (cooperative strategy)
Strategic competition policy (non-cooperative strategy)	A 5/B 5 (W = 10)	A 15/B 0 (W = 15)
International competition policy (cooperative strategy)	A 0/B 15 (W = 15)	A 10/B 10 (W = 20)

Source: Budzinski (2003b: 7)

[91] See Budzinski (2003b: 4–10). Independently, Durand et al. (2004: 7–8) develop a similar line of argumentation with regard to export cartel exemptions.

(regional) competition law enforced by a national (regional) authority with a view on world welfare or whether some international agreements are enforced by a supranational agency. The decisive insight from modelling strategic competition policies as a PD game, points to the possibility of rational national behaviour leading to an inferior equilibrium in the absence of an international arrangement. If country A decides upon its competition policy strategy unilaterally and without knowing in which competition policy strategy country B engages, then it is perfectly individual-rational for A to choose the non-cooperative strategy (that is, to engage in a strategic competition policy). If B chooses the cooperative strategy, A gains a welfare pay-off of 15, the corresponding pay-off of B is zero with world-welfare (W) being 15.[92] If A had engaged in the cooperative strategy, its pay-off would have been 10 (a minus of 5). Furthermore, if B also chooses the non-cooperative strategy, A is also better off. A gains 'only' 5 but – given the non-cooperative performance of B – choosing the cooperative strategy would have reduced this pay-off to zero.

Therefore, irrespective of the strategy B chooses, A is individually always better off engaging in a strategic competition policy at the expense of world welfare. Strategic competition policy is the individually superior (and, therefore, rational) choice as long as the two countries decide upon their strategies without mutual ('international') coordination and thus, do not know in advance (or with a sufficient security) what strategy the interacting one will choose. Since B's situation is exactly the same, without international coordination rational jurisdictional behaviour will lead to the inferior equilibrium (W = 10), which is suboptimal (inefficient) from a world-welfare point of view. The superior equilibrium of cooperative strategies (W = 20) can – in this very simple model – only be achieved by some kind of international coordination,[93] which credibly commits the players to the cooperative strategy.

However, it would be oversimplifying to conclude the necessity of an international level of competition policy authority to erode the incentives for strategic competition policy from the one-shot game. The theory of repeated games offers more complex but also more comprehensive results. With regard to international competition policy, a repeated game approach shows that a self-enforcing cooperative solution is possible if the national (regional) competition policy jurisdictions repeatedly interact (Cabral 2003, 2004). In a variant of the folk theorem (Friedman 1971), a dynamic equilibrium emerges in which

---

[92] If individual rational behaviour is assumed, the welfare pay-offs of B and W do not influence A's decision.

[93] 'International coordination' must be interpreted in a very broad sense here. The model tells nothing about the type of international coordination (substantive international law, minimum standards, international procedural rules, cooperation agreements, and so on), which would be sufficient to escape from the PD situation.

the players discount future pay-offs and develop stabilising strategies of mutual modes of reaction to defecting and cooperating behaviours.[94] A mutual concession equilibrium may result, which incrementally but asymptotically enlarges towards an efficient international competition policy coordination (in terms of maximising world welfare). In other words, repeated interaction can lead in the long run to the (imperfect) self-enforcement of the mutually cooperative strategy.

However, there are some qualifications concerning this optimistic result. First of all, the infinite horizon of the supergame is crucial. With a finite number of stages, the famous chain-store paradox (Selten 1978) offers scope for the sustainability of strategic competition policies (non-cooperative strategy). Since any punishment strategy relies on disciplining effects in future stages, the final stage (n) will rationally be played non-cooperatively (similar to the one-shot game). As rational players anticipate this in advance, they will defect in the ($n - 1$) stage, rationally anticipating this even in the ($n - 2$) stage, and so on. Therefore, in finite supergames, strategic competition policy remains a rational strategy.

Secondly, in regard to infinite supergames, the cooperative result becomes possible but not certain. The cooperative trajectory is only one of a continuum of possible equilibrium solutions (multiple equilibria), including more non-cooperative ones as well. Moreover, a number of rather specific assumptions are necessary to secure the pro self-enforcement result, including – among many – symmetric and undistorted information, objective rationality, stable and symmetric discount rates, strict limitation of the number of players, stationary regulatory and business environments,[95] and a strict welfare orientation of the deciding competition agencies. The latter implies the absence of political and lobbyism-biased interests, which are the main driving forces of strategic competition policies in the real world (as discussed in the following

---

94 For instance, Cabral (2004: 3) introduces to his model the following rules: (1) play starts in the cooperative phase; (2) play continues in the cooperative phase as long as players choose the designated cooperative action; (3) play switches to the start of the punishment (non-cooperative) phase whenever a player chooses an action different from the designated action for whatever phase play is on; and (4) starting from the punishment phase, play reverts to the cooperative phase after a defined number of periods.

95 For instance, there is evidence in the literature that the competition policy strategy of the US has changed with the respective administration, for example, from the Reagan and Bush Sr Administrations to the Clinton Administration as well as from the latter to the Bush Jr Administration. See, with differing weight of the presidencies' influence compared to other factors, Krattenmaker and Pitofsky (1988), Mueller (1996), Coate (2000), Kovacic and Shapiro (2000), Ghosal and Gallo (2001), Litan and Shapiro (2001), Davidow (2002, 2004), Leary (2002), and Kovacic (2003).

paragraphs). Therefore, the nonetheless most valuable insights from dynamic game theory offer 'only' the basic possibility of a self-organisational minimisation of strategic competition policies but neither certainty nor sufficient probabilities in real-world conditions. It would be negligent to waive antitrust internationalisation because of the mere possibility that among the large number of trajectories the cooperative one will materialise. Some type of international framework is necessary to ensure that the players waive discriminating competition policy strategies.[96]

1.3.3 The political economy of real-world strategic competition policies

However, similar to strategic trade policy, cases in which national and global welfare run into opposite directions are likely to be exceptions in the real world. More often than not, a case will produce the same results on national and global welfare. As with strategic trade policy, the conditions under which global welfare reducing strategic competition policies really increase national (regional) welfare are rather narrow.[97] Moreover, the case for a positive net effect on national welfare becomes further aggravated if retaliation by the exploited jurisdictions is considered. As the game-theoretic reformulation in the preceding section has demonstrated, the disadvantaged interacting jurisdiction can – reciprocally – engage in similar strategies with the consequence of suboptimal outcomes for everyone. In fact, the large majority of cases (cartels, mergers, and so on) will either improve or deteriorate both national and global competition and, therefore, no economic rationale for strategic policies occurs. However, even in such cases, there might be a political rationality for strategic competition policies that reduces both national and global welfare.

Accordingly, most real-world cases of strategic competition policy are probably related to lobbyism-biased strategies. Strategic competition policies are likely to occur as soon as they are rational in the eyes of the policymakers. As public choice theory convincingly demonstrates, policies that decrease national welfare can be politically rational if they serve lobby interests. Generally, groups of producers can exert more lobby pressure on politicians than consumers (due to their poor degrees of both homogeneity and organisation), so that enterprise- or industry-favouring strategic competition policies at the expense of foreign enterprises, foreign consumers, and domestic consumers can become possible.[98]

---

96 However, the insights of game theory do not demand any specific type of international framework. Perhaps, even rather informal institutions may be sufficient to grant the emergence of a cooperative trajectory.

97 See with regard to strategic trade policy, Krugman (1987) and Kemp and Shimomura (2002).

98 See, on differing lobby abilities of social groups, Olson (1965). The interrela-

Although the strategic (mis-)use of antitrust policy does not increase domestic welfare (even if the interacting jurisdictions waived employing reciprocal instruments) any more, the PD game effectively runs in a similar way to the preceding section. The numbers in Table 3.2 are not economically true any more since jurisdiction A's gain is less than 10 now (say pay-off = 9) if A employs a strategic competition policy while B plays the cooperative strategy. Thus, economically, choosing the non-cooperative strategy is not rational. However, if politicians maximise their individual welfare, the pay-off matrix may look identical to Table 3.2 in the eyes of the policy-makers. The economic gain of playing non-cooperatively (9) is now raised by the political gain of benefiting influential lobbyism groups (for example bundles of votes or improved career perspectives), say pay-off = 6, so that the sum of economic and political pay-offs reinstalls the PD game as it is discussed in the preceding chapter. Moreover, the policy-makers may try to sell the context of policy decision and action in the way of the PD game in order to reduce negative responses from less organised domestic groups (consumers, for instance). What is described here in economic terms is, for instance, the claim of a lobbyism-biased national policy-maker that a national merger would secure domestic jobs and/or create a national champion, thus, benefiting domestic welfare, although, in reality, only supracompetitive profits of the lobbying industry are secured – with anticompetitive consequences in particular for the domestic economy. Likelihood and impact of such lobbyism biases can be reduced, however, if either courts play an important role and/or competition agencies are independent from the political process.[99]

1.3.4 Do strategic competition policies violate WTO trade rules?

Since strategic competition policies represent state action[100] that blesses private action, which harms foreigners, and, thereby, distorts trade, one can argue whether international trade regulations (in the context of the WTO)

tion of protectionist interests, competition, and international trade is explored by Vanberg (2000, 2001).

[99] Central bank independence can serve as a paragon for a competition agency independence. See, for example, Schmidt (2001). If courts instead of agencies play the dominating role in a competition policy regime, the symmetry of decision-making is an important feature. For instance, if courts only decide on prohibitions but not on clearances and exemptions, significant scope for selectively lenient competition policy to promote national enterprises in international markets remains. See for more abstract comparative analyses of different antitrust regime types, Gerber (1998b) and Trebilcock and Iacobucci (2002).

[100] As opposed to private anticompetitive actions, which are predominantly addressed in sections 1.1 and 1.2 of this chapter.

prohibit such strategies. This is intensively discussed in the literature[101] with the dominant though not unanimously consensual result that no sufficient prevention of strategic competition policies can be achieved by international trade rules (in the absence of complementing international competition rules).[102] Particularly the famous Kodak–Fuji case has empirically demonstrated considerable limits (Baron 1997; Zanettin 2002: 243–245; Fox 2003c).

The US company Kodak, in a joint action with US officials (more precisely the US Trade Representative), complained about foreclosed market access to Japan. The dominant domestic competitor, Fujifilm, was said to have vertically cartelised the Japanese market for photographic film and paper by operating an exclusionary distribution system.[103] The US side suspected that the cartelised structures were deliberately tolerated by the Japanese Fair Trade Commission and the Japanese government since they had the same deterring effect on market access as the trade barriers (tariffs), which only a short time before had to be removed in the context of GATT/WTO provisions. Thus, the vertical cartel was viewed to be a politically encouraged, supported, and facilitated substitute for the protectionist trade policy instruments that had been employed before. A combination of the application of protectionist-interpreted domestic laws (large stores law, premiums law), an opaque Cabinet directive, and strategically motivated selective nonenforcement of the existing Japanese anticartel laws was assumed. Eventually, the WTO panel ruled that the US had not sufficiently demonstrated: (1) that imported photographic film and paper were treated different from domestic products; and (2) why the single-brand distribution in the Japanese market sensitively relies on continuing government intervention and not on economic forces instead. In particular, the first argument explains the difference between the trade and the competition perspective. From the WTO trade perspective it is decisive whether any discrimination between domestic and foreign enterprises can be identified. If market access is generally anticompetitively restricted, that is, both against foreign and new domestic competitors, no trade problem arises.[104] Thus, the

---

101 See, for example, Hoekman and Mavroidis (1994), Hoekman (1997), Iacobucci (1997), Drexl (1999), Fox (1999b), Lloyd and Vautier (1999: 175–183), and Kennedy (2001: 311–332).

102 'In theory, WTO members have an obligation not to discriminate in their competition rules against foreigners, but in practice, this obligation has proven unenforceable' Stephan (2004: 86).

103 One finds disputing opinions in the literature whether this exclusive dealing is an inefficient organisation existing only to constitute an entry barrier (Stephan 2004: 78–79) or efficiency reasoning may speak in favour of it (Zanettin 2002: 243–244).

104 This does not imply that the panel answered the question of the existence of an anticompetitive vertical integration in the affirmative. On the contrary, the panel pointed to the fact that in the US market itself, single-brand distribution had become the dominating vertical arrangement. See Lloyd and Vautier (1999: 180).

proceedings within the WTO indicated that indirect protectionist state action is generally difficult to handle under international trade law.[105] Competition policy issues (that is, deliberately allowing private anticompetitive arrangements and practices), in particular, cannot be adequately treated.

1.3.5 Concluding remarks

Eventually, the occurrence of strategic competition policy leads to distortions of international competition, which are intentionally caused by the national and regional competition policy regimes. Only an international arrangement – irrespective of its design or degree of formality – is able to effectively exclude strategic competition policies and, thus, grant a coherent and non-discriminating control of cross-border anticompetitive market behaviour. Without some kind of antitrust internationalisation, the perverse phenomenon that competition policy intentionally restricts competition causes significant welfare losses on a global scale. Voluntary renunciations of strategic options are both highly unlikely to appear and unlikely to last/be sustainable without the binding force of an international arrangement.

However, as the following section explores, the 'natural antithesis' – to shift competition policy competences altogether to an international authority, enforcing international laws – is also characterised by considerable limits.

2. THE LIMITS OF A UNIFORM WORLDWIDE COMPETITION POLICY REGIME

With a uniform worldwide competition policy regime, I denote the (extreme) idea of having a world competition code enforced by a global competition authority. This regime would replace the existing national and regional ones. Once the latter are viewed to be insufficient to protect international competition adequately and efficiently (which is the result of section 1 of this chapter), a centralisation of competition lawmaking and policy competences at a single authority on a supranational level would be an obvious response to global market integration in order to guarantee a global 'level playing field'. However, even many proponents of an international competition policy regime oppose such extremely centralised solutions against the background of both practical and theoretical arguments.[106] Those arguments demonstrate the

---

[105] For more details, see Hoekman and Mavroidis (1994), Hoekman (1997), Iacobucci (1997), Drexl (1999), Fox (1999b, 2003c), Lloyd and Vautier (1999), Kennedy (2001), and Zanettin (2002).

[106] Contrary to the arguments discussed (and rejected) in section 1 of this chapter, they do not argue that an international regime is superfluous because either compe-

limits of centralising competition law and policy to a full extent on a global or near-global level. However, they do not automatically apply to more complex institutional designs of an international competition policy regime, which include significant decentralised competences.

This section summarises the major arguments against an uniform global regime as they are presented in the literature. I start with a very brief analysis of the feasibility of such a regime, that is, looking at the political problems of sovereignty transfer (section 2.1), before I briefly review well-known public choice deficiencies of centralised global governance (section 2.2). Finally, I briefly explore some dynamic and evolutionary arguments (section 2.3).

2.1 Supranational Governance and National Sovereignty

In order to create a uniform worldwide regime, nation states and confederations of nations would have to transfer their competences in competition law and policymaking to the chosen supranational body.[107] However, they may be very reluctant to do so. As section 1.3 of this chapter has shown, competition policy represents a policy field of significant strategic interests, which politicians might not want to lose. Powerful jurisdictions have low incentives to give up their sovereignty over antitrust issues, since their abilities to extraterritorially enforce their domestic competition rules is comparatively good. Consequently, they gain relatively little from a global regime but lose considerable scope for strategic policies. Less powerful jurisdictions might also be reluctant, although they gain over-proportionally. However, they might be suspicious whether the global agency really will act neutrally or, instead, will be captured by the interests of the big jurisdictions (most likely the biggest financiers).[108]

Notwithstanding such fears, international economic rules and centralised supranational governance have successfully been implemented, for instance in regard to trade policy competences. However, the contemporary degree

tition policy becomes unnecessary in the face of global market liberalisation altogether or national/regional competition policy suffices to deal with cross-border antitrust cases. However, '[e]ven if uncoordinated national regimes are inefficient, it does not follow that an international regime will be more efficient' (McGinnis 2004: 127). That would mean ignoring the substantial costs of international centralisation.

107 See on sovereignty, antitrust, and public international law, for example, Dabbah (2003: 139–158).

108 See for literature emphasising that diverging interests render any multilateral agreement on uniform world antitrust impossible, for example, First (1998), Ullrich (1998), Kaiser and Vosgerau (2000), Tarullo (2000), Swaine (2003), and Tay and Willmann (2005). A very differentiated approach with an integrative analysis of the relevant arguments (and non-simplistic conclusions) is provided by Guzman (1998, 2001).

of power by the WTO (which still does not represent a complete uniformity) has developed incrementally from less uniform, less harmonised and less centralised regimes – starting with the GATT agreement (1946–1948).[109] Generally, the reluctance to transfer sovereignty rights to an international body is stronger the more uniform and centralised the international regime is designed.

Quite typically – and in accordance with its general attitude towards centralised supranational governance – the US has long been the main opponent of an international regime. However, its faith in being the uncontested number one antitrust jurisdiction in the world – a position that eroded any incentive to engage in internationalisation efforts – has been shattered significantly with the uprising importance and self-confidence of EU competition policy. The EU's prohibition of the all-US GE–Honeywell merger in 2001 marked a peak in this development as well as the beginning of (modest) modifications of the previous US rejection of an international antitrust regime.[110] Contrarily – and again in accordance with its more general attitude – the EU has always been the major proponent of the internationalisation of competition policy. This is most likely rooted in the experiences with the unique process of European political and economic integration.[111] Within the – most heterogeneous – group of smaller and developing countries no clear position is obtained. On the one hand, a lot of them propose an internationalisation of competition policy on the grounds of their struggle to cope with anticompetitive practices of multinational enterprises. On the other hand, fear is widespread that the powerful industrial nations will design or capture such an international regime to the disadvantage particularly of the developing countries – as, in the eyes of many developing countries, they have done with

109 Additionally, and perhaps even more important, the situation at the end of the Second World War represented a unique time slot for internationalisation because the collective experience of the horrors of worldwide war temporarily downscaled national sovereignty interests. This time-frame lasted long enough to release the self-perpetuating and self-energising forces of international trade liberalisation (GATT/WTO) and – at least for some decades – international currency coordination (IMF, WBG) but not long enough to allow for the realisation of the additionally introduced conceptions of an international competition policy regime (ITO). See section 2.3 of Chapter 4 for more details.

110 Most recently, the US Antitrust Modernization Commission (2007: 213–240) has recommended the development of a centralised international pre-merger notification system.

111 See on the general positions of the US and the EU the representative article by Keohane (2002) and with regard to competition policy, for example, Gerber (1999, 2003), Holmes (2002), Damro (2004), and Weinrauch (2004: 152–160). See additionally Aigner (2004: 11–20, 48–62) and the literature cited therein.

the WTO Trade-Related Aspects of Intellectual Property Rights (TRIPS) arrangement.[112]

A related argument points to the process of consensus finding, which is necessary to establish uniform global competition law and enforcement. This would require long and costly negotiations in which strategic considerations would probably dominate the competitive adequacy of the discussed rules and enforcement systems. In the course of bargaining, insufficient and inefficient global institutions and organisations may not be a too unlikely result. The situation becomes complicated because of missing consensus on basic competition policy principles among the existing national and regional competition policy regimes, further widening the room for the injection of strategic purposes.

Although the arguments presented in this section principally apply to any kind of internationalisation that includes the transfer of sovereignty rights (any kind of binding agreements), a uniform regime is particularly affected. In such a regime, the waiver of national competition policy competences is complete, implying that no residuals for national competition policy making remain. Therefore, the hurdle for international consensus is particularly high. Additionally, the existing national (regional) agencies become omitted, wherefore their support and constructive participation cannot be expected. The self-interest of national competition policy authorities only favours such steps of internationalisation, which contribute to their individual power and prestige. This includes mutual assistance regarding extraterritorial enforcement as well as voluntary interagency cooperation concerning cartel prosecution and agenda setting in international antitrust debates. However, it clearly excludes substantial harmonisation and international uniformity with competent international authorities.[113] Consequently, a very practical argument against a uniform global competition policy regime is that it is simply not feasible.

2.2 Public Choice Problems of a Uniform Regime

Apart from the feasibility, arguments against a uniform regime usually draw on public choice considerations. This includes two lines of argument: (1) government failure; and (2) political economy of bureaucracy. Both types

---

[112] See on the developing countries' position towards international antitrust, Cook (2002), Hoekman and Mavroidis (2003), Swaine (2003), Hoekman and Saggi (2004), Owen (2004), and Stewart (2004). See also section 2.3 of Chapter 4.

[113] See Tarullo (2000) and Weber Waller (2003: 432–436). Furthermore, cooperative national antitrust agencies may be very much needed in the course of international antitrust regime building in order to draw on their experience and knowledge about adequate regime design and policy practices.

of problems also occur with national authorities and politics but are believed to be more severe on a global dimension.[114]

The first line of argument emphasises that a uniform global regime shifts government failure from the national to the global level, thereby increasing its dimension and impact. Thus, severe negative welfare implications of government failure would have to be expected if a uniform worldwide regime was established. Having only one global authority additionally implies that the corrective of occurring governance failure through the action of concurrently competent authorities is not available any more.[115] Secondly, a world competition agency would represent a giant bureaucracy, bringing with it the typical problems of bureaucratic rationality on a corresponding scale. Most generally, the costs and deficiencies of bureaucracy like budget maximisation, slowed-down procedures, growing weight of non-productive activities (directed towards internal administration), sclerotic procedures and decision pattern, dynamically deteriorating flexibility, hostility towards innovation, and so on, increase over-proportionally with the size of the bureaucracy.[116] As a likely result, the capacities for the effective protection of international competition will decrease while budget and costs increase. These administrative inefficiencies will not only cause considerable costs for taxpayers but most probably also harm enterprises. Facing a worldwide antitrust bureaucracy, enterprises must expect increasing red tape including more and more demanding mandatory forms, less service, longer time schedules, and so on. Thus, a welfare-reducing bureaucratic burden on business activities in competition is a likely result.

In economic terms, a uniform worldwide competition policy regime creates significant agency costs.[117] There are two dimensions of principal–agent relations, which explain disadvantages of a uniform global regime. The first one analyses the world competition agency as an agent of the citizens of the states as the principals (for example, Stephan 2004: 77–79), whereas the second one analyses competition agencies as principals and the regulated (colluding or merging) enterprises as agents (for example, Smets and Van Cayseele 1995). In the first case, the principals – the citizens of the states (incompletely and distortedly) represented by their governments – have to:

---

[114] See for the following argumentation, for example, Smets and Van Cayseele (1995), Van den Bergh (1996), McGinnis (2004: 126–130) and Stephan (2004: 71–85).

[115] See, for example, Meessen (1989), Nicolaides (1992) and Stephan (2000, 2004). This is related to the idea of beneficial institutional competition. See section 3 of this chapter for an elaborate discussion.

[116] In the words of Stephan (2004: 81): 'Bureaucratic rationality typically masks a powerful urge for aggrandizement.'

[117] See Smets and Van Cayseele (1995), Van den Bergh (1996), McGinnis (2004) and Stephan (2004: 77–79).

- *ex ante* limit the agent's discretion, that is, the ability of the global competition agency to follow its own goals (budget and power maximisation, and so on) at the expense of the principals' goals (tying); and/or;
- *ex post* supervise the agent's performance, that is, to detect and sanction any behaviour of the global competition agency that deviates from the principals' goals (monitoring).

Otherwise, the principals would have to tolerate the outcomes, irrespective of their deficiencies.

However, both tying and monitoring are more difficult in regard to a global competition agency than in regard to national agencies. The 'distance' between the agent and the principals is longer and the multitude of principals most probably increases the heterogeneity of their interests, creating additional discretionary elbowroom for the agent. Notwithstanding the fact that these problems have been manageable in other contexts of global governance, Stephan (2004: 78) identifies two antitrust-specific features, which exacerbate the agency problem:

- the absence of consensus on elementary competition policy principles both in science and in policy complicates tying; and
- monitoring is likely to reveal that – in specific cases – some states could be individually better off if they had been engaged in national (for example, strategic) competition policy.

In the second case (competition agency as principal, enterprises as agents), it is again the 'distance' between principal and agents that aggravates the agency problems. A world competition agency is more likely to suffer from strategic (misleading) information provided by the colluding or merging enterprises. The problem of asymmetric information is less severe with national (regional) competition agencies because they are 'closer to the markets', thus they possess better abilities to monitor the enterprises' informational behaviour.

An argument related to agency problems is lobbyism. However, the literature is ambivalent about the likelihood of an agency becoming captured in relation to its characteristic 'national/regional' versus 'international/global'. On the one hand, the citizens of states may be better able to control rent-seeking influences on national competition agencies than on international ones. Higher transparency and more direct influence on the agency might, thus, allow a comparatively better protection against lobbyism in the case of national (regional) competition agencies.[118] On the other hand, it might be

---

[118] Regulatory capture as a disadvantage of an international competition agency is emphasised, for example, by Neven and Röller (2000: 847–848) and Stephan (2004).

more difficult for lobby groups to capture a supranational competition agency than national or regional ones, which are more focused on the location in which the interest group predominantly acts (for example, Smets and Van Cayseele 1995: 438–439).

Altogether, a uniform global competition policy regime raises significant and severe public choice problems. As section 1.2.2 of this chapter has demonstrated, the 'regime' of uncoordinated and concurrently applied national (regional) competition policies also causes significant administrative costs in terms of effort multiplication at competition agencies and increasing transaction costs for enterprises. According to some authors, the administrative costs of the uniform regime tend to overcompensate the ones of the uncoordinated regime (for example, McGinnis 2004; Stephan 2004). However, this is difficult to estimate with sufficient precision and security. Nevertheless, the fact that a uniform regime also causes considerable costs and inefficiencies encourages the search for intermediate solutions between the extremes.

2.3 Overall Adequacy of Centralised Global Competition Governance

Next to lacking feasibility and considerable bureaucratic burden, there are doubts whether a uniform regime is adequate to govern competition. Four lines of objections can be raised:

- *Adequacy in relation to market size*. There is no doubt that market globalisation is a forceful process with remarkable dynamics. The number of markets which have cross-border characteristics is rapidly increasing and so is business activity – as sections 1 and 2 of Chapter 2 have clearly demonstrated. However, this does not mean that all markets internationalise and will become cross-border or even global ones in the course of time. Instead, regional, national and local markets will prevail for a number of reasons, among them being non-tradable goods, transportation costs, currency costs, language barriers (for example, books markets) as well as regional, local, and cultural consumer preferences. When anticompetitive arrangements and practices occur in such markets, a global competition agency is the inadequate authority to adequately govern them. Subsidiarity alone demands the prevalence of competition policy competences on national or regional levels.
- *Adequacy in relation to competition policy preferences* (for example, Ullrich 1998). Next to consumer preferences about goods, citizen preferences about competition policy matter significantly. Citizens of different jurisdictions can have diverging majority preferences about elementary competition policy characteristics, for example, the goal(s) of competition policy, its relation to other political and societal goals,

the borderline between fair and unfair (legitimate and illegitimate) means of competitive interaction and business behaviour, the extent of competition as a coordination device (for instance, with regard to the inclusion of markets for health and education), the degree of intervention and the weight of individual freedom, and so on. The currently existing, significantly diverging national (regional) competition policy regimes may at least partly correspond to such different preferences about competition policy of the respective citizens. With a uniform global competition policy regime, the prevailing diversity of competition cultures and rule, law, and policy design becomes eroded, implying that many jurisdictions would have to give up their preferred variant of practising competition policy. This would be inadequate, in particular if intermediate solutions (between the uniform and the uncoordinated regime) are considered as alternatives.

- *Adequacy in relation to competition policy knowledge.* Next to diverging preferences, the existing variance of competition policies reflects the diversity of competition theories in economics (Burton 1994; Budzinski 2007). If there is no certainty about the best competition theory, the one chosen by a uniform regime might be inferior and no corrective mechanism (comparative performance of other regimes relying on different theories) is available any more (for example, Hauser and Schoene 1994; Freytag and Zimmermann 1998; Kerber 2003). An uniform regime erodes regulatory alternatives. This argument is related to the idea of a beneficial institutional competition as a way to create knowledge about better institutions and policies. However, a detailed analysis is needed to evaluate the importance and the limitations of this argument. This is provided in section 3 of this chapter, deriving only limited scope for institutional competition between competition policy regimes.
- *Adequacy in relation to changing environments.*[119] Competition policy faces permanently evolving environments in regard to three dimensions. First, the competitively interacting enterprises are creative and, therefore, innovate on anticompetitive arrangements and practices. Secondly, from time to time, the evolution of technologies challenges the orthodox assessment of modes of business behaviour in regard to their anti- or procompetitive effects. Thirdly, scientific knowledge about competition and competition policy evolves, hopefully producing improved knowledge. All three types of environmental changes can render previously

[119] See Kovacic (1992, 1996), Van den Bergh (1996), Budzinski (2002b, 2002c: 117–119), Kerber (2003), and Kerber and Budzinski (2003, 2004).

well-working antitrust instruments obsolete and inadequate and, thus, demand competition agencies to respond and adapt their laws, policies, analysis and assessment techniques, and so on. A uniform regime, however, offers comparatively few channels through which innovation can enter the system. In other words, a uniform regime tends to be rather sclerotic and obsolete solutions are more likely to persist than in regimes in which scope for norm entrepreneurs remains (Wigger 2004a). However, this also depends on the design of the uniform system, that is, the extent to which external experts or independent courts are allowed to influence the global agency.

Altogether, a coexistence of an international competition policy and national (regional) competition policies are better suited to match overall adequacy of competition governance.

Eventually, the extreme variant of internationalising competition policy – establishing worldwide applicable antitrust laws, which are exclusively enforced by a global competition agency and abolish national (regional) competition policies – produces a number of disadvantages. Apart from the high hurdles for international consensus such a regime erects, shortcomings in regard to efficiency and adequacy emerge. The inefficiencies of the uncoordinated extraterritorial application of national competition laws becomes substituted by the inefficiencies of worldwide bureaucracy. Additionally, the improvements concerning the governance of cross-border arrangements and practices come at the expense of the governance of national, regional and local markets. Moreover, it remains doubtful whether a uniform regime can be sufficiently flexible and open to innovation. Consequently, both of the extremes are characterised by significant and considerable disadvantages, which overcompensate their main advantage – being simple in design. Thus, more complex intermediate solutions offer room for improvements. Before I explain more closely what characterises such intermediate regimes, a distinct escape from this dualism is discussed. It shifts the concept of competition as a coordination device to the level of institutions and regimes. If competition is advantageous in coordinating producers and consumers on 'ordinary' goods markets, why not let competition coordinate competition policy jurisdictions?

3. DOES COMPETITION OF COMPETITION POLICY REGIMES PROVIDE AN ESCAPE?

Predominantly in the economic literature on the pros and cons of an international competition policy, the specific idea of a competition of competition policy regimes is brought forward – and either praised as beneficial or condemned as destructive.[120] This line of thought draws on the more general theory of institutional competition, which applies the concept of market competition to selection processes of institutional arrangements.[121] Most generally, the concept of institutional competition – synonyms are systems competition, regime competition, order competition and regulatory competition – constructs markets for institutions (systems of rules: law, regulation, and so on) with governments being suppliers and citizens (taxpayers) as well as market participants (enterprises, investors, labour, consumers, and so on) representing the demand side. However, there is no coherent body of theory but a variety of considerably different concepts and models, applied to such different fields like fiscal federalism, corporate laws, labour standards, environmental regulation and many more.

With regard to competition of competition policy regimes, most of the literature lacks clarity concerning the nature of institutional competition. However, there are significant differences in the concepts of institutional competition as, for example, applied to competition between corporate laws (that is, enterprises can choose each law irrespective of their location) or competition between social systems (implying that enterprises must and will change locations in order to evade restrictive or inefficient rules, thereby generating incentives for domestic politicians to create 'better' social systems). Not only with regard to antitrust competition, it makes a difference which concept of regulatory competition serves as a basis for argumentation. In order to provide a thorough reasoning concerning the importance of competition-of-competition-policies arguments, different types of institutional competition have to be distinguished.

---

[120] See Easterbrook (1983), Meessen (1989, 2000), Nicolaides (1992, 1994), Hauser and Schoene (1994), Smets and Van Cayseele (1995), De Léon (1997), Rosenthal and Nicolaides (1997), Ackermann (1998), Freytag and Zimmermann (1998), Sinn (1999), Fox (2000a), Stephan (2000, 2004), Guzman (2001), Isele (2003), Kerber and Budzinski (2003, 2004), and Möschel (2005a, 2005b).

[121] It is impossible to provide a comprehensive overview. See among many others the more conceptual and elementary discussions by and in Kenyon and Kincaid (1991), Sinn (1992), Vihanto (1992), Vanberg and Kerber (1994), Gerken (1995), Breton (1996), Cassel (1996), Kerber (1998, 2000b), Streit and Wohlgemuth (1999), Stephan (2000), Vanberg (2000), and Van den Bergh (2000). Among the critical aspects, one of the most important concerns whether the idea of market competition is a good enough analogue to what is called institutional competition. See, reflecting this, for example, Sinn (1990), Tirole (1994), and Kiwit and Voigt (1998). Seminal contributions arguing in favour of modelling states or governments as analogues to enterprises (a prerequisite of modelling competition between governments according to the paragon of competition between enterprises) and analysing institutions and laws as products are, for example, Ostrom et al. (1961) and Romano (1985).

Table 3.3 Four basic types of regulatory competition

Type of regulatory competition	Mobility of Information/ theories	Goods/ services	Factors of production	Institutions
(I)	X	–	–	–
(II)	X	X	–	–
(III)	X	X	X	–
(IV)	X	X	X	X

Source: Budzinski and Kerber (2003: 414, 2004: 33)

Following Kerber and Budzinski (2003, 2004), four basic types of regulatory competition can be identified, which yield very different results in regard to their workability and effects (see also: Kerber 2000a). The criterion for delimitating these four types is the extent of actual mobility between the competing jurisdictions (see Table 3.3). The most restrictive type (I) allows only for information to be mobile between the competing regimes. Type (II) additionally allows goods to be mobile (exports and imports) and type (III) includes factor mobility (capital and labour). The most comprehensive one is type (IV), which additionally allows a somewhat virtual mobility of institutions (for example, competition rules) themselves. Mobility of rules means that they can be applied irrespective of their origin (so that their application is neither bound territorially nor jurisdictionally). This analytical framework makes it possible to shed some light on the prospects and limits of any competition of competition policy regimes. In doing so, I briefly discuss each type of regulatory competition in regard to competition of competition policy regimes.

3.1 Type (I) Regulatory Antitrust Competition via Mutual Learning

Type (I) regulatory competition (Kerber and Budzinski 2003: 417–424, 2004: 36–40) assumes that information is the only mobile element. This means that jurisdictions can observe each other but do not interact otherwise. For the sake of analysis, it is assumed that the jurisdictions do not influence each other's economic welfare.[122] How can there be something like competition of competition policy regimes under these assumptions? Each jurisdiction carries out its

[122] These very restrictive assumptions are relaxed in the other types.

own competition policy, differing from the other ones in regard to substantial rules (legal texts, standards, official guidelines, and so on), procedural rules (filing requirements, deadlines, time schedules, investigation rights, confidentiality rules, and so on), organisation of the regime (public versus private enforcement, agency versus court system, degree of independence of agencies and courts, instances for appeal and revision, and so on), economic theories applied by the authorities (efficiency versus other goals, qualitative versus quantitative analysis, static/stationary versus dynamic/evolutionary effects, role of pro-market versus market-sceptical ideologies, schools of economic thought, and so on), and techniques, practices and methods (defining relevant markets, determining market shares, estimate turnovers, design of leniency programmes, and so on). The way competition policy is practised in the different regimes will affect the outcome, for example, in terms of welfare but also in terms of market dynamics, enterprise and consumers' confidence, safeness and soundness of the procedures, and so on. These differences are observable and cause mutual learning. The comparative performance of the different regimes provides incentives to learn from each other, be it through the imitation of superior elements of foreign regimes or through the creation of new solutions inspired by mutual observation. One of the most simple variants is to avoid mistakes others have made. In evolutionary terms, type (I) regulatory competition allows for experimentation with different solutions in regard to the above presented dimensions of competition policy regimes. This can be beneficial since the 'practice test' of standards, procedures, theories, and techniques is likely to reveal knowledge, which was not obtainable otherwise.[123]

With regard to competition policy regimes, mutual learning has always been important and significant until now. A large number of discourses on regime evolution and reforms of competition rules, enforcement strategies, applied theories and techniques, and so on have relied on observations of foreign regimes. For instance, the innovation of modern competition policy by the establishment of US antitrust policy at the end of the nineteenth century

[123] 'Although theoretical and empirical studies can provide valuable information from which we learn extensively, we have to accept that the above-mentioned knowledge problems exist in relation to nearly all of these elements of competition law regimes. Although there is a wide-spread consensus on some basic elements, like the positive assessment of the existence of merger reviews or the prohibition of hardcore cartels, our knowledge about the best set of criteria for reviewing mergers or exempting cartels or about the most appropriate procedural rules is rather limited. Therefore, experiences with already implemented rules, established competition authorities, and applied theories and practices are an important source of valuable information' Kerber and Budzinski (2003: 419–420). This line of argumentation is related to the fundamental knowledge problem and the impossibility of centralising coordination knowledge, which Hayek (1937, 1945, 1975) emphasises.

itself represents an excellent example. In the second half of the twentieth century, it diffused into many industrialised countries, and since the 1990s also into an increasing number of developing countries. Another example is represented by the evolution of the European competition policy regime. In general, until the 1980s, the European competition policy regime learned much from the more developed German regime, whereas now, starting in the 1990s, the German regime predominantly imitates the European one.[124] Additionally, the introduction of leniency programmes in the context of cartel prosecution in the US in the early 1990s has led to imitation processes by the other countries, including the EU. Similarly, the most recent reform of the EU merger control regime has sometimes been interpreted as an imitation of superior US solutions.[125]

Of course, mutual observation (and, thus, type (I) regulatory competition) is only one among many sources of learning and regime development. Scientific knowledge and expertise as well as interpretative efforts of courts and judges, political ideologies, suggestions of parties and interests groups (and many more) also influence this process. However, they may also profit from type (I) regulatory competition in terms of richer experiences as sources of inspiration, ideas and academic knowledge. Furthermore, one must emphasise that mutual learning does not inevitably lead towards superior solutions:

- The transplanting of particular rules, standards, practices, or policy instruments from one competition policy regime to another can cause compatibility problems with other parts of the legal system of the imitating jurisdiction.[126] The same institutions can have very different effects

---

[124] For an empirical review of the development and spreading of competition policy from its beginnings to the 1990s, see Gerber (1998a). The development of European competition policy with respect to the role of influential actors and interest groups is discussed by Budzinski and Christiansen (2005b).

[125] The standard for prohibiting mergers changed from the European-style dominance test to the newly created SIEC-test ('Substantial Impediment of Effective Competition'), which is believed by some to be closer to the US-style SLC-test ('Substantial Lessening of Competition'). Furthermore, the so-called 'more-economic approach' is said by some to imitate the US practice of using quantitative analysis in a rule-of-reason fashion. However, SIEC may still diverge considerably from SLC (and, thus, represent an – US inspired? – innovation rather than an imitation) and quantitative price theory can be applied in very different manners. See in favour of the imitation hypothesis, for example, Gifford and Kudrle (2003), more sceptical, for example, Zimmer (2004) and emphasising the discreteness of the European approach, Neven (2006) and Röller and De la Mano (2006). General overviews on the 2004 merger control reform are provided by, for example, Díaz (2004), Lyons (2004), Budzinski and Christiansen (2005a), and Christiansen (2006).

[126] This is related to problems of path-dependency. See with respect to regulatory competition of corporate laws, Heine and Kerber (2003).

in different jurisdictions due to the different institutional, political, and cultural environments, wherefore the imitation of a foreign solution, which yields better results abroad, is no guarantee for domestic improvement. Adjustments are necessary which may cause incremental innovation.

- The comparative assessment of the performance of competition policy regimes can suffer from errors or identification problems. When a jurisdiction performs better than others, the willing-to-learn jurisdictions have to disentangle its complex competition policy regime in order to identify the part that makes the difference.
- There can be a difference between institutions that are superior from an academic competition or welfare point of view and institutions that are superior in the eyes of the policy-makers. Type (I) regulatory competition provides incentives to learn according to the goals pursued by the relevant agents. Depending on imperfections of the political competition, policy-makers may refuse to learn competition-improving strategies. Instead, the influence of interests groups may induce them to learn better ways of restricting competition, discriminate in favour of the lobby groups, and so on.[127] However, there is a counterargument. In comparison to the no-institutional-competition case, type (I) regime competition provides more transparency on what can be done, what are the related outcomes, and how the different institutions are assessed (including controversial assessment by domestic and foreign politicians and interests groups). Thereby, domestic agents interested in improvements in competition – academic experts, consumers, lawyers, judges, maybe officials of competition agencies – dispose over better access to pro-competition arguments.

The main result is that even this indirect type of institutional competition – mutual learning – can produce effects. On average, these effects tend to improve competition policy regimes and, maybe more importantly, preserve the ability and openness for further learning. Such an error tolerance is particularly important in view of the imperfectness of all knowledge and learning. The latter is also true for the no-regime-competition case, albeit with significantly less error tolerance and openness to future change. However, it remains a rather indirect type of institutional competition and the incentives for policy-makers

---

[127] Note, however, that this is limited to discriminating strategies among domestic market participants, since it is assumed that no exchange other than information takes place between the jurisdictions. Therefore, no strategic competition policies as discussed in section 1.3 of this chapter can be learned in this setting.

to learn from superior solutions might be weak in a number of cases. The anecdotal evidence briefly presented above shows that it, nevertheless, has some empirical relevance.

3.2 Type (II) Regulatory Antitrust Competition via International Trade

Type (II) competition of competition policy regimes allows for information and goods/services to be mobile across jurisdictions (Kerber and Budzinski 2003: 424–433; 2004: 40–46). International trade adds to the effectiveness of institutional competition via effects on the comparative competitiveness of enterprises from trading jurisdictions. Since the domestic competition policy regime influences the international competitiveness of domestic firms, success or failure in international trade represents a considerable additional feedback mechanism and governments have incentives to consider the international competitiveness of domestic industries and enterprises in their decisions upon the domestic competition policy.

With the inclusion of international competitiveness considerations, two different effects can be identified, depending on the respective views of what promotes international competitiveness:

- If international competitiveness is believed to be increased by intensive competition on domestic markets,[128] type (II) regulatory antitrust competition provides incentives for pro-competition competition policy regimes. In tendency, the capabilities of the domestic regime to protect competition on domestic markets improves.
- If international competitiveness is believed to be improved by protecting domestic industries or enterprises from competition on domestic markets, type (II) regulatory antitrust competition provides incentives for strategically discriminating competition policy regimes. The protection of the competitive forces in domestic markets is, in tendency, weakened in favour of strategic competition policies (beggar-thy-neighbour strategies, and so on).

In both cases, mutual learning reinforces the incentives. Thus, in combination with international trade, learning how to restrict competition can occur.

From a pro-competition perspective, competition of competition policy

[128] The rationale for this strategy is that: (1) domestic enterprises/industries are more fit for worldwide competition if they are used to sharp domestic competition; and (2) competitive markets for intermediate goods and factors of production allow for cost advantages for domestic industries on international markets.

regimes via international trade can improve or deteriorate the competing regimes. It depends on what policy-makers believe promotes international competitiveness. However, the analysis of strategic competition policies in section 1.3 of this chapter has demonstrated that self-reinforcing feedback mechanisms provide rationales for anti-competition strategies (from the agents' individual perspectives). Type (II) regulatory competition has the potential to aggravate that problem. On the other side, if countries with high domestic antitrust standards performed systematically better on international goods markets, type (II) institutional competition would work towards improvements of competition policy regimes.

Type (II) institutional antitrust competition still is a comparatively indirect one. Therefore, its effects are limited but not insignificant. The first best choice to influence export–import relations are trade policy instruments such as tariffs, contingents, and so on. However, these instruments have become rather restricted in the course of the GATT/WTO process of trade liberalisation. Thus, competition policy instruments can gain attractiveness. Yet, even then, international competitiveness depends on many more influences (for example, exchange rate evolution, tax systems, availability of production factors, labour quality, workability of monetary and capital systems, and so on) than competition policy.

3.3 Type (III) Regulatory Antitrust Competition via Locational Competition

If, in addition to information and goods/services, factors of production are assumed to be mobile across jurisdictions, then direct institutional competition becomes possible. Enterprises, investors and workers can now choose the most appropriate competition policy regime by moving into that jurisdiction. Locational competition emerges, that is, countries are competing with each other to attract mobile factors (Kerber and Budzinski 2003: 434–438, 2004: 46–49). In fact, this is the type of institutional antitrust competition, which most of the literature implicitly addresses. In contrast to 'good old' international trade, the increasing mobility of factors, in particular the increasing mobility of enterprises and 'the capital' is distinctive for modern globalisation of markets. Since type (III) regime competition provides a more direct competitive interaction, its effects are believed to be far stronger than with type (II). This raises hopes and fears of either a race-to-the-top (Meessen 1989, 2000; Hauser and Schoene 1994; De Léon 1997; Freytag and Zimmermann 1998) or a race-to-the-bottom (Sinn 1990, 1999; Ackermann 1998) of competition policy regimes. More pronounced, two strategies corresponding to the type (II) discussion can be derived:

- A jurisdiction can improve its attractiveness as a location for business activities by securing intensive competition on domestic markets.[129] Enterprises may favour such a jurisdiction because they: (1) can expect to be protected against anticompetitive strategies from competitors; and (2) profit from competitive factors markets and markets for intermediate goods (implying lower prices). Thus, a pro-competition antitrust regime is reinforced by type (III) institutional competition.
- If enterprises value the possibility of engaging in restrictions of competition highly, jurisdictions improve their attractiveness by offering generally lax competition policy regimes or those with lots of exemptions, selective non-enforcement, casual arrangements, and so on. To obtain supracompetitive profits can be a very strong motivation for factors of production to choose a location. Thus, a competition-reducing antitrust regime is reinforced by type (III) institutional competition.

Whether type (III) institutional competition tends to improve or deteriorate competing competition policy regimes depends on the preferences of mobile factors. If the mobility of enterprises is generally higher than the one of labour and additionally increases with the size of the enterprises (in tendency implying also increasing possibilities to restrict competition and to monopolise), type (III) regulatory antitrust competition includes considerable threats of increasing discrimination and decreasing pro-competition policies.

However, the race-to-the-top/race-to-the-bottom terminology tends to overestimate the effectiveness of type (III) competition of competition policy regimes. Since enterprises cannot choose between competition policy regimes alone but are forced to choose between the complete package of regulations (including tax systems, company laws, environmental laws, consumer protection standards, and so on) related to the competing locations, the importance of competition policy for the locational decision becomes limited. Moreover, mobility is costly and the benefits of locational change must overcompensate its costs.

3.4 Type (IV) Regulatory Antitrust Competition via Choice of Law

The most direct and most comprehensive type of institutional competition adds the mobility of institutions themselves. Without having to physically change their location (and irrespective of the relevant geographical markets), enterprises can choose the competition policy regime under which their behav-

---

129 Thus, type (III) regulatory competition is about the international competitiveness of jurisdictions, whereas type (II) regulatory competition is about the international competitiveness of enterprises and industries.

iour and arrangements shall be regulated (Kerber and Budzinski 2003: 438–440, 2004: 49–51). This type (IV) regulatory competition dominates the elaborate debate on competition of corporate laws. However, in regard to antitrust, an acceptable application of type (IV) regulatory competition seems implausible.

Competition law concerns itself with injuries to third parties not involved in the competition-violating arrangement (for example, consumers harmed by a cartel, society harmed by reduced innovation activity in the future, and so on). No contractual links between anticompetitively behaving enterprises and harmed market participants exist. Instead, significant externalities occur because of jurisdiction-shopping by enterprises. Moreover, there is no workable mechanism that would force the respective enterprises to internalise these costs.[130]

Eventually, the differentiated analysis of competition of competition policy regimes reveals only very limited scope for this kind of argument. Overall institutional competition (type (IV)) is not applicable to competition policy. In the other cases, the effects are ambivalent and the case for an improvement of competition rules and policies is not very clear. Both type (III) and type (II) would need an accompanying institutional framework – second-order competition rules for the competition of competition policies[131] – in order to prevent destructive developments. The relative best result derives from the most indirect variant. Type (I) offers beneficial effects of mutual learning, in particular if the other types are restricted and effective only in a limited way. However, competition is very indirect with type (I), so that one can argue to abandon the term 'competition' in this case. Instead, 'advantages of decentralism of institutions' also adequately describe the beneficial effects of type (I). In the following chapters of this book, the type (I)-related arguments will be further discussed under the label of decentralism versus centralism of institutions and the term 'competition of competition policy' will not play a significant role.

Furthermore, this is justified because of the ambivalent implications of the competition-of-competition-policy-regimes debate for the question of the internationalisation of competition policy. At first glance, competition of competition policy regimes – albeit limited in its application – presents an argument against an international regime. Obviously, the latter would restrict or even abolish (in the case of an uniform regime) antitrust competition. However, the uncoordinated 'system' in which every jurisdiction engages in extraterritorial enforcement via the effects doctrine virtually has the same

---

130 See even Stephan (2000: 186–187, 199) who otherwise is a clear proponent of regulatory competition.

131 Implying an infinite regress: why not allow for an institutional competition for the second-order competition rules, and so on.

effect. The effects doctrine significantly reduces the scope for types (II) and (III) competition since any enterprise behaviour or arrangement that affects international or foreign markets becomes additionally regulated by foreign competition authorities. If a country allowed cartels, relaxed merger control or included an efficiency defence with the intention of increasing international competitiveness, this would become countervailed by the affected jurisdictions – at least, if extraterritorial application and enforcement worked perfectly without restrictions. Thus, the differentiated analysis of competition of competition policy regimes reveals that transition from the uncoordinated 'regime' to an international regime does not necessarily reduce the scope for beneficial effects of institutional competition. Instead, this depends on the design of the international regime and its degree of centralism respectively. Again, it becomes clear that not the extreme solutions but an analysis of intermediate and more complex variants of international competition policy represent the most promising field of research.

4. CONCLUDING REMARKS: COMPETENCE ALLOCATION AS A PROBLEM

As the discussion in this chapter has clearly demonstrated, neither the waiver of any international regime (that is, any international coordination of competition policy) nor the theoretical concept of an uniform worldwide competition policy regime (that is, global antitrust laws enforced by a global authority) represent sufficient and/or practicable responds to the ongoing globalisation of competition. This result stands in accordance with the vast majority of the literature cited in this chapter, which powerfully points to the shortcomings of both extreme solutions. However, a systematic theory-based analysis of midway solutions is lacking in the overwhelming majority of contributions to this issue, irrespective of the disciplinary background of the authors (legal sciences, economics, political sciences, and so on).[132]

Solutions which create a truly international competition policy regime without eroding the scope for national and regional antitrust regimes need to be analysed. Thus, the 'midway' comprises a matrix of regime designs, which combine elements of centralism and decentralism in order to create a complex but coherent system of competition policies.[133] On the one hand, the implementation of some kind of serious and effective international coordination of

[132] It is not necessary to quote the rare exceptions here because they are extensively discussed in the following chapters.

[133] For a visualisation, see Budzinski (2002b: 487).

otherwise decentralised competition policies represents something like a minimum requirement. On the other hand, national and regional antitrust authorities must retain at least some substantial competences in order to sustain the preservation of the merits of decentralism within the regime.

The main common feature of such intermediate designs of competition policy regimes is their relatively higher degree of complexity (compared to the extreme solutions), that is, a larger variety of interrelated institutions and organisations[134] and the emergence of a division of competences between the elements of the complex system. It is this last aspect which introduces the problem of competence allocation as a crucial issue of international competition policy between extreme centralism and extreme decentralism. The allocation of competences represents: (1) the distinguishing characteristic of the high number of thinkable intermediate regime designs; and (2) the decisive factor for achieving and securing the necessary integration of coherence and flexibility of the regime, or, in other – though not congruent – words, the integration of the benefits of centralised and decentralised regime elements. Therefore, a theory-based analysis of midway international competition policy regimes must focus on the theoretical analysis of competence allocation. In particular, the rules and institutional arrangements, which can be implemented to create a deliberate and intentional governance of competence allocation within complex regimes, must be analysed systematically. However, such an analysis is currently missing in the academic literature on international antitrust. The following chapters contribute to filling this gap by presenting a theory-based, comparative analysis of rules for the allocation of competences in complex competition policy regimes. In doing so, the theoretical input into the discussion on the design of international competition policy is enriched and further research stimulated.

Since the analysis deals with rules for competence allocation, the modern theory of institutional economics represents an appropriate background. In the next chapter, the available theories are tailored to the problem of the governance of international competition. A theory of multilevel systems of competition institutions is derived and existing regimes are described and analysed in order to demonstrate the capacity of the theory. Afterwards, in Chapter 5, the actual comparative analysis of alternative rules for the allocation of competences is presented.

---

134 I refer to the standard definitions of 'institution' (system of rules) and 'organisation' (groups of individuals bound by some common objective) in new institutional economics. See, for example, North (1990).

4. Towards an international multilevel system of competition policies

The first part of this chapter is dedicated to the development of the analytical framework, which is needed for the comparative analysis in Chapter 5. Following a very brief overview on intermediate governance concepts in the sense of the outline in Chapter 3 (section 1.1), the concept of multilevel systems of institutions is characterised in brief (section 1.2). Afterwards, the analytical framework is discussed in detail (section 1.3), thereby deriving the relevant criteria for the comparative analysis of specific competence allocation rules in Chapter 5 (section 1.4). In the second part of this chapter, the developed analytical framework is applied to describe the existing competition policy systems and their evolution. Starting with the US antitrust system (section 2.1), I address a selection of different national and supranational antitrust regimes, namely the EU competition policy system (section 2.2), the (suggested) WTO Regime (section 2.3), and the international competition network (section 2.4). Eventually, the specific problem of having a multitude of agencies and institutions at the international level itself is discussed (section 2.5). The motivation for discussing the real-world regimes at this point of analysis (and not, as some readers may have expected, in Chapter 3), stems from wanting to apply the framework developed in the first part of this chapter in order to characterise the existing regimes in a way and in a language that facilitates the identification of their competence allocation rules and their deficiencies. This could not have been done before thoroughly introducing the concept of multilevel systems. Section 3 summarises the most important results of this chapter and leads over into the next chapter.

1. THE CONCEPT OF MULTILEVEL SYSTEMS OF INSTITUTIONS – GENERAL IDEA AND WORKING PROPERTIES

1.1 Governance Concepts between Centralism and Decentralism: A Brief Overview

The need to escape the dilemma of choosing between extreme decentralism (waiver of governance internationalisation) and extreme centralism (global government) as possible responses to the globalisation of governance objectives occurs in many policy fields[1] and has stimulated research on intermediate concepts of international governance. In particular, concepts of network governance have gained increasing popularity within various disciplines, for example, political, legal, and social sciences.[2] In this context, the term 'participatory governance' is also popular. A related strand of economic literature deals with innovation networks and addresses the interplay of intrafirm, interfirm, and public–private governance.[3] Out of real-world governance problems within a enlarged EU most recently emerged the so-called 'open method of coordination', which represents an alternative approach to midway governance.[4] All of these approaches are motivated by the desire to create coherent regimes for international governance without eroding the diversity of players, institutions and responsibilities. In other words, the combination of coherence and diversity[5] is striven for (Budzinski 2002b, 2003b).

However, all these approaches remain rather vague in regard to an economic analysis of competence allocation and no one analyses specific rules for the allocation of competences from an economic perspective. Notwithstanding, those theories and concepts offer most valuable insights and at least the network approaches can be viewed to be influential on practical international competition policy.[6]

Additionally, there are several preceding or accompanying academic contributions to a network governance perspective on international competition

---

[1] Examples include diverse things such as the governance of international environmental problems, labour standards, health and epidemics (nuclear, chemical, and biological), armament, terrorism and international crime, ethnic conflicts, human rights, protection of intellectual property, and financial markets regulation.

[2] See for instance Rosenau and Czempiel (1992), Ladeur (1997), Messner (1997), Young (1999), Slaughter (2000), Raustiala (2002), Fuchs (2004) and the chapters in Marin and Mayntz (1991) and Héritier (2002). This discourse is linked – more often implicitly than explicitly – to concepts of network governance and virtual or borderless types of organisation in business economics. See, for example, Davidow and Malone (1992), Jarillo (1993), Picot et al. (1996), Safarian (1997), and García-Canal et al. (2002).

[3] See as representatives for many others, Cimoli and Dosi (1995), Edquist (1997), Lundvall (1992), Nelson and Rosenberg (1993), Niosi and Bellon (1996), Calbay (2004), and Lundvall and Borrás (2005).

[4] See with respect to a more general interpretation (not restricted to EU issues), for example, Régent (2002) and Kerber and Eckardt (2005, 2007) as well as the literature cited therein.

[5] In other words: the cohabitation of coherence and diversity (Forrester 2005).

[6] They can serve as a theoretical background to describe the international competition network (for example, Budzinski 2003b, 2004c). Section 2.4 of this chapter addresses this issue from the theoretical perspective suggested in this book.

policy. Tarullo (2000: 495) develops a regulatory-convergence approach in which systematic network cooperation provides 'a mechanism for structuring and monitoring the mutual expectations of states' in order to make national regulations more congruent across interacting jurisdictions. He vehemently argues in favour of a participation of the existing antitrust agencies in the process of generating an international regime. The latter should be built upon the experience of the national agencies with systematic interaction of their officials being the driving force to incremental convergence. However, it remains unclear whether the network character has a long-term perspective or is only seen as a temporary need to overcome (non-beneficial) resistances against centralised international governance.

In a compatible approach, Maher (2002: 114) views competition policy networks to be an important regime-building factor and, in this sense, 'a prerequisite to any greater internationalisation'. The agenda-setting and debate-framing role of networks coincides with the interplay of transgovernmental networks (that is, horizontal, decentralised and informal coordination by officials from national and regional competition authorities) and epistemic communities (defined as knowledge-based networks of specialists[7]) to form driving forces of regime-creation. Consequently, the emphasis is predominantly on the way towards international competition governance and to a lesser extent on the sustainable design of the regime.

First (1998, 2003) also focuses on identifying superior avenues towards an international competition policy regime. He develops an interesting and challenging concept of mapping the existing antitrust networks. In doing so, he emphasises the fact that a number of existing antitrust regimes do not correspond to the extreme regime designs discussed in Chapter 3 but, instead, must be characterised as complex institutional arrangements ('networks') themselves. This represents an important insight to which the line of argument in this chapter will continually refer. However, against the background of the US experience, First (1999, 2003) also presents more principal arguments in favour of decentralised regime elements.[8] Similar to O'Connor (2002), the idea of having a common law of international antitrust with case law evolution as a driving-force is prominent. Eventually, both authors apply the American concept of antitrust federalism in a non-imperialistic way to the problem of international antitrust. According to O'Connor (2002), enforce-

[7] The network members share beliefs about causalities, validity standards, underlying elementary values, and policy goals. See on the role of epistemic communities in international competition governance, Maher (2002: 118–121).

[8] 'My overall view is that for a system of antitrust enforcement to remain dynamic, overcentralization must be avoided and some degree of chaos tolerated', First (2003: 24).

ment networks play the decisive role in approaching coherence in the face of diverging laws.

Taking a rather broad perspective, Piilola (2003) provides a comparative analysis of different substreams of network governance theory and their implications for international antitrust. He concludes that a mixed network of cooperative intergovernmental relations, transgovernmental networks (formed by officials of national antitrust agencies), and transnational networks (consisting of nongovernmental organisations and non-state actors, particularly business and consumer organisations) presents the only sufficient design for an international competition policy regime. 'Ideally, the international antitrust architecture would be designed through active, open, transparent, and cooperative dialogue in which all levels of governance participate' (Piilola 2003: 249). Unfortunately, the reasoning for the desirability of such a mixed network is not accompanied by details of its design, mechanisms, and workability conditions – not to mention competence allocation.

The most valuable insights, which are offered by the above outline of the literature, will selectively flow into the analysis presented below. However, these papers cannot serve as a theoretical background, since they do not address the rules of competence allocation. It is the innovative contribution of this book to add an explicit economic analysis of competence allocation rules, thereby, providing additional insights for the design of an international competition policy regime.

In order to directly address the problem of competence allocation, which was identified as being central at the end of the preceding chapter, I turn to a different theory – multilevel systems of institutions and agencies[9] – which can also serve as a framework for analysing intermediate institutional arrangements, combining coherence and diversity or balancing centralising with decentralising elements and forces. Its main advantages for my purposes – in comparison to the above outline of network theories – are the enhanced possibility of drawing on (both traditional and evolutionary) economic concepts and the superior capacity for providing a framework for a comparative analysis of specific institutional arrangements determining (statically and dynamically) competence allocation. However, the concepts of networks and multilevel systems are neither opposed nor incompatible. With regard to the purpose of my analysis, the multilevel system framework can be viewed as an extension and generalisation of the network approach,

---

[9] This is not identical with the multi-level governance approach from political science. See, for example, Marks (1996), Hooghe and Marks (2001), and Neyer (2003). This EU-centred approach is more closely related to the above mentioned open-method-of-coordination approach.

which focuses more closely on the character and effects of the relations between the agents involved.[10]

1.2 Multilevel Systems and the Economics of Federalism

1.2.1 Introductory remarks on multilevel systems

The concept of multilevel systems represents an analytical framework to describe and model complex regimes, which include of a multitude of interrelated institutions and organisations. Generally speaking, a system consists of elements and interrelations (or, synonymously, interconnections). If the (interrelated) elements are located on more than one level, a multilevel system is constituted. Within such a system, interrelations occur regarding two dimensions: vertical interrelations between elements on different levels and horizontal interrelations between elements of one and the same level. Theoretically, diagonal interrelations between non-vertically interrelated elements of different levels are also possible. If they occur comprehensively, a true network result. Thus, networks (as discussed in section 1.1 of this chapter) qualify as an extreme variant of a multilevel system.

Figure 4.1 shows a stylised multilevel system with focus on horizontal and vertical interrelations. Although it does not represent a necessary condition, multilevel systems, more often than not, possess only one element on the top level and an increasing number of elements on downward levels.[11]

With respect to complex international competition policy regimes, possible levels are global, regional-supranational, national, regional-subnational, and local. The elements are competition policy authorities (antitrust agencies, competent ministries, courts, and so on) and antitrust institutions (substantive rules, procedural rules, assessment techniques, enforcement practices, and so on). Thus, in Figure 4.1, level 1 could include a World Antitrust Agency and/or a World Competition Code, whereas level 2 could represent the competition policies of federal unions and association of nations (like the EU Competition Policy) and level 3 could carry the competition policies of nation-states. In order to constitute a system, however, these elements have to be interrelated.

---

[10] In Budzinski (2003b), where my analysis is predominantly based on network governance, I outline the multilevel approach as an 'extended framework for analysis' (ibid.: 39).

[11] The characterisations 'upward' and 'downward' refer to the visualisation of a multilevel system according to Figure 4.1 and do not imply assessments of importance or superiority versus inferiority. In particular, no prejudice about the competence (neither in a positive nor in a normative sense) of a level to exert jurisdiction over an antitrust case is implied. In the context of this book, top-down only means from centralised to decentralised, for example, from global to local. This notice should be particularly remembered in the context of section 2 of this chapter.

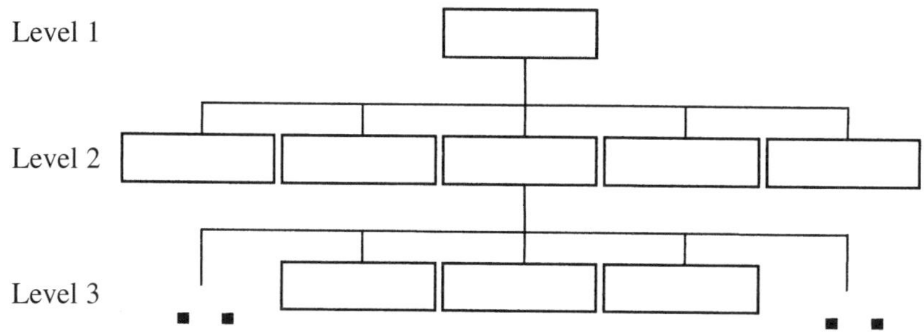

Source: Kerber (1999: 252; 2003: 275)

Figure 4.1 Stylised multilevel system

These interrelations are represented by the allocation and delimitation of competition policy competences.

Thus, the concept of multilevel systems inherently includes the problem of competence allocation and, therefore, represents an appropriate framework for the analysis of competence delimitation rules. Competence allocation plays an important role with regard to the performance of the system as a whole. It is sensitive for the sustainable integration of coherence and diversity. The analysis in the preceding chapter of the pros and cons of having an international competition policy regime has yielded a case for intermediate solutions between extreme centralism and extreme decentralism. Complex regimes, which combine beneficial elements of centralised and decentralised institutions, are more adequate to cope with the challenges of antitrust internationalisation. A complex but coherent international competition policy regime, preserving intra-regime diversity, is on the agenda. The concept of multilevel systems allows for a systematic, theory-based analysis of such regimes. Complexity and diversity are explicitly modelled by the existence of more than one level of jurisdiction and the possibility of having more than one institution/agency at each level (variety of elements). Coherence is represented in the system by the vertical and horizontal interrelations between the elements, that is, by the design of the interfaces. In other words, the allocation and delimitation of competences decides whether coherence within the system can be achieved without eroding the multilevel character. Thus, the choice of the rules, which determine competence allocation and delimitation, represent a decisive problem in regard to the workability of a multilevel system.

In the framework of multilevel systems, the problem of competence allocation and delimitation possesses a number of dimensions:

- Vertical and horizontal allocation of competences (dimension I): competences are allocated vertically between the levels (which is the competent level?) and horizontally among the authorities and institutions of the same level (which is the competent institution/authority on a specific level?). Additionally, problems of diagonal delimitation can occur in the case of allocative effects between a jurisdiction on a downward level and a jurisdiction on an upward level if the two jurisdictions are not vertically interrelated.[12]
- Institutional and enforcement competences (dimension II): competition policy regimes can consist of a number of institutional competences. The competence to create, implement and shape competition rules (dimension IIa) can be differently allocated than the competence to apply antitrust institutions (dimension IIb) or the competence to enforce the applied rules (dimension IIc). Moreover, substantive rules and procedural rules can be distinguished and allocated in a different way. Regarding any specific antitrust case, it must be decided, which institution (set of competition rules) is applied and which agency is responsible. For instance, a downward level agency can be competent in enforcing the institutions of an upward level agency. Or, an upward level agency only consists of procedural rules to enforce downward level substantive institutions. Similarly, on one and the same level agency A (institution Φ) can be competent in moulding substantive rules, whereas agency B (institution Ω) is responsible for applying them (for example, a domestic institution might be applied by a foreign agency). Consequently, the competence allocation regarding rule-making can differ from the one regarding rule application and enforcement.[13]
- Exclusive and concurrent allocation of competences (dimension III): the competence to exert jurisdiction over a specific antitrust case can be exclusively allocated to one institution and one agency. For instance, a specific case may fall exclusively under the European competition rules and jurisdiction is exclusively allocated to the European Commission. If competence allocation and delimitation is ambiguous, concurrent jurisdiction emerges. For instance, the German Cartel Office might want to challenge a cartel, applying European competition rules. At the same time, the US Federal Trade Commission pursues the same cartel under federal US laws.

---

[12] Imagine, for example, the question of competence allocation between the EU (supranational but regionally limited level) and Canada (national level but not within the regional scope of the EU).

[13] Section 2 of this chapter presents a number of real-world examples.

- Sustainable and temporary competence allocation (dimension IV): balancing centralising and decentralising forces within the system is a dynamic problem. Multilevel systems evolve along with competence allocation and delimitation. This can lead to two kinds of deficiency: (1) a creeping process of centralisation, incrementally eroding the benefits of having decentralised elements; and (2) a creeping process of decay, incrementally eroding the benefits of having centralised elements. Therefore, the allocation and delimitation of competences must not only focus on stationary combination of advantages of centralism and decentralism. It must also secure the sustainability of the system by controlling and balancing the centralising and decentralising forces. However, this need not imply that the once-implemented allocation and delimitation of competences must not be changed.

In order to speak meaningfully of competence allocation and delimitation, two extreme variants must be excluded. No meaningful competence allocation emerges if: (1) no authority and no institution has jurisdiction about antitrust cases, that is, there are no competition policy competences in the world at all; and (2) every authority and every institution has jurisdiction on all the antitrust cases, that is, there is no single case in which at least one institution or authority is not competent. Theoretically, these two variants can be viewed as extreme allocations of competences (to no one and to every one). However, in these extreme constellations, no differences between jurisdictions exist, wherefore no complex system is constituted. Distinguishable elements and interrelations are constitutive for a system because otherwise no borderline between the system and its environment is constituted or can be identified.

Consequently, the perspective of multilevel systems allows for a direct analysis of the (implicit or explicit) rules, which determine competence allocation and its evolution within a given multilevel system. In order to comparatively evaluate different rules for the allocation and delimitation of competences, criteria are needed, which operationalise these different dimensions and allow for normative conclusions.

1.2.2 The economics of federalism as a theoretical foundation for a theory of competence allocation in multilevel systems

The economics of federalism provide an adequate theoretical ingredient in order to derive criteria for the allocation and delimitation of competition policy competences. This theory developed from the narrower context of the provision and financing of government services. 'The traditional theory of fiscal federalism lays out a general normative framework for the assignment of functions to different levels of government and the appropriate fiscal instruments for carrying out these functions' (Oates 1999: 1121). Although the narrowly understood theory of fiscal federalism already entails a number of the most important insights, the modern economics of federalism[14] considerably extends the scope of analysis. In a more comprehensive approach towards a theory of regulatory federalism, it enquires 'which functions and instruments are best centralized and which are best placed in the sphere of decentralized levels of government' (Oates 1999: 1120). Thus, federalism is not about unconditional merits of decentralisation, instead, the 'basic issue is one of aligning responsibilities and . . . instruments with the proper level of government' (Oates 1999: 1120). This refers to research about: (1) assessing 'the advantage of a federal system compared to a unitary system'; and (2) 'the various possibilities to shape federal arrangements' (both quotations: Feld et al. 2004: 5). Furthermore, the economics of federalism stresses the importance of analysing both the horizontal and vertical dimension of interacting governments (Salmon 1987, 2000; Breton 1996: 184–194, 240–262).

Regarding the analysis of the allocation and delimitation of competition policy competences, the taxation side of the economics of federalism is less interesting than concepts of regulatory federalism.[15] The latter is well-suited to serve as a theoretical foundation since the comparative analysis of competence allocation rules, which is attempted in this book, belongs to research about alternative designs of federal arrangements (as outlined in the preceding paragraph). Moreover, the economic theory of regulatory federalism has yielded outcomes that are capable of serving as a background against which criteria for the evaluation of alternative federal arrangements can be derived. These results, however, must be understood more in the way of general guidelines instead of firm principles (Oates 1999: 1122, 1145) and do not relate explicitly to competence allocation rules in competition policy systems. Therefore, they cannot be directly transmitted to antitrust issues but require an antitrust-specific analysis, which is provided in section 1.3 of this chapter.

The major insight of the traditional fiscal federalism approach represents 'the presumption that the provision of public services should be located at the lowest level of government encompassing, in a spatial sense, the relevant benefits and costs' (Oates (1999: 1122). In other words, the question which externalities arise through centralised governance compared with decentralised competences (in a disaggregated approach, that is, regarding specific public goods) lies at the heart of the traditional theory (Breton 1996: 197–203; Feld et al. 2004: 3). Obviously, the emergence of externalities if governments are decentralised tends to favour centralisation. Nevertheless, the focus on externalities somewhat limits centralisation because – in a rather crude

---

14 See, for example, Breton (1996), Inman and Rubinfeld (1997), Qian and Weingast (1997), Oates (1999), Bird (2000), Scott (2000), and Feld et al. (2004).

15 See for a seminal overview on (narrowly defined) fiscal federalism, Oates (1999: 1124–1130).

version[16] – it represents a necessary condition for assigning competences to upward level governments: only if decentralised governments generate externalities, a centralisation can be beneficial.

Otherwise, decentralisation is viewed to be advantageous. This can be traced back to a number of reasons and arguments. First, differences in preferences tend to favour decentralisation.[17] As Oates (1999: 1120) maintains, the 'hope is that state and local governments, being closer to the people, will be more responsive to the particular preferences of their constituencies.' An information asymmetry between centralised and localised governments concerning knowledge about local preferences drives this effect. Secondly, a related line of argument concerns cost differentials. Differences in the production costs for public goods between governments on different levels as well as between governments within a given level also tend to favour decentralisation because of efficiency considerations and comparable information asymmetries (for example, Breton 1996: 204–209; Oates 1999: 1120–1124; Ogawa 2001). However, these aspects have to be complemented by the consideration of coordination costs between governments, which might entail a disadvantage of decentralisation under specific conditions.[18]

Thirdly, federalism might represent an advantageous regulatory framework concerning the limitation of Leviathan. Decentralised governments constrain each other, thereby, preventing a misuse of government power and preserving market institutions (Weingast 1995; Qian and Weingast 1997). One important aspect in this discussion is that the scope for lobbyism may be limited with a multitude of decentralised governments. However, this is an ambiguous argument since decentralised governments may also prefer to follow local interests and engage in protectionist policies.[19]

Fourthly and finally, decentralised governments allow for a beneficial laboratory federalism (Oates 1999: 1131–1134).[20] Having competent governments

---

[16] In the context of this book, it is impossible to reproduce comprehensively the elaborate and highly differentiated insights of the economics of federalism. Therefore, the summary of central features of the economics of federalism necessarily remains somewhat stylised.

[17] See, for example, Salmon (1987), Hamlin (1991: 194–199), Inman and Rubinfeld (1997), and Scott (2000: 193–197).

[18] See, for example, Breton (1996: 209–221) and Scott (2000: 187). For instance, too many decision-makers may create incoherent outcomes or tend to block and paralyse each other. See Feld et al. (2004: 10–11).

[19] See concerning this controversy, for example, Weingast (1995), Qian and Weingast (1997), Oates (1999: 1138–1141), Besley and Coate (2003), and Feld et al. (2004: 9–10).

[20] Comparable arguments are stressed by, for example, Salmon (1987, 2000), Inman and Rubinfeld (1997), O'Connor (2002: 427–429), Feld et al. (2004: 8–9), Kerber (2005), and Kotsogiannis and Schwager (2006).

on various levels of jurisdiction allows for decentralised experimentation with new regulatory solutions for economic problems. In particular, non-standard and innovative solutions can prove their capacities with geographically limited impact before being adopted countrywide (what, otherwise, is unlikely to happen at all). In other words, mutual learning becomes possible, promoting the horizontal and vertical diffusion of successful policies. The major mechanism for this phenomenon is type (I) regulatory competition (yardstick competition) because only this type occurs both in the horizontal and the vertical dimension (Salmon 2000: 239). Additionally, type (III) regulatory competition (voting by feet) is considered, which, however, only works horizontally.[21]

In summary, the economics of federalism provide a number of arguments concerning advantages and disadvantages of centralism and decentralism. In complete accordance with the world-antitrust-related analysis in Chapter 3, it can be concluded that neither unlimited decentralism nor total centralism represent beneficial arrangements. Again, the difficulty is to combine centralising and decentralising forces in order to reap their respective benefits.[22] However, the economic arguments that are raised in the regulatory federalism framework can be employed to evaluate the comparative performance of alternative federal arrangements. Regarding the context of multilevel systems of institutions, this is sufficient in order to compare alternative competence allocations. By focusing on competence allocation rules, additional advantages can be reaped. Each competence allocation and delimitation rule encompasses a group of related competence allocations with similar economic effects. Therefore, a comparative analysis of rules for the allocation and delimitation of competences, which is based on economic criteria derived from the economics of federalism, allows for a more comprehensive coverage of principal options – of course, without providing completeness. Nevertheless, this extended coverage of underlying competence allocations (and conceivable federal arrangements) alleviates the 'problem' that 'only' comparative conclusions (as opposed to general and definite conclusions regarding optimum solutions) are currently possible.

Before the analysis can proceed, however, the outlined basic features and results of the economics of federalism must be transmitted to competition policy institutions and agencies. Thereafter, criteria for the comparative evaluation of competence allocation rules in multilevel systems of competition policies can be derived.

---

[21] The exceptional case of type (IV) regulatory competition (direct choice of law) is neglected in this chapter since its principal inadequacy for competition policy was demonstrated in section 3 of Chapter 3.

[22] On this 'dilemma' in the economics of federalism debate see, for example, Oates (1999), Feld et al. (2004), and Figueiredo and Weingast (2005).

1.3 A Theory of Competence Allocation in Multilevel Systems of Competition Institutions

As argued in section 1.1 of this chapter, competence allocation is crucial for the long-run workability of a multilevel system of institutions and agencies. It can have very different designs with respectively differing performances of the system. Therefore, a theory is needed, which allows for normative conclusions about the adequacy of a specific competence allocation in regard to the system's performance. More precisely, the theory should permit comparative evaluation of the rules that allocate and delimitate competences within the multilevel system. In order to provide a theory-based list of criteria for respective evaluative assessments, the insights from the economics of federalism, outlined above, are applied to the context of multilevel competition policies. Each aspect allows for the derivation of a criterion, which, subsequently, serves to comparatively evaluate these rules (in Chapter 5).[23]

1.3.1 Externalities and spillovers

Whenever an incongruity between the geographical scope of an antitrust case and the territorial scope of the competition policy jurisdiction emerges, spillovers and externalities are likely to occur. An externality results if the decision of a competent antitrust authority causes costs or benefits, which are carried by other jurisdictions and, therefore, fall outside the calculations of the deciding authority.

If the territorial scope of the competent jurisdiction is smaller than the geographic scope of the antitrust case (that is, the relevant affected markets), its decisions can generate negative or positive externalities. Positive externalities arise if the competent authority effectively solves the problem for itself as well as for the other affected jurisdictions. In this case, the competent authority provides a public good (protection of competition) for the other jurisdictions, which can take a free-riding position, that is, the competent jurisdiction cannot force them to pay for the provision of the public good. According to

[23] Similar (though not identical) criteria are analysed by Van den Bergh (1996, 2000), Kerber (2000a: 84–88, 2003: 284–295), Van den Bergh and Camesasca (2001: 127–136), Grundmann and Kerber (2002), Kerber and Heine (2002), and Heine (2003: 40–49). While Van den Bergh (1996), Van den Bergh and Camesasca (2001), and Kerber (2003) discuss competition policy issues, the other contributions are either more general or refer to other fields of law and economics, for example, Grundmann and Kerber (2002) discuss contract laws and Heine (2003) analyses corporate laws. Methodologically differing (though not incompatible) approaches to antitrust federalism are provided by Easterbrook (1983), Fox (2000a), Guzman (2001), and Wood (2003b).

standard economic theory, this reduces the incentives to provide such goods (here: protection of competition) and leads to a reduction of welfare.[24]

Negative externalities arise if the competent jurisdiction protects its domestic markets but ignores anticompetitive effects on foreign markets. This can occur through discretion of the competent authority or because antitrust institutions in the competent jurisdiction demand a focus on domestic welfare only.[25] Moreover, the competent jurisdiction could also engage in strategic competition policies (by discretion of the authority[26] or institutionally prescribed[27]). In doing so, it not only forgoes protecting foreign market competition but actively generates restrictions on it.[28] However, even if one abstracts from strategic intentions, national antitrust authorities (targeting national welfare) may come to decisions which differ from and are incompatible with each other and the one of a (hypothetical) world authority (targeting world welfare). Economic theory demonstrates that, from a world welfare perspective, suboptimal policy outcomes result as soon as consumers and producers are asymmetrically distributed across jurisdictions. For instance, jurisdictions with more producers than consumers may rationally pursue gradually more lenient competition policies because the benefits for the producers outweigh the disadvantages for consumers. Vice versa, jurisdictions with a higher weight on consumers compared to producers may rationally employ stricter competition standards. Consequently, inbound focused national competition policy will allow some arrangements which would be prohibited by a world welfare oriented authority, and restrict some arrangements, which would remain unchallenged by a world authority because of their aggregate net benefits. However, an allegedly anticompetitive arrangement (for example, a merger) or practice in a truly international market cannot be separated between the jurisdictions that the markets overlaps. Thus, inbound focused national competition policy produces external effects on other jurisdictions, adversely affecting world welfare. These effects even occur under rather strict assumptions, that is, the jurisdictions can be completely identical except of the

---

[24] For instance, since a world-welfare-oriented national competition policy authority does not get any reward for its engagement when others insist on their 'national markets only' view, rational jurisdictions will be reluctant to provide positive externalities.

[25] The loopholes of both the EU and US regime regarding anticompetitive effects on markets in developing countries might serve as an example. See section 1.2.2 of Chapter 3.

[26] For instance, discriminating application of antitrust laws or selective non-enforcement.

[27] An example for such an institution is the general exemption of export cartels from the cartel prohibition.

[28] See section 1.3 of Chapter 3.

consumer producer relations.[29] For instance, this implies that welfare-reducing externalities and spillovers can theoretically even occur if national competition laws are completely harmonised as long as national (regional) welfare is the exclusive goal of competition policy.[30]

Spillovers between jurisdictions can be horizontal or vertical. A striking example of horizontal negative externalities is the widespread extraterritorial enforcement of domestic antitrust rules.[31] However, vertical problems can also arise. The competent jurisdiction may be a state authority and may generate (positive or negative) externalities on the federal level.[32]

If the territorial scope of the competent jurisdiction is larger than the geographic scope of the antitrust issue, principally the same problems arise, albeit restricted to vertical spillovers. Again, the competent jurisdiction can do the job for the downward level, thus generating an incentive problem. It can also generate negative externalities, for instance, if significant local anticompetitive effects arise but the competent jurisdiction ignores every case that has no territory-wide effects.[33] The competent jurisdiction may even promote a local monopoly because it views it to be a better territory-wide competitor. Thus, it might accept the loss of consumers' rent in the local jurisdiction because from its viewpoint the loss is – perhaps only theoretically but not practically – overcompensated by beneficial effects on the upward level.

The problem becomes aggravated if externalities arise in a regime with concurrent antitrust competences. Now, every acting jurisdiction can simultaneously cause externalities and become a victim of externalities from other jurisdictions. In such settings, jurisdictional conflicts are generated, which is a quite typical feature of the uncoordinated extraterritorial-antitrust-enforcement regime prevailing in the current antitrust world.

The consequences of externalities and spillovers due to decentralised competition policy competences in regard to centralism versus decentralism of

---

[29] Strictly speaking, this is only true for the total welfare standard. Haucap et al. (2006) argue that a widespread (unilateral) application of the consumer surplus standard would reduce the number of cases in which the sign of the changes of national and global welfare diverges, thereby linking the two lines of welfare standard discussions, which are presented above.

[30] See on the whole paragraph, for example, Barros and Cabral (1994), Head and Ries (1997), Guzman (1998: 1512–1524, 2004: 101–108), Falvey and Lloyd (1999), Sykes (1999), Neven and Röller (2000, 2003), and Klodt (2005).

[31] See section 1.2.2 of Chapter 3 as well as section 2.1.1 of Chapter 5.

[32] In the context of the US Antitrust System, a vital discussion about disturbances of federal antitrust caused by State competences is ongoing. See section 2.1 of this chapter.

[33] For instance, a world cartel office might not be interested in price-fixing if it is strictly limited to a (albeit distinctive) local market in Angola.

antitrust are explored in a number of quantitative economic analysis. Barros and Cabral (1994) and Head and Ries (1997) both offer models that rely on the standard framework of the modern oligopoly theory of mergers.[34] Thus, their analyses are reduced to international merger control, although Head and Ries (1997: 1106) emphasise that horizontal alliances are likely to be subject to similar effects. Furthermore, this framework assumes (among other things) that enterprises only engage in profitable mergers,[35] products are homogeneous, and external effects represent a major driving force of welfare effects.[36] In both papers, the distribution of producers and consumers across jurisdictions plays the decisive role. Barros and Cabral (1994) derive from their model that the decisions of national competition authorities differ from the ones of a supranational type as soon as an asymmetric distribution of producers and consumers occurs. In this more realistic case, both the welfare effects of mergers across jurisdictions and the relative weight, which competition authorities ascribe to producer and consumer surplus, differ. In the model of Head and Ries (1997), no difference between the aggregate decisions of national competition authorities and a hypothetical world competition bureau would arise if all affected countries had effective jurisdiction over the respective mergers.[37] However, if the power to exert jurisdiction over a specific merger depends on the location of the headquarters of the merging enterprises and if consumers and producers are allocated asymmetrically across jurisdictions, then a significant number of world welfare reducing mergers would not be blocked by the national authorities, although they would be challenged by the world competition bureau. As a very generalised consequence of both models, in a world of imperfect extraterritorial antitrust enforcement and asymmetric countries, a world competition bureau represents the superior solution in order to internalise negative externalities resulting from national competition policies.

An empirical analysis, which is based on this Farrell–Shapiro-type of models, is provided by Beelders and Özden (2001). They estimate the relation

---

[34] The landmark model is Farrell and Shapiro (1990).

[35] This is due to a rather strict concept of rationality in Farrell and Shapiro (1990). However, the empirical evidence in regard to cross-border mergers suggests that this is a heroic assumption (see section 1 of Chapter 2). The big share of inefficient mergers can mean that: (1) managers and other decision-makers are not as rational as assumed (bounded rationality, subjective rationality, knowledge problems, and so on); (2) share- and stakeholders pursue self-interests; or (3) synergy potentials are difficult to materialise due to post-merger-management imperfections.

[36] In Farrell and Shapiro (1990), (positive and negative) external effects of a merger on remaining competitors and on consumers are analysed. With the extension to include transborder mergers, external effects on other jurisdictions emerge.

[37] Although it is not mentioned by Head and Ries (1997), this describes the situation of perfect application of the effects doctrine by all interacting jurisdictions.

of specific merger characteristics with the likelihood of (extended) review by the European Commission. Only mergers with the participation of at least one US enterprise are included in the data. This limitation should serve as a proxy for the generation of externalities by the European merger review. The results are as follows (Beelders and Özden 2001: 18–23):

- The probability of review is significantly increased if the acquired company is European.
- The probability of review is positively related to the presence of both the acquired and the acquiring firm in Europe.
- The probability of review is positively related to the market shares of US firms in Europe in the affected industries.
- The probability of review increases with the size of the merger.
- The presence of the acquired and the acquiring firms in the US is insignificant.
- The market shares of European firms in the US are insignificant.
- The nationality of the acquired company is insignificant.

Despite far-reaching interpretations by the authors of this study, the results mainly confirm that EU merger control tries to protect competition in the Common Market – as it is demanded by law – and not in foreign markets like the US markets. Moreover, larger mergers are more often challenged than smaller ones, which stands in accordance with the codified review thresholds and the probability of pre-analysis dominance concerns. Additionally, there are more or less plain shadows of a (strategic) home bias.[38]

Another treatment of the problem of international merger control with rather similar results is presented by Tay and Willmann (2005). The main formal difference is that they do not assume a specific model of oligopolistic competition or specific market structures. In a two-country model with homogeneous products and where only profitable mergers are allowed, Tay and Willmann (2005) analyse the effects of a merger on three participating groups: the merging enterprises (denoted 'insiders'), other suppliers ('outsiders'), and the buyers of the product. They present a comparative analysis of the aggregated welfare

[38] This is further supported by Schinkel et al. (2004), who empirically derive that the chance of success for appeal against competition decisions of the European Commission is significantly higher in cases with non-European companies than it is in purely European cases. However, Bergman et al. (2004: 19) find that the participation of at least one US firm even reduces the probability of a merger prohibition by the Commission. Lindsay et al. (2003: 682) do not find a significant influence of the involvement of US firms on the European Commission's merger decisions. All three of these studies are more inbound focused on European competition policy and international implications represent only by-products.

effects of three different competition policy regimes. According to their model, the 'symmetric and non-cooperative territoriality regime', that is, a national competition authority has jurisdiction on mergers located within its territory and there is no coordination between the national authorities of the two countries, leads to an inefficient lax competition policy towards cross-border mergers. The second regime, the 'non-cooperative extraterritorial enforcement regime', that is, both national authorities perfectly apply the effects doctrine without any coordination, generates a 'global' policy, which is inefficiently strict. In terms of welfare, both regimes are inferior compared to the 'global authority regime' because this third regime type perfectly internalises negative externalities. However, since powerful countries lose from the implementation of the global authority regime,[39] a consensus for such a regime can only be achieved by unrealistic high side-payments (Tay and Willmann 2005). Altogether, the paper summarises the well-known results from the non-quantitative literature (albeit in a much more shallow way) that the waiver of extraterritorial enforcement implies severe loopholes in the protection of competition, whereas perfect extraterritorial enforcement favours the relative strictest competition agency (among the affected ones) and imperfect extraterritorial enforcement advantages powerful jurisdictions as they can successfully engage in strategic competition policies. In a rather indirect way, the PD character of the implementation game of the global regime is also included.

Drawing more on international economics than on industrial economics, a two-country static general equilibrium model of international competition policy is provided by Kaiser and Vosgerau (2000). Different from the preceding ones, this comparatively complex model is not limited to merger control. The effects of competition policy are explicitly modelled by a price(p)-marginal cost(c)-margin (denoted ß): $p = ßc$, with $ß > 1$, implying that effective competition policy minimises the term: $(ß - 1)$. In the otherwise perfect equilibrium setting (for example, full-employment, internationally equalising prices, cleared markets, atomistic, price-taking demand side, and so on), Pareto-social welfare functions are optimised: (1) for each country; and (2) for the two-country world economy. Not surprisingly, the 'uncoordinated national competition policies' setting is efficient in the case of autarky but inefficient in the case of international trade. More challenging are the results from the world-economy analysis. Here, the model produces multiple solutions, which are subsequently reduced by Kaiser and Vosgerau (2000: 44–46) against the

[39] In order to derive this result, Tay and Willmann (2005) introduce an asymmetric and non-cooperative regime in which the powerful country can exert jurisdiction extraterritorially, whereas the other country involuntarily sticks with the territoriality principle.

background of the Euler theorem, isolating the most rigorously competitive solution. Paying attention to these additional assumptions and restrictions, a worldwide coordination of competition policies becomes second-best efficient. However, similar to the precedingly reviewed models, only small countries gain unambiguously, whereas the effect of large countries is ambivalent because of deteriorating terms of trade. This is due to the fact that, without coordination, large countries have the power to influence world market prices and, thus, behave monopolistically against the smaller countries. This 'strategic' advantage gets lost with the internationalisation of competition policy.

Another externalities-focused quantitative approach can be found in two related papers by Neven and Röller (2000, 2003). Their two-country model with a homogeneous commodity does not depend on specific market structures or models of competition. In order to 'investigate how different rules to allocate jurisdiction will affect the outcome' (Neven and Röller 2000: 850) in terms of welfare but also in terms of jurisdictional conflicts, they assume that mergers are prohibited if they exceed defined market shares. The two jurisdictions differ in regard to geographic market definition and it is sufficient if one jurisdiction bans the merger (perfect application of the effects doctrine). Although Neven and Röller (2000: 849) emphasise the importance of (more complex) rules for the allocation of jurisdiction, they effectively compare the simultaneous (uncoordinated) assertion of jurisdiction on the basis of the effects doctrine with the authority of a centralised world antitrust agency.[40] Their analysis yields the following results (Neven and Röller 2000: 852–854, 2003: 240–247):

- The more similar the effects of a merger are in the two countries, the less conflicts arise.
- If both countries view the common ('world') market as the relevant market, then no conflicts arise and the allocation of jurisdiction does not matter.
- If both countries conclude different market definitions, then scope for conflict emerges.
- Conflict is less likely with extreme merger control rules (that is, very lenient or very strict thresholds) than with moderate standards.

Altogether, the framework of Neven and Röller (2000, 2003) implies that economic integration alleviates competition policy conflicts rather than

40 In the context of this chapter's analysis, this represents a comparison of the extreme regimes (no international coordination versus uniform world antitrust). However, they depart from some of the other papers by explicitly modelling effects doctrine-based jurisdiction.

generating or exacerbating them. This is because international economic integration (globalisation) makes the effects of mergers on different jurisdictions more congruent.[41] The counterintuitive result that the internationalisation of competition alleviates jurisdictional conflicts between national competition policies is, technically, rooted in the sensitive role of market definitions in the model. The frequent empirical emergence of antitrust conflicts particularly in global industries (Boeing–MDD, GE–Honeywell, and so on[42]) can, in the context of the model, only be traced back to exogenous factors, which were by assumption excluded from the model. In particular, the pursuit of objectives, which antitrust authorities should not pursue from a purely competition policy perspective (for example, industrial policy considerations, strategic competition policies), is identified as a probable candidate (Neven and Röller 2003: 240).

Altogether, according to standard economic theory, an internalisation of external effects enhances welfare (Pigou 1920). Popular internationalisation strategies in regard to goods' markets are taxes and bargaining. The former needs an upward jurisdictional level, which re-prices the activities on downward levels in a mandatory way, whereas the latter relies on voluntary contracts, which represent a cooperative solution.[43] This points to different ways to internalise externalities. In the context of competition policy, the first strategy implies that an upward level jurisdiction chooses the competent downward level jurisdiction (either with or without the opportunity of choosing itself). The second strategy hints at cooperative solutions through bargaining between the jurisdictions, either horizontally on the same level (for example, bilateral cooperation) or vertically between levels (cooperative federalism).[44]

When applied to competence allocation in antitrust multilevel systems, an internalisation is achieved if congruency is given between the geographic scope of a competition problem and the territorial scope of the competent jurisdiction. Consequently, and most generally speaking, the competence to deal with an antitrust issue should be allocated to the jurisdictional level, which has the highest degree of congruency with the territorial or geographi-

---

[41] This is further explored and emphasised if the supply-side globalisation, which dominates the reviewed models, is complemented by a demand-side globalisation (Haucap et al. 2006).

[42] See the overview in section 1.2.2 of Chapter 3 (Table 3.1).

[43] See the seminal contribution of Coase (1960). Note, however, that – according to Coase (1960) – the absence of transaction costs is sensitive to the superiority of the contractual solution in comparison to the tax solution.

[44] These brief remarks only outline possible internalisation strategies and, thus, remain rather vague. However, in Chapter 5, concrete competence allocation rules are analysed regarding their internalisation capacities.

cal scope of the problem. Therefore, this points towards an upward allocation of competences if antitrust cases affect: (1) several markets in different jurisdictions on downward levels; or (2) international markets. However, it also encompasses an argument for downward allocation if 'merely' national or regional markets are affected.

1.3.2 Efficiencies in terms of production, transaction, and administrative costs

Competition policy causes a number of costs, wherefore the economical organisation of competition policy procedures becomes a relevant aspect. If practising competition policy is characterised by economies of scale, then implications for the allocation of competences arise. Additionally, competence allocation obviously influences the amount of transaction and administrative costs.

By first looking at static economies of scale, it is clear that the fixed costs[45] of competition policy like the drafting and implementation of laws, the decision processes of the legislators, and the building up of specific human capital (legal scholars, lawyers, judges, the staff of competition authorities and courts, and so on) are very high. In contrast, the variable costs of applying the rules are comparatively small, leading to decreasing marginal costs. Consequently, an upward allocation of competences, that is, centralisation of competences at the top-level, economises on the fixed costs; the average cost of practising competition policy with a specific institution and through a specific authority declines with an increasing number of cases.

Regarding dynamic economies of scale, a more differentiated situation emerges. On the one hand, the quality of legal regimes improves with the number of cases that have been decided on its basis. Cumulating experience and knowledge, a higher predictability because of well-established reference cases as well as an increased stabilisation of expectations dynamically improve the applicability and workability of a specific combination of antitrust institution and authority. This also points towards a centralisation of competences because fewer regimes within the multilevel system imply a higher number of cases for each regime and, thus, improved economies. However, on the other hand, if path-dependencies are considered, severe problems arise (Heine and Kerber 2002). Lock-in effects may lead to inefficient paths with the consequence that deficient institutions and insufficient authorities persist in spite of increasing case numbers. Such sclerotic paths can be more easily challenged if alternative regimes are available within the multilevel system. This points towards some decentralisation of competences and may even favour some degree of concurrent competences.

---

[45] One may also speak of setup costs.

In summary, competition policy is characterised by economies of scale, implying an upward allocation of competences. However, centralisation should not be complete in order to avoid incontestable lock-ins. Altogether, economies of scale represent a somewhat ambivalent criterion but tends to favour upward allocation.

Next to economies of scale, administrative and transaction costs that do not relate to extra benefits represent sources of inefficiencies. The more institutions and authorities of the multilevel system deal with one and the same antitrust case, the more such costs are generated. This comprises both transaction costs for enterprises[46] (multiple filings, knowledge about different legal regimes, increasing legal uncertainty, and so on) and administrative costs for competition authorities and, eventually, taxpayers (parallel fact finding, parallel review procedures, and so on).[47] Generally speaking, transaction and administrative costs increase with the complexity and opaqueness of the competition policy system. However, different from the economies-of-scale argument, centralisation of competences is not a necessary condition for this kind of efficiency. A clearcut competence allocation is beneficial, but this does not imply that one and the same combination of institution and authority (preferably at the top level) must be competent. Each case has to be allocated unambiguously and exclusively to one jurisdictional level (clearcut vertical allocation) and, on the chosen level, one specific authority, applying one institution, is exclusively competent (clearcut horizontal allocation). One can call this criterion the one-stop-shop principle. However, the one-stop-shop principle does not demand a top-level-centred allocation (all cases to the same level and the same authority and institution[48]) and, consequently, it is not inevitably a centralisation principle.

1.3.3 Preference orientation

In democratic societies, the preferences of the citizens are the normative standard to answer the question of which goals and objectives a competition policy system should pursue. The first step is to assume that the preferences of the citizens can be transferred into antitrust policy through the democratic process (some majority–minority rules) without distortion (perfect principal–agent relation).[49] In this case, different preferences in different jurisdictions lead to different competition policies. These preference differences between jurisdic-

---

[46] These transactions include, for example, mergers and acquisitions as well as procompetitive cooperations.

[47] See section 1.2.2 of Chapter 3.

[48] Exactly this would be necessary to reap economies of scale.

[49] See section 1.3.4 of this chapter for the important case of distorted principal–agent relations.

tions can be rooted in deviating cultural and/or societal environments.[50] According to the respective preferences of the citizens, the desired objectives of competition policies may refer to such diverse things as economic efficiency according to the total welfare standard, economic efficiency according to the consumer welfare standard, fairness, protection of small business, economic freedom, social and ecological responsibility, static versus dynamic welfare, and many more. A crucial aspect is that, irrespective of whether one believes it to be 'right' or 'wrong' from the perspective of economic theory,[51] each of these objectives is legitimate if it corresponds to the preferences of the citizens. For instance, each society must inevitably make a value judgement about the borderline between legitimate competitive behaviour and unfair competition (for example, according to its moral standards).[52] The argument remains valid even if one assumes (for the sake of the argument) that there would be an ultimately 'right' competition theory – say, efficiency. The reason is that citizens may be rationally willing to accept a loss in welfare if they can have desired objectives be better fulfilled. In economic terms, the principals can be willing to pay (in terms of reduced material welfare) for having fair competition.

Interjurisdictionally differing preferences demand a decentralisation of competences (downward allocation of competences). Obviously, a uniform competition policy on the global level is less capable of representing heterogeneous preferences about, for example, supplier concentration, the value of economic freedom, or fairness standards of the downward jurisdictions and their citizens. The more centralised competence allocation is, the farther away the competent authorities and institutions are from the preferences of the principals.

1.3.4 Agency problems and lobbyism

However, the assumption that preferences are represented undistorted by the agents is rather ambitious. This leads to the political economy of competition

---

[50] See comprehensively Ullrich (1998) as well as Rosenthal and Nicolaides (1997), Fikentscher (1998, 2003), Haley (1998), Iyori (1999), Eguchi (2003), and Immenga (2004).

[51] Moreover, Budzinski (2007) demonstrates that there neither is, nor can ever be, an ultimately 'right' competition theory. Besides, the frontiers between total welfare standard and consumer welfare standard cut through the hardcore of mainstream economics. See, for example, Chang et al. (2002), Lyons (2003), Werden (2004), Neven and Röller (2005), Salop (2005), Farrell and Katz (2006), Haucap et al. (2006), and Heyer (2006). Eventually, it remains a normative decision whether or not one accepts redistributional effects from consumers to producers.

[52] Societies with deviating cultural backgrounds may find different modes of behaviour acceptable. See also the landmark contribution by Fox (2003b).

policy and lobbyism (imperfect principal–agent relations). Unfortunately, the context of 'centralisation versus decentralisation' and the extent of rent-seeking activities is ambivalent. On the one hand, decentralised competences may increase the ability of the citizens to control rent-seeking influences on their agents. Probably, information asymmetries between the principals and the agents are smaller, leading to improved control abilities for the citizens (McGinnis 2004; Stephan 2004).

In a related line of argumentation (but different application of the principal–agent approach), regulatory information asymmetries between the enterprises (as agents) and the competition authorities (as principals) can be reduced if the authorities are 'closer to the markets' (Smets and Van Cayseele 1995; Van den Bergh 1996). Smets and Van Cayseele (1995) analyse the scope for a supranational competition policy in a principle–agent model with asymmetric information. The competition authorities (national or supranational) are the principal and the merging enterprises are the agents, which have better information about the case facts. The resulting optimal control problem has two contradictory dimensions:

- Decentralised competition authorities can reduce the scope for merging enterprises to provide strategic ('misleading') information to the authority because they are 'closer to the markets'. Therefore, an international regime implies an aggravation of the principal–agent problem.
- For practically the same reasons, the national authorities can more easily be captured by lobbyism than a supranational authority. Thus, the danger of discrimination in favour of domestic enterprises arises in the absence of an international regime.

As a consequence, Smets and Van Cayseele (1995: 438–439) argue in favour of a two-level system to balance the contradictory effects. To the supranational authority, they assign the task of supervising the national authorities, which remain responsible for the actual case analysis. However, it remains open: (1) how and in which cases the supranational authority should effectively exercise its supervision; (2) why mandatory cooperation between the national authorities does not suffice in overcoming the lobbyism problem; and (3) how the complex regime can be quantitatively modelled. Altogether, there are arguments in favour of the hypothesis that agency problems can be reduced (albeit not erased) by a downward allocation of competences.

On the other hand, it might be more difficult for interest groups to capture supranational authorities with centralised competences than decentralised ones (Smets and Van Cayseele 1995; Neven and Röller 2000: 847–848). Competition policy agencies on more regional or local levels may be more prone to regional or local interests. Due to the lower degree of organisation and the worse ability to organise interests, consumer interests usually experience less influence than producer interests.[53] Moreover, the best organised producers more often than not win the lobby game, causing biased competition policy at the expense of the losers. Consequently, the suggestion of Piilola (2003: 216–218, 243–246), who explicitly demands the participation of business and its federations as well as consumer organisations in order to influence the shaping and design of international antitrust rules, must be rejected. Instead, the problem of lobbyism implies the exclusion of those groups from competition policy competences. The main reason is that there simply is no mechanism for reliably preventing business from misusing its influence at the expense of less organised groups or the public good.[54]

In summary, competence allocation should promote the preference conformity of competition policy, which points towards decentralisation of competences. Additionally, a minimisation of lobbyism is beneficial.

1.3.5 Institutional evolution and adaptability

Every multilevel competition policy system is confronted with a permanently changing environment. This introduces an evolutionary perspective, which has been neglected so far. An antitrust system needs adaptability through institutional and organisational evolution in order to cope with the evolution of its environment. There are two dimensions of evolutionary change to which competition policy systems must be responsive:

- First, competition policy deals with creative enterprises, which can innovate on anticompetitive arrangements and practices (evolutionary character of market competition; external evolution). An inflexible regime loses competence in protecting competition in the course of time because of its deficient ability to adapt to new market conditions. This aspect includes technological change, which can be a driving force of evolving and innovative (pro- and anti-) competitive market behaviour.[55]

53 A group possesses superior capabilities to effectively organise their interests (higher organisationability) if the interests are more homogeneous, the participants know each other, and experienced organisation structures are available. See Olson (1965).

54 Becker's (1983) landmark idea of having a competition of pressure groups, generating optimal regulatory outcomes, is sensitive to a significant number of assumptions that do not meet real world governance problems and situations. Therefore, it is not applicable in a realistic way regarding the problem of competence allocation and delimitation.

55 A recent example is the vital discussion on the implications of worldwide internet access to basic antitrust issues like market definition and the meaning of potential competition. See, for example, Ordover and Baumol (1988), Audretsch et al. (2001), Pleatsikas and Teece (2001), Posner (2001), Shapiro (2002), Röller and Wey (2003), and Ahlborn et al. (2004).

- Secondly, the theoretical knowledge about competition and antitrust (competition economics) is fallible and evolves (evolutionary character of the scientific competition of ideas; internal evolution). The state of competition economics is characterised by a significant variety with divergent views both within the: orthodoxy; and between competition economics paradigms. There are significantly divergent views among orthodox industrial economists on fundamental issues of competition (empirical proof: Aiginger et al. 1998 and 2001). These include several core issues like the importance of predation and entry deterrence, the goals of antitrust policy, the impact and development of industry concentration, and the meaning of the standard oligopoly models (Bertrand- and Cournot-competition) for real-world markets. The lack of consensual industrial economic competition theory is further demonstrated by the high-profile controversies among famous industrial economists about how to assess cases like Microsoft (for example, Fisher and Rubinfeld 2001; Gilbert and Katz 2001; Evans et al. 2005), GE/Honeywell (see section 1.2.2 in Chapter 3) or Oracle (Budzinski and Christiansen 2007). Probably, one should not go as far as Fisher's (1991: 207) 'second organizing principle' that suggests that 'the principal result of theory is to show that nearly anything can happen'. However, any claim that industrial economics would have provided a unambiguous manual to the 'right' competition policy cannot be sustained – even if competition economics could been reduced to theoretical industrial economics. Furthermore, such a reduction would be highly problematic against the background of alternative and partly incompatible competition economics concepts like Chicago-styled free market antitrust economics, theories of workable competition, Ordoliberalism, game-theoretic industrial economics, econometric-empirical industrial economics, Schumpeterian innovation and dynamic competition economics, market process and evolutionary theories of competition, and so on.[56]

The kaleidoscopic picture of the current competition economics world (Fox 2001; Immenga 2004; Budzinski 2007) raises the question of how this state should be assessed. In other words, what is the assessment of this existing theory pluralism in competition economics? Does it represent a principal deficiency, a temporary imperfection, or a sustainable and beneficial situation?[57]

---

56 See Burton (1994), Audretsch (1998), Budzinski (2003a, 2007), Fox (2003b), and Kerber and Schwalbe (2007).

57 See on the following paragraphs, Budzinski (2007).

Incapacity of competition economics? One could argue that the existing theory pluralism simply represents overwhelming evidence for the incapacity of competition economics, pointing to the necessity of new and more research efforts. When it comes to the evaluation of scientific disciplines, their state of the art, and their evolution, the (meta-) theory of science is addressed. Against the background of modern reasoning, however, the radical position of equalling diversity with incapacity has no backing.

Selection of superior theories? A more sophisticated and less destructive perspective treats theory pluralism as a temporary imperfection on the avenue towards the ultimate, 'right' competition theory. According to this view, the present pluralism of competition policy paradigms will be overcome by a scientific selection process that incrementally rules out inferior theories in favour of the most superior one. The underlying idea is a concept of continuous improvement of scientific knowledge, which implies that new theories are generally better (that is, representing improved knowledge) than older ones. This notion is very common within the discipline although the mechanisms, which are believed to drive the selection process, differ significantly. Drawing on the paragon of natural sciences, many proponents believe that economic reality will select the most appropriate theory, whereas others believe that theoretical rigour (drawing on the paragon of ideal sciences like mathematics) to be the best selection mechanism. While the latter would expect theoretical convergence to appear through intrascientific quality control (for example, refereed journals), the former would focus on comparative evaluations of the performance of markets and economies with differing institutional frameworks and policy programmes. The common denominator of these approaches, however, is the opinion that there is a diversity reducing selection process of theories, eventually leading to the identification of the best competition theory and policy paradigm.

The popular opinion that high standards for rigorous theoretical analysis will inevitably cause a convergence of views on competition theory – if rigorously interpreted – has an interesting implication. The idea that an unambiguous expert consensus would be a natural consequence of deepened research depends on an underlying assumption about the nature of real world evolution. It can only be true in a deterministic world in which theories and models could be capable of providing a true, ultimate description or explanation of reality. Only if ultimate explanations exist, sustainable and homogenising convergence towards the (unchanging) truth is at least theoretically possible. In a non-deterministic world (which is not following some foreordination), theories cannot be an exact copy of reality but (must) simplify things in order to isolate specific effects, thus representing simplifying heuristics of complex real-world phenomena. However, if this is true, the degrees of freedom to apply theories to real-world cases remain inevitably high enough to allow for deviating interpretations and conclusions. By developing these theories and models (or, theoretically, even by developing only one of them), thereby imperfectly approaching reality, an open menu of different directions is at the scientists' disposal and, in doing so, creates divergent views. In summary, the ideal of an economic consensus, which allows for 'objective' solutions of antitrust cases, remains impossible in an indeterministic world. Due to the fact that even scientists are confronted with and influenced by special interests, such a consensus would be illusionary even in a deterministic world.

Notwithstanding this implication, the importance of the described intrascientific selection processes is not principally challenged. However, concluding a temporary character of theory pluralism and an inherent tendency towards convergence becomes less obvious, leading towards the question of whether diversity may have a more than temporary function.

A sustainable role for theory pluralism? Drawing on modern contributions to the metatheory of science, another way of dealing with theory pluralism emerges. Diversity of competition theories can be regarded as a sustainable imperative of science instead of a temporary phenomenon or an evidence of incapacity. Real sciences (like economics) develop by testing theories and hypotheses on reality, thereby weakening theories with little or doubtful explanatory power and strengthening the 'better' ones. Up to this argument, this notion is perfectly compatible with the notion of temporary imperfections on the way to the truth. However, the selection process is both incomplete (Karl R. Popper) and imperfect (Thomas S. Kuhn), making the disposability of alternative theories a sustainable and fundamental characteristic instead of a temporary imperfection.

According to Popper (1959, 1962, 1972), scientific progress is characterised by a fundamental asymmetry: theories can only be proved to be false but never to be true. Empirical evidence can only refute/disprove theories but never prove them. Therefore, all scientific knowledge remains preliminary and fallible at any time. Irrespective of the amount of supporting evidence, it can never be scientifically excluded that the next experiment represents a counter-example and proves the theory at least situationally wrong.[58] Popper's legacy

[58] Originally, Popper believed that the refutation of a theory is always definite because one counter-example should be sufficient to prove a theory wrong. However, although this appeared to be suitable for natural sciences, it did not fit for social sciences in which any real-world theory represents a small part of a complex system of interacting effects. Thus, in social sciences, counter-examples can result from an inseparable overlay of another effect. Furthermore, in the face of modern quantum theory in physics, it seems doubtful whether the unambiguousness of counter-examples can be unexceptionally upheld in natural sciences.

implies that there cannot be an ultimate theory, instead, scientific progress is a never-ending process. A competition theory that has proven perfectly suitable until today can be set to refutation by tomorrow's empirical evidence. Concerning social sciences, this argument becomes reinforced by the inherently evolutionary character of social interaction: contrary to physics, the environment of economic analysis changes over short periods of times, that is, that the object of analysis endogenously produces changes in its working mechanisms, underlying patterns, and performances. This can render good theories obsolete. Social science theories are not only fallible due to previously undiscovered empirical evidence but, additionally, due to previously non-existing evidence that is (permanently) created by the object of analysis itself.

The paradigm theory of scientific progress (Kuhn 1962) waters down the case for continuous improvement of scientific insights even more. Not only is scientific knowledge always and inevitably fallible, beyond it, the process of the selection of ideas itself is imperfect and does not always select the better theories. Instead, disciplines of science are most of the time characterised by the domination of a specific paradigm that moulds the questions actually asked, the methods applied, and the answers deemed acceptable as well as defining the common world view, the basic (often implicit) assumptions, and so on. These common values influence how reality is perceived and shape the resulting theories since 'the empirical world can be known only through the filter of a theory; thus, facts are theory-laden' (Wilber 2003).

This paradigm, the contemporary orthodoxy, is persistent, that is, that other approaches might be neglected even if they produce new knowledge. According to Kuhn (1962), a paradigm is able to become dominant because it possesses superiority concerning the research on a specific group of problems that are contemporarily very urgent and not sufficiently addressed by other theories. However, once a paradigm dominates, path-dependencies and lock-ins arise. Scientific resources including manpower concentrate on orthodox research because that offers the best possibilities for careers and further resources. This is reinforced by a growing monoculture in the education of students and young scholars, so that knowledge about alternative approaches becomes neglected and devastated irrespective of its future potentials. Since careers, prestige, success, and resources are bound to the domination of the paradigm, this can become combined with active defence strategies of the proponents to deter heterodox scientists and their ideas. If the paradigm grows older, its capacity to solve scientific problems usually begins to decline because the problems, which fit well into its explanatory framework, are exploited, and neglected problems (that do not fit well into the paradigm) grow in relative importance. Thus, the combination of explanatory power, self-reinforcing effects, and defence policy that keeps the paradigm dominating tends to incrementally shift to the defence side over time, resulting in slowdowns of scientific progress or even in net regress due to the obstruction of non-orthodox research. Eventually, the paradigm will fall and be replaced by a new one. However, this can take a significant time in which theories, which may be obsolete and which cannot claim to have become selected because of their superiority, dominate. During this time, scientific knowledge is shaped by the common world view of the paradigm and its associated value judgements. Scientific research within a paradigmatic 'research programme' is limited to alterations of the 'protection belt' of supplemental theories and assumptions that leave the hard core untouched (Lakatos 1970).

After all, the contemporary metatheoretical insights (Chalmers 1990, 1995) that: (1) there cannot be anything like an ultimate paradigm; and (2) the dominating paradigm at a specific time need not consist of superior theories[59] render a convergence of competition theories towards some sort of an ultimate competition theory not only improbable but also inadequate. Since: (1) there cannot be an ultimate knowledge on market competition; and (2) the selection process is imperfect, a lock-in to one overall dominating theory does not represent scientific progress but, instead, the frustration of progress in knowledge. Instead of theory pluralism, a monoculture of competition economics would represent an inefficient state of the discipline since the output (production of new ideas, theories) is restricted.[60] Therefore, sustainable pluralism of competition theories is an imperative for science and no temporary problem on the path to the ultimate solution. This assessment is perfectly compatible with the (temporary) dominance of one competition theory paradigm. However, it cannot be claimed that a dominating paradigm represents the ultimate theory and, thus, renders theory pluralism obsolete. Such a claim has to be refuted because it would confuse the 'victory' or domination of a scientific paradigm with scientific advancement, which would be a variant of the natural fallacy (that is, deriving a normative assessment from a positive fact).

In summary, although majority opinions (the 'mainstream') may serve as useful guidelines for competition policy practice (in order to draw on what most experts currently believe to be the best available theory), this must not be confused with superiority of a paradigm from a meta-theoretical perspective. Scientific knowledge is always fallible and provisional. Furthermore, the

[59] According to Lakatos (1978), who combines lines of argument by Popper and Kuhn, the superiority of paradigms (research programmes) can only be evaluated historically. Comparative assessments (in regard to superiority) of contemporary or future research programmes are not possible in a scientific way.

[60] It is important to emphasise that output restrictions occur both quantitatively and qualitatively since research activities are channelled to a narrow programme by the dominating paradigm. Instead of exploring a wide variety of paths to new insights, only a few parts that are very near to each other are explored.

scientific community innovates on competition economics, for instance creating new theories or changing comparative evaluations of existing paradigms. Consequently, it is beneficial if a competition policy regime maintains openness and responsiveness to new knowledge from academic competition economics.

In order to secure adaptability, permanent learning processes have to be facilitated within the multilevel system. This means offering channels through which innovative ideas can be injected into the system. A decentralised allocation of competences, securing a sustainable role of institutional and organisational diversity, produces more interfaces with the academic sphere and allows for more and more diverse scientific ideas to enter the system (Kovacic 1992, 1996). This argument is strengthened when theoretical aspects of learning are introduced. With sustainable diversity within the system, different institutions and practices can be tested on reality, producing knowledge-generating feedback, in particular through their comparative performance. The crucial aspect is that institutional and organisational diversity allows for parallel experiments with different solutions, whereas a uniform regime is limited to sequential experiments.[61] Consequently, competence allocations that produce vertical and horizontal diversity allow for a higher rate of learning than more centralised competence allocations. The better ability to learn improves the adaptability of the system.

Parallel experimentation can take place both between horizontally related institutions and authorities and between vertically related levels. It significantly improves mutual learning. Therefore, this argument promotes competences on downward levels but it does not exclude competences on upward levels. However, the maintenance of decentralised elements is crucial for securing resonance ability, reaction flexibility, error tolerance, and innovation permeability. Without sufficient adaptability, a competition policy system is unlikely to be able to cope adequately with future challenges.

1.4 Criteria for the Evaluation of Rules for the Allocation of Competences

The five dimensions of economic effects of competence allocations in multilevel competition policy systems, which are analysed in the preceding section, put

---

[61] On the advantages of parallel experimentation in comparison to sequential experimentation see Vanberg and Kerber (1994), Kerber (2003, 2005), and Kerber and Budzinski (2004). This argument is related to type (I) competition of competition policy regimes. See section 3 of Chapter 3. More intuitively, the idea that a variety of laws and enforcers is likely to produce and facilitate creativeness, innovativeness, and adaptability to change is also explored, for instance, by Wils (2002) and Virtanen (2004). A typical variant is Venit (2003: 562) who argues that controlled diversity in the application of competition laws 'may enhance product quality and benefit consumers in ways not fully anticipated.'

up an analytical framework, which allows for the derivation of a set of criteria. These economic criteria can be used for a comparative evaluation of different rules for the allocation and delimitation of competences within multilevel systems with regard to their economic performance.[62]

The allocation and delimitation of competences within a multilevel system is guided by explicit or implicit rules. These rules: (1) assign competences to authorities and institutions (both horizontally and vertically); and (2) determine (horizontal and vertical) competence interfaces. The resulting allocation and delimitation of competences has a decisive influence on the performance of the multilevel competition policy system. It best promotes a sound multilevel system (that is, a balance of centralising and decentralising forces; combination of coherence and diversity) if the rules governing competence allocation meet the list of criteria (Figure 4.2), derived from economic effects, to the highest degree.

Before the comparative evaluation of competence allocation rules is carried out (in Chapter 5), the framework of multilevel systems of competition policies is applied to a number of existing antitrust regimes, in which competence allocation has proved to be a crucial problem in recent decades.

---

[62] The criteria derived in this book differ somewhat from the one's introduced by Conrad (2005: 75–77). He analyses design-proposals for complete regimes against the background of: (1) their contribution to international allocative efficiency and the international freedom of competition; (2) public acceptance; (3) political acceptance; and (4) organisational expense – with declining weight. Obviously, Conrad's fourth criterion belongs to efficiency (section 1.3.2 of this chapter), although the concept of institutional efficiency is more comprehensive in my analysis. The second and third one are captured by preference conformity (section 1.3.3 of this chapter). Eventually, the first and most important criterion in Conrad's scheme is partly mirrored (albeit in a somewhat narrower way) in the more precise and superiorly operational criterion of internalisation of external effects. However, Conrad's variant considerably extends the externality-focused view, although it remains rather vague what exactly could be additional applicable aspects in his analysis. It seems to include the dimension of identifying better or best competition rules in the sense of guaranteeing (stationary) allocative efficiency. This is explicitly excluded in my analysis due to the principal reasoning about scientific diversity and limited institutional knowledge (see section 3 of Chapter 3, and section 1.3.5 of this chapter). As a natural consequence of mixing issues of competence allocation (who makes/applies/enforces competition rules) with issues of institutional quality (what is the right substantive-material design/content of competition rules), Conrad neglects the evolutionary criterion developed in section 1.3.5 of this chapter. In part, this reflects the fundamental difference of focusing on regime proposals as a whole (Conrad) and competence allocation rules as decisive elements of competition policy regimes (Budzinski). As a logical result, the comparative evaluations carried out by Conrad (2005: 77–101) and Budzinski (Chapter 5) are not compatible.

List of criteria
• Internalisation of external effects • Cost efficiency: economies of scale and one-stop-shop principle • Preference conformity • Minimisation of lobbyism • Adaptability

Figure 4.2 Criteria for the comparative evaluation of competence allocation rules

2. EXISTING MULTILEVEL COMPETITION POLICY REGIMES – AN ANALYTICAL OVERVIEW

The two most important competition policy regimes in the world today – the US Antitrust System (section 2.1) and the EU Competition Policy System (section 2.2) – can be described and analysed in terms of multilevel systems. One advantage of referring to this analytical framework is that the dynamics of the systems regarding competence allocation – or centralisation and decentralisation respectively – can be analysed in a theory-driven, integrated way. Next to these two acting competition policy regimes, the two approaches to create a global antitrust regime, which are currently concurring, can also be analysed against the background of this framework. This offers valuable insights on the merits and problems, which the WTO Competition Regime (section 2.3), on the one hand, and the International Competition Network (section 2.4), on the other hand, raise. Finally, some remarks on the world competition order as a whole (section 2.5) conclude this section.

The pattern of analysis is the same in the first four subsections. First, the respective regimes are described in the language of multilevel systems. Secondly, the state of competence allocation and delimitation is identified. Thirdly, the previous evolution, current problems, and future challenges of competence allocation within those systems are analysed. In contrast, a precise evaluation of specific competence allocation rules according to the above derived criteria (and, thereby, an evaluation of the advantages and disadvantages of the described regimes) lies at the heart of Chapter 5 and is suspended in the following subsections.

2.1 The US Antitrust System: Ongoing Discussion about Federalism?

The US Antitrust System has a federal structure, which has developed through the long history of the world's effectively oldest antitrust regime.[63] Antitrust competences are allocated both to the federal level and the states. Additionally, private enforcement plays an important role (see Figure 4.3).

At the top level, there are the federal antitrust institutions like the Sherman Act, the Clayton Act, the federal Merger Guidelines, and so on. They are enforced on the federal level by two federal agencies, namely the Antitrust Division of the US Department of Justice and the Federal Trade Commission (FTC; established in 1914). They enforce the federal antitrust institutions, specifically the Sherman Act (1890) and the Clayton Act (1914).[64] The former prohibits contracts, arrangements, or conspiracies in restraint of trade as well as monopolisation and attempts to monopolise, while the latter focuses on merger control, price discrimination, tying, and exclusive dealing. The Antitrust Division and FTC as general competition authorities are complemented by several industry-specific regulatory agencies with significant competences in antitrust issues, in particular merger control, codified and explained in the respective regulatory institutions. Prominent examples include the Securities and Exchange Commission (SEC), the Federal Energy Regulatory Commission (FERC), and the Federal Communication Commission (FCC).[65] With regard to the enforcement of the general antitrust laws, an asymmetric allocation of decision competences must be noticed. The federal agencies can challenge alleged anticompetitive business arrangements and practices by filing a suit against them. Thus, the ultimate decision about a

---

[63] On the historical origins and development of the US Antitrust System see Mueller (1996), Kovacic and Shapiro (2000), Peritz (2000), Wells (2002), and with regard to the theory of institutional change, Neugebauer (2004: 76–99). Modern overviews include Kaserman and Mayo (1995), Hovenkamp (1999), Lin et al. (2000), and Sullivan and Grimes (2000).

[64] A number of additional Acts (like the Federal Trade Commission Act, the Robinson–Patman Act, the Hart–Scott–Rodino Antitrust Improvements Act, and many more) complement and interpret these two basic antitrust laws. See Kaserman and Mayo (1995), Hovenkamp (1999) and Sullivan and Grimes (2000) for more details.

[65] For instance, the FCC generally prohibits mergers in telecommunications if the buying company comes from abroad and is state-owned (more than 25% of the shares), unless the foreign corporate interest is consistent with the public interest. It also disposes over the discretionary power to allow exemptions. Another example: the US Department of Transportation is exclusively authorised to approve certain types of horizontal agreements between airlines. For overviews on the complex interrelation of antitrust and regulatory institutions, agencies and policies in the US see Kaserman and Mayo (1995: 441–448), Hovenkamp (1999: 698–720), Sullivan and Grimes (2000: 697–798), and Kovacic (2004: 318–320).

prohibition is made by the courts.[66] If the agencies waive bringing an arrangement or practice to the courts, this de facto implies an allowance. A court review of this implicit decision only occurs if other private parties file a suit.[67]

The second level is represented by the states and their competition policy institutions.[68] In principle, the states have the competence to implement their own antitrust institutions. However, only some of them have designed their laws in a way which substantively deviates from the federal laws. The states' attorneys general enforce the state antitrust laws, that is, they bring respective cases to the competent courts.[69] However, they also have competence to enforce the federal antitrust laws. By doing so, they are technically considered private persons, wherefore the term 'quasi-public enforcement' is commonly used (Hovenkamp 1999: 590–591).

Additionally, a third level is constituted by private litigation, meaning that purchasers, consumers, competitors, subcontractors, and so on, also have standing to bring antitrust cases to the courts. More precisely, the antitrust injury doctrine requires any private plaintiff to show that his or her injury reflects the anticompetitive effect of the violation of the competition rules.[70]

The allocation of competences to enforce the federal antitrust institutions is split between the federal agencies (Hovenkamp 1999: 584–590). Public enforcement of the Sherman Act lies predominantly in the authority of the Antitrust Division. However, the FTC's task to challenge unfair methods of competition constitutes its competence in Sherman Act issues because 'unfair methods of competition' is interpreted in a way that includes everything in the Sherman Act plus a few additional practices. Regarding the Clayton Act, the FTC and the Antitrust Division share concurrent enforcement competence. However, procedures by both agencies regarding the same case are actively avoided. For this purpose, they have developed cooperative clearance proce-

---

[66] Binding out-of-court settlements between the antitrust agencies and the involved enterprises, so-called consent decrees, must be approved by the competent court.

[67] However, this procedure does not centre around the reasons of the federal authorities to waive challenging the practice or arrangement but represents an independent proceeding.

[68] See for the whole paragraph, Hovenkamp (1999: 721–745) and Sullivan and Grimes (2000: 902–906).

[69] Very rarely, even local antitrust enforcement occurs. For instance, the Los Angeles District Attorney's office runs an Antitrust Section as a part of its Consumer Protection Division. See Sullivan and Grimes (2000: 904–905).

[70] This is a very general description that does not cover the specific interpretations and limitations regarding indirectly affected purchasers or umbrella plaintiffs. See, in more detail, Hovenkamp (1999: 592–639) and Sullivan and Grimes (2000: 907–967).

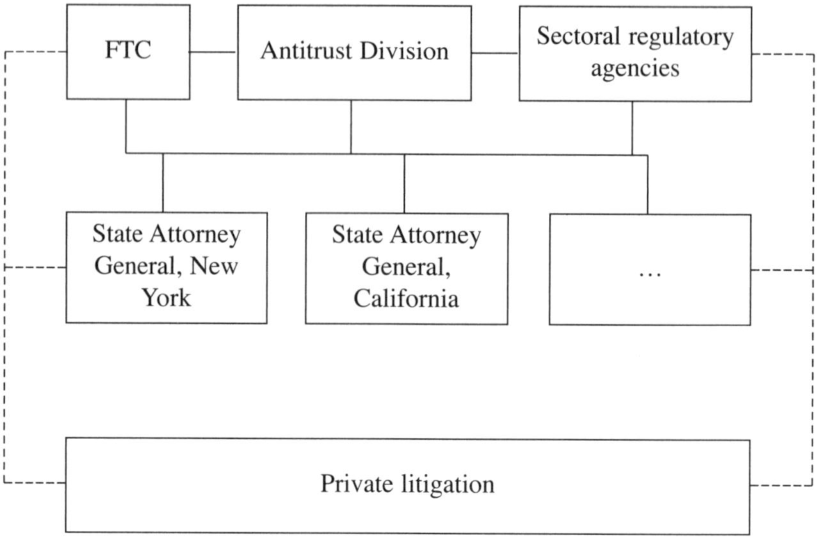

Figure 4.3 The stylised US antitrust system

dures, in which, after mutual notifying, cases are consensually allocated based on considerations of expertise, staff availability, and so on. Cases involving criminal sanctions are generally allocated to the Antitrust Division.

Regarding the allocation and delimitation of competences between the federal and the state level, the interstate commerce clause plays an important role.[71] In theory, according to the clause, a case is allocated to the federal level whenever it touches interstate commerce. Then, the state level would be reduced to purely intrastate anticompetitive arrangements and practices. However, in the course of time, the interstate commerce clause has been interpreted by the courts in a much broader manner, maintaining considerable extraterritorial scope for state antitrust policies. According to case law, the interstate commerce clause limits state antitrust policy only insofar as: (1) no contact of the challenged business activities with the state's territory can be identified; (2) inconsistent rules are forced upon a nationwide and networked

[71] For descriptions and analyses of the state and interplay of US antitrust policy at the federal, state, and local level, see Easterbrook (1983), Kovacic (1992, 1996, 2004), Kaserman and Mayo (1995), Hovenkamp (1999: 721–745), Ginsburg and Angstreich (2000), and Sullivan and Grimes (2000: 536–556, 887–967). The whole paragraph draws on these sources.

market;[72] or (3) the state laws differ significantly from the federal laws if both the extraterritorial impact is more significant than the intraterritorial one and the federal policy would be de facto undermined. However, court decisions about the competence of state antitrust policy are made on a case-by-case basis. On the other hand, the scope of federal antitrust policy is limited by the interstate commerce clause because federal policy is not competent in purely intrastate cases.

In summary, a significant overlapping of competences must be noted. This leads to both frequent conflicts between, and cumulating effects of, federal and state antitrust policy, as was evidenced, for instance, in the more recent cases of Microsoft and Illinois Brick, as well as in the tobacco cases. In order to reduce the resulting problems, the federal agencies and the National Association of Attorneys General (NAAG) have entered into a procedural agreement regarding merger cases (Antitrust Division 1998). However, the voluntary character of the coordination agreement reduces its scope to cases where no divergence of interests is involved. An example of the divergences between federal and state antitrust enforcement are the issued guidelines on horizontal mergers and vertical restraints, which deviate considerably from each other, with the state guidelines (issued by the NAAG) generally being more strict than the federal ones.

Among the state antitrust enforcers, cooperative coordination takes place through the NAAG Multistate Antitrust Task Force (established in 1983). However, the cooperation is voluntary and based on similar interests. For instance, in the Microsoft case, a number of states (with the domestic states of Microsoft competitors and buyers among them) cooperated on attacking the alleged anticompetitive behaviour of the software quasi-monopolist, whereas some states took the side of the defendants (among them Microsoft's home state).[73] In order for this to be comprehensive, it must be remarked that – naturally – no formal or systematic coordination between public and private enforcement exists.

Altogether, the US antitrust system lacks a clearcut competence allocation. The considerable overlap of antitrust competences and the resulting conflicts and cumulating procedures fuel an ongoing vital and controversial discussion about limiting the scope for state antitrust policies and implementing less ambiguous competence delimitation rules.[74] Arguments against

---

72 Instituted examples are the major national sports league as long as uniform governance is economically essential (Hovenkamp 1999: 742).

73 For an empirical generalisation see Posner (2004: 263).

74 See – with varying degrees of rigour and compromise – contra extensive state antitrust competences, Flexner and Racanelli (1994), Rose (1994), Zimmerman (1999), Epstein and Greve (2004), and Posner (2004) and pro state antitrust competences

the current degree of decentralised competences with fuzzy delimitation are as follows:

- The state attorneys general do not have enough resources at their disposal for complex antitrust investigations.
- They are dominated by political career interests because they are elected and often potential rivals to the acting governors.
- Incentives for discriminatory antitrust, that is, at the expense of non-resident enterprises and taxpayers are more effective.
- An inconsistent regulatory framework for business activities results.
- Increasing coordination costs and more lengthy proceedings harm both business and taxpayers.

In defence of state antitrust competences, the following arguments are raised:

- It provides a countervailing power for (interest-biased) federal antitrust and its errors.
- Innovative antitrust doctrines or methods are generated.
- Beneficial experimentation with different ideas and concepts (laboratory federalism) as well as institutional and interjurisdictional competition is allowed and maintained.
- State antitrust enforcement is better suited for regional and local cases.
- Institutional comparative advantages can be reaped.

Not surprisingly, the arguments are essentially the same as in the discussion about the pros and cons of an international competition policy regime. Some contributors even call for a domestic US antitrust network, which copies basic elements of prominent international approaches (First 2003: 28–29; Kovacic 2004).

The fierce controversy on the future of US antitrust federalism has culminated in the establishment of an Antitrust Modernization Commission (AMC) with a reform of the division of labour in antitrust enforcement and of the reach of state and federal antitrust laws being among its major topics (Antitrust Division 2005). In its final report of 2 April 2007, the AMC (2007) recommends.

Easterbrook (1983), Barnes (1988), Kovacic (1996, 2004), Burns (2000), First (2001b), and Grimes (2003). See also Lande (1990), Ehle (1998), Ginsburg and Angstreich (2000), Slot (2002), Hahn and Layne-Farrar (2003), Adkinson (2004), and De Bow (2004).

- eliminating inefficiencies resulting from dual federal enforcement, however, dual enforcement should not be disestablished;
- improving coordination between state and federal enforcement, in particular to enhance cooperation between the two levels and work towards substantive harmonisation, especially in regard to merger review;
- modestly modifying the rules of private enforcement.[75]

It remains to be seen whether legislative acts will follow the recommendations. In summary, competence allocation and delimitation represents a most important and controversial subject within the US antitrust community.

2.2 The EU Competition Policy System and its Reform Dynamics

In contrast to the US antitrust system, the EU competition policy system includes a truly supranational level,[76] albeit with regionally limited extent.[77] Competition policy was on the agenda of the European integration process right from the beginning. The European Coal and Steel Community (ECSC), founded in 1951 (Treaty of Paris), contained a general prohibition of

[75] See for controversial discussions of the work of the AMC, Hovenkamp (2005), Cengiz (2006), and Sagers (2006).

[76] Next to the elaborated competition policy system of the EU, a number of other regional economic associations (free trade areas, tariff unions, and so on) contain more or less rudimental provisions on competition policy. Among them are the Andean Community and the UEMOA (Union Economique et Monétaire Ouest Africaine), which each possess their own supranational competition agency, as well as the NAFTA, Mercosur, APEC, ASEAN, and Caricom (Carribean islands). The new South African economic community (COMESA) is also planning to implement some kind of common competition policy. See Tavares de Araujo and Tineo (1998), Lloyd and Vautier (1999), Vautier (2001), Rimoldi de Ladmann (2002), Jenny (2003b), Lloyd (2003), Drexl (2005), and with specific reference to most recent centralization tendencies in competence allocation within UEMOA, Bakhoum (2006).

[77] The territorial reach is continuously increasing. The founding members Belgium, France, Germany, Italy, Luxembourg, and the Netherlands were supplemented by Austria, Denmark, Finland, Greece, Ireland, Portugal, Spain, Sweden, and the UK in the course of the twentieth century. Since 1 May 2004, Cyprus, the Czech Republic, Estonia, Hungary, Latvia, Lithuania, Malta, Poland, Slovakia, and Slovenia have joined the community, January 2007 saw Bulgaria and Romania joining. Possible new members in the course of the upcoming decade include Croatia, with the status of Turkey (as an applicant for almost 20 years now) remaining more or less unclear. Switzerland and Norway are virtually ready to join, however, a majority of citizens in these two countries have voted against an EU membership. Altogether, the EU has expanded to approximately 450 million inhabitants and a territory of approximately 4 million km^2.

anti-competitive arrangements[78] and attempted to regulate mergers and practices related to powerful market positions in these sectors. However, the provisions were not only guided by the desire to protect competition, but also by the motivation to control strategically important, war-sensitive industries through a supranational authority (the ECSC High Authority). Therefore, the High Authority and the governments (in their role of mandatory consultants) enjoyed considerable degrees of discretion and, in specific situations, would have been competent to regulate prices and quantities in these sectors.[79]

When the EU[80] was founded in 1957 (Treaty of Rome), the sector-specific antitrust provisions of the ECSC became generalised and modified in a competition-oriented way and, thus, created competition policy competences at a supranational level. From 1957 on, the European competition rules consist of a general cartel prohibition with exceptions (Art. 81, previously Art. 85 EC), an abuse prohibition for market-dominant enterprises (Art. 82, previously Art. 86 EC), control provisions in regard to public enterprises (Art. 86, previously Art. 90 EC), and rules to limit anticompetitive state aids (Art. 87, previously Art. 92 EC). Until today, these substantive rules have remained unchanged. However, they have been complemented by EU merger control rules in 1989 (European Community Merger Regulation,[81] (ECMR), which were substantially revised in 2004[82] and complemented by Horizontal Merger Guidelines.[83] In terms of substantive law,[84] the old EU merger control regime focused on the creation and strengthening of dominant market positions as the prohibition criterion for mergers, whereas the new regime implemented the

78 In particular, according to Art. 65, § 1, interfirm agreements, which: (1) fix or influence prices; (2) restrict or control production, technical development or investments; and (3) allocate markets, products, customers, or sources of supply, were banned.

79 See, in more detail, Gerber (1998a: 335–342). Some of the provisions can be viewed to be anticompetitive rather than procompetitive. See Bulmer (1994: 427–428).

80 However, the original name was European Economic Community (EEC), a term, which was later succeeded by European Community (EC) and eventually by European Union (EU; Amsterdam Treaty in 1997). Despite the historical inaccurateness, I use the term 'European Union' and the abbreviation, EU, to denote the European integration project at any time of its existence.

81 Council Regulation (EEC) No 4064/89 of 21 December 1989 on the control of concentrations between undertakings: [1989] OJ L 395/1.

82 Council Regulation (EC) No 139/2004 of 20 January 2004 on the control of concentrations between undertakings (the EC Merger Regulation): [2004] OJ L 24/1.

83 Guidelines on the Assessment of Horizontal Mergers under the Council Regulation on the Control of Concentrations between Undertakings: [2004] OJ C 31/5. See for analyses Ridyard (2004) and Voigt and Schmidt (2004b).

84 The reform also touches competence allocation issues. This is explored later in this section.

all-new SIEC test, according to which, all mergers which create significant impediments to effective competition, are banned. The guidelines specify that the EU merger review shall rely more closely on quantitative industrial economics. In this context an economic expert staff was implemented, that was initially headed by Lars-Hendrik Röller (Professor of Economics with the Humboldt-University in Berlin), and since 2006 is by Damien Neven.[85] However, the dualism of competition policy goals in the EU Competition Policy System has been left untouched in the recent reforms. Next to the protection of competition for the welfare of the consumers, the promotion of economic integration in the community has always played an important role.

The relevant institutions at the European level of the EU Competition Policy System are supplemented by the European Commission as the acting competition policy agency. The actual work is done by the Competition Directorate but the decisions are made by the Commission as a whole. Judicial review is provided by the European courts, namely the European Court of First Instance and the European Court of Justice (ECJ). These are the elements of the top level of the EU competition policy system, but what are their competences? The European Commission does not possess definitive rule-making competences. Instead, the European Council or the Council of Ministers, respectively, eventually decide upon the competition rules.[86] However, the European Commission disposes over comparatively extensive decision and enforcement competences, since it both reviews alleged anticompetitive cases and decides on them. It can approve and prohibit cases, place sanctions and fees, demand modifications and dictate conditions. The courts become involved only if the regulated companies (or their competitors, suppliers, and

---

85 In particular, unilateral effects of mergers in heterogeneous oligopolies and enhanced and specified considerations of efficiency effects of mergers shall be introduced. See on the substantive elements of the recent reform and their implications in more detail, Díaz (2004), Lyons (2004), Monti (2004a), Schmidt (2004), Voigt and Schmidt (2004a, 2005), Zimmer (2004), Budzinski and Christiansen (2005a), Levy (2005), Schwalbe (2005), Christiansen (2006), Neven (2006), and Röller and De la Mano (2006). The implications of the appointment of Röller as the first chief economist against the background of his scientific legacy are further explored by Stevenson and Filippi (2004). A comprehensive summary of the controversial lines of argumentation during the reform process provide the chapters in Drauz and Reynolds (2003). For theory-driven analyses of institutional change during the history of modern European competition policy see, for example, Neugebauer (2004: 99–122) and Budzinski and Christiansen (2005b).

86 The European Council consists of the leaders of government of the Member States, whereas the Council of Ministers consists of the respective members of government, which are responsible for a specific policy field. In the case of competition policy, these are most generally the ministers of economic affairs.

consumers[87]) file an appeal against the Commission's decision. Additionally, the Commission can influence the rule-making process through its agenda-setting power due to its right of initiative in the legislative process (Peters 1994).

The second level of the EU competition policy system consists of the antitrust institutions and authorities of the Member States, which have considerable scope for the application of their national laws. For instance, in Germany, the *Bundeskartellamt* (Federal Cartel Office of Germany) enforces the German Act against Restrictions of Competition (*Gesetz gegen Wettbewerbsbeschränkungen* (GWB), implemented in 1958)[88] independently from the government.[89] Another institution is the German Act against Unfair Competition (*Gesetz gegen den unlauteren Wettbewerb* (UWG), implemented in 1909, substantially reformed in 2004).[90] Additionally, there are sector-specific regulatory agencies and institutions with competition policy competences in regard to telecommunications, banking, and energy.[91] Almost every Member State has its own antitrust institutions and authorities, albeit in different shape, design, and extension.[92]

---

[87] Historically, most cases have been appeals against merger prohibitions or (the size of) penalties. However, in the recent Impala case, the European Court of First Instance annulled the EC's unconditional clearance of the Sony-BMG music joint venture (Aigner et al. 2006). See on the limited – though increasing – role of private enforcement within the EU competition policy system, Venit (2003: 570–572), Wils (2003b), McCurdy (2004), Jones (2005), van Gerven (2005), Komninos (2006), and Wigger (2006). The acting Commissioner, Neelie Kroes, views an increased role of private antitrust enforcement within the EU to be one out of three major goals of her term. See Kroes (2005: 2).

[88] The GWB includes provisions against cartels and market power abuse as well as merger control rules. See Gerber (1998a: 266–333), Stockmann (2001), and Kerber (2002).

[89] The German Minister of Economic Affairs, though, can exceptionally overrule the Cartel Office in the name of the overwhelming public good (§§ 8 (cartel exemptions) and 42 (merger control) of the GWB). See, on the ministerial exemption in German competition policy, for example, Kühn (1997: 133–135).

[90] The UWG includes provisions against unfair modes of behaviour in competition, for example, misleading information and advertising, reviling and denouncing competitors, economic espionage, misuse of consumers' trust, and calculated/unobjective/intentional handicapping of competitors. See Finger and Schmieder (2005).

[91] See Haucap and Kruse (2004) and generally, on the interrelation of antitrust and sector-specific regulatory agencies, Hewitt (1999). Currently, there are no such regulatory agencies at the European level.

[92] See exemplarily for UK competition policy, Miller (2002), Suzuki (2002), and Zahariadis (2004), and for the case of France Jenny (1995), Gerber (1998a: 403–405) and Parmentier (2002). Regarding other EU countries see, for example, Gerber (1998a: 405–413), Martin (1998), and Vedder (2004).

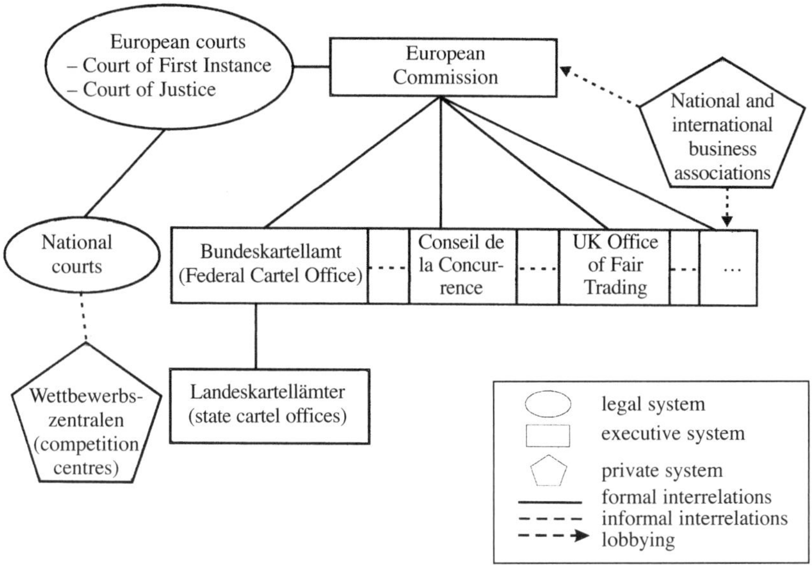

Source: A slightly different variant is included in Budzinski and Christiansen (2005b)

Figure 4.4 The stylised EU competition policy system

Without attempting to be comprehensive, this brief overview demonstrates the high degree of complexity of the EU competition policy system, which is also illustrated by Figure 4.4. In some cases, even a third, subnational level with (minor) competition policy competences exists. In Germany, to continue the above chosen example, there are *Landeskartellämter* (State cartel offices) with limited enforcement power. Moreover, the federal UWG provisions are generally enforced through private litigation before regional courts. In this context, local *Wettbewerbszentralen* (competition centres), representing private enforcement associations (more often than not consisting of business representatives), are the main driving-force of enforcement.

After having described the elements of the EU competition policy system, I now address their interrelations. Within such a complex system, competence allocation represents an important issue.[93] Consequently, it has been controversially discussed from the start of the integration project until the most

[93] In the words of Fingleton (2005: 12): 'The decision to allocate a case may well have consequences for how the case is investigated, appraised and ultimately dealt with'.

recent reforms – and the controversy is most likely to last into the future (Budzinski and Christiansen 2005b; Budzinski 2006). However, I concentrate on the allocation and delimitation of competences between the two top levels – European level and level of the Member States – and on cartel policy and merger control. In doing so, all the important features become clear. In order to keep the analysis workable, therefore, I skip subnational levels and abuse of market dominance.

With regard to cartel policy, the institutional allocation and delimitation of competences between the EU and the Member States follows a rather general rule. According to Art. 81 EC, the European competition rules have to be applied whenever cartel-like interfirm arrangements 'affect trade between Member States'. This general rule is also called effects of trade concept or interstate trade criterion. However, it is less clearcut as it appears at first glance and its interpretation has been subject to considerable dynamics. As a very general tendency, the scope of community competition rules has expanded at the expense of national rules in the course of time (Burnley 2002a: 217–220). For instance, interpretations of interstate effects have increasingly covered any influence on the trade flows within the EU even if the effects are indirect or potential. Additionally, the notion of the criterion has expanded beyond the simple movement of goods to comprise all kinds of cross-border economic activity including services and the establishment of industries and enterprises. Moreover, the ECJ has explicitly affirmed the priority of European competition rules over national ones in cases of conflict. In the landmark Walt Wilhelm judgment of 1969, the court clearly supported centralisation at the European level for the first time. Furthermore, in the Delimitis judgment of 1991, it maintained that national courts were obliged to halt proceedings in certain cases and wait for the decision at the EU level. In the 2000 Masterfoods judgment, the court went even further by stating that national courts were to avoid rulings that would conflict with a subsequent decision according to European rules (for an overview, see Goyder 2003: 440–444, 462–463). An additional effect was generated by the increasing significance of cross-border business activity following the deepening economic integration and the completion of the EU Common Market. Altogether, a creeping centralisation of cartel policy competences resulted.

Notwithstanding, the vagueness of the interstate criterion has remained. Recognising this, the Commission recently issued a Notice on the interpretation of the effect-on-trade concept.[94] It develops the so-called 'not appreciably affecting trade' rule (NAAT rule), which effectively represents a combination

[94] Commission Notice – Guidelines on the effect on trade concept contained in Articles 81 and 82 of the Treaty, [2004] OJ C 101/81.

of market share and turnover figures without constructing a precise quantitative threshold. This interpretation guideline may contribute to a clarification of the competence allocation rule. However, it also possesses a number of shortcomings, for instance, the inclusion of market shares (which implies the need to define markets first – an ambitious and controversial issue) and the non-binding character (even on the Commission, which emphasises the necessity of case-by-case analyses).

Concerning cartel policy enforcement, the recent reforms of European competition policy caused significant changes in competence allocation. Until May 2004, enforcement competence allocation was determined by the 'old' Cartel Enforcement Regulation of 1962.[95] It implemented a so-called centralised ex ante authorisation regime, which assigned the exclusive competence to grant exemptions from the general cartel prohibition (according to Art. 81(3) EC) to the European Commission. All interfirm arrangements, which fulfilled the interstate trade criterion, had to be notified to the Commission. While the general cartel prohibition of Art. 8(1) EC is directly applicable in all Member States, the Commission held the monopoly for exempting specific types of arrangements, which serve the consumers, promote innovation and economic development, are cartel-specific, and do not comprehensively impede competition between the collaborating enterprises. The national competition authorities (NCAs), on the other hand, have the exclusive right to apply their domestic competition rules to domestic interfirm arrangements, that is, such that do not effect trade between the Member States.

However, the Commission was unsatisfied with the old regime because it felt that it wasted too much time on reviewing procompetitive interfirm collaborations in order to exempt them from the cartel prohibition. In the face of the increasing importance of international hardcore cartels like the vitamins cartels, the Commission argued that it would be more effective in terms of protection of competition if it used these resources to detect and fight hardcore cartels. Moreover, from the viewpoint of the Commission, the ex ante authorisation regime was ineffective in this respect since hardcore cartels – per se illegal without exemptions – were not notified but instead pursued in secret (Nicolaides 2002: 42–44; Venit 2003: 548–559; Wils 2004: 669–672, 675–679).

Consequently, the old Enforcement Regulation was replaced in May 2004 by a new one.[96] The reform implemented a regime change. The centralised ex

95 EEC Council: Regulation No 17: First Regulation implementing Articles 85 and 86 of the Treaty, [1962] OJ 13/204. See Gerber (1998a: 348–351, 394–401), Ehlermann (2000: 540–546), and Wils (2002, 2004).

96 Council Regulation (EC) No 1/2003 of 16 December 2002 on the implementation of the rules on competition laid down in Articles 81 and 82 of the Treaty: [2003] OJ L 1/1.

ante authorisation regime was replaced by a decentralised ex post control regime. This significant change in competence allocation raised a vital academic discussion.[97] Instead of having to notify cooperative arrangements and awaiting approval by the Commission, enterprises now self-assess their arrangements. If they believe that the conditions of Art. 81(3) EC are met, they can enter into the arrangements without having to make notification to any competition policy authority. This corresponds to the opinion of the Commission that only legal interfirm agreements will be notified to the authorities anyhow. With the regime switch, the enforcement monopoly of the Commission is also suspended. After the reform, the national competition authorities and the national courts are also entitled to apply Art, 81(3) EC and, thus, decide on cartel exemptions. As a consequence, cartel enforcement competences have been decentralised through the reform. However, this explicit decentralisation of enforcement competences is accompanied by a more implicit centralisation on the institutional side.[98] The jurisdiction of European competition rules is de facto expanded, since national authorities are now obliged to deal with domestic cases, which might affect interstate trade solely on the grounds of European law. Additionally, increased rights to overrule national proceedings for the Commission and comprehensive information obligations for the NCAs contribute to the picture. To some extent, the Commission managed to delegate the cumbersome fieldwork to the national level while reserving the important powers for itself, leading some commentators to speak of a 'political masterstroke' (Riley 2003: 672) and 'increased dominance' (Wilks 2005: 438) by the Commission. In the end, the scope for applying national law becomes further marginalised in competition policy practice.

---

[97] See, among many others, German Monopolies Commission (1999), Temple Lang (1999), Ehlermann (2000), Gerber (2001), Kingston (2001), Mavroidis and Neven (2001), Burnley (2002a), Nicolaides (2002), Wils (2002, 2003a, 2004), Barros (2003), Calvani (2003), Venit (2003), DeKeyser and Laurila (2004), Forrester (2004), Lenaerts and Gerard (2004), Virtanen (2004), Wigger (2004b), Bloom (2005), Böge (2005a), Schaub (2005), and Wilks (2005). Critics point to the danger of: (1) inconsistent treatments of similar cases in individual Member States due to differences in competition policy traditions and procedural rules (in particular with regard to the new EU Member States in Eastern Europe with their rather short history of market economy); (2) a loss of legal certainty; (3) enhanced scope for forum shopping by enterprises; and (4) an overall decline of the competitive standards were feared as possible reform consequences. However, the self-reinforcing implications for the inherent vagueness of the basic competence allocation rule (interstate trade criterion) is barely subject to critical review. See, for exceptions, Mavroidis and Neven (2001), Burnley (2002a), and Budzinski (2006).

[98] See, on the following, Kingston (2001), Lever (2002), Riley (2003), Forrester (2004), Budzinski and Christiansen (2005b), Fingleton (2005), Smits (2005), and Wilks (2005).

In principle, competence allocation in EU merger control follows a similar criterion like cartel policy. However, in the ECMR, the delimitation of competences is much more specified. As a general rule, the Commission and the EU institutions are exclusively competent for every merger that has a Community dimension. All other mergers within the EU fall under the competence of the Member States and their institutions and authorities. The concept of having a clearcut vertical allocation of competences with either the EU level or the Member States level being exclusively competent is called the one-stop-shop principle (for example, Brittan 1990). In order to operationalise the community dimension concept, the Merger Regulation contains quantitative thresholds that decide to which level a specific merger case is allocated. These thresholds apply to turnovers, following the intuition that the likelihood of a merger having a Community dimension increases with its size, which is approximately measurable by the turnovers of the participating enterprises.[99] According to Art. 1 of the ECMR, a merger falls exclusively under the jurisdiction of the EU level if either (cumulative conditions):

- the combined aggregate worldwide turnover of all the enterprises concerned exceeds €5000 million;
- the aggregate communitywide turnover of each of at least two of the enterprises concerned exceeds €250 million;
- unless each of the enterprises concerned achieves more than two-thirds of its aggregate communitywide turnover within one and the same Member State;

or

- the combined aggregate worldwide turnover of all the enterprises concerned exceeds €2500 million;
- in each of at least three Member States, the combined aggregate turnover of all the enterprises concerned exceeds €100 million;
- in each of at least three Member States, the aggregate turnover of each of at least two of the enterprises concerned exceeds €25 million;
- the aggregate communitywide turnover of each of at least two of the enterprises concerned exceeds €100 million;
- unless each of the enterprises concerned achieves more than two-thirds of its aggregate communitywide turnover within one and the same Member State.

---

[99] However, turnover thresholds represent a rather crude proxy for the dimension of a merger in terms of affected markets. The pros and cons of turnover thresholds as a competence allocation rule are discussed in more detail in sections 1.1.3 and 2.2 of Chapter 5.

All mergers, which do not meet these thresholds, are subject to the merger laws and authorities of the Member States according to their individual notification and review thresholds (which differ significantly between the Member States).[100]

These turnover thresholds alone would constitute an unambiguous competence allocation. However, the one-stop-shop principle falls short if a specific merger does not meet the thresholds but has to be notified (according to national law) to more than one Member State authority. In such cases, multiple parallel proceedings can occur, something which has always generated a vital discussion on the appropriateness of competence allocation and delimitation in EU merger control. The other way around, it was also argued that some of mergers that meet the thresholds should better be subject to national rules because anticompetitive concerns affect only or predominantly one Member State.

These problems of competence allocation according to turnover thresholds led to the introduction of a referral regime.[101] The old Merger Regulation entailed only provisions for post-notification referrals, that is, Member States could: (1) request a downward referral of a merger notified by the Commission; and (2) jointly refer a merger upward, which did not meet the thresholds but of which the NCAs thought should be a Community case. In the first case, the Commission enjoyed a veto right and in the second case, the referrals were non-mandatory. This reallocation of merger control competences was assessed both by academics and practitioners to be ineffective. Multiple filings and reviews on the Member State level increased since the late 1990s[102] and more dynamics were to be expected in the face of the enlargement to 25 members. Moreover, both upward and downward referrals were rare as both the Commission and the NCAs were reluctant to engage in post-notification referrals (European Commission 2001b; Bright and Persson 2003; Domínguez Pérez and Burnley 2003). Therefore, the reform of competence allocation was a major issue in the 2004 reform of the EU merger control regime.

During the reform process, a number of interesting and innovative ideas on

---

[100] See generally on jurisdiction in merger control within the EU, Morgan (2001), Burnley (2002b), Drauz (2003), Budzinski and Christiansen (2005b), and Budzinski (2006).

[101] See on the 'old' referral regime, for example, Hirsbrunner (1999), Morgan (2001), Bright and Persson (2003), and Domínguez Pérez and Burnley (2003).

[102] According to Bright and Persson (2003: 492), the ratio between multiple filings and EU notifications was 62 per cent in 2000, with a figure of 35 per cent in regard to multiple filings in three or more Member States. Total numbers of multiple filings reached almost 300 cases between 1992 and 2000.

how to design competence allocation and delimitation were discussed.[103] However, in the end, the turnover thresholds are left untouched and the referral regime is reformed instead.[104] In order to become more 'streamlined', post-notification referrals are modestly enhanced and pre-notification referrals are introduced. However, no mandatory referrals were agreed upon. Regarding post-notification referrals,[105] a right of initiative for the Commission to invite a Member State request for downward referral complements the existing rules. Additionally, the formal requirements are alleviated (for example, shortened deadlines, simplified formal criteria, less administrative efforts, and so on).[106] However, the Member State is not obliged to request (following a respective invitation by the Commission) and, as it was before, the Commission may veto downward referrals at its discretion (at least, if it had not invited a request). The major innovation is the introduction of pre-notifications referrals (Art. 4(4–5) of the ECMR). The merging enterprises are entitled to request pre-notification referrals, that is, in cases where the thresholds are met, enterprises may vote for Member State competence and vice versa. Only requests according to the following reasons are allowed:

- in case of pre-notification downward referrals, the merger must raise concerns that it significantly affects competition in a market within a Member State, which presents all the characteristics of a distinct market; and
- in case of pre-notification upward referrals, the merger must be subject to review in at least three Member States.

However, three veto rights are implemented:

- in case of pre-notification downward referrals, the Commission can veto (without being obliged to give reasons);

[103] See the overview discussions by Drauz (2003) and van Gerwen (2003). Section 1 of Chapter 5 draws on some of these ideas, which are – subsequently – thoroughly analysed and evaluated in section 2 of Chapter 5.

[104] See, on the reform aspects concerning competence allocation, Broberg (2002), Schaub (2002), Klees (2003: 197–200), Domínguez Pérez and Burnley (2003), Drauz (2003), Díaz (2004: 179–184), Schmidt (2004: 1556–1563), Budzinski and Christiansen (2005a, 2005b), Levy (2005: 111–112), Soames and Maudhuit (2005: 58–64), and Budzinski (2006).

[105] Art. 9 of the ECMR addresses post-notification downward referrals, whereas Art. 22 of the ECMR addresses post-notification upward referrals.

[106] See Commission Notice on Case Referral in Respect of Concentrations, available at http://europa.eu.int/comm/competition/mergers/legislation/consultation/case_allocation_tru.pdf, to be published in the *Official Journal*.

- in case of pre-notification downward referrals, the Member State concerned can veto; and
- in case of pre-notification upward referrals, each Member State concerned can veto.[107]

Altogether, one is forced to cast doubt upon the effectiveness of the reform. First, it is not convincing why merging enterprises shall decide about regulatory competence allocation (Stockmann 2003). Secondly, it remains unclear why competence reallocation is improved since no mandatory referrals (but extensive veto rights instead) are introduced. Thirdly, competence allocation seems unnecessarily complicated.[108] In summary, one can predict that competence allocation will remain on the reform agenda of EU merger control.[109]

To some extent, the Commission seems to acknowledge the deficiencies of the reform. At least, this would explain why the Commission finds it necessary to introduce networks between competition agencies within the EU – both in cartel enforcement policy and in merger control[110] – in order to create a soft

---

[107] That means for instance, that if a merger does not meet the thresholds but is subject to reviews in, for example, 11 Member States, the veto of one of those Member States (even if all the others want to refer) suffices to suspend the one-stop-shop principle. More probable than not, such cases will happen in the EU-27.

[108] Easier solutions were discussed but discarded because of party interests. See Budzinski and Christiansen (2005b). Moreover, sections 1.2.3 and 2.7 of Chapter 5 demonstrate that simpler rules are not inevitably less effective. See, with respect to the EU merger control reform, Budzinski (2006).

[109] See Budzinski and Christiansen (2005b) and Budzinski (2006). For a contrary statement see Schmidt (2004: 1563), who claims that the reformed referral regime provides 'an efficient, sufficiently predictable and flexible mechanism for ensuring the allocation of cases to the most appropriate authority.' She assigns both 'significant enhancement of proper case allocation and huge savings of time and expenses' (Schmidt 2004: 1563) to the new pre-notification referral rules (see, however, the contrary assessment by Soames and Maudhuit (2005: 62–63)). However, Schmidt does not deal with the disadvantages that are outlined in this section . Instead, she addresses alleged problems of switching jurisdictions (that is, a pre-notification downward referral may be allocated upwardly again by a post-notification upward referral – this, indeed, seems an extraordinary and rarely relevant aspect because the extensive veto rights can much more easily prevent any pre-notification referral) and the exact design of the Form RS (which is the administrative form to be submitted in cases of pre-notification referral requests), including the related information requirements (perhaps implying some aspects of self-incrimination by the submitting enterprises). According to her view, these problems 'are far outweighed by the huge advantages of the possibility of requesting pre-notification referrals' (Schmidt 2004: 1563). However, from an economic perspective, different concerns have to be raised (see discussion and text accompanying this footnote).

[110] Both recital 15 of Regulation No 1/2003 and recital 14 of the new ECMR explicitly call for the formation of a 'network' consisting of the Commission and the

guide towards more efficient competence allocation. As an overall principle for soft allocation, the centre of gravity principle is introduced. However, its content remains rather vague by simply stating that any anticompetitive arrangement or practice should be located – without mandatory character – 'where the main effects will be felt' (Monti 2004b: 496).[111]

Thus, in 2004, the European Competition Network (ECN)[112] was formally introduced, comprising the Commission and the competition authorities of the (now) 25 member states.[113] The explicit aim of the network as a 'forum for discussion and cooperation' (para 1) in regard to cartel policy is 'to ensure both an efficient division of work and an effective and consistent application of EC competition rules' (para 3). Thus, the ECN is explicitly implemented to heal some of the deficiencies in competence allocation, which may arise as a consequence of the new decentralised enforcement regime. Due to a closer cooperation within the ECN, deviating interpretations of cases and laws by the NCAs shall be avoided. Instead, consensual assessments about the application of EU rules shall be achieved through permanent cooperative interaction of the antitrust officials. However, it can be suspected that the ECN will also serve as an improved information medium and early warning system in case of deviation by NCAs. This promotes (re-)centralisation because the Commission can take over competence from the national authorities at any time.[114] Hence, the cooperation forum ECN might effectively help the Commission to prevent decentralised enforcement from becoming 'too' decentralized, that is jeopardising the Commission's monopoly of rule-interpretation. Some commentators

---

NCAs acting 'in close cooperation'. However, it is not clear whether these should be different networks or not.

111 See for critical comments, Smits (2005: 175–180) and Wilks (2005: 440–445).

112 Commission Notice on Cooperation within the Network of Competition Authorities: [2004] OJ C 101/43. See, for analyses, Monti (2004a), Virtanen (2004), Wils (2004: 699–705), Böge (2005a), Budzinski and Christiansen (2005b), Forrester (2005), Fingleton (2005), Gerber (2005), Schaub (2005), Smits (2005), and Wilks (2005).

113 However, even before the first introduction of the ECN (in 2002), the Commission and the NCAs cooperated in a more or less formal framework in the context of the Advisory Committee on Restrictive Practices and Monopolies, the Advisory Committee on Concentrations, and the Network of European Competition Authorities (ECA-Network; horizontal network of national competition authorities within the EU). Additionally, informal and mutual cooperation and exchange of information and opinion have increased in the course of time. See, for example, Bright and Persson (2003).

114 The Commission Note states the Commission 'has the ultimate but not the sole responsibility for developing policy and safeguarding consistency' (para 43). Consequently, some commentators expect the Commission to want merely to shift routine work to the NCAs without offering them real participation. See, for example, Kingston (2001) and Fingleton (2005).

even fear that the NCAs might become 'automaton satellites' of the Commission.[115]

Concerning merger policy, the respective network shall enhance efficiency and effectiveness of the referral process in order to achieve a 'more streamlined system of referrals' (Drauz 2003: 22). Again, this does not give the impression of a sound post-reform competence allocation regime. The ECN shall improve the referral regime by facilitating both upward and downward referrals due to the enhanced and deepened cooperation. Consensual arrangements shall secure that 'a case is dealt with by the most appropriate authority, . . . with a view to ensuring that multiple notifications of a given concentration are avoided to the greatest extent possible . . .' (Recital 14 of the ECMR). The guiding principles include that 'cases involving local markets or distinct national markets in not more than two Member States should, as a general rule, be reviewed by the national competition authorities' (Drauz 2003: 25). In other words, the upward referrals (centralising competences) shall – in the Commission's opinion – be interpreted much more strictly than in the wording of the Regulation. Similar to cartel policy, a continued pressure for the reform of the allocation and delimitation of competences can be predicted.

In summary, competence allocation represents an important issue in the development of the EU competition policy system. It plays an important role in ongoing reform activities and significantly influences the performance of the system. The strong and not completed reform discussion in this area, combined with rather ambiguous (re-)allocation principles of the ECN, indicates that the current rules for the allocation and delimitation of competences are not satisfactory.[116] Most recently, a new controversy about the competence allocation in merger control arose around the two-thirds rule within the turnover thresholds, which was viewed to favour economic patriotism by Member States, leading to calls for more centralisation (Nourry and Jung 2006; Scott 2006).

2.3 The WTO Competition Regime: Creating an Additional Level of Antitrust Jurisdiction?

Long before the WTO was implemented in 1995 to succeed the GATT (since

---

115 See Fingleton (2005) and additionally Kingston (2001), Forrester (2004), and Smits (2005).

116 In a broader context, there is a more general debate on the vertical allocation of competences within the EU, which significantly extends the antitrust perspective and, therefore, is not explored in this book. For more information see, for example, Von Bogdandy and Bast (2002). However, this also points towards a broader application scope for the multilevel system concept.

1947) as the governing supranational institution and organisation regarding international trade, the first attempts to deal with competition policy issues on a supranational level had been undertaken. As early as in 1927, the World Economic Conference (in Geneva) under the framework of the League of Nations addressed the problem of international cartels, discussing calls for coordinated international anticartel policy efforts. However, since there was not even a basic consensus on the economic effects of cartels, which were viewed to be legitimate means of economic organisation in a number of countries at that time,[117] the conference yielded no real chance for success. At this point in history, among the major trading nations, only Canada (since 1889) and the US (since 1890) had an acting and effective antitrust law at their disposal.[118] However, although this scenario had not changed much, the implementation of international competition rules entered the international policy agenda again – and this time more systematically – in the 1940s in the context of the creation of the post-war world economic order.

In order to promote free trade and global economic relations, which were seen as major contributions to sustainable worldwide freedom, welfare and peace, institutions and organisations responsible for the governance of both real and monetary cross-national economic activities were created. The monetary side included the still extant IMF and the WBG, which were needed to manage the Bretton Woods system. The latter was an international currency regime that determined exchange rates of national currencies in relation to the US dollar, which was fixed in relation to gold.[119] This regime of fixed

---

[117] Cartels (including even horizontal price-fixing arrangements) were viewed as: (1) a legitimate part of the freedom of business; and (2) an effective instrument against the permanent thread of deflation (because of their price-stabilising effects), which was inherent to the contemporary gold standard currency system. However, concerns about the negative welfare effects of cartels incrementally started becoming popular around the world since the early 1900s.

[118] See generally, for the American development, Peritz (2000) and Wells (2002: 4–89) as well as for the European developments, Gerber (1998a: 16–164). The 1927 World Economic Conference is discussed, for example, by Günther (1961), Rahl (1970: 417–418), Nörr and Waibel (2001: 345–365), Wells (2002: 10–11), Wilson (2003: 212), and Podszun (2003: 65).

[119] The Bretton Woods system lasted until 1970 (de facto) or 1974 (de jure), when the fixed exchange rates were abandoned. Regimes of fixed exchange rates must rely on similar economic developments of the participating economies (in particular inflation rates but also in regard to economic growth) as a necessary condition for their frictionless workability. However, due to the starting positions after the Second World War (Continental Europe and Japan undervalued because of the war damages; Latin American countries overvalued), the inclusion of an increasing number of developing countries (which got rid of their status as colonies), and recessive economic developments including inflation in both the US and the UK, this condition was not met to an

currency exchange rates, created in order to prevent the harmful and aggressive depreciation runs (which had characterised the period of the Great Depression from 1929 until the end of the 1930s), were to be complemented by an International Trade Organization (ITO), governing an international trade and competition regime. The constituting Havana Charter (1948) comprised rules both against public and private restraints of cross-border competition. The rules on public trade restrictions had been implemented in advance (1946–1948), codified in the GATT as an interim institution (to become Chapter 4 of the Havana Charter on ratification). Thus, when the Charter failed to be ratified by its originally most prominent supporter, the US, and subsequently became abandoned in the early 1950s, 'only' the rules against private anticompetitive arrangements and practices (laid out in Chapter 5, Art. 46–54 of the Havana Charter) did not come into force.[120] However, as the stillborn ITO is clearly a direct predecessor of the WTO, the defunct Havana Charter belongs to the history of a WTO competition regime.

An ITO regime would have included consultation, complaint, and investigation mechanisms (Art. 47–48 of the Havana Charter), which comprised a, albeit relatively weak, dispute settlement regime. On the substantive side, members were obliged (Art. 50 of the Havana Charter) to fight restrictive business practices with cross-border effects by domestic enterprises, which 'restrain competition, limit access to markets, or foster monopolistic control' (Art. 46 of the Havana Charter[121]). If the members fail to comply, the ITO would have stepped in. In particular, international price-fixing, quota, market division, and discrimination cartels along with abuse of property rights were banned.

In the face of the ITO failure, the United Nations (UN) with US governmental support attempted to implement a more informal international competition policy regime in 1953.[122] A United Nations Draft Convention was approved by the UN Economic and Social Council. Similar to the Havana Charter, it was designed to challenge business practices, which restrain competition, limit access to markets, or foster monopolistic control. A new international agency, consisting of a secretariat, an investigation division, and

---

ever-increasing degree. The oil crisis of 1973–1974 only marks the death blow for an inherently deficient regime. However, both the IMF and the WBG survived the regime change towards flexible exchange rates and, especially in the case of the IMF, have found new tasks related to development policy and the prevention of, and intervention into, economic crisis.

120 See on the Havana Charter in more detail, Wood (1992: 281–284), Straw (1997: 35–38), Kennedy (2001: 122–128) and Wells (2002: 116–125).

121 Citation follows Kennedy (2001: 124).

122 See on the following, Günther (1961), Rahl (1970: 425–427), Timberg (1973) and Scherer (1994: 39–41).

a representative body (in which each member would have had one vote) was to be implemented. It was to receive complaints, supervise investigations by the national authorities, and issue recommendations for appropriate actions to be carried out by the national authorities. These recommendations were to leave some discretionary scope for member countries in order to comply with their own constitution, law, and economic system but would have possessed a comparatively high binding force. However, the convention failed to be ratified by a sufficient number of UN members just like the Havana Charter. Again, the failure of the US to ratify the convention, following resistance from the US business community and criticism of the one-vote-per-member provision, represented its eventual failure in 1955.

After decades of deadlock, international competition rules within the GATT/WTO context came back onto the agenda in the mid-1990s. First, a group of academic antitrust experts, called the Munich Group, issued a Draft International Antitrust Code (DIAC) as an academic blueprint for an international antitrust regime (Fikentscher and Immenga 1995; Fikentscher 1994, 1999; Drexl 2003). Although the proposal itself did not stand a chance to become realised and instead received vigorous criticism (for example, Phillips 1994; Gifford 1997), it fuelled the comeback of a viable discussion about international competition rules. Following the report of an appointed expert group,[123] the EU and its Member States initiated a WTO Working Group on the Interaction of Trade and Competition (WG) at the Singapore Ministerial Conference (1996). This working group was assigned the task of providing the grounds for subsequent negotiations on internationally binding minimum standards for competition rules and antitrust enforcement, including dispute settlement. On its way towards creating consensus on complementing the trade-focused (that is, public restraints of cross-border competition) WTO by implementing rules against private anticompetitive arrangements and practices, the working group engaged in: (1) generating knowledge about trade–competition interfaces; (2) information sharing; and (3) assisting the implementation of national competition rules in developing countries.[124] The

[123] See Brittan and van Miert (1996) and Petersmann (1999: 50–56). A number of members of the Munich Group were participating in this expert group.

[124] In particular, regarding this aspect, the working group had been very successful. For instance, the number of countries with (albeit more or less effective) competition policy regimes increased from less than 50 to more than 90 between 1992 and 2003, covering approximately 90 per cent of world trade. See Palim (1998), Wood (2003b: 102), Davidow and Shapiro (2003: 53), and Basedow (2004: 321, 334). While the number keeps increasing, it is difficult to assess to which percentage these newly introduced competition policy regimes are workable and provide an effective protection of competition. However, one can state with sufficient certainty that the number of workable and effective regimes is also increasing.

activities of the working group revived an intensive and controversial academic and political discussion about the adequacy of the WTO to accommodate competition rules and antitrust enforcement as well as on the benefits of international competition rules and their different design options (minimum standards, fully-fledged rules, enforcement assistance, and so on) and degree of binding character.[125]

While the EU, Japan, and the majority of both Southeast Asian[126] and Middle and East European countries represented the major supporters of WTO antitrust competences, the United States and a majority of developing countries opposed this concept. Until most recently, the United States resisted any approach towards binding international competition rules and favoured unilateral antitrust enforcement complemented by case-by-case bilateral cooperation instead.[127] The main US arguments against a WTO solution are that: (1) the WTO is simply too large and too heterogeneous to produce sound competition rules through consensus-oriented negotiations; (2) competition issues will become intertwined with other, non-competition issues to form packages for bargaining processes (with the danger of sacrificing competition on the altar of trade problems); (3) WTO (trade) experts do not have available sufficient expertise in the area of antitrust issues (and are ill-equipped to handle complex economic issues); and (4) the protection of sensitive confidential

---

125 See, for example, Scherer (1994), Fox and Ordover (1995), Jacquemin (1995), Petersmann (1996, 1999, 2004), Fox (1997, 1998a), Hoekman (1997), First (1998, 1999), Freytag and Zimmermann (1998), Drexl (1999, 2003), Gerber (1999), Hudec (1999), Jenny (1999, 2003a, 2003b), Kerber (1999, 2003), Lloyd and Vautier (1999: 153–183), Sykes (1999), ICPAC (2000), Tarullo (2000), Wins (2000), Amato (2001), Anderson (2001), Bercero and Amarasinha (2001), Kennedy (2001: 179–200), Mitchell (2001), Anderson and Holmes 2002), Holmes (2002), Clarke and Evenett (2003), Dabbah (2003: 206–286), Davidow and Shapiro (2003), Graham (2003), Janow (2003), Podszun (2003), Wilson (2003), Wood (2003b), Budzinski (2004a), Hoekman and Saggi (2004), H. Lee (2003), Lo (2004), McGinnis (2004), Neugebauer (2004: 223–232), Trebilcock and Iacobucci (2004), Weinrauch (2004: 127–150, 161–185), Worm (2004: 181–194), Conrad (2005), Klodt (2005: 67–86), and Bode and Budzinski (2006).

126 For instance, Korea has always been a vivid proponent of a WTO Competition Regime. See, for example, Jenny (2004: 652).

127 See, for example, Klein (1996) and Melamed (1997). Doern (1996b: 307) concludes: 'The United States (. . .) has already given ample indication of its desire to export its competition policy system elsewhere (. . .).' During the last 5 years, multilateral cooperation has become the new US strategy. See section 2.4. of this chapter. See also for modest and cautious moves towards enhanced multilateral coordination (albeit on a voluntary basis) ICPAC (2000), Epstein and Greve (2004), and Wood (2004). Discussions of the US position towards international antitrust provide, for example, Gerber (1999), Holmes (2002), Davidow and Shapiro (2003: 55–57), and Damro (2004: 277–280).

business information cannot be adequately managed by WTO bureaucrats.[128] A number of developing countries, however, expressed fears that an international antitrust regime within the WTO framework could be misused by the industrialised countries to prevent industries in developing countries from becoming internationally competitive.[129] As a result of the academic and political controversies, the EU, Japan and others presented a modified, less-ambitious proposal, which was eventually adopted by the WTO Ministerial Conference at Doha (Qatar, November 2001) in the so-called Doha Declaration.[130]

With the Doha Declaration, the WTO members agreed to start negotiations on a WTO Agreement on a Multilateral Framework on Competition Policy after the Cancún Conference (in September 2003), albeit subject to the approval of this conference. According to the adopted modified proposal, a to-be-negotiated WTO Competition Policy Regime ought to consist of the following main elements:

- a set of core principles of competition policy including the WTO principles of transparency, non-discrimination, and procedural fairness;
- a binding commitment by the member states to fight hardcore cartels;
- support for the introduction and development of effective competition institutions in developing countries through technical assistance and experience exchange;

---

[128] See ICPAC (2000: 259–277), Wilson (2003: 236–240), and Wood (2003b: 104–108). However, while the second argument indeed represents a WTO-inherent problem, this is not so clear in regard to the others. The first one, for instance, occurs whenever a consensus about antitrust issues is to be achieved. Indeed, the third and fourth ones point towards the necessity of modifying WTO procedures in accordance with the specific characteristics of antitrust cases but it is difficult to see why this should be a fundamental argument against a WTO solution. In particular the argument that the WTO does not consist of enough antitrust experts seems strange since no one would cast doubts on: (1) the necessity to build up an expert staff for a WTO Competition Committee; and (2) the fact that trade issues also include complex economics.

[129] See generally, on the controversy about the importance and shape of adequate competition policies in developing countries, for example, Correa (1999), Cook (2002), Hoekman and Mavroidis (2003), Hoekman and Saggi (2004), Owen (2004), and Phillips (2004). Although this infant-industry-protection related argument is highly doubtful from an economics perspective, it nevertheless developed impact on the negotiations of a WTO competition agreement.

[130] WTO Ministerial Declaration 14 November 2001, WT/MIN (01)/DEC/1 (20 November 2001). See for descriptive analyses of the declaration, for example, Clarke and Evenett (2003), Fox (2003c), Jenny (2003a, 2004), Budzinski (2004a), and Bode and Budzinski (2006). The following paragraph also draws on these sources.

- modalities for voluntary cooperation on competition policy issues between WTO members in order to facilitate worldwide cooperation between antitrust authorities;
- the creation and establishment of a standing WTO Competition Policy Committee in order to supervise the commitments of the members and provide dispute settlement; and
- securing a continuous review and development of its international competition policy approach.

However, the Cancún Ministerial Conference failed to achieve any consensual agreement about the so-called Singapore issues.[131] However, more important for the failure of the conference were more principal divergences and disagreements between industrialised and developing countries, mainly on market access in agriculture. Diverging opinions on international competition rules did not seem to be among the most controversial issues and, to some extent, became involved in the main conflict as a side-show. In a bargaining game, the competition issue somehow went to the dogs of agricultural disputes, in particular as no consensus about an unbundling of the Singapore issues could be achieved. With the Cancún failure, the future of the WTO avenue towards an international competition policy regime has become very insecure.[132] More clouds over WTO competition policy prospects result from the fact that competition policy (like investment and transparency in government procurement) was excluded from the Geneva 'July 2004 package', which is designed to resume the strive for consensus among WTO members (WTO 2004a, 2004b; Bode and Budzinski 2006).

Altogether, the WTO eventually represents a comparatively centralised approach, which shifts significant competences upwards to the supranational WTO level (see Figure 4.5). Mandatory general competition rules on a global level represent the eventual goal of the WTO avenue. This remains true even in the face of the very modest Doha Declaration, although the chairman of the WG emphasises that 'these current proposals have very little in common with calls for development of a detailed multilateral "code" on competition policy . . . or related calls for the establishment of an international competition law enforcement agency . . .', but, instead, 'are less ambitious than elements that

131 The Singapore issues, namely competition, investment, transparency in government procurement and facilitation of trade in protected sectors, resulted from an agreement about packaging controversial issues, which was reached during the WTO Ministerial Conference in Singapore in 1996. See Woolcock (2003).

132 See, on the Cancún failure with respect to competition policy, Woolcock (2003), Amarasinha (2004), Drexl (2004), Hoekman and Saggi (2004), Jenny (2004), Petersmann (2004), and Stewart (2004).

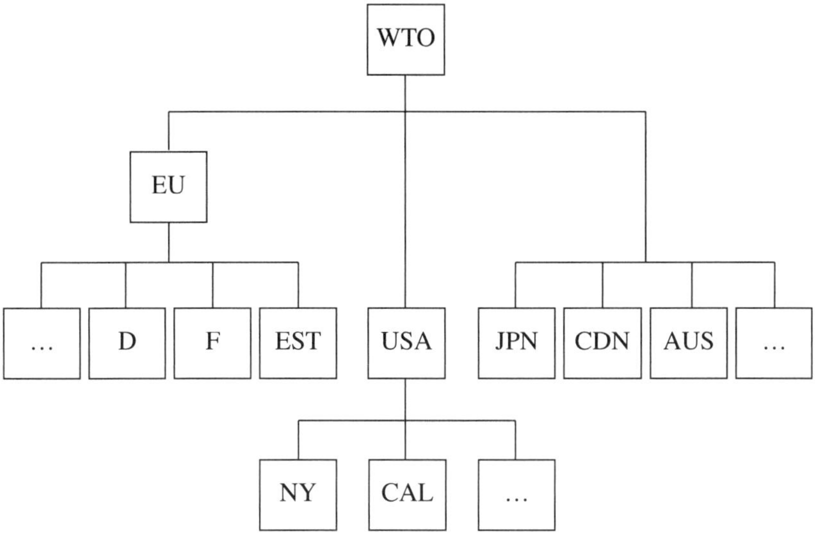

Figure 4.5 The WTO competition regime

were proposed in the past . . . they do not aim at a comprehensive "harmonization" of competition law . . .', instead much 'emphasis would be placed on voluntary cooperation (. . .) and the exchange of national experience' (Jenny 2003a: 622). However, the Doha Declaration must be viewed only as a first step along an avenue towards more ambitious goals. Or, as Eleanor Fox (2003c: 913) puts it, the declaration represents 'the seeds of a new charter'.

A WTO Competition Policy Regime along the lines of the Doha Declaration would constitute a top level with competences in supervision of the lower levels and dispute settlements. Minimum standard competition rules would de facto be allocated to the top level, although in the shape of requirements that the national and regional institutions would have to meet. However, the detailed (vertical) allocation of competences between the WTO and its members belongs to the issues, which would have to be clarified during concrete negotiations. Therefore, only more or less vague principles (non-discrimination, transparency, and procedural fairness), which desperately need further interpretation,[133] are available at this point in time. If the dispute settlement competence is directed towards 'compliance of lower-level decisions with WTO standards', an antitrust case would be allocated to the WTO-level whenever a conflict on its regulation occurs.[134] If the supervision competence

[133] See section 1.1.4 of Chapter 5 for an exemplary interpretation.
[134] This calls for a clarification of what exactly constitutes a conflict.

follows the same path, WTO substantial competences could be considerable. A different interpretation is to understand the dispute settlement competence as directed towards 'choosing the best-competent lead jurisdiction', that is, a competence of allocating cases but not of – de facto – deciding cases. The centralising implications would be reduced.

2.4 The International Competition Network: A Virtual Global Level?

The International Competition Network (ICN), founded in late 2001, represents a different approach to the governance of global competition. Waiving binding international rules as the ultimate goals, the ICN attempts to provide effective governance through voluntary multilateral cooperation. In the face of the failure of the Havana Charter and related approaches, cooperative solutions have some history as second-best approaches in international competition policy.

For instance, the Organisation for Economic Co-operation and Development (OECD) engaged in several attempts to create a multinational framework for voluntary antitrust cooperation and convergence. Its efforts began in 1967 with far-reaching goals. The OECD Competition Law and Policy Committee intended: (1) to provide periodic examinations of national competition policy systems; (2) to produce collective reports on substantive issues in competition law (such as predatory pricing or franchising); and (3) to implement consensually policy recommendations. However, only the first goal was realised, whereas the latter two were eventually dropped by the OECD due to notorious lack of success. In the meantime, the OECD Global Forum on Competition succeeded the Committee early in 2001 and its contemporary targets are less ambitious, that is, limited to the publication of background papers on national competition policy systems and the organisation of round tables to discuss important international problems of competition policy without attempting to resolve divergent national views and approaches.[135]

Another example is the initiative of the United Nations Conference on Trade and Development (UNCTAD). It enacted a Restrictive Business Practices Code in 1980 in order to promote procompetitive conduct by multinational enterprises, especially towards developing countries. It attempted to ban – among other things – price-fixing agreements, market division and quota cartels, and boycotts. However, the comparatively ambitious code lacked enforceability and, consequently, failed to develop significant practical influence.[136]

---

[135] See, on the OECD efforts, Vogelaar (1980), Straw (1997: 40–43), Lloyd and Vautier (1999: 131–138), Winslow (2001), Wells (2002), Zanettin (2002: 53–57), First (2003), Jenny (2003b), Podszun (2003: 68–72, 117–118), and Wood (2003a: 310–312).

[136] See Baade (1980), Davidow (1980), Brusick (1983), Lloyd and Vautier (1999: 127–130), Wins (2000: 93–96), Wells (2002), First (2003), Podszun (2003: 119–120), and Wilson (2003: 213–214).

Thus, the ICN currently represents the dominating informal approach to design a coherent international regime of competition governance without enacting binding supranational rules or a forceful supranational authority. The genesis of the ICN lies in the suggestion of an informal Global Competition Initiative (GCI) by the International Competition Policy Advisory Committee (ICPAC) to the US Department of Justice.[137] It developed its concept deliberately as an explicit alternative to a WTO regime and the US quickly adopted the initiative. Its proponents hailed the potentials of progress, which could be achieved without the formal and, therefore, sometimes awkward WTO mechanisms,[138] whereas sceptics interpreted the initiative simply as a means to avoid a binding WTO solution.[139] In spite of being the main proponent of a WTO solution, the EU joined the initiative[140] and many other antitrust jurisdictions followed – a process, which eventually led to the establishment of the ICN in October 2001.[141]

The ICN is a network of competition authorities from around the world with close interaction of other public and private players that are concerned with international antitrust issues. Calling itself a virtual organisation, which is neither based on an international contract, nor has its own administrative staff or budget, the ICN is led by a steering group consisting of member authorities. Its chair and all secretarial functions (and their budgeting) rotate among the members. Since September 2004, the president of the

137 See ICPAC (2000), Klein (2000), and Janow and Lewis (2001). The committee consisted of four academics of which two can be called leading antitrust experts (political scientist Merit Janow and legal scientist Eleanor M. Fox), additionally one labour economist (emeritus John T. Dunlop) and one professor of business administration (David B. Yoffie); five lawyers and legal practitioners; three industry lobbyists; one representative of The Markle Foundation. It has to be noted that no antitrust economist is among the ICPAC members.

138 See ICPAC (2000: 259–277). However, one of the most prominent ICPAC members, Eleanor M. Fox, disagreed with the anti-WTO-position. See ICPAC (2000: 303–305).

139 'The inconsistent treatment of the drawbacks of the existing institutions (they are deficient either because they adopt enforceable rules or because they do not) leads one to suspect that the main reason for embracing the Global Competition Initiative was strategic, an "anything but" strategy. . . . U.S. antitrust policy makers [have realized] that . . . further international cooperation is "inevitable". A strategy of resistance to these developments would only leave matters in the hands of others, particularly the EC. Thus, the choice was for "anything but", and, particularly, "anything but" the WTO, the institution preferred by the EC' First (2003: 35).

140 See, for a critical analysis of the 'evolving stance' of the EU, Davison and Johnson (2002).

141 For comprehensive analyses of the ICN, see Budzinski (2003b, 2004c), Finckenstein (2003), Graham (2003), Janow (2003), Todino (2003), and Böge (2005b, 2005c).

Bundeskartellamt, Ulf Böge, has held the chair,[142] while the Canadian Competition Bureau remains responsible for the administration. Annual conferences of all member authorities represent the major 'decision body'.

The main goal of the ICN is the promotion of the cooperation of competition authorities worldwide in order to diminish potential conflicts arising from different views and interpretations of antitrust cases and to create a common competition culture. Instead of aiming to introduce mandatory international competition rules or to constitute an antitrust authority itself, the ICN strives to initiate projects on relevant competition policy issues in order to develop consensus-based recommendations for its members. Compliance with these consensually developed and adopted (on the annual conferences) best practice recommendations and guidelines is completely voluntary. Nonetheless, convergence of national and regional competition policies, primarily concerning procedural issues – but in the long-run also concerning substantive issues – is on the agenda. Peer pressure through publication and transparency of superior antitrust practices, which have been consensually acknowledged as superior, should promote a widespread adoption of the ICN best practice recommendations by the member authorities. Up to March 2005, competition agencies from more than 70 jurisdictions (more than three-quarters of worldwide existing ones) had joined the ICN.[143]

The best practice recommendations and guidelines are compiled by substantial working groups (WGs), which review and comparatively evaluate the current practices of the member authorities. They constitute themselves project-oriented and, if necessary, expire with the agreed-upon recommendations. Thus, they have a temporary character but with an ex ante undetermined term. Additionally, administrative working groups address problems of internal governance. Currently, the ICN consists of four substantial and three administrative WGs, see the overview in Figure 4.6.

An exemplar for the achievements and the types of consensual recommendations, the ICN – in its current shape – is capable of generating, the work of the most elaborate working group, the WG Mergers, is briefly described in the following. Merger control issues are viewed to be the most contentious ones in international antitrust. Enhancing the efficiency of control procedures for

[142] He succeeds Fernando Sanchez Ugarte (Mexican Federal Competition Commission, 2003–2004) and Konrad von Finckenstein (Canadian Bureau of Competition, 2001–2003).

[143] This includes the international competition authorities of the EU, the EFTA, and the Andean Community. The number of member agencies is even higher than the number of participating jurisdictions because some jurisdictions have more than one competition agency (as, for instance, the US; see section 2.1 of this chapter). Currently, Africa remains the only continent with negligible participation in the ICN.

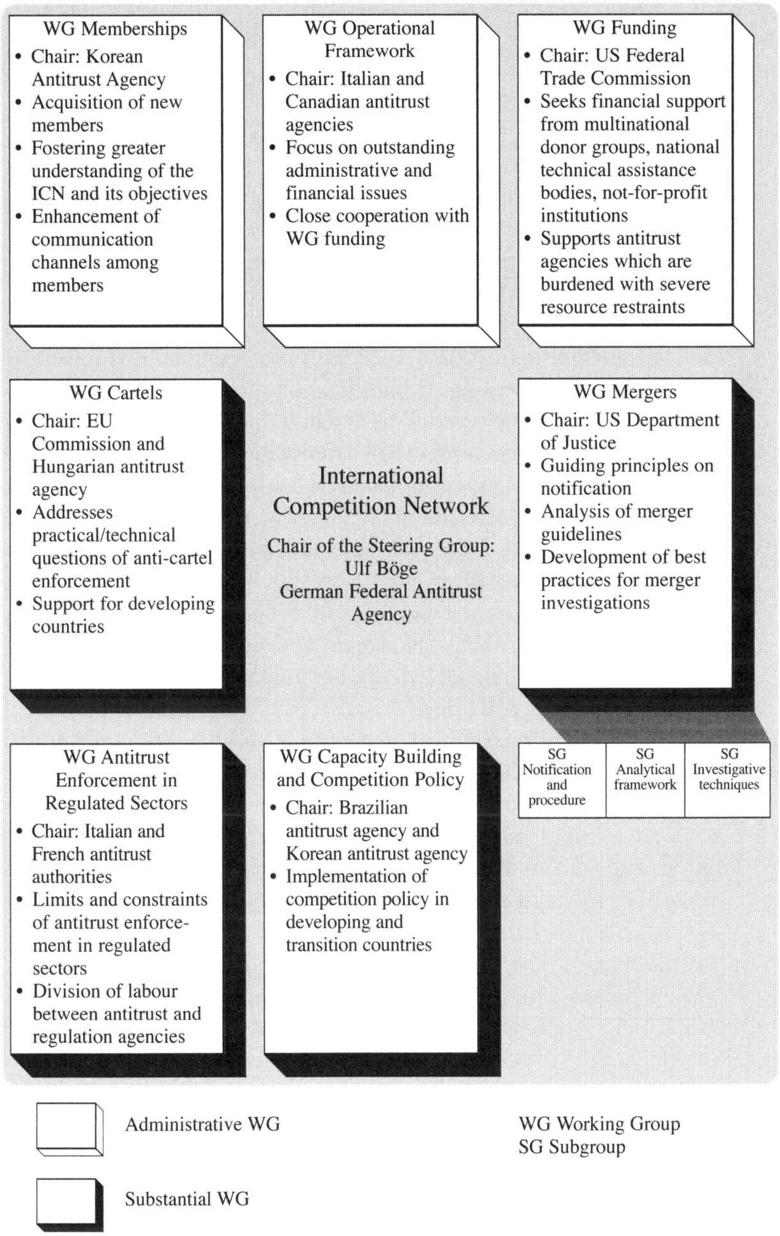

Source: translated from Budzinski and Aigner (2004: 26)

Figure 4.6 Working Groups of the International Competition Network 2005

cross-border mergers by reducing transaction costs both for merging companies and for participating competition agencies and avoiding jurisdictional conflicts are the main objectives of the three subgroups (SGs), which constitute the ICN's merger governance system:

- The SG 'Merger Notification and Review Procedures' has developed eight guiding principles that each merger control regime should consider: (1) sovereignty; (2) transparency; (3) non-discrimination on the basis of nationality; (4) procedural fairness; (5) efficient, timely, and effective review; (6) coordination; (7) convergence; and (8) protection of confidential information. Additionally, a set of recommended practices for merger notification procedures has been published. It includes best practices concerning: (1) notification thresholds; (2) the timing of notification and review periods; (3) requirements for initial notification; (4) the appropriate nexus between a transaction's effects and the reviewing jurisdiction; and (5) continual reviews of merger control procedures with periodical evaluations of the state of convergence towards ICN best practices (ICN 2004). These guidelines attempt to significantly reduce transaction costs resulting from differing notification and review procedures. In order to continue and deepen the procedural convergence, information about the merger review procedures are collected and published to create knowledge about remaining inconsistencies.
- The SG 'Analytical Review Framework' collects and compiles information about the substantive standards for prohibiting anticompetitive mergers. One of its main goals is to provide model merger guidelines. In doing so, the SG has presented an interim report (ICN 2003a), which reviews existing merger guidelines of member countries, compiling information about their common features and main differences with regard to: (1) market definition; (2) unilateral effects; (3) coordinated effects; (4) barriers to entry; and (5) the consideration of efficiencies. Furthermore, it has initiated a best-practice discussion on the substantive standards for prohibiting anticompetitive mergers, especially 'substantial lessening of competition', 'creation or strengthening of dominant market positions', and 'public interest'.
- The SG 'Investigative Techniques' attempts to provide a best practice manual for investigating mergers including methods for gathering reliable information and for coordinating interagency information sharing including the protection of confidential business data. It has published a comprehensive compendium on the current practices of the member agencies (ICN 2003b), which shall serve as the basic source for the upcoming process of evaluation.

A considerable number of the adopted best practice recommendations remain rather vague and non-conflicting. For instance, it seems rather unproblematic to agree upon transparency or procedural fairness. However, among the working results are also more ambitious elements, like the – still ongoing – discussion about substantial merger prohibition standards or the guidelines on the appropriate nexus between a transaction's effects and the reviewing jurisdiction. The latter may seem harmless at first glance but includes far-reaching implications as the (horizontal) allocation of review competences is addressed. However, the impressive agenda of the ICN – despite its brief history – demonstrates that a significant number of practical problems in international antitrust are located below the level of material law and conflicts of interests. A lot of recommendations may sound self-evident and most naturally, however, they were obviously not realised in advance of ICN governance.

As the ICN represents a variant of network governance,[144] it does not constitute an additional international level like a WTO Competition Regime would. Instead, the national and supranational (in the sense of regional as differentiated from global) competition authorities, which form the network, become horizontally interwoven.[145] Nevertheless, the problem of competence allocation lies at the heart of the ICN. By addressing problems like conflict reduction, appropriate nexus to an antitrust case as a precondition for claiming jurisdiction, and so on, the network attempts to solve competence allocation problems. The difference is that it does so in an informal way. However, by moving away from bilateral to multilateral cooperation, an additional level emerges, albeit a virtual one that does not include formal/mandatory competences. Nevertheless, the network interrelations are managed through a common forum, which, moreover, presents its own recommendations and (non-committal) guidelines for institutional arrangements and practices in antitrust policy. Eventually, the central and sensitive condition for the viability of the ICN as an international regime is whether the problem of competence allocation can be solved to a sufficient degree in an informal way. If it cannot provide a sufficiently workable competence allocation, the internal dynamics of the network are likely to overemphasise the decentralising forces at the expense of coherence and the ICN is destined to decay. Otherwise, one

---

[144] Thus, it represents an application of the theories discussed in section 1.1 of this chapter.

[145] Strictly speaking, the network consists of horizontal interrelations (for example, between the antitrust authorities of Korea and Brazil), vertical interrelations (for example, between the antitrust authorities of the EU and Germany, which are both and separately members of the ICN), and lateral interrelations (for example, between the antitrust authorities of France and the Andean Community).

should not underestimate the power of informal governance modes to develop their own enforceability and self-reinforcement in the course of time.

2.5 Avenues towards and State of the World Competition Order: Some Brief Remarks

Looking at the picture of international antitrust, one can identify two major alternative avenues towards an effective regime – the WTO approach and the ICN concept.[146] Additionally, efforts from the OECD and the UNCTAD are still viable although their importance for the academic and political discussion process has ceased in recent years. Rudimentary competition policy aspects can also be found in the current practice of the international monetary policy organisations, namely the IMF and the WBG. Having lost most of their original tasks in the context of the Bretton Woods regime of fixed exchange rates, both are now – with at least partly overlapping activities – focusing on economic policy advice and financial support, addressing developing countries and regions, which suffer from economic crisis. Supporting the creation and implementation of institutional frameworks for competitive market economies (including competition rules) belong to their consultancy agenda but play relatively less important roles compared to issues like investment and growth, trade flows, monetary stability, and so on. The kaleidoscope of competition policy activities at the supranational level becomes complemented by international competition policies with a regional scope, like the EU competition policy system or the antitrust authorities of the Andean Community and UEMOA.

Despite the considerable variety of activities, it is currently not possible to predict which avenue will lead to an effective regime or how long this will take. Moreover, the failure of the avenues is among the options. Thus, the state of the world competition order is still fundamentally characterised by the anarchic regime of the principally independent application of the effects doctrine by the existing antitrust jurisdictions. Nevertheless, the problems of such a 'regime' are increasingly realised and motivated both the WTO and the ICN approach. However, effective coordination remains voluntary and at the discretion of the acting jurisdictions. No mandatory international coordination

[146] It is not my intention to provide a systematic comparison of the two avenues in this chapter because: (1) central design elements are still variable/fluid; and (2) an analytical concept of a sound international competition policy system results from of the analysis in Chapter 5. However, I have provided provisional comparative evaluations in other publications. For descriptive and analytical comparisons of WTO and ICN as international competition policy regimes see Graham (2003), Janow (2003), Budzinski (2004a), and Bode and Budzinski (2006).

of antitrust policies has occurred until now – apart from regional regimes. Consequently, research on the effects and dynamics of theoretically possible intermediate regimes (between centralism and decentralism) is urgent and represents an important input both for academic discourse and the policy process. The current avenues – as they are at the moment – are all deficient in healing the problems outlined in Chapter 3, although they may develop potential to do so. However, the latter can only come as the consequence of significant reforms and developments of the contemporary state of play.

3. CONCLUDING REMARKS

The introduction of the economic concept of multilevel systems of competition policy institutions and agencies allows for more systematic reformulation of: (1) the two major players in international antitrust (the US antitrust system and the EU ccompetition policy system); and (2) the two major avenues towards an effective international regime (the WTO competition regime and the ICN). In particular, the internal dynamics and working properties of the regimes as multilevel systems become explicit. The major insight is that the allocation and delimitation of competences matters significantly for the workability and the evolution of the existing systems (US and EU). In both cases, competence allocation is among the most pressing problems and reform discussions include the struggle for (re-allocating) competences in prominent roles. Consequently, the rules, which decide the allocation of competences and both vertically and horizontally delimits them from each other, are major issues of reform calls. In the EU, all the competence allocation rules – interstate trade criterion, turnover thresholds, and the referral regime – and their deficiencies have been targets of the modernisation process. However, as the results do not show significant improvements, the reform discussion is unlikely to stop at that issue. Similarly, the largely overlapping competences within the US system are both vigorously criticised and defended and a modernisation process on competition allocation rules has just started, for instance, targeting the interstate commerce clause.

The problems with competence allocation in the existing multilevel antitrust systems underline the importance of competence allocation rules for the creation and implementation of a workable international regime. However, both major avenues – ICN and WTO – remain widely silent on these crucial questions. Yet, the examples of the US and the EU systems indicate that the problem of allocating and delimitating competition policy competences is more sensitive for the success of a coherent but non-centralistic international regime than problems of substantive law, like the harmonisation of merger prohibition standards or conditions for cartel exemptions. This is why a thorough analysis of competence allocation rules regarding their economic effects offers important insights for designing a complex international regime between the extreme solutions – or, in other words, combining elements of centralism and decentralism. Focusing on competence allocation rules instead of discussing whole regime types, which – except of the extreme types – are not separable in a clearcut way, allows for conclusions concerning both contemporary avenues (WTO and ICN) and, as a by-product, regarding the ongoing controversy about American and European antitrust federalism. Therefore, the institutional-economic implications of different rules for the vertical and horizontal allocation and delimitation of competences are analysed in the following chapter.

5. A comparative analysis of different rules for the allocation and delimitation of competences

The first section of this chapter presents and basically characterises the type of rules for the allocation and delimitation of competences, which are comparatively analysed thereafter. Some of these rules originate from the practices of non-coordinated antitrust extraterritorialism, within the existing US and EU multilevel systems, and of the current avenues towards an international regime (WTO and ICN). They are described and characterised according to their competence allocating and delimitating quality in section 1.1. Additionally, a number of rules derived from the academic discussion on supranational competition policy are explicated (section 1.2).[1] Section 2 analyses the comparative performance of the resulting competence allocations according to the set of economic criteria derived in Chapter 4. A comparative conclusion sheds more light on the politically relevant results (section 3), from which are drawn policy conclusions for designing a coherent, decentralised, and evolutionary multilevel system of competition policies for the world economy (Chapter 6).

1. DESIGN OPTIONS FOR RULES FOR THE ALLOCATION OF COMPETENCES

Since real-world competence allocation rules can be governed by a mixed (and possibly incoherent) set of rules, the following two sections isolate such types

[1] There are a few studies that review more or less comprehensively, selected academic proposals for an international competition policy regime. See, for example, Wins (2000) and Wilson (2003). Conrad (2005: 75–101) introduces an analytical and systematic scheme in order to evaluate different proposals according to the criteria: (1) organisational expense; (2) loss of sovereignty; (3) international allocative efficiency and freedom of competition; and (4) public acceptance level. However, none of the studies explicitly addresses the role of competence allocation and, therefore, fails to identify and comparatively evaluate the elements which are responsible for the performance of a complex regime or regime proposal.

of rules, which lead to distinguishable competence allocations and delimitations. In doing so, the content of the rules must be somewhat stylised while combinations of rules are excluded from the analysis. Otherwise, the sample of rules would be too large to present a compact and manageable analysis in section 2. However, both section 3 of Chapter 5 and Chapter 6 look at the tribute paid for this reduction of complexity and reintroduce some hitherto neglected elements into the analysis, which prove valuable in providing policy conclusions. Nevertheless, comprehensiveness in regard to thinkable competence allocation rules cannot be claimed. Instead, the choice of rules reflects their importance in the discourse on international competition policy.[2]

In section 1.2 of Chapter 4, a number of dimensions of competence allocation were identified, namely:

- horizontal and vertical allocation of competences (dimension I);
- institutional and enforcement competence allocation (dimension II), which can be subdivided into rule-making (dimension IIa), rule-application (dimension IIb), and enforcement competences (dimension IIc);
- exclusive and concurrent competences (dimension III); and
- development of competence allocation in the face of globalisation of markets and business activities (dimension IV).

In the following two subsections, each stylised competence allocation and delimitation rule is first of all described and secondly, characterised according to these four dimensions.

In coherence with the analysis of sections 2.1 to 2.5 of Chapter 4, I assume that an international competition policy regime has roughly the shape of one jurisdiction on the supranational-global level (as the top level) and a number of horizontally interrelated jurisdictions on the national and (supranational) regional levels. Note, however, that this shape does not prescribe which competences are ascribed to each level (vertical allocation of competences) or among one level's jurisdictions (horizontal allocation of competences). For instance, the competences assigned to the top level may also be zero (as with the effects doctrine-based regime).

2 However, the method of analysis, which is developed and explored here, can easily be used to discuss any additional type of rule. Providing an economic framework for the comparative analysis of competence allocating and delimitating institutions represents a major goal of this book.

1.1 Stylised Rules Extracted from Existing Regimes

1.1.1 The effects doctrine

Despite the ongoing WTO and ICN efforts, the currently dominating 'regime' in international antitrust is the non-coordinated extraterritorial application of national and regional competition laws by national and regional authorities, supplemented by discretionary interjurisdictional cooperation. In this regime, competence allocation is determined by the effects doctrine. Since it represents the most important competence allocation rule in present day international competition policy, it is the first rule chosen for analysis. The effects doctrine allocates the competence to handle an antitrust case non-exclusively to every jurisdiction whose internal markets are affected by the case.[3] This implies that the competence to deal with an anticompetitive arrangement or practice is neither connected to the location of the arrangement or practice, nor to the countries of origin of the colluding, merging, or power abusing enterprises. In its pure variant, the effects doctrine includes no mandatory minimum nexus between the effects of a business arrangement or practice and the internal markets of the jurisdiction-claiming authority. Each jurisdiction decides autonomously about the standard for sufficient inbound effectiveness. In an extreme scenario, this can involve cases with only potential or virtual nexus to the respective jurisdiction like in the – eventually turned-down – Empagran case.[4] Of course, jurisdictions can also – voluntarily and non-binding – waive to investigate and decide a case and – without coordination – rely on other jurisdiction's competence instead:

- Dimension I: the effects doctrine predominantly addresses the horizontal allocation of competences within a jurisdictional level. This includes diagonal allocation, for example, between the EU and the Japanese competition policies. Vertical competence allocation between the levels is not possible because each case that affects a downward jurisdictional

---

[3] For descriptions, definitions, and legal implications of the effects doctrine, see Castel (1984), Rishikesh (1991), Immenga (1994), Torremans (1996), Basedow (1998), Griffin (1999), Pavic (2001), Zanettin (2002: 7–52), Fox (2003a), Hovenkamp (2003), and Podszun (2003: 17–33). See section 1.2.2 of Chapter 3 on its origins and spreading.

[4] See section 1.2.2 of Chapter 3. Against the background of the total welfare standard, the effects doctrine could even be extended to cases in which domestic producers are hurt by foreign practices in foreign markets (for example, entry deterrence abroad). The sum of domestic producer and consumer rent becomes reduced if export activities are anticompetitively distorted. Of course, extraterritorial enforcement would be even more difficult than in 'real' inbound cases – however, not necessarily impossible, among other things, in respect to damage suits.

market automatically also effects the upward jurisdiction's internal markets. This implies that the supranational top level is not equipped with competences other than mutual recognition.

- Dimension II: each jurisdiction, which is competent to deal with an anticompetitive arrangement or practice (because it affects its internal markets), applies and enforces its own competition rules (dimensions IIb and IIc). Regarding rule-making competences (dimension IIa), no provisions about competent levels are made by the effects doctrine.
- Dimension III: an exclusive competence is only generated if an anticompetitive arrangement or practice has effects on only the markets within one jurisdiction. Otherwise, concurrent allocations of competences result.
- Dimension IV: under the effects doctrine, processes of decay are more probable than centralisation processes. The number of participating jurisdictions increases with economic development and globalisation. Thus, it is hard to see how the allocation of cases should evolve towards a less scattered allocation. In this sense, competence allocation according to the effects doctrine tends to increase its degree of dissipation.

1.1.2 Interstate commerce clause, interstate trade criterion, and community dimension

Both in the US antitrust system and in the EU competition policy system, competence allocation relies on similar elementary principles. The simple idea is that anticompetitive arrangements and practices, which affect the trade between the downward level jurisdictions, are allocated to the federal or union's level, whereas all else remains under the jurisdiction of the downward level (for example, Easterbrook 1983; Burnley 2002a, 2002b; Budzinski and Christiansen 2005b). In the US, the interstate commerce clause represents the respective value, while, in the EU, the interstate trade criterion (regarding cartel policy) and community dimension (regarding merger control) belong to this category of competence allocation rules.

However, so-styled competence allocation and delimitation rules leave an important aspect imprecise: when does a specific anticompetitive arrangement or business practice affect interjurisdictional trade? To some extent, interjurisdictional trade or community dimension represents more a desired outcome of competence allocation than an applicable rule. One most important question remains unsolved: which concrete competence rule(s) generate a competence allocation according to these three similar stipulations. Thus, it comes as no surprise that in both competition policy regimes additional competence allocation rules have been developed (or are under controversial discussion in the context of the respective modernisation processes) in order to interpret and operationalise interstate commerce, interstate trade, or community dimension.[5] An important role of interpreting the general rules is played by the courts and the case law evolution driven by them. To some extent, interpretations and qualifications have been made on a case-by-case basis with ambiguous prospects regarding their potential to become generalised.

Due to the problems reported above with an interstate commerce clause, interstate trade criterion, and community dimension, I limit my analysis to the rules, which specify these general provisions. Taken from the practice of EU competition policy, I discuss turnover thresholds in the following subsection. A number of alternative rules, partly stemming from the reform debates, are discussed in section 1.2 of this chapter.

1.1.3 Turnover thresholds

In the EU competition policy system, turnover thresholds are used as a proxy for the likelihood of effectiveness of an interstate trade or community dimension both in merger control and – only recently – in cartel policy.[6] In a generalised way, the competence allocation rule reads as follows. If specific turnover figures are met or exceeded, the competence to deal with an anticompetitive arrangement or practice is allocated to the upward level. All other cases are dealt with by the downward jurisdictions:[7]

- Dimension I: EU-styled turnover thresholds address the vertical allocation of competences ('vertical threshold') and remain silent on horizontal issues. However, horizontal allocation can be introduced if, additionally, specific turnover figures have to be met or exceeded as a general precondition for a (downward) jurisdiction to claim competence over an anticompetitive arrangement or practice. This would imply that a case that does not meet the threshold of the upward level is allocated to those downward jurisdictions in whose internal markets the downward level threshold ('horizontal threshold') is met. Thus, a two-tiered turnover threshold rule would emerge.
- Dimension II: institutional and enforcement competences are not differentiated in the basic concept. Rule-making, rule-application, and enforcement competences are all allocated in the same way. However,

[5] See the respective discussion in sections 2.1 and 2.2 of Chapter 4.

[6] See section 2.2 of Chapter 4 for a detailed description of the turnover threshold that delineate EU mergers from national ones. As also explored there, the Commission currently attempts to establish a more technical interpretation of the interstate trade concept regarding cartel policy, which includes turnover figures, through its respective guidelines.

[7] See, for example, Burnley (2002b), Drauz (2003), Heimler (2003), Van Gerwen (2003), Budzinski and Christiansen (2005b), and Budzinski (2006).

turnover thresholds as a competence allocation rule are also compatible with an exclusive limitation for enforcement competences, that is, meeting the thresholds decides about the competent agency (dimension IIc) but not about the to-be-applied institution (dimension IIb).

- Dimension III: the effect with regard to exclusivity and concurrence of competences is asymmetric. If an anticompetitive arrangement or practice meets or exceeds the vertical-oriented threshold, it is exclusively allocated to the upward level. However, cases below this threshold are concurrently allocated among the downward jurisdictions. With the two-tiered threshold, the number of jurisdictions, which share competences, becomes limited by the downward level threshold (depending on its strictness) but not to zero.
- Dimension IV: economic growth and accelerating market globalisation lead to creeping centralisation of competence allocation if the turnover thresholds remain unchanged. Inflation implies similar effects if the thresholds are defined in nominal figures. Therefore, it is likely that more cases become allocated to the upward level over the course of time.

1.1.4 Nondiscrimination rule

The principle of nondiscrimination or national treatment principle belongs to the most important and fundamental principles of the GATT–WTO framework for international trade. It is codified in Art. III of the GATT and would have become a major principle of the ITO framework for trade and competition in the world economy as laid out in the defunct Havana Charter.[8] Thus, it represents an obvious choice for the analysis in this book. Regarding international antitrust, an extended and modified nondiscrimination rule could incorporate the following elements.[9] Competition policy regimes are not allowed to discriminate between domestic and foreign producers and consumers.[10] In particular, they must not favour domestic consumers and/or producers at the expense of foreign ones or disadvantage foreign consumers and/or producers compared to domestic ones. This includes not only the design of the national and regional competition rules but also the way they are enforced. Both a supervision or complaint and a sanction mechanism to identify and stop discriminating antitrust policies complement the antitrust nondiscrimination principle:

---

[8] See section 2.3 of Chapter 4.

[9] For the purposes of this analysis, the WTO-styled nondiscrimination principle is combined with elements from the Havana Charter and from the suggestion of an antitrust national treatment principle by Trebilcock and Iacobucci (2004). See also Iacobucci (1997) and Trebilcock and Howse (1998).

[10] The inclusion of consumers represents an important extension of the trade-oriented variant of the nondiscrimination concept.

- Dimension I: the nondiscrimination rule includes both horizontal and vertical allocation effects. Horizontally, the competence to claim extraterritorial jurisdiction is limited by the legitimate interest of the foreign jurisdictions to design their domestic laws according to their own preferences (as long as they are non-discriminatory).[11] Vertically, an upward allocation of competences to a supranational level is implied with regard to (alleged) discriminations and anticompetitive arrangements or practices that generate conflicting competition policies on the downward level. Additionally, diagonal effects are also possible and run similar to the horizontal ones.
- Dimension II: the rule-making competences of each jurisdiction are limited to institutional arrangements that are nondiscriminatory. This excludes a number of popular rule designs, for example, the exemption of pure export cartels from the general prohibition of cartels and surrogates. Nevertheless, rule-making competences (dimension IIa) remain exclusively on the downward (national and regional) levels – the (supranational) level gains no competence to create, design, and implement its own institutions (perhaps apart from informal procedural rules concerning conflict resolution proceedings). In cases of discrimination and conflict, the upward level gains application and enforcement competences, however, in a limited sense. Only conflict resolution competences are assigned to the upward level, irrespective of whether they follow complaints by downward jurisdictions or result from supervision. This can mean competences to decide which institutions of which downward jurisdictions apply to a specific anticompetitive arrangement or practice (dimension IIb). It can also cover decisions

---

[11] See Trebilcock and Iacobucci (2004: 154–167). They construct the example that specific national competition rules (for instance on vertical restraints) lead to a de facto entry barrier to the respective markets. However, if the rules are the same for foreign and domestic potential entrants, the nondiscrimination rule is not violated and, therefore, the home authority of the foreign deterred entrant cannot claim (extraterritorial) jurisdiction over this case. See Trebilcock and Iacobucci (2004: 158–159). The same would be true – although not reported in Trebilcock and Iacobucci (2004) if country A exempts an industry from the cartel prohibition irrespective of the nationality of the producers (thus, not discriminating between domestic and foreign ones) and this would lead (maybe among other interfirm arrangements) to an export cartel. However, a pure export cartel exemption (meaning that inbound cartels stay prohibited) violates the nondiscrimination rule because it discriminates against foreign consumers. See Trebilcock and Iacobucci (2004: 158–159).

These explanations of the allocation principle interfere with the analysis of this rule in section 2.3 of this chapter, wherefore these aspects will enter the agenda again over there. However, it seems important to clarify these implications of the nondiscrimination rule in advance, and worth paying the price of limited redundancy.

about enforcement competences (dimension IIc). However, the upward level neither directly applies downward institutions, nor directly enforces them, although by determining which one(s) prevail in conflict cases, an indirect application and enforcement as a choice between downwardly created alternatives results. Additionally, an indirect rule-making competence may occur because the upward level decides whether complained-about competition rules or antitrust practices of downward jurisdictions violate the nondiscrimination principle or not – which can be a controversial matter. However, the upward level can only negatively condemn specific provisions but it cannot prescribe specifically designed rules.

- Dimension III: exclusive competence on the national or regional levels only occurs with regard to purely domestic business arrangements without participation of foreign producers and without effects on foreign consumers. Otherwise, discrimination claims and inbound effects from the perspective of other jurisdictions generate concurrent competences. On the supranational level, exclusive conflict resolution competences exist.
- Dimension IV: the number of cases, which are effectively (albeit indirectly) decided on the supranational level, depends on the number of discriminatory provisions and practices in the national and regional competition policy regimes. However, such provisions should cease over the course of time because of the complaint, supervision, and sanction mechanism. A contrary effect may arise if the globalisation of business activities leads to an increasing number of interjurisdictional antitrust conflicts about non-discriminatory decisions.

1.1.5 Best practice recommendations and peer pressure

The inclusion of ICN-styled best practice recommendations and peer pressure[12] in these lists of competence allocation rules is more problematic than with the other selected competence allocation rules. In a formal understanding, competences are not allocated since nobody is forced to abstain from antitrust competences. However, if one allows or concedes more informal governance concepts – relying on persuasion, insight, and voluntary compliance – to produce real effects, then it is possible to characterise the underlying principles as institutional arrangements to allocate competences in an informal way. Furthermore, it is useful to integrate the idea of 'soft' governance in the comparative analysis. Therefore, its inclusion – despite being potentially controversial – improves the overall results of the theoretical analysis in this chapter.

---

12 See section 2.4 of Chapter 4.

In order to generate a stylised rule, one can codify the competence allocation mechanism as a combination of consensual best practice recommendations and interjurisdictional peer pressure to comply voluntarily with these best practices.[13] One interpretation may be to view this as a framework for an organised yardstick competition or competition of ideas[14] for the practical, objective identification of superior antitrust solutions. An antitrust-improving process of mutual learning is facilitated because it is organised by an international network:

- Dimension I: the ICN creates what is, in effect, a virtual supranational level, which consists of emergent phenomena of the horizontal and diagonal interrelations. No explicit competences are allocated to that level. However, indirect and informal competences emerge through the factual effects of the public ICN best practice recommendations once they are consensually adopted by the downward jurisdictions. Similarly, the horizontal allocation of competences consists of no explicit limitations of jurisdiction. Again, informal peer pressure to adopt the identified best practices (that is, not to stick to practices which have been publicly identified to be inferior) should cause a horizontal allocation of competences according to best practices about a sufficient nexus[15] between an anticompetitive arrangement or practice and jurisdiction.
- Dimension II: formally, the rule-making, rule-application, and enforcement competences of the national and supranational-regional competition policy regimes within the ICN are left untouched. However, the best practice recommendations target predominantly the rule-making competence as well as enforcement (dimensions IIa and IIc). The jurisdictions shall be convinced to voluntarily redesign their competition rules according to the ICN benchmark and voluntarily mould their enforcement practice according to the ICN guidelines. If effective, this implies considerable (albeit informal) allocation effects on rule-making and enforcement competences. As far as one can now see, rule-application remains untouched (dimension IIb).
- Dimension III: best practice recommendations and peer pressure generally lead to concurrent competition policy competences. Exceptions include the competence to propose best practices (supranational level)

[13] See for this interpretation and its economic rationale, Budzinski (2003b: 36–39, 2004a: 90, 94–96, 2004b: 75–78, 2004c: 228, 230–235).

[14] See section 3 of Chapter 3.

[15] See section 2.4 of Chapter 4. Until now, guidelines on this crucial aspect remain rather vague and in a provisional shape. Therefore, it is difficult to be precise about the effects.

and implications from the yet-to-be-specified best practice recommendations about the appropriate nexus between anticompetitive effects and jurisdiction.
- Dimension IV: the evolution of competence allocation largely depends on the effectiveness of the informal allocation principle. In advance, neither an increasing scattering of antitrust competences nor a gradual extension of supranational competences (perhaps through an exclusive interpretation competence with regard to the adopted best practices) can be ruled out.[16] If tendencies towards harmonisation arise, then the process belongs to the type of so-called bottom-up harmonisation (because of the decentralised competence allocation) or best-rule harmonisation (First 1998) (because individual insight is the major driving-force).[17]

1.2 Stylised Rules Derived from Literature

1.2.1 Principle of origin and location doctrine

The first rule taken from the academic literature is the location doctrine as an antitrust-related variant of the principle of origin. Each competition policy regime has jurisdiction over anticompetitive arrangements and practices, which originate from its territory, irrespective of the location of the anticompetitive effects.[18] Consequently and contrary to the effects doctrine, outbound anticompetitive arrangements and practices fall under the domestic jurisdiction (instead of inbound arrangements in the case of the effects doctrine). If domestic enterprises form a price-fixing cartel or an anticompetitive merger, the domestic antitrust authorities apply their domestic antitrust institutions in order to protect competition both on domestic and foreign or international markets. This implies that jurisdictional competition policy regimes no longer focus on domestic welfare alone but include the effects on foreign and global welfare in their decisions:

---

[16] This area of tension is addressed in more detail in section 2.4 of this chapter.

[17] This type of ex post harmonisation stands in contrast to top-down harmonisation through international contractual negotiations or mandatory (minimum) standards set by an international organisation (ex ante harmonisation). See for comparative discussions First (1998) and Wegner (2003). Sometimes the contrast is emphasised by referring to market-based harmonisation as opposed to policy-determined harmonisation.

[18] This is often more implicitly included in the literature that sceptically reviews the effects doctrine. See with explicit reference to a location principle, for example, Kerber (1999: 259–260) and Wins (2000: 145–147). See also Fox and Ordover (1995), Fox (1997, 1998a), Basedow (1998), and Durand et al. (2004).

- Dimension I: the location principle predominantly targets the horizontal allocation of competences, with diagonal effects being easily includable. Vertical competence allocation is not addressed as long as a territorial focus prevails. If, however, the origin of anticompetitively acting enterprises relates to institutional issues instead, for example, incorporation according to federal or state law,[19] then vertical effects may arise. For instance, anticompetitive arrangements or practices on the French market by an enterprise, which is incorporated according to EU corporate law (the new SE), fall under the jurisdiction of the European Commission and the EU competition rules (thus, are allocated upwardly to the regional-supranational level), whereas identical arrangements or practices by a Spain-incorporated enterprise fall under the jurisdiction of Spanish authorities and institutions (thus, are allocated to the national level).
- Dimension II: principally, institutional and enforcement competences remain together in the hands of the respectively competent jurisdiction. However, while this is robust regarding rule-making and enforcement competences (dimensions IIa and IIc), rule-application can deviate from the above formulated principle (dimension IIb). An alternative design of the location principle could include that national competition policy regimes protect foreign markets by applying the competition rules of the antitrust regime of the affected foreign markets instead of its own institutions (Basedow 1998: 38–40; Kerber 1999: 261).
- Dimension III: whenever the enterprises, which collude to form an anticompetitive arrangement or practice, originate from one and the same jurisdiction, exclusive competences for the respective domestic antitrust regime result. If the respective arrangements and practices have cross-border origins (not effects) instead, concurrent competences occur. In cases of the latter type, all competition policy regimes, in which at least one participating enterprise is resident or incorporated, have jurisdiction.
- Dimension IV: the ongoing process of the globalisation of business activities is likely to increase the frequency of the occurrence of inter-firm alliances, arrangements, cooperations, mergers, and so on, with participants from different countries. Therefore, the allocation of competences will predictably develop a more scattered picture in the course of time.

---

[19] Assume an enterprise can choose whether to incorporate according to national laws or according to the European Company Statute (SE). Such a vertical competition of corporate laws is intensively discussed in the respective literature, see, for example, da Costa and Bilreiro (2003), Enriques (2003), and Heine (2003).

1.2.2 The relevant markets rule

From a strictly internalisation-focused point of view, the competence over an anticompetitive arrangement or practice should be allocated to the jurisdiction, which just covers the relevant anticompetitively affected geographic market.[20] Thus, the relevant markets rule implies an optimisation of the congruency between affected market and jurisdiction. Consequently, the assignment of jurisdiction follows the definition of the relevant geographic market according to the respective standard economic instruments:

- Dimension I: the relevant markets rule addresses both the horizontal and the vertical allocation of competences. Horizontally, jurisdiction is delimitated by the geographical reach of the affected market. Note that if the relevant market exceeds the territory of a specific competition policy regime, no jurisdiction is assigned to that regime. This leads on to the vertical implications. The vertical allocation of competences starts with the geographically smallest regime and compares it to the geographical extension of the relevant market. Whenever the relevant market is larger than the territory of the jurisdictional unit, say national countries, an upward allocation of competences, for example, to the regional supranational level results. This procedure stops at the first antitrust regime, which covers the complete relevant market.[21]
- Dimension II: the pure version of the relevant markets rule allocates the institutional and enforcement competences as one integrated bundle.
- Dimension III: principally, exclusive competence over an anticompetitive arrangement or practice results from the relevant markets rule as long as exactly one market is anticompetitively affected. In such cases, there exists exactly one regime, which territorially just includes the geographically relevant market. However, if more than one relevant product market is anticompetitively affected, concurrent competences can occur. In particular, mergers of large and diversified companies regularly affect a multitude of relevant product markets with differing geographic extensions. Applying the relevant markets rule to such cases

---

[20] Astonishingly enough, though, this rather obvious principle is not prominently discussed in the literature – including the economic contributions. Similarly, relevant markets do not play a significant role in the existing multilevel systems of competition policies (as discussed in Chapter 4). Within the EU system, for instance, a vague reference to geographically relevant markets can only be found in the merger control referral regime (that is, concerning the post-notification re-allocation of competences), where downward referrals demand a distinct national markets to be negatively affected by the combination (Art. 9 of the ECMR). However, as the analysis in section 2.6 of this chapter indicates, there may be some convincing practical reason for this.

[21] Thus, this procedure incorporates the subsidiarity principle.

allows for different conclusions. First, the whole case is treated by all competition policy regimes, which house at least one of the defined relevant product markets. Secondly, the competence could be allocated to the regime, which just covers the geographically largest market among the affected ones. Thirdly, the respective antitrust case could be divided into market-related subcases, which, subsequently, are allocated to the respective antitrust regimes.

- Dimension IV: if relevant markets become more and more internationalised in the course of trade liberalisation and the globalisation of business activities and competition, then an increasing number of cases will be allocated to upward levels. It is unlikely, however, that this process will completely erode the scope for cases, which effects are limited to national or regional markets. The development of the importance of cases with concurrent competences depends on business strategies, for instance, the current tendency towards core competence-enhancing alliances and mergers should reduce the scope for concurrent antitrust competences, whereas diversification as the dominant business strategy would enhance it.

1.2.3 X-plus rule

Out of the controversial debate about the reform of the EU merger control and the division of labour between national and community level emerged a new proposal for a rule for the allocation and delimitation of competences: the 3-plus rule.[22] Like turnover thresholds, it served as an alternative proxy for the likelihood of effects on interstate trade or community dimension in merger control and in cartel policy.[23] In a more generalised manner, the *X-plus rule* implies that each anticompetitive arrangement and practice, which would be subject to review by X or more downward (for example, national or regional)

---

22 This represented the preferred competence allocation rule by several contributions. See, for example, BDI (2002), Burnley (2002b: 272–273), Díaz (2004: 184), as well as in tendency, Van Gerwen (2003) and Budzinski and Christiansen (2005b); more sceptical, Drauz (2003) and Stockmann (2003). However, this rule was eventually not adopted and an amendment of the referral regime was preferred instead. See also section 2.2 of Chapter 4.

23 While the X-plus rule was intensively discussed during the merger control reform process, its relation to cartel policy emerges more recently in the shadows of the ECN. In a notice concerning the intra-network cooperation, the Commission explained its view that a cartel, which – as a general rule – infringes competition in more than three Member States, is 'well-placed' at the EU level. See Commission Notice on Cooperation within the Network of Competition Authorities: [2004] OJ C 101/43 (paras 8–15). See also Budzinski and Christiansen (2005b), Schaub (2005), and Smits (2005: 175–180).

competition policy regimes, is automatically allocated to the upward (for example, international) level.[24] All other cases are allocated to the downward level and reviewed according to the respective institutions by the respective authorities. Obviously, both the value of X and the inequality in terms of size, economic importance, business activity, and so on of the constituting jurisdictions[25] are crucial issues regarding the effects of such a competence allocation rule:

- Dimension I: the X-plus rule addresses the vertical allocation of competences, whereas the horizontal and diagonal delimitation of competences is left untouched and must be designed according to other principles.
- Dimension II: in its pure variant, the X-plus rule allocates institutional and enforcement competences as a bundle.
- Dimension III: the X-plus rule implies an asymmetry in regard to exclusivity and concurrence of competences. If the rule is met, exclusive competence for the upward level results. However, if less than X, downward level regimes claim jurisdiction over a specific anticompetitive arrangement or practice, concurrent competences by these regimes arises. It depends on the value of X, how large the share of concurrent competences in comparison to exclusive competences is. Purely national cases generate exclusive competences for the respective national regime.
- Dimension IV: if business activities tend to affect the markets of more and more antitrust regimes on the national level, an increasing number of anticompetitive arrangements and practices will be allocated to supranational levels in the course of time. The dynamics of this development depend on the degree of openness and involvement into international trade flows of national economies (and, in particular, small economies[26]) as well as on the value of X.

---

[24] In the case of the EU Competition Policy System, X = 3 would have implied that each merger, which would have to be notified to three or more Member States, is automatically defined to have community dimension and, consequently, allocated to the community level.

[25] Drawing on contemporary nations, X = 3 may mean an arrangement affects the US, Japan, and Russia as well as Estonia, Luxembourg, and the Bahamas. In other words, the number of consumers suffering from anticompetitive business arrangements, which is necessary to constitute an upward competence, can differ considerably. However, I abstract from the theoretical alternative of evenly designed downward level jurisdictions (for example, countries) and, instead, accept the imbalance of intralevel jurisdiction (country) characteristics as a matter of fact in a historically path-dependent world.

[26] The smaller the involved national economies are, the faster and the more often the number of X is achieved.

1.2.4 Voluntary lead jurisdiction (advanced comity principle)

Principally, the comity principles stem from the bilateral interagency cooperation agreements, which have been frequently implemented to supplement the otherwise uncoordinated application of the effects doctrine.[27] However, the advanced comity principle, which represents the core element of the voluntary lead jurisdiction rule, significantly extends the comity principles incorporated in those agreements.[28] If an anticompetitive arrangement or practice is to be reviewed by more than one competition policy regime (according to their respective standards), the affected jurisdictions appoint a lead jurisdiction, whose antitrust authority is designated to play the role of a coordinating agency (Campbell and Trebilcock (1993: 149–150, 1997: 109–110; Rowley et al. 2000: 27–28). The latter implies that the lead jurisdiction does not suspend the reviews of the other involved jurisdictions. Instead, it coordinates their reviews, that is, it collects and distributes information from the interacting agencies and, thereby, ensuring mutual comity (that is, mutual respect for each other's legitimate interests). Eventually, the coordinating agency compiles a common but non-binding recommendation regarding remedies, which integrates the competition-oriented interests of the participating jurisdictions, in order to generate a coherent treatment of a specific international anticompetitive arrangement or practice. According to the advanced comity concept, the lead jurisdiction role should be assigned to the one whose authorities are best equipped to enforce sanctions (if necessary):

- Dimension I: the advanced comity principle is predominantly about the horizontal and the diagonal allocation of competences. Vertical effects can also occur, for example, if a specific anticompetitive arrangement or practice affects among others both the federal US institutions and agencies and the ones of the State of New York.[29] However, they are more of a by-product.
- Dimension II: the rule-making competences of the participating jurisdictions is not touched (dimension IIa). Theoretically, the same is true for rule-application (dimension IIb). However, a coherent result of the

[27] See section 1.2.3 of Chapter 3, where the shortcomings of the bilateral approaches and the failure to effectively exercise ambitious comity principles are discussed.

[28] This is why the advanced comity principle as a variant of the lead jurisdiction model, which is developed and proposed in the academic literature, is not discussed in section 1.1 of this chapter.

[29] A precondition is that the internal vertical allocation of competences within the US antitrust system generates concurrent competences – as it currently is. See section 2.1 of Chapter 4.

common, coordinated review and governance procedure can, in practice, require some jurisdictions to waive the application of certain parts of their institutions due to comity considerations. Enforcement competences are allocated to the lead jurisdiction in the common interest of all participants because it is the best suited to enforce the commonly adopted sanctions (dimension IIc). However, this does not exclude the possibility that the lead jurisdiction calls on some of the interacting agencies for assistance concerning specific elements of the sanctions.

- Dimension III: since the lead jurisdiction predominantly has a coordinating function, concurrent competences principally prevail. Only with regard to enforcement is something close to exclusive competences allocated to the lead jurisdiction.
- Dimension IV: the allocation of competences is not significantly influenced by further market globalisation except for a more frequent necessity to agree upon a lead jurisdiction and – possibly – an increasing number of participating agencies.

1.2.5 Mandatory lead jurisdiction

The last competition allocation and delimitation mechanism also focuses on identifying a lead jurisdiction. However, an international panel or agency is introduced, which decides about competence allocation – and only competence allocation. This means that no substantive provisions, no minimum standards for competition rules (à la nondiscrimination), or comparative evaluations of national antitrust policies are provided by the international level. The only task for the supranational agency or panel is to choose the competent lead jurisdiction with regard to a specific anticompetitive arrangement or practice.[30] According to the primary effects clause, the jurisdiction should qualify as the lead jurisdiction, which is most impacted by an anticompetitive arrangement or practice.[31] 'Most impacted' is meant to be assessed against the background of the largest share of consumption of the anticompetitively affected product markets.[32] So, the competence to deal with

---

30 This represents a modified version of the suggestion by Campbell and Trebilcock (1993: 150–153, 1997: 110–112).

31 From an academic perspective, the ECN's 'centre of gravity principle' could be interpreted very similarly (in particular against the background that the ECN itself does not provide a conclusive interpretation). However, in the practice of network cooperation considerably deviating outcomes are not unlikely. Perhaps, in the end of the day, the similarities to the advanced comity principle will be more apparent. See on the centre of gravity principle in the context of the ECN, Monti (2004b: 496).

32 '[T]he choice of lead jurisdiction should reflect the concern for consumers that animates competition policy. The country that represents the largest share of consumption should presumably be the lead jurisdiction.' Trebilcock and Iacobucci

this case is allocated to the internationally chosen lead jurisdiction (both regarding authority and institution), which is obliged to pay attention to anticompetitive effects in other jurisdictions and entitled to call on other antitrust regimes for assistance. If an anticompetitive arrangement or practice has effects solely within one country, the primary effects clause automatically assigns all competences to this country without the necessity of involving the international panel:

- Dimension I: the primary effects clause addresses the horizontal allocation of competences because only the competition policy regime with the most impacted markets is competent to review a specific anticompetitive arrangement or practice. Diagonal effects are treated the same way. In a limited sense, the vertical allocation of competences is also addressed since an upward level is regularly competent to decide on the appropriate lead jurisdiction.
- Dimension II: the rule-making competences of the national and regional-supranational regimes is left untouched, whereas the supranational level does not get substantive rule-making competence (dimension IIa). The enforcement competences are allocated to the lead jurisdiction (dimension IIc), which applies its own antitrust institutions. However, the decision concerning which competition rules are applied to a specific anticompetitive arrangement or practice is effectively allocated to the supranational level (dimension IIb) because it is there the decision about the lead jurisdiction is made.
- Dimension III: the mandatory lead jurisdiction model leads to an exclusive allocation of competences. After the supranational level has exerted its exclusive competence to appoint the lead jurisdiction, the latter has exclusive competence to deal with the respective case. Anticompetitive arrangements and practices, which affect only markets in one antitrust jurisdiction, fall under the exclusive competence of this jurisdiction. In the pure variant of the primary effects clause, no concurrent competences arise.
- Dimension IV: if the most impacted competition policy regime is identified via the absolute share of consumption, most cases will be allocated to large jurisdictions with large internal markets and lots of consumers. Further market globalisation will only reinforce this development.

(2004: 166). In particular, non-competition aspects like employment or industrial policy considerations must not play any role regarding the appointment of the lead jurisdiction. See Campbell and Trebilcock (1997: 112).

2. AN INSTITUTIONAL-ECONOMIC ANALYSIS OF COMPETENCE-ALLOCATING RULES

Following the introduction and descriptive characterisation of the rules for the allocation and delimitation of competences in the previous section, these rules are now analysed against the background of the economic criteria derived in section 1 of Chapter 4.[33] I continue using the sequential order of the previous section and the comparative element is introduced in two ways. First, sporadic backward references compare rules with already analysed ones and, secondly and more importantly, a comparative conclusion is presented in section 3 of this chapter.

2.1 The Effects Doctrine

2.1.1 Internalisation of external effects

The non-coordinated application of the effects doctrine does not contribute to the internalisation of negative or positive externalities. The exclusive focus on domestic effects ignores outbound effects and denies their inclusion in the analysis and decision practice of the domestic authorities. Furthermore, the inbound-focused decision is enforced extraterritorially without comity to outbound effects. More precisely, neither the (anti-) competitive effects of a reviewed business practice or arrangement on foreign or international markets, nor the effects of the domestic antitrust policy on other jurisdictions are considered. Thus, the non-coordinated application of the effects doctrine itself generates negative externalities, that is, causes costs – for instance in terms of welfare losses – in foreign jurisdictions.

Positive externalities can also emerge if a jurisdiction effectively protects competition not only in its domestic markets but also, in doing so, in international and/or foreign markets. However, the incentives to engage in such modes of beneficially extraterritorial antitrust policy are low since no reward can be expected. Therefore, positive externalities will be rather insignificant and only emerge as (inevitable) by-products of inbound-focused policies.

Moreover, the effects doctrine facilitates strategic competition policies and, therefore, can be applied with the intention of causing negative externalities (thereby, further reducing the incentives to provide positive externalities). First, the effects doctrine can be applied discriminatorily to disadvantage foreign competitors at the benefit of domestic business. For instance, a jurisdiction can attempt to block an efficiency-enhancing merger between foreign companies in order to improve the relative competitiveness of domestic

---

33 See Figure 4.2 in section 1.4 of Chapter 4.

competitors. Other examples include the intentional promotion of purely outbound restrictions (for example, export cartels) in order to shift foreign consumers' rent to that of domestic producers'. Secondly, the effects doctrine provides countries with an asymmetric power regarding international economic relations. Countries or federations, which exert jurisdiction over large, important internal markets are powerful enough to impose their antitrust policy on foreign companies and jurisdictions. However, small countries and developing countries frequently experience powerlessness against inbound restrictions of competition from abroad. This can be particularly difficult if the respective countries depend on specific imports.[34]

The last aspect points towards the frequent emergence of jurisdictional conflicts as a consequence of the non-coordinated application of the effects doctrine. Such conflicts are only 'resolved' if two asymmetrically powerful jurisdictions are involved, with the powerful jurisdiction prevailing. However, the asymmetric allocation of enforcement power is not systematically correlated to welfare-enhancing antitrust decisions. Jurisdictional conflicts, while resulting from externalities, can produce additional negative external effects if other areas of international economic relations become affected in the course of the struggle for power. For instance, the EU–US conflict on the Boeing–MDD merger demonstrated that countries might attempt to improve their bargaining position by extending the conflict on trade issues.[35]

In summary, the effects doctrine performs very badly in regard to the internationalisation of externalities. This includes horizontal ones – as discussed above – and also vertical ones, since the effects doctrine does not apply to vertical interrelations.

2.1.2 Efficiency: economies of scale and the one-stop-shop principle

Concerning the cost efficiency of an international competition policy, an allocation of competences according to the effects doctrine is characterised by a number of deficiencies. An economisation on economies of scale is not introduced. Since each country sticks to its independent regime, no economic benefits of centralisation can be obtained. This includes both static and dynamic economies of scale. This negative assessment can only be toned down mildly in two aspects. First, the coexistence of numerous antitrust regimes with their own considerable fixed costs is attenuated (though not erased) by the fact that smaller countries often simply copy the laws of the 'market leaders' or even rely on their decisions (that is, copying the decisions of the leading

34 See, with examples, section 1.2.2 of Chapter 3.
35 See section 1.2.2 of Chapter 3.

authorities).[36] Secondly, the large variety of decentralised antitrust regimes may represent an effective protection against institutional lock-ins.

However, more severe problems arise with regard to compliance costs of enterprises and administrative costs for taxpayers. An effects doctrine-based allocation and delimitation of competences does not fulfil the one-stop-shop principle in the slightest extent. Concurrent competences are the dominating case as soon as a business practice or arrangement has cross-border effects. Internationally competing enterprises must notify to and comply with large numbers of antitrust regimes, each diverging in procedural and substantial issues from the others, while the burden falls on procompetitive arrangements and practices as well as on anticompetitive ones. Cumulating and contradictory verdicts, sanctions, and remedies by concurrently competent authorities further aggravate the efficiency record. The extra costs of doing business internationally, caused by the effects doctrine-based competence allocation, may well reduce international business activity and, thereby, the intensity of international competition. Relative welfare losses are a likely consequence.[37]

Furthermore, parallel proceedings in numerous jurisdictions cause inefficient burdens on taxpayers. Although this cannot be a priori maintained in regard to independent decisions by regional or national competition policy authorities, the parallel and non-coordinated efforts regarding detection, information gathering, fact finding, hearings, generation of evidence (including economic expertise like econometric studies), and so on are less likely to produce any extra benefit. Altogether, significant inefficiencies must be diagnosed.

2.1.3 Preference conformity

Theoretically, an effects doctrine-based competence allocation allows for a high degree of preference conformity. Each country produces its own competition policy regime with its own rules and practices. Depending on the workability of a specific country's political process, differences in the so-resulting competition policy regimes should reflect differing preferences about competition and antitrust.

However, a qualification is necessary with regard to the practical effects. Due to the extraterritorial enforcement of foreign antitrust rules, a country may not be able to completely enforce its own – preferred – competition policies.

---

36 For instance, Switzerland was often said to waive an own active competition policy because it believed the large neighbours (EU, Germany) would automatically protect competition on the Swiss markets in the course of their regular antitrust activities.

37 See also the empirical evidence presented by Evenett (2002).

For instance, one national competition policy regime (A) may want to adhere to the total welfare standard, while another regime (B) focuses on consumer welfare. Consequently, the first regime promotes a specific efficiency-enhancing merger between domestic enterprises because the gain in producers' welfare outweighs the loss in consumers' welfare (say, for the sake of argument, on a worldwide scale as well as in every affected country). However, this merger becomes blocked by the other regime because of its negative consequences for consumers' welfare. Although sovereign in theory, regime A cannot 'live' its preferred antitrust policy, that is, accounting for efficiency considerations, because of the extraterritorial enforcement of regime B's competition rules. The comprehensive and unilateral employment of the effects doctrine practically leads to an individual veto right for each affected country regarding the practical allowance of international interfirm arrangements and practices (similarly: Heyer 2005: 401). This represents a de facto restriction of preference conformity.

However, one must emphasise that the limited and incomplete power to extraterritorially enforce national or regional competition rules reduces the scope for vetoing business combinations and arrangements from abroad and desired by foreign jurisdictions. Altogether, the degree of preference conformity remains considerable if competences are allocated according to the effects doctrine.

2.1.4 Minimisation of lobbyism

The effects doctrine demands an inbound-focused view. Therefore, an identification of the domestic antitrust authorities with policy strategies, which are beneficial for domestic producers and consumers is promoted. Consequently, no inherent barrier against strategic competition policies exists. This relates to the influence of lobbyism. If beggar-thy-neighbour strategies are generally viewed to be legitimate, better organised groups can more easily sell their private interests to the authorities by presenting them as having overall domestic benefits.[38] Additionally, self-interested politicians may find it more comfortable to justify discriminating or biased policies in such an environment. Since competitive effects are sometimes difficult to estimate objectively (making it impossible to unambiguously detach vested interests), considerable scope for lobbyism results.

However, the degree to which the decentralised antitrust jurisdictions are vulnerable to lobbyism will significantly differ. It largely depends on the respective domestic political systems and institutional conditions. For

[38] See for the interrelation of economically rational and politically rational strategic competition policies sections 1.3.2 and 1.3.3 of Chapter 3.

instance, an independent antitrust authority[39] or a court-dominated system are likely to significantly reduce the scope for lobbyism-biased antitrust policies.

2.1.5 Adaptability

Due to the strongly decentralised competence allocation, which results from the effects doctrine, considerable scope for parallel experimentation with different competition rules, policy strategies, and antitrust practices is created. Each country is free to act according to its state of knowledge and experience. Moreover, the extraterritorial application of national and regional competition rules to inbound business arrangements and practices generates an interplay between the unilaterally acting jurisdictions. Since foreign antitrust policies affect domestic enterprises, for instance, if a domestic alliance or merger is blocked by a foreign antitrust authority, an incentive to notice and deal with foreign competition rules and antitrust practices exists. This is important because it strengthens the possibility of mutual learning, which requires (an existing incentive for) comparative assessments of foreign and domestic solutions. In this sense, conflicts might serve as a catalyst for learning processes because they intensify the mutual dealing with alternative antitrust policies.[40] Notwithstanding this, jurisdictional conflicts produce a number of undesirable outcomes,[41] where learning process may be costly in an effects doctrine-based competence allocation. Moreover, the content of the learning process need not be beneficial since an effects doctrine regime creates incentives to learn about discriminatory and distortionary antitrust strategies (Kerber and Budzinski 2004: 39). Apart from jurisdictional conflicts, however, incentives for mutual learning are rather weak.[42]

Yet, there might be an additional exception to the generally positive assessment of the adaptability of an effects-doctrine-based allocation of competences. Among the innovative anticompetitive modes of enterprise behaviour,

---

39 This points towards the independence from government, following the paragon of central bank independence (as with the European System of Central Banks), to exclude the misuse of competition policy instruments by lobbyism-biased politicians.

40 For instance, the EU–US conflicts on the Boeing–MDD and the proposed GE–Honeywell merger may have intensified the efforts for antitrust convergence between the two jurisdictions. See for such an opinion in tendency, for example, Akbar (2002) and Gifford and Kudrle (2003). However, first, it is a one-sided convergence process (the EU copying the US practice) and, secondly, it remains doubtful whether substantial convergence is really achieved. In the face of the important role played by national interests in both cases, similar conflicts can be expected for the future if similarly sensible cases arise.

41 See section 1.2.2 of Chapter 3 and section 2.1.1 of this chapter.

42 See section 3 of Chapter 3.

a considerable number might relate to cross-border restrictive practices and arrangements. Highly decentralised competition policy regimes have significant difficulties to deal with such types of anticompetitive arrangements without creating considerable loopholes.[43] Learning abilities and responsiveness regarding such types of anticompetitive arrangement and practices might be limited if competence allocation solely depends on the effects doctrine.

2.2 Turnover Thresholds

2.2.1 Internalisation of external effects

A competence allocation based on turnover thresholds provides some internalisation of external effects both in vertical and in horizontal perspective. Regarding the vertical allocation of competences, the idea is that the larger an arrangement or practice is in terms of the turnovers of the participating enterprises, the more likely are cross-border effects, wherefore arrangements that meet or exceed a defined vertical threshold are upwardly allocated to a supranational level. Since a specific anticompetitive arrangement or practice is allocated either exclusively to the international level or exclusively to the national level, vertical jurisdictional conflicts are unlikely to occur.

With regard to horizontal competence allocation, a very low threshold, instead, would allow for a more virtual market tangency to generate jurisdiction over a specific arrangement. In doing so, competition policy regimes, which do not experience a sufficient amount of domestic turnovers by the colluding or merging enterprises, are excluded from reviewing the arrangement. This reduces the scope for externalities, albeit not to zero, because it reduces the number of competition policy regimes that are competent to deal with a below-the-vertical-threshold case.

The quality of the internalisation of externalities by the horizontal allocation of competences obviously depends on the appropriateness of the horizontal threshold. If the turnover threshold, which must be met or exceeded in order to constitute jurisdiction of a downward level authority, reflects a sufficient nexus between the anticompetitive arrangement or practice and the competent jurisdictions, a reduction of horizontal conflicts might be achieved. A very low threshold, instead, would allow for more virtual market affections to generate jurisdiction, whereas a more ambitious threshold further reduces spillovers but, instead, increases the danger of creating loopholes (that is, specific cases fall under no jurisdiction at all because of their dispersed effects).

---

43 See section 1.2.2 of Chapter 3.

However, turnover thresholds represent a rather crude proxy for the geographic extent of the economic effects of an anticompetitive arrangement or practice. Therefore, only an imperfect internalisation will occur with regard to the vertical allocation of competences. Irrespective of the exact figures of the vertical turnover threshold, some cases will be misallocated. Some of the arrangements and practices that meet or exceed the threshold will, nevertheless, exclusively affect markets on the downward level. According to the turnover-threshold-based competence allocation, they will be allocated to an upward level although they could have been appropriately treated on the downward level. Thereby, positive externalities are generated because the upward level authority must provide antitrust policy on behalf of the downward ones. Similarly, there can be cases where the threshold is not met but there are effects on suprajurisdictional markets with respect to the downward level jurisdictions. This could be the case, for instance, in markets, which are generally characterised by small or medium-sized companies, but, nonetheless, have cross-border dimensions or are subject to internationalisation processes. In such cases, scope for negative externalities arise since the case is reviewed on the downward level although the geographic scope of the case exceeds the one of the then competent jurisdictions.[44]

2.2.2 Efficiency: economies of scale and the one-stop-shop principle

Competence allocation according to turnover thresholds allows for economies of scale if the vertical turnover thresholds lead to a considerable centralisation of competences at the upward level. This does not seem too unrealistic, in particular against the background of ongoing market enlargement (due to globalisation) with its inherent tendency towards larger enterprises. Regarding the horizontal allocation of competences, this kind of efficiency is not enhanced because no downward jurisdiction can increase the number of cases for which it is competent. On the contrary, some cases are lost to the upward level and others due to the horizontal threshold (preventing jurisdiction in cases of a rather minor nexus to an anticompetitive arrangement or practice). Furthermore, considerable centralisation can incrementally marginalise downward level competences,[45] thus, enhancing the danger of institutional lock-ins. Strong tendencies towards centralisation can result from inappropriate thresholds. However, even once appropriate but static turnover thresholds (in partic-

44 The experience with turnover thresholds as a competence allocation rule in EU merger control supports the described externality problems from case misallocation. See in more detail section 2.2 of Chapter 4.

45 To some extent, this reflects the development in the EU Competition Policy System. See section 2.2 of Chapter 4.

ular when defined in nominal figures) can develop to become inappropriate in the course of time.

A one-stop shop is always created by turnover thresholds if an anticompetitive arrangement or practice meets or exceeds the (vertical) threshold and, consequently, is exclusively allocated to the upward level. Otherwise, concurrent competences remain possible. The extent of multiple reviews on the downward level depends: (1) on the figures of the vertical threshold; and (2) on the figures of the horizontal threshold. The first aspect highlights how many cases are allocated to the downward level at all, whereas the second aspect determines how many downward jurisdictions are competent. With low horizontal thresholds, the problem of multiple reviews is considerable, causing inefficient burden on business and taxpayers. This case is even stronger if no horizontal threshold exists at all or its design is in the autonomous competence of the downward jurisdiction respectively.[46] An ambitious and harmonised horizontal threshold, on the other hand, would reduce this problem, albeit not to zero.

In summary, turnover thresholds as competence-allocating rules lead to mixed results regarding efficiency aspects. A crucial problem is inefficiencies resulting from concurrent jurisdiction over below-the-vertical-threshold cases. Although this problem can potentially be reduced by proper threshold designs, the identification and implementation of such appropriate designs may be rather difficult in reality. At least the experiences within the EU competition policy system indicate this. A likely consequence is the implementation of a referral system in order to reallocate cases and correct shortcomings of the initial competence allocation. This leads to an increase in complexity that can develop considerable negative impact in regard to procedural efficiency (Budzinski and Christiansen 2005b; Budzinski 2006).

2.2.3 Preference conformity

To some extent, preference conformity may decrease because of the described likelihood of centralisation tendencies. Differences in preferences about competition policy cannot be adequately reflected in those cases that are allocated to the international level. Additionally, an international bureaucracy

---

[46] The latter is the case in the EU competition policy system. Among the Member States, notification rules for mergers, for instance, differ significantly. Some Member States have turnover thresholds (with varying degrees of strictness), other market share thresholds (Greece, Spain, Portugal, Latvia, Poland, Slovak Republic and Slovenia) or a 'share of supply' criterion (the UK), and sometimes a reference to a specific national jurisdictional nexus is completely lacking. See Drauz (2003: 20). As a consequence, the problem of multiple filings and reviews is viewed to be a major driving force of the recent reforms of EU merger control. See section 2.2 of Chapter 3.

comes into force, which is further from the citizens and, therefore, agency problems may increase. A crucial aspect is that all competences are upwardly allocated and no splitting of competences occurs (in the pure variant, which is discussed in this section). The negative effect is particularly severe if predominantly national cases exceed the turnover thresholds and, therefore, an international jurisdiction becomes exclusively competent.

However, if considerable competences remain with national and regional competition policy regimes, that is, a considerable number of cases are allocated to downward levels, then scope for inter-jurisdictionally differing antitrust policies is maintained. The performance of turnover-threshold-based competence allocation regarding this criterion significantly depends on the dynamics of the inherent tendencies towards centralisation.

The introduction of a two-tiered threshold further reduces the scope of jurisdiction for an individual downward level competition policy regime. It becomes barred from exercising jurisdiction over anticompetitive arrangements and practices, which affect its inbound markets only in a minor way. Yet, that jurisdiction might, nonetheless, prefer to claim jurisdiction.

2.2.4 Minimisation of lobbyism

In a turnover thresholds-based competence allocation, no explicit safeguard against distortionary influence through lobbyism exists. However, the scope for lobbyism-biased local competition policy strategies is limited because most anticompetitive arrangements and practices with significant cross-border effects will be allocated to a supranational level. Consequently, they are reviewed and governed according to an international welfare standard, which erodes the case for beggar-thy-neighbour strategies of the different types. However, a – maybe not insignificant – residual remains since there can be anticompetitive arrangements or practices with significant cross-border effects, which do not meet the vertical threshold. Again, the results depend on the degree to which the horizontal threshold prevents jurisdictions without a sufficient nexus to the reviewed anticompetitive arrangement or practice from acquiring competences.

It is difficult to assess whether a (centralised) international authority, which is likely to gain a considerable share of (exclusive) competences according to the turnover threshold rule, is more prone to lobbyistic capture than (decentralised) national or local authorities.[47] Therefore, having both more centralised competition policy regimes on upward levels and more decentralised competition policy competences on downward levels might represent an error-tolerant solution, in particular if the levels are vertically interrelated.

47 See, on the ambivalence of this problem, section 1.3.4 of Chapter 4.

However, if a centralised authority becomes captured, the consequences are more severe than with a more decentralised allocation of competences.

2.2.5 Adaptability

Competence allocation according to turnover thresholds can provide a considerable variety of antitrust institutions and practices. The international level and all the jurisdictions on the national and regional levels produce their own competition rules and policies. Principally, they are autonomously competent in shaping and developing their institutions and practices. Moreover, the interaction of the different competition policy regimes with their institutions and agencies becomes more explicit, so that incentives for mutual learning are enhanced. Altogether, significant scope for parallel experimentation and a variety of channels for the injection of innovation can be expected, leading to a high adaptability of the resulting system.

However, this positive assessment must be abandoned if the centralising forces dominate the system's evolution. If the competences of the downward levels are marginalised and omitted because an ever-increasing number of cases are allocated upwards, then incentives for an ostensibly 'spontaneous harmonisation' of the national and regional institutions and agencies emerge.[48] If there is no considerable scope for distinct national competition policies, why not simply copy the supranational provisions or give up national efforts altogether? At least this saves administrative costs. However, antitrust diversity is effectively eroded. As in regard to other criteria, the performance of the turnover-thresholds-based competence allocation sensitively depends on the establishment of thresholds that effectively limit centralisation tendencies.

The case for an (explicit or implicit) top-down harmonisation might become strengthened by the vertical interrelation of the levels of jurisdiction. If in cases of conflict,[49] the laws of the upward level break the laws of the downward level, tendencies towards harmonising the downward level competition rules according to the upward level standard can be fuelled.[50] This can be reinforced if incompatible competition rules and antitrust practices among

---

48 Vedder (2004) describes the ostensibly voluntary adaptation of EU-styled competition rules by the (old and new) EU Member States in similar terms. However, in the light of the recent modernisation, which contributes to substantive centralisation and, in effect, reinforces the process of diminishing the importance of national antitrust laws, one must cast doubts on the spontaneity or voluntariness of this process.

49 Despite a comparably clearcut vertical threshold, such conflicts may not be completely avoidable in practice.

50 The development of the EU competition policy system offers a striking example. See section 2.2 of Chapter 4. An elaborate analysis of driving forces for and interests in centralisation in the EU competition policy system is provided by Budzinski and Christiansen (2005b).

decentralised competition policy regimes on the downward level aggravate the governance of below-the-threshold cases, which, nevertheless, affect several jurisdictions.

2.3 The Nondiscrimination Rule

2.3.1 Internalisation of external effects

The discriminatory employment of competition policy instruments as well as discriminatory competition rules are prohibited by the nondiscrimination rule. If the anti-discrimination provision works effectively, that is, it is adequately reflected in the decentralised competition policy regimes, then this should reduce a significant number of external effects and avoid considerable numbers of jurisdictional conflicts. All kinds of intentionally strategic antitrust policies are excluded. Cases in which antitrust authorities selectively non-enforce their competition laws or promote domestic champions fall under the discrimination ban as well as antitrust provisions like the general exemption (or even active promotion) of pure export cartels.

However, negative externalities can also occur without strategic intention. As it was outlined in the previous analysis,[51] the focus on domestic welfare, combined with an asymmetric distribution of producers and consumers and/or with asymmetric anticompetitive impacts (efficiencies are predominantly realised in one regime, whereas the anticompetitive burden predominantly falls on another), can lead to externalities and cause incompatible and conflicting decisions by the respective jurisdictional antitrust authorities. Such cases do not involve a discriminatory treatment of foreigners and, thus, are not covered by the non-discrimination rule. For instance, a non-hardcore cartel (say, a strategic alliance in regard to innovation) may generate efficiencies, which outweigh its anticompetitive impact, and which predominantly occur in one country. Assume further that in another country, significant parts of the anticompetitive impact of the interfirm arrangement are felt. Even if neither one of the two involved agencies cares about the nationality of the cooperating enterprises (that is, whether they are domestic or foreign companies), the inbound focus on national welfare alone would lead to contradictory outcomes. The first jurisdiction would allow the arrangement, while the second one would challenge it.

In the pure variant of the nondiscrimination rule, some types of jurisdictional conflicts remain unsolved. The reason is that the inbound focus of national welfare prevails. However, one could be tempted to suppose that it would be not too ambitious to simply extend the conflict resolution mecha-

---

51 See section 1.2.1 of Chapter 3 and in particular, section 1.3.1 of Chapter 4.

nism of the international level, so that it does not only cover conflicts due to discriminatory antitrust but also addresses conflicts which are generated otherwise. Yet, the crucial problem is the missing standard against which such conflicts should be cleared. The international authorities only have competence to decide whether an antitrust rule or practice discriminates against foreign consumers or producers – and this standard fails in the exemplary type of conflict.[52] Therefore, it would take more than minor modifications to solve these shortcomings.

The extent to which an internalisation of externalities can be achieved by a nondiscrimination rule-based competence allocation depends on the effectiveness of the upward level supervision and resolution mechanism. Only if the upward level – through an international agency or panel: (1) can independently decide, (1a) what constitutes a discrimination and (1b) which downward jurisdiction violates that standard; (2) effectively force downward jurisdictions to comply to these rulings through mandatory provisions; and (3) can effectively sanction non-compliance, then successful internalisation can prevail in the face of interest-driven conflicts, based on industrial policy considerations and politico-economic deficiencies.

2.3.2 Efficiency: economies of scale and the one-stop-shop principle

Since the upward level only decides about the discriminatory character of a provision or decision, no centralisation of the production of competition law and its application occurs. The indirect effects on the allocation of substantial competences by the power: (1) to determine what is discriminatory, and (2) to clear competence clashes, are unlikely to produce significant scale economies.

Similarly, no one-stop shop is created. International business arrangements and practices, which affect a number of national and regional competition policy regimes, fall under the jurisdiction of each regime's rules and authorities. The involved enterprises are protected from non-discriminatory treatment, however, this does not exclude the respective country's jurisdiction over the arrangement or practice. A horizontal multiplication of parallel procedures results.

Even if a specific case finds its way to the upward level – whether through complaint about discriminatory treatment or through supervision – violations

---

52 An additional introduction of a world welfare standard, which could serve as such a standard, implies a significant departure from the pure nondiscrimination rule since this would erode the freedom of the downward competition policy regimes to implement socially desired but welfare-reducing competition rules. Consequently, the example, which was reported above in section 1.1.4 (n. 11), would be suspended with significant effects on the performance of the nondiscrimination rule in regard to the other economic criteria.

of the one-stop-shop principles are not avoided in most cases. There may be circumstances in which the upward level procedure leads to the rejection of some downward authorities' competence claims, causing an incomplete reduction in concurrently competent jurisdictions. However, in the vast majority of proceedings, upward level decisions 'only' alter the way in which specific downward jurisdictions deal with a given anticompetitive arrangement or practice – without denying their principal competence to deal with this arrangement.

In summary, competence allocation according to the nondiscrimination rule does not significantly reduce multiple reviews of one and the same business arrangement or practice. Sometimes, even more inefficiencies may be generated by the upward resolution procedure because the total time of the proceedings is increased and legal insecurity enhanced. In addition to the initial review and decision procedure on the downward level, the upward procedure plus – if the initial decision is rejected on the grounds of discriminatory treatment – a new downward procedure have to pass before a final and definite decision (with which the affected enterprises can reliably deal) is made.

2.3.3 Preference conformity

This criterion is fulfilled to a large degree by the nondiscrimination rule. Except (anyhow non-generalisable) preferences for discriminatory rules and policies, each jurisdiction is free to design and shape its own competition rules and policy practices according to the respective local preferences.[53] This even covers the inclusion of non-competition elements in antitrust rules and policy as long as they apply to domestic and foreign market participants in the same way.

2.3.4 Minimisation of lobbyism

As lobbyism is essentially directed towards the creation of discrimination in favour of the lobbyists (and, consequently, against someone else who bears the costs of the rents, which are redirected to the lobbying groups), the performance of a nondiscrimination rule-based competence allocation should be rather good. Depending on the effectiveness of the enforcement by the upward level, the scope for lobbyism with cross-border effects is considerably reduced. However, this does not apply to purely domestic lobbyism activities whose discriminatory effects completely fall on residents of the respective jurisdiction. Nevertheless, a large number of lobbyism-distorted national or regional competition rules are likely to fall under the nondiscrimination

[53] Of course, the usual objections regarding the imperfection of the domestic political competition apply.

verdict in the course of time – particularly in the face of ongoing market globalisation. To some extent, the nondiscrimination rule can work as an external safeguard against lobbyism bias in antitrust for the downward level competition policy regimes.[54]

A different question is whether the upwardly allocated supervision and resolution mechanisms can be prone to capture. Generally, there is the usual ambivalence to this problem.[55] Obviously, institutional arrangements that strengthen the independence of the upward level authorities could be helpful. Altogether, no compelling reason why lobbyism should easily succeed in capturing the supranational level can be presented.

2.3.5 Adaptability

Since only discriminatory rules and practices are excluded from the menu of theoretically selectable competition rules and practices, no important barriers against a significant variety and diversity of antitrust policies are introduced. Although there are a multitude of discriminatory provisions and practices both in antitrust history and contemporary competition policy regimes, which would all be eroded in an effective international nondiscrimination regime, an indefinite number of possible rule-designs and practice-options remain on the agenda. Additionally, the introduction of new, innovative ones is not hindered in the face of decentralised rule-making and enforcement competences, offering comprehensive scope for parallel experimentation and mutual learning.

The tendency towards harmonisation should be insignificant in the dynamics of a competence allocation according to the nondiscrimination principle. Only if the upward level massively over-interprets its role to identify and eliminate discriminatory rules and practices would harmonising effects occur. This could be the case if it de facto prescribes narrow standards for competition rules and practices that do not violate the (in an excessive way comprehensively defined) nondiscrimination provision. However, such a scenario seems rather unrealistic. However, any extension of the indirectly substantial competences of the supranational level, for instance in the context of conflict resolution and the related extension of its supervision and decision competences (for example, towards a world welfare standard), can increase the likelihood of de facto centralising forces.

---

[54] In a similar way, the GATT and WTO provisions have always been used by politicians as an 'external-pressure' justification against domestic lobbying for protection. Of course, this does not represent a perfect safeguard.

[55] See sections 1.3.4 of Chapter 4 and 2.2.4 of this chapter.

2.4 Best Practice Recommendations and Peer Pressure

2.4.1 Internalisation of external effects

At first glance, it seems doubtful whether a completely informal and voluntary process of interaction can contribute to the internalisation of externalities. However, economic theory provides a rationale for the possible effectiveness of best practice recommendations, combined with peer pressure. Systematic and permanent interaction of competition policy-makers through an informal and voluntary cooperation forum contributes to the generation of common perspectives on antitrust issues (Maher 2002) and a process of cognitive convergence (Tarullo 2000: 495; Budzinski 2004c: 228, 230–231) results, through which jurisdictional conflicts become reduced. Repetitive interaction (potentially) creates substantial trust over time, thereby, stabilising mutual expectations and generating path dependencies as well as routine behaviour. The existence and effectiveness of such phenomena is comprehensively backed by modern experimental economics, in particular, regarding the economic theory of reciprocity and trust.[56] Generally speaking, their results show that repetitive social exchange facilitates and increases stable voluntary cooperation by generating substantial trust among the network members. Deviating, non-cooperative behaviour becomes aggravated because the (experimentally well supported) human preference for fairness and retaliation produces cognitive barriers against such modes of behaviour. However, it is important to emphasise that deviation only becomes impeded, not excluded.

As a consequence, the different national and regional competition policy regimes with their overlapping and concurrent competences might be made more congruent without formally eroding the sovereign competences of the decentralised jurisdictions. Within the cooperative network, cognitive convergence and the stabilisation of mutual expectations can promote the emergence of a 'common competition culture' among the antitrust authorities, facilitating consensual assessments of competition policy standards, rules, and practices. Thus, a variant of (voluntary) bottom-up harmonisation reduces the scope for possible conflicts on competition policy matters and contributes to the internalisation of externalities.

However, the potential of cognitive convergence through cooperative interaction to reduce antitrust conflicts is somewhat limited. It can be supposed in particular that those conflicts which do not involve severe political and non-competition interests become soluble. If conflicts are fuelled by non-competition interests and/or political-economic considerations, the voluntary character of

---

[56] See, for landmark contributions, Güth and Kliemt (1994), Gächter et al. (1996), Güth et al. (1997), and Fehr and Gächter (2000).

the best practice recommendations and the public 'shame effect' (peer pressure) of defection and deviation may be too weak (even in combination) to provide a protective belt against such influences. This is reinforced by the fact that the antitrust authorities (willing-to-cooperate) are predominantly not acting independently of their governments. Without mandatory provisions or binding institutional arrangements, compliance with best practices and peer pressure might be sacrificed to (ostensibly) pressing political issues. This may affect few cases in terms of numbers. However, these few cases are probably the ones with particularly severe impact on international competition like the famous EU–US conflicts on the Boeing–McDonnell Douglas merger and the proposed GE–Honeywell merger.[57]

However, the remaining conflict reduction potential must not be neglected. According to antitrust practitioners, 'pure' antitrust conflicts (without other than competition-oriented arguments) represent a large share of total conflicts about cross-border competition policy cases.[58] Thus, despite not representing a complete solution, a considerable benefit with regard to externalities might be achieved. Eventually, the remaining shortcomings result from the missing switch to a cosmopolitan perspective. In its pure variant, best practice recommendations and peer pressure do not challenge the principal inbound focus of national and regional competition policy regimes.

2.4.2 Efficiency: economies of scale and the one-stop-shop principle

Due to the informality of the competence allocation according to best practice recommendations and peer pressure, a considerable economisation on scale effects seems implausible. However, if a significant tendency towards a best practices harmonisation occurs, the exchange of experiences with the consequently dominating type of law may be facilitated. To some extent, 'switching costs' for law consumers and producers might be reduced along with path-dependencies. Yet, such effects are likely to be limited because of: (1) the fragility of the voluntary harmonisation process; and (2) the problem of legal transplants and their fit into the legal and institutional environment of the respective countries.

Regarding the one-stop-shop principle, no convincing performance can be expected either. The number of competent jurisdictions (concerning a specific cross-border business arrangement or practice) is not reduced. The exceptional case would be if an ambitious best practice recommendation about the sufficient nexus between challenged anticompetitive arrangements and practices and competent competition policy regimes could be consensually agreed

---

57 See section 1.2.2 of Chapter 3 on these conflicting merger cases.

58 See, for example, Schaub (2001). See also the line of argumentation in section 1.2.2 of Chapter 3.

upon, with widespread adoption. Then, an incomplete and imperfect approximation towards a one-stop shop might be possible.

However, even in the absence of such an ambitious nexus principle (whose voluntary and consensual adoption does not seem to be too realistic anyhow), considerable efficiencies with respect to the multiple reviews problem can be realised. In particular concerning merger control issues, an efficiency-enhancing procedural convergence can be achieved. The less ambitious harmonisation of notification requirements, filing prerequisites, time schedules, and so on, as well as the enlarged sharing and exchange of information and deepened cooperation in investigation matters offers significant potentials for increased efficiency regarding two dimensions:

- It decreases administrative costs because the effort of parallel investigating agencies is reduced if these procedures are carried out cooperatively instead of independently from each other.
- The bureaucratic burden, which multijurisdictional merger review imposes on enterprises doing business internationally, becomes reduced, albeit not to zero.

The improvements can be significant, since the increase in transaction costs caused by mere procedural differences of competition policy regimes is particularly deficient because it is not connected to any benefits in terms of an improved protection of competition. Moreover, for the majority of enterprises in international markets, these administrative costs (including legal uncertainty and uncertainty about the definite time schedule of the aggregated review procedure) are even more important than those because of substantive differences (Rowley et al. 2000). The reason is that the vast majority of mergers and alliances (non-hardcore cartels) with effects in different jurisdictional markets do not cause competitive concerns in any jurisdiction and, thus, only face procedural inefficiencies. More often than not, the meaning of mere procedural convergence is neglected or underestimated.

2.4.3 Preference conformity

Competence allocation according to best practice recommendations and peer pressure does not move any binding competences away from the decentralised units on downward levels. Therefore, preference conformity can potentially be fulfilled to an acceptable degree.[59]

---

[59] Again, the usual disclaimer regarding the imperfection of the political systems applies.

This assessment remains valid even in the face of best practice harmonisation. Although the national and regional differences in the design and shape of competition rules and policy practices vanish, no violation of the preference conformity criterion arises. The reason is that harmonisation comes as a consequence of insight and happens on a completely voluntary basis. In the absence of any top-down mandatory enforcement, a bottom-up process of consensual identification of superior solutions and subsequent voluntary adoption follows the (represented) decentralised preferences. Moreover, each jurisdiction can suspend the once-adopted best practices rules and practices at its disposal.

2.4.4 Minimisation of lobbyism

As it is argued above in the context of the conflict reduction potential,[60] the voluntary character of a competence allocation according to best practice recommendations and peer pressure provides no protection against the injection of lobbyism-driven policy strategies and elements into the overall regime. The independence lacked by the participating antitrust authorities creates scope for them to get captured by national and regional interest groups (for instance, via political influence).

However, this applies 'only' to each of the authorities individually. The whole network should be less prone to capture because of its heterogeneous character. One must cast doubts on the success of a strategy to capture all or at least a sufficient number of network participants in order to drive the inherently complex network dynamics towards the benefits of the lobbying group.

2.4.5 Adaptability

At first glance, the competence allocation according to best practice recommendations and peer pressure seems to promote adaptability. Diversity plays an important role and harmonisation is not dictated but evolves bottom-up and without an explicit centralisation of competences. However, a closer look on the sustainable role of diversity reveals that the idea of promoting best rule harmonisation incorporates an inconsistency (Budzinski 2004a: 94–96; 2004c: 233–235).

The combination of best practice recommendations and peer pressure can be viewed as an instrument to promote a beneficial yardstick competition[61] in order to benefit from the dispersed antitrust knowledge and experience of the regional and national competition policy regimes. Yardstick competition between competition policy regimes also takes place without any international coordination. However, its effectiveness is usually restricted and limited due

---

60 See section 2.4.1 of this chapter.

61 See sections 3 of Chapter 3 and 1.1.5 of this chapter. See also Kerber and Budzinski (2003, 2004).

to information deficits and asymmetries about foreign institutions and their comparative efficiency as well as small incentives to imitate superior foreign solutions. Here, the cooperative forum (network) plays an important role in providing information intermediation (best practice recommendations) and imitation incentives (peer pressure). The systematic review of member agencies' practices provides information about the diversity of available options for organising competition policy procedures and, thus, increases transparency. Moreover, the evaluation of the practices facilitates assessments of the relative performance of different institutions and practices. Consequently, the identification and publication of benchmark solutions promotes mutual learning among the agencies and intensifies the institutional yardstick competition. The fact that superior solutions are identified and proposed puts pressure on the member agencies to adopt/imitate these benchmarks and, thereby, improves the diffusion of superior solutions. Thereby, the effectiveness of yardstick competition is enhanced.

However, both from a stationary and an evolutionary perspective, obstacles arise as to whether this organised yardstick competition can fulfil the expectations in terms of providing an instrument in order to optimise on the decentralised knowledge about competition policy without having to bear the costs of centralisation:

- Starting from a stationary perspective, the main obstacle is represented by the question whether overall best practices can actually exist.[62] The participants of the network operate in strongly differing economic and institutional environments. For instance, it seems doubtful that practices, which serve as benchmarks for industrialised countries' competition policy regimes are also superior with regard to antitrust in developing countries or such in transition. Some sort of a 'geography of best practice clusters' would be needed.
- Switching to an evolutionary perspective, the above mentioned inherent inconsistency of the treatment of diversity becomes clear. Yardstick competition via best practice recommendations and peer pressure relies on institutional diversity to identify and select benchmark solutions. It is genuinely the comparative evaluation of the diversity of institutions and practices which constitutes the advantages of best practice identification and subsequent peer pressure harmonisation. However, this diversity only plays a temporary role. Once the best practices are identified, the diversity – which has been so useful up to now – becomes eroded by the process of best rule harmonisation. If the diffusion of

---

62 See – albeit with respect to a different context – Hanushek (2004).

proposed best practices via yardstick competition and peer pressure worked perfectly, the process of mutual learning would cease when all jurisdictions have adopted the best practices and diversity of competition rules and antitrust practices has been replaced by a self-organised harmonisation. The latter may well represent a superior harmonisation strategy but this does not unambiguously imply that paying the price of harmonisation can be avoided.

The eventual erosion of institutional diversity proves costly as soon as once-defined best practices are rendered obsolete by either a changing business environment (new, non-anticipatable anticompetitive arrangements and practices) or a changing academic environment (new theories)[63] – both demanding a responsive adjustment of the acting competition policy regimes (Budzinski 2002c: 121–122, 2003b: 35). However, they then live in an antitrust 'monoculture' with a significant reduction of the number of acceptable alternatives (Maher 2002: 117–118). The flexibility and innovativeness of the best-practice harmonised regime may additionally suffer from a culture of consensus, which develops to be a barrier against innovation (as a departure from the status-quo consensus), and institutional conservatism (Tarullo 2000: 497; Budzinski 2002c, 2003b: 33–36). If a successful best practice harmonisation should occur, such a culture of consensus represents an indispensable ingredient.

In summary, the competence allocation according to best practice recommendations and peer pressure suffers from an inconsistency. If diversity is indispensable to derive best practices, why then erode this source of benefits in the subsequent harmonisation process? As a consequence, institutional evolution does not play a sustainable role in the dynamics of this competence allocation rule. However, the power and realisation probability of completely consensual and voluntary harmonisation forces are rather insecure. Therefore, in practice, the ineffectiveness of best practice recommendations and peer pressure – with a subsequent decay of instituted competence allocation – seems to be at least as likely as the (perhaps more academic) harmonisation variant.

2.5 Principle of Origin and Location Doctrine

2.5.1 Internalisation of external effects

Since according to the location doctrine outbound anticompetitive arrangements and practices fall under domestic jurisdiction, the internalisation of negative externalities is explicitly addressed. Instead of focusing exclu-

---

63 See section 1.3.5 of Chapter 4.

sively on effects on domestic markets, the competent antitrust authorities review a given arrangement or practice with regard to the anticompetitive impacts on all affected markets, irrespective of their territorial location or geographical reach.

Therefore, the location principle offers considerable scope to reduce some of the most important and conflicting competition policy strategies with negative spillover effects. For instance, export cartel exemptions are incompatible with the location principle as are beggar-thy-neighbour strategies in general. With the introduction of a location principle-based competence allocation, the national welfare orientation of the acting antitrust authorities becomes surmounted without the necessity to implement a supranational authority. Moreover, the production of positive externalities is promoted and institutionalised because domestic antitrust authorities must now protect foreign and international markets.

A residual for negative externalities remains if the domestic antitrust authorities apply their own competition rules and procedures to outbound anticompetitive effects. The reason is that, in this case, the level playing field of the foreign countries' market can be distorted. For instance, a domestic vertical arrangement may be prohibited because the respective jurisdictions' competition rules are hostile towards vertical integration and combination. The same arrangement between foreign enterprises, however, may be allowed (without any strategic intention) since it falls under the jurisdiction of their country of origin and, in this country, competition laws may emphasise the efficiency-enhancing effects of vertical combinations and, consequently, the respective authorities do not challenge them (irrespective of whether they are inbound or outbound in direction). In summary, a competence allocation according to the location principle can lead to situations in which similar business arrangements or practices in the same markets are treated differently because of different countries of origin. Thereby, artificial distortions of competition might be generated.

However, as laid out in section 1.2.1 of this chapter, a modest modification of the location doctrine may solve this problem. If domestic antitrust authorities always apply the competition rules of the affected markets, negative externalities of the above described type can be reduced. A merger between two Australian companies with effects on Australian and Japanese markets would be subject to review by the Australian antitrust authorities. They would govern the merger regarding its Australian anticompetitive impact according to Australian competition rules and regarding its Japanese effects according to Japanese competition rules. Of course, this complicates the task of the competent authorities, which have to apply several differing antitrust laws and are in need of the respective expertise. However, since the antitrust authorities of the other affected countries (Japan in my example) should be interested in an effective protection of their domestic markets, this ought to be a classic case for frictionless and conflict-free interagency cooperation. Nevertheless, some inconsistencies remain since the way in which the competition rules of country X are applied by: (1) itself; and (2) the other countries Y and Z may differ markedly.

More severe shortcomings of the conflict-reducing potential of the location doctrine can result from the sensitive role of enforceability. This does not refer to the enforceability of competition rules against anticompetitively behaving enterprises[64] but to the enforceability of a fair outbound perspective of national and regional antitrust authorities. In other words, from an economic perspective it is not trivial to rely on the production of positive externalities by the competent jurisdictions at the non-rewarded benefit for foreign ones.[65] Since only the home authorities of enterprises from a given country are competent to review, modify, and/or challenge an arrangement or practice, the incentives for strategic competition policy are high. Everything depends on the existence of an effective control and sanction mechanism, which guarantees that outbound effects are really treated in the interest of the affected country. Otherwise, anti-contractual (defecting) behaviour may be cheap. Consequently, the addition of extra elements becomes necessary. For instance, a supranational supervision and sanction mechanism – perhaps comparable to the nondiscrimination rule – could serve to safeguard the decentralised application of the location principle.[66]

Eventually, scope for jurisdictional conflicts remains in cases in which the participating enterprises originate from different countries. Then, all countries, which accommodate at least one of the participants, can claim jurisdiction and may derive – according to their domestic rules – conflicting decisions, compulsory modifications, and remedies.

In summary, a location doctrine-based competence allocation offers considerable theoretical scope for the reduction of negative externalities. However, a number of practical shortcomings pour a lot of water into the wine and lead to a more cautious and more conditioned assessment of the conflict-reducing potentials of the location principle.

---

64 Since every antitrust authority exclusively deals with domestic enterprises, this enforceability is comparatively superior because no sovereign actions abroad are involved (as with the effects doctrine, for instance).

65 Incentive problems regarding the location doctrine are also emphasised by Worm (2004: 138–141, 203).

66 However, this reduces one of the advantages of the location doctrine in terms of feasibility and international consensus: the absence of any supranational compulsion. See also section 2.5.4 of this chapter.

2.5.2 Efficiency: economies of scale and the one-stop-shop principle

Since neither a centralisation, nor an accumulation of competition policy competences is induced by a location doctrine-based competence allocation, economies in the production of competition policy cannot be expected.

A one-stop shop results whenever an anticompetitive arrangement or practice with cross-border effects is performed by enterprises from one and the same jurisdiction. This is always the case with the international abuse of market power by one dominating company. For instance, against the background of the location principle, the Microsoft case would have fallen exclusively under the jurisdiction of the US authorities (albeit with them having to take a different perspective on the effects). Furthermore, until now, a significant share of the mergers with cross-border effects consisted of companies from the same country.[67] While the effects doctrine denies a one-stop shop in such cases, the location principle realises it.

However, looking towards likely future developments, it is not too speculative to assume that international anticompetitive arrangements in effect will increasingly be composed of participants from different countries. The vitamins cartels offer a striking example and the increasing involvement and integration of newly industrialised countries further support this hypothesis. If this is true, more often than not a one-stop shop will not be the outcome of a location-principle-based competence allocation. However, the number of jurisdictions competent for a given arrangement or practice should lie considerably below that of an effects-based competence allocation. For instance, an international merger will usually affect a lot more markets than it will involve companies from different countries. This advantage of the location principle should be sustainable.

2.5.3 Preference conformity

With a location doctrine-based competence allocation, competition policy competences remain decentralised and close to the citizens. Apart from the usual disclaimer regarding political deficiencies, a high degree of preference conformity of the jurisdictional competition rules and practices seems plausible.

However, if foreign competition rules must be applied by the domestic antitrust authorities when dealing with outbound anticompetitive arrangements or practices, minor restrictions on the freedom of competition policy design result. Competition policy regimes are not free to handle outbound arrangements between domestic enterprises in the way the citizens would prefer to do so. If outbound arrangements or practices are handled according

---

67 See Table 2.5 in section 2.3 of Chapter 2.

to domestic rules – but with the focus on foreign or international welfare – potential preference conformity is enhanced.

Yet, in this case, a more important drawback results from the impossibility of dealing with inbound anticompetitive arrangements and practices from abroad according to one's own preferences. This would be better fulfilled if the foreign jurisdictions apply domestic rules if the domestic markets are affected. If it is plausible that the protection of competition on domestic markets is more important in the preferences of the citizens than the protection of competition on foreign markets, then the variant in which the countries of origin apply the laws of destination (affect markets) is superior regarding preference conformity.

2.5.4 Minimisation of lobbyism

As argued above in section 2.5.1 of this chapter, the extent of lobbyism is a crucial problem if competition policy competences are allocated and delimitated according to the location principle. The central task is to ensure that antitrust authorities do not misuse their competence to regulate (both anti- and pro-)competitive impacts on foreign or international markets to favour domestic interests at the expense of foreign and/or global welfare. Of course, the conceptual idea demands that antitrust authorities act in the interest of the protection of competition on each affected market and without reference to discriminating or distortionary vested interests. However, the incentive to give in to lobbyistic pressure in the face of a sufficient competence looks quite considerable.

Perhaps, the tendency towards lobbyism bias could be significantly reduced if an international agreement on effective sanctions for defecting behaviour would complement the location principle. Note, however, that this implies the introduction of an upward level with considerable competences – or, in other words, a combination with a nondiscrimination rule or something similar. Thus, this supplement is not trivial. A more modest modification of the competence allocating rule would be to introduce competition agency independence in order to protect the acting antitrust authorities from being influenced by (short-run) vote-maximising politicians. An international agreement on institutionalising and securing competition agency independence might be sufficient to solve the lobbyism problem and would not add considerable centralism.

2.5.5 Adaptability

With regard to adaptability, a location-principle-based competence allocation performs rather similar to an effects-doctrine-based competence allocation. The decentralised competence allocation offers considerable scope for parallel experimentation with different competition rules and practices.

Furthermore, the extraterritorial effects of national and regional competition rules and their application to outbound business arrangements and practices generates an interplay between the jurisdictions, which enhances the incentives for mutual learning via comparative assessments of foreign and domestic solutions.

Yet again, the same qualification as with the effects doctrine must be raised. Among the innovative anticompetitive modes of enterprise behaviour, a considerable number might relate to cross-border restrictive practices and arrangements. Highly decentralised competition policy regimes have significant difficulties dealing with such types of anticompetitive arrangements without creating considerable loopholes. Learning abilities and responsiveness regarding such types of anticompetitive arrangement and practices might be limited, if competence allocation solely depends on the location principle. Furthermore, since interjurisdictional interaction predominantly relies upon jurisdictional conflict, mutual learning entails considerable costs.

2.6 The Relevant Markets Rule

2.6.1 Internalisation of external effects

Since a competence allocation according to the relevant markets rule optimises the geographical congruency between affected markets and jurisdictions, it minimises both negative and positive externalities. The degree of internalisation depends on the way competences for multimarket cases are allocated.[68]

- If the complete multimarket arrangement or practice is reviewed by each competition policy regime, which inhabits at least one of the affected relevant markets, cumulating, conflicting, or incompatible decisions can result.
- If review and decision competences are exclusively allocated to the jurisdiction just covering the largest of the relevant markets, no conflicts emerge. However, the competent jurisdiction is expected to provide positive externalities for the other affected jurisdictions.
- If competences on the multimarket arrangement or practice are split according to a market-based subdivision of the governed business arrangement or practice, a far-reaching internalisation of externalities, which leaves only very limited scope for externalities, can be achieved. Although none of the relevant markets falls under the jurisdiction of

68 See the analysis of dimension III in section 1.2.2 of this chapter.

more than one competition policy regime, the combination of the remedies may, nevertheless, cause accumulations, conflicts, or incompatibilities in rather rare cases.

However, it must be remarked that the analysis of problems stemming from multimarket cases represents an advanced critique. All the other analysed competence allocation rules produce externality problems on far less sophisticated levels of analysis. In summary, therefore, a competence allocation according to the relevant markets rule comparatively internalises externalities to a superior degree. This indicates potential for a *ceteris paribus* maximisation of world welfare.

2.6.2 Efficiency: economies of scale and the one-stop-shop principle

Although the relevant markets rule, if it worked perfectly, could be expected to produce superior results in terms of welfare, a serious practical efficiency concern must be raised. A competence allocation of this type is based on the definition and delimitation of relevant markets. Eventually, geographical relevant markets are the decisive factor but in order for them to be clearly defined, more often than not the definition and delimitation of relevant product markets is also necessary. Despite the existence of elaborated and well-applied quantitative methods (such as the standard small but significant non-transitory increase in price (SSNIP) or hypothetical monopolist test[69]), the delimitation of the relevant markets represents an issue of controversy in significant numbers of antitrust cases. There are a number of reasons for this. First, even with quantitative methods there remains considerable scope for value judgements since available empirical data are incomplete and partly hypothetical. Furthermore, the tests themselves contain arbitrary elements. Secondly, market delineations themselves can be subject to (hardly anticipatably) change in the course of time. Thirdly, the eventual market delineation defines to a significant extent the seriousness of the (anti-)competitive impact.[70]

To decide about the allocation of competences on the basis of a complicate, ambiguous, and controversial criterion, like market delineation, generates considerable costs concerning the subsequent antitrust procedure;[71]

---

69 This test is widely viewed to be a 'conceptual framework'. See the following citations.

70 See, for example, Werden and Froeb (1993), Massey (2000), Häckner (2001), Haldrup (2003), Engel (2004), and Kerber and Schwalbe (2007).

71 Requirements to undertake substantive analysis in order to decide about notification and jurisdiction 'generate considerable uncertainty because market definition is such a subjective, fact-intensive and economics-intensive process – the absolute opposite of what business needs to ascertain legal obligations in time constrained situations', Rowley et al. (2000: 17).

- First, it takes time and effort to derive a thorough market delineation and it remains unclear who shall be responsible for doing this and how the jurisdiction which is competent for market delineation, is determined.
- Secondly, if, in the course of the proceedings, an erroneous market delineation is made (for example, by a court of appeal), the implication is not only a correction of the antitrust authority's decision but a switch in the competent jurisdiction. The complete procedure becomes obsolete and a new one starts from the beginning. Obviously, significant negative effects on transaction costs and procedural efficiency result.

The impracticability of a relevant markets-based competence allocation distorts the otherwise fitting results concerning the one-stop-shop principle.[72] Even regarding multimarket arrangements and practices, a one-stop shop is realised if competences are allocated to the competition policy regime, which just covers the largest among the affected relevant markets. If the arrangement or practice is divided into subcases and competences are accordingly split, a number of smaller one-stop shops result as, technically, the complete case is divided into a number of subcases, which each are reviewed by only one competition policy regime. However, concurrent competences occur if each jurisdiction, which inhabits at least one affected relevant market can claim jurisdiction over the complete case.

2.6.3 Preference conformity

The competent jurisdiction is the one whose territory just covers the geographic extent of the affected relevant market. This implies that all kinds of competition policy competences are allocated as a bundle. Consequently, some centralisation occurs. Jurisdictions on downward, decentralised levels lose competence over anticompetitive arrangements and practices that do affect their internal markets but also the markets of horizontally related ones. This means that local preferences are comprehensively excluded if markets are larger than local. In the course of market globalisation, a dynamic tendency towards centralisation of competences and a process of the erosion of conformity to decentralised preferences cannot be ruled out. Moreover, a growing international bureaucracy with its inherent agency problems is implied.

However, due to the implicit inclusion of the subsidiarity concept, preference conformity is fulfilled in the sense of a comprehensive congruency

[72] This impracticability is the wisdom behind more or less crude proxies for relevant markets like turnover thresholds (see sections 1.1.3 and 2.2 of this chapter) or the X-plus rule (see sections 1.2.3 and 2.7 of this chapter). They are easier to determine and less subject to controversy and produce outcomes which approximately and imperfectly meet the ones of the relevant markets rule.

between the territorial extent of the competent jurisdiction and the affected relevant markets. One can cast doubts on the sense of geographically subdividing preferences within identified relevant markets. Instead, competition on geographically relevant markets can be treated as an indivisible entity. Furthermore, no interjurisdictional restrictions on the individual design of competition rules and practices are introduced. Consequently, local antitrust cases can be governed according to local competition rules and policy practices.

2.6.4 Minimisation of lobbyism

The relevant markets rule does not provide any safeguard against distortionary influence through lobbyism. Looking at the resulting allocation of competition policy competences as a whole, some limiting effects can be expected from the vertical interrelation of different competition policy regimes. On the one hand, it seems implausible for someone to capture the complete competition policy system. On the other hand, balancing effects due to the comparatively close interrelation between supranational, national, and regional jurisdiction may alleviate the impact of singular captures on the overall system.

If competent antitrust authorities get captured by lobbyism, the distortionary effects will predominantly impact on the respective jurisdiction. Cross-border effects from lobbyism can only occur in the case of multimarket arrangements or practices. More precisely, the first (each jurisdiction with domestic affected relevant markets is competent) and the second (the largest affected relevant market determines the competent jurisdiction) variants to deal with multimarket arrangements and practices, offer (albeit) limited scope for lobbyism-biased, not purely inward competition policy strategies. The third one, subdividing the case and splitting competences, reduces this scope significantly.

2.6.5 Adaptability

A competence allocation according to the relevant markets rule includes decentralised competences and a considerable diversity of acting competition policy regimes. Although the process of market internalisation implies an increased upward allocation of cases, diversity and decentralism are unlikely to be comprehensively eroded. As long as regional and local markets still exist, scope for downward level competition policy is maintained. Altogether, a relevant markets-based competence allocation should perform well in terms of adaptability.

However, similar to the analysis of turnover thresholds as a competence allocation rule, tendencies towards top-down harmonisation can result from the deep vertical interrelation of the jurisdictional levels.[73] This represents a non-negligible qualification to the otherwise positive assessment.

[73] See section 2.2.5 of this chapter.

2.7 X-plus Rule

2.7.1 Internalisation of external effects

Competence allocation according to the X-plus rule provides an incomplete and imperfect internalisation of externalities. The idea is that anticompetitive arrangements and practices with cross-border effects should be allocated upwards, whereas other cases should remain on downward levels. As a simple proxy for market affection serves the number of jurisdictions, in which a specific arrangement or practice would be subject to review. If this number exceeds a defined value of X, it is assumed that it generates with a sufficient probability, significant cross-border spillovers which justify its upward allocation.

With reference to an effects doctrine-based competence allocation, this clearly represents an improvement. However, several shortcomings have to be considered:

- Depending on the value of X (assume X > 2), there can be cases where fewer than X countries are affected in terms of review competences but, nonetheless, significant cross-border effects including jurisdictional conflicts emerge. Two affected countries can be enough to generate externalities.
- The other way around, anticompetitive arrangements and practices, which would be subject to review in X or more countries, need not necessarily produce cross-jurisdictional spillovers with regard to the downward level. Assume a merger or an interfirm alliance, which affects three distinct product markets – say, one in Estonia, the second in Portugal, and the third in Ireland – maybe, through three distinct subsidiaries. Assume further that each market is purely regional and X = 3. Although no externalities in terms of market interaction are produced, jurisdiction is allocated to the supranational-regional (here: EU) level because the arrangement would be subject to review in three countries.
- The number of downward level competition policy regimes, which would be competent to review a specific anticompetitive arrangement or practice, depends on the respective national or regional notification and taking up rules. They can differ significantly and need not always refer to rational, sensible and sufficient standards for the nexus between an arrangement's or practice's effects and jurisdiction.

In summary, an X-plus rule-based competence allocation provides considerable internalisation of externalities, albeit not a perfect one. Errors can occur in both directions. Their impact and meaning depends on the value of X and on the notification and taking up thresholds in the downward-level jurisdictions. Very low thresholds would imply that even more virtual market affections generate jurisdiction in the respective countries or regions, whereas more ambitious thresholds contribute to an advanced reduction of spillovers but increase the danger of loopholes (missing jurisdiction over an anticompetitive arrangement or practice due to its dispersed effects). The X-plus rule – in its pure variant – lacks provisions for the horizontal allocation and delimitation of competences, in particular on the downward levels. This clearly must be assessed as a weak point.

2.7.2 Efficiency: economies of scale and the one-stop-shop principle

The X-plus rule is very simple one, which – similar to turnover thresholds (or even beyond them) – has the potential to heal the deficiency of the relevant markets rule in terms of practicability. Its efficiency of application is remarkable.

Economies of scale can probably be reaped to a considerable extent since some centralisation of competences on the upward level will result. Regarding supranational competition policy, the number of cases decided on the international level increase with the number of jurisdictions on the downward level and decrease with an increasing value of X. These efficiency gains through the vertical allocation of competences are not complemented by similar horizontal effects since horizontal competence allocation issues are not addressed.

A one-stop shop is created whenever an anticompetitive arrangement or practice sufficiently affects X or more countries (according to their respective rules, the design of which belonging to their exclusive and decentralised competence) and, consequently, is exclusively allocated upwards to the international level. Arrangements and practices that fail to affect X countries fall under the concurrent jurisdiction of the affected countries (number < X). Obviously, the extent of and the scope for multiple review and concurrent competences sensitively depends on and is effectively limited by the value of X.

2.7.3 Preference conformity

A significant share of antitrust cases become allocated to an upward and more distant level. This implies considerable potential for decreasing preference conformity. However, a number of antitrust cases with predominantly local effects should remain within the decentralised competences of downward levels. Again, the value of X represents the crucial issue. A very small X, in particular when combined with a large number of horizontally interwoven downward jurisdictions, is likely to generate considerable centralising forces, which tend to erode preference conformity. Furthermore, the differing size of the jurisdictions, which can constitute the necessary value of X, creates frictions. If X is met because X large downward level jurisdictions are affected, the consequence for preference conformity is obviously different from the case where X small downward level jurisdictions are affected. Moreover, an asymmetric combination of jurisdictions in order to meet X reinforces the problem that preferences of citizens experience different weights depending on the size of the jurisdiction they inhabit.

Since all competences are allocated as a bundle and no compulsory limitations on rule-making, rule-application and enforcement are introduced, the downward jurisdictions are principally free to design their competition policy regimes according to the preferences of their citizens. Thus, regarding the remaining scope of decentralised antitrust policy, preference conformity should be high. However, if tendencies towards centralisation are strong, comprehensive competition policy competences are allocated upwards to supranational levels, perhaps even marginalising decentralised competition policy regimes on national and infranational levels in the face of market globalisation. A powerful international bureaucracy, including its inherent agency problems, occurs as a consequence.

2.7.4 Minimisation of lobbyism

Competence allocation according to the X-plus rule does not include an explicit safeguard against distortionary influence through lobbyism. However, the scope for lobbyism-biased competition policy strategies is limited because most anticompetitive arrangements and practices with significant cross-border effects are allocated upwardly to a level which comprises the largest affected markets (in geographic terms). However, a residual remains since there can be anticompetitive arrangements or practices with significant cross-border spillovers between less than X downward jurisdictions. Next to the value of X, the performance of the competence allocation depends on the degree to which jurisdictions without a sufficient nexus to the reviewed anticompetitive arrangement of practice are prevented (or, more detailed, bar themselves) from acquiring competences.

It is difficult to assess whether a (centralised) international authority, which is likely to gain a considerable share of (exclusive) competences according to the X-plus rule, is more prone to lobbyistic capture than (decentralised) national or local authorities.[74] Thus, balancing competences between the vertically interrelated levels might be a good idea in order to limit the impact that individual lobby biases can exert on the system as a whole. However, this balance might capsize towards overcentralisation in the course of time. Furthermore, if centralised authorities become captured, then the consequences are more severe than with a more decentralised allocation of competences.

---

74 See on the ambivalence of this problem, section 1.3.4 of Chapter 4.

2.7.5 Adaptability

A competence allocation according to the X-plus rule implies a viable multi-level system with a certain diversity of jurisdictions with own competition rules and practices. This should allow for benefits from parallel experiments and mutual learning. Moreover, permeability and resonance ability for both international and local innovations on anticompetitive modes of behaviour are included. Therefore, adaptability should be rather high.

However, two crucial aspects deserve attention which possess potential to reinforce inherent tendencies towards top-down harmonisation similar to a turnover-threshold-based competence allocation:

- The concrete value of X is decisive for the balance of centralising and decentralising forces. In particular, if X is close to two, considerable dynamics towards centralism can be expected. The subsequent (and maybe creeping) marginalisation of downward competition policy competences incrementally erodes adaptability.
- Missing provisions for the horizontal delimitation of competences in the sense of excluding jurisdiction, which lack a sufficient nexus to the effects of a given anticompetitive arrangement or practice, harm adaptability. The reason is that they enhance the number of decentralised competition policy regimes claiming jurisdiction over a given case and, thus, contribute to a rapid meeting of X (which is not justified in terms of spillovers[75]).

With a sensible X, sustainable scope for national, regional, and local antitrust competences should be maintained and sufficient institutional diversity secured. However, there is a price to pay. Without some binding standards for a sufficient nexus between decentralised, downward level competition policy regimes and the anticompetitive impact of business arrangements and practices, a domination of centralising forces is difficult to prevent. Thus, a harmonisation of notification, filing, and taking up rules – though reducing institutional diversity to some extent – may contribute to preserving diversity of competition regimes, (other) rules, and practices.

2.8 Voluntary Lead Jurisdiction (Advanced Comity Principle)

2.8.1 Internalisation of external effects

Through a competence allocation according to the advanced comity principle, the internalisation of negative externalities is targeted by the definition of a

[75] See section 2.7.1 of this chapter.

lead jurisdiction, whose competition authority acts as a coordinating agency. In doing so, the chosen agency leads and coordinates the review of the respective anticompetitive arrangement or practice with cross-border effects. Its goal is to provide a recommendation that respects the competition interests of each affected jurisdiction and represents a coherent remedy of the anticompetitive concern. Consequently, the leading agency is expected to provide a positive externality (that is, protect the markets of the other affected jurisdictions).

If the advanced comity principle worked smoothly, the reduction of negative externalities should be considerable. The lead jurisdiction as a mediator can reduce conflict potentials by providing a fair compromise for diverging interests in a specific case. However, it must weigh its own interests equally to each foreign jurisdictional interest, which might be a quite optimistic assumption, in particular if the respective antitrust authority is not independent from other policy instances. From an economic perspective, the incentive to provide this positive externality represents a crucial aspect. The reward of the lead jurisdiction could be the expectation that, in other cases, the interacting jurisdictions will behave reciprocally when they are assigned the leading role. Particularly in multistage games, patterns of mutual cooperation and trust may emerge.[76] However, the emergence and prevalence of a cooperative trajectory is not guaranteed since trajectories with domination of mutual defection also represent equilibrium solutions.[77]

The lack of compulsory and mandatory elements casts shadows over the likelihood of diminishing conflicts and negative externalities. If more than one country believes itself to have vital interests in governing a specific business arrangement or practice, it will be difficult to achieve consensus on the leading agency. Moreover, the selection criterion 'best equipped agency in terms of enforcement' (see section 1.2.4 of this chapter) does not exclude ambiguity. Even if a leading authority is selected and even if it fulfils its coordination and recommendation task, the adoption of the recommended remedies and sanctions remains voluntary. Again, this offers scope for defecting behaviour by the participating authorities, whether it be due to deviating opinions and competition interests, or whether it be due to political or other non-competition influences.[78]

---

76 Again Güth and Kliemt (1994), Gächter et al. (1996), Güth et al. (1997), and Fehr and Gächter (2000) offer the relevant theoretical insights regarding the economics of trust and reciprocity, combined with experimental and laboratory evidence. An optimistic game-theoretic model of the emergence of stable cooperative equilibria (mutual concession equilibrium) is provided for international merger control by Cabral (2003, 2004). Although the type of cooperation is not specified in these papers, limited analogies to the lead jurisdiction concept (advanced comity principle) can be drawn.

77 See also section 1.3.2 of Chapter 3.

78 The analysis in Chapter 3 clearly demonstrates that conflicting assessments

In summary, a theoretically high potential becomes contrasted with doubts about practical workability. Only cross-border antitrust cases, which do not involve serious national or regional interests, are likely to profit from improved governance if competence allocation follows the described advanced comity principle.

2.8.2 Efficiency: economies of scale and the one-stop-shop principle

Cost efficiency gains from an advanced comity-principle-based competence allocation include the significant reduction of multiple efforts by the reviewing antitrust authorities. If nothing else, the coordinating agency improves the information exchange and renders parallel administrative action regarding investigation, fact finding, and so on, unnecessary on a large scale. This may represent a significant improvement for taxpayers but also for enterprises facing notification and filing fees.

Additionally, reviewed enterprises gain a central agency to which they turn and with which they negotiate. Regarding the proceedings, a one-stop shop becomes realised – or at least something very close to it. However, it remains an imperfect one-stop shop due to the non-binding character of the final recommendation by the leading agency. The other participating authorities can join the recommended decision but are also free to refuse and impose their own sanctions and remedies. A coherent treatment of a given cross-border business arrangement or practice becomes more likely but not guaranteed and may be difficult to expect ex ante. Much depends on the degree of cooperation between the antitrust authorities.

As with economies of scale, the rule, according to which the relatively best equipped agency shall be assigned the leading role, should lead to concentration of coordination tasks at a small number of big competition policy regimes. In terms of investigation and review techniques, economies can be realised. Regarding enforcement (and appeal), economies can be reaped if more often than not the participating authorities accept the recommendations of the lead jurisdiction and waive their own enforcement actions. However, the extent of this remains insecure.

2.8.3 Preference conformity

If the advanced comity principle worked perfectly, preference conformity would be fulfilled. Ideally, the leading agency coordinates the reviews of the

---

by decentralised antitrust authorities can result from very different reasons, including adherence to different competition economics, asymmetrical effects on different countries, and differing judgements about imprecise and insecure (because future-oriented) expectations about market dynamics and developments. Even without strategic interests, defecting behaviour can occur.

decentralised competition policy regimes in a frictionless way and compiles a decision recommendation, which respects the preferences of each participating regime. Furthermore, the freedom of the claiming jurisdiction over a given anticompetitive arrangement or practice is not limited, wherefore participation in the coordinated review procedure is not externally excluded.

However, as soon as the participating jurisdictions perform according to mutually incompatible preferences, it becomes an impossible task for the coordinating agency to generate a common decision recommendation, which fulfils each jurisdiction's preferences. In practice, therefore, either some limitations to preference conformity occur or the competence allocation rule will fail to produce significant effects at all.

Apart from the problems of compatibility and coherence of the coordinated outcome, competences principally remain decentralised and comparatively close to the citizens. This is particularly true for rule-making and application competences (including the freedom for locally preferred limits of competition), whereas enforcement competences are partly transferred to the leading agency according to the 'best equipped criterion' for the selection of the lead jurisdiction – albeit on a voluntary basis. If the eventual governance outcome is in the interest of the non-leading jurisdiction, this improved enforcement power serves its preferences. If not, an adoption of the recommended sanctions and remedies would reduce preference conformity.

2.8.4 Minimisation of lobbyism

Since no international level or supranational authority is introduced, lobbyism remains an issue with which the national and regional competition policy regimes each have to deal on their own. This implies that an international protection against local biases is lacking. If a national or regional antitrust authority is entitled to be the coordinating jurisdiction, it also becomes obliged to abstain from a national or regional focus. Instead, the legitimate interests of foreign jurisdictions should be equally taken into account. However, lobbyistic capture can render such a stance improbable. Without sufficient independence of decentralised competition policy authorities, lobbyism is likely directly or indirectly (via vote-maximising politicians) to distort the cooperative process.

2.8.5 Adaptability

A competence allocation based on the advanced comity principle performs well in regard to adaptability. Since competences are only temporarily allocated to (and concentrated at) one leading agency, the diversity of institutions and practices is not too limited. It is essential, however, that a considerable number of decentralised competition policy regimes qualify as lead jurisdiction from time to time and no monopoly or duopoly of possible lead jurisdictions emerges.

The process of mutual learning is promoted by the intense interaction of competition policy regimes. The coordinating agency (lead jurisdiction) is obliged to consider effects on foreign markets according to the institutions and policies of the competent jurisdictions. Similarly, the participating jurisdictions interact with the coordinating agency and learn about their institutions and practices as well as about the ones of the other participating jurisdictions. Thus, transparency about different goals, institutional arrangements and antitrust practices is enhanced and incentives for mutual learning are improved.

The doubts regarding the workability of the voluntary cooperation do not principally disturb adaptability since no centralising force results – neither from the decay of cooperation, nor from stable and sound cooperation. In summary, a positive assessment can be derived.

2.9 Mandatory Lead Jurisdiction Model

2.9.1 Internalisation of external effects

According to this advanced type of lead jurisdiction model, the competence to select the lead jurisdiction is allocated to the supranational level. An international authority identifies the jurisdiction whose markets bear the most severe (anti-)competitive impact of a given cross-border business arrangement or practice and assigns the exclusive competence to deal with this case to this jurisdiction. By implementing an exclusive competence over antitrust cases with cross-border effects, conflicts on antitrust become reduced. At least, this covers conflicts in terms of contradicting or cumulating decisions, sanctions, and remedies of decentralised antitrust authorities. However, it does not exclude conflicts in terms of a lack of satisfaction and explicit disagreement of an also-impacted jurisdiction with the way the case is handled by the lead jurisdiction. More importantly, the inclusion of negative externalities in terms of welfare reducing effects in also-impacted countries is not secured.

Whether the lead jurisdiction, which is selected by the international authority, manages to avoid negative externalities, depends on its ability and willingness to provide positive externalities. In other words, the competent jurisdiction must internalise spillover effects by protecting also-affected foreign markets with the same rigour as its domestic markets. Ideally, the selected lead jurisdiction should review and govern a given anticompetitive arrangement or practice according to its world welfare implications. In doing so, it is expected to provide a good for the other jurisdictions without being directly rewarded. An incentive problem may result.

The crucial aspect is supervision. In the pure variant, the mandatory lead jurisdiction model does not include a supervision and sanction mechanism, which is implemented on the international level. If dissatisfied also-impacted jurisdictions had a chance to appeal a lead jurisdiction's decision[79] and if the international agency had (additional) supervision and/or sanction mechanisms[80] against defecting lead jurisdictions, the performance of the resulting competition policy system in terms of the externality criterion would be significantly improved.

2.9.2 Efficiency: economies of scale and the one-stop-shop principle

A competence allocation according to the mandatory lead jurisdiction model offers scope for significant economies of scale. The reason is that a process of concentration of antitrust procedures is likely to occur. Following the 'share-of-consumption' test,[81] jurisdictions with big domestic markets and large numbers of domestic consumers are most likely to 'attract' considerable numbers of cross-border antitrust cases. It is not difficult to imagine an oligopolistic structure of the 'market for lead jurisdiction' as a consequence. Dynamic diseconomies, like lock-in effects, are less likely unless a monopolistic structure results.

The performance of a mandatory lead jurisdiction model-based competence allocation concerning the one-stop-shop principle is remarkably good. Business arrangements and practices with cross-border effects are reviewed and treated by one single competition policy regime and its competent antitrust authority. Concurrent substantive competences are effectively excluded.

2.9.3 Preference conformity

Each jurisdiction on the downward levels sustains its competences to design and shape its own competition rules and antitrust practices. However, whether it can apply its rules to a given anticompetitive arrangement or practice depends in cases with cross-border effects on the decision of the international panel. In the pure variant of the primary effects clause, the jurisdiction which is most severely impacted, is appointed as the lead jurisdiction and gains exclusive competences. The also-affected competition policy regimes participate in the proceedings as the lead jurisdiction attempts to include their interests and competitive concerns in review and decision. However, they cannot secure preference conformal outcomes by themselves any more. Note that in particular preferences for non-competition elements or preferences for non-

[79] This could imply having an international instance of appeals. However, this would introduce a number of additional problems, for example, regarding the substantive standards and laws according to which the authority should decide.

[80] For instance, defecting lead jurisdiction could be banned from being appointed as a lead jurisdiction.

[81] See section 1.2.5 of this chapter.

mainstream theories or techniques – whether outdated or innovative – are likely to be neglected by a lead jurisdiction, which focuses on world welfare and current standards.[82]

Limits to preference conformity may be particularly marked for small jurisdictions with few consumers as they: (1) are probably seldom appointed to serve as lead jurisdiction; and (2) experience relatively few purely domestic antitrust cases without cross-border effects. Consequently, the dependence on benevolent decisions by other jurisdictions becomes comparatively strong.

2.9.4 Minimisation of lobbyism

Lobbyistic capture of a national or regional antitrust authority becomes particularly severe within a competence allocation according to the primary effects clause if the captured agency is the one of the lead jurisdiction. Compared to other international competition policy systems, which rely on national and regional decision-making, direct or indirect lobbyism-bias of antitrust policy is neither more, nor less likely. However, due to the exclusive competence and responsibility of an appointed lead jurisdiction, no correction mechanism exists – whether through concurrent competences or through an upward level supervision. Additionally, the concentration of powers over a given case at one downward jurisdiction and the absence of error tolerance makes influence more interesting and rewarding for non-benevolent politicians or regulated enterprises.

However, referring to the system as whole, incomplete relief can be drawn from the facts that: (1) the selected lead jurisdiction changes from case to case; and (2) the jurisdiction is selected which is inhabited by most of the affected consumers (and not the one where the anticompetitively acting enterprises are located). If the conjecture is plausible that national and regional authorities are more prone to capture by local residents than by foreigners, the interests of the consumers have some likelihood of outweighing lobbyism-bias. According to economic theory, an ambivalent assessment of the question whether the international competence allocation panel may be more prone to lobbyism-bias than national and regional efforts remains.[83]

2.9.5 Adaptability

Although each cross-border anticompetitive arrangement and practice is handled by only one antitrust authority, the limitations of regime diversity are comparatively negligible. The reason is that the exclusively competent jurisdiction is not located at an upward, centralised (global) level but on down-

[82] It would be even more problematic, if the lead jurisdiction itself adheres to dubious practices.

[83] See section 1.3.4 of Chapter 4.

ward, decentralised (national and regional) levels. Consequently, there is diversity of decentralised competition policy regimes, which potentially all qualify to be lead jurisdiction from time to time. Thus, exclusive competence over cross-border effects is case-specific and temporary. Different anticompetitive arrangements and practices cause differing impacts on jurisdiction-internal markets, wherefore different regimes with differing institutions and practices will become competent in the course of time.

Mutual learning is promoted by the interaction of the temporarily and case-specifically competent jurisdictions with the also-impacted ones. Thereby, transparency of the diversity of institutions and practices itself as well as of comparative performances of these institutions and practices is enhanced. Interacting decentralised competition policy regimes experience the advantages and disadvantages of other (lead) jurisdictions' competition rules and antitrust practices because they affect domestic competition. The changing lead jurisdiction and the absence of restrictions on the decentralised competition policy regimes by the upward level (which has no substantive competences) offer numerous channels for the injection of antitrust innovations and ensure considerable flexibility for the international competition policy system as a whole.

However, the need for a qualification occurs, if the 'market for lead jurisdiction' becomes rather narrow. According to the primary effects clause, the 'most impacted' jurisdiction is the one with the largest share-of-consumption of the anticompetitively affected goods market(s).[84] This favours downward level jurisdictions with large internal markets and high numbers of consumers over small market economies when it comes to the appointment of lead jurisdictions. In the face of an increasing market globalisation, this could imply an oligopoly of jurisdictions, with the oligopolists being the only jurisdictions regularly selected to serve as lead jurisdiction. In an extreme case, a duopoly of the US and the EU could be imaginable.[85] This would reduce de facto diversity.

[84] See section 1.2.5 of this chapter.

[85] However, upcoming global players like China, India, Russia, or Brazil as well as smaller but self-confident antitrust jurisdictions like Australia, Japan, Korea, Canada, or Germany render this scenario not too realistic. See also, generally, Drexl (2005) and with respect to the antitrust ambitions of specific ones of the listed countries Doern (1996a), Sanekata and Wilks (1996), Clark (2000), Hellmann (2001), Lee (2002), Hutchins (2004), Letin (2004), Reynolds (2004), Bhattacharjea and Nanda (2005), First and Shiraishi (2005), Owen et al. (2005), and Williams (2005).

3. A COMPARATIVE CONCLUSION

The results of the preceding analysis are summarised in Table 5.1. Assessed against each other, the performance of the stylised competence allocation rules is presented according to each economic criterion. The order of the respective evaluations can be explained in the following way.

3.1 Internalisation of External Effects

Regarding the internalisation-of-externalities criterion and spillover effects, a competence allocation according to the relevant markets rule offers the best performance. If the competent jurisdiction exactly covers the relevant geographic market affected by the anticompetitive arrangement or practice, then the antitrust authority with the most comprehensive incentives to objectively include all welfare effects in its analysis becomes exclusively competent.[86] Next best in performance are the competence allocation rules, which represent proxies of the relevant markets rule, namely turnover thresholds and the X-plus rule. Being imperfect proxies for allocating competences according to geographically relevant markets, the derived competence allocations produce a manageable number of misallocations. Consequently, internalisation of externalities is imperfect but, nonetheless, significantly high. It is difficult to assess which one of the two proxies is better suited to approximate affected markets. If the downward level consists of national competition policy regimes and the upward one of international ones, the X-plus rule may serve in a better way to indicate an effect on interstate commerce or trade. If a specific anticompetitive arrangement or practice affects markets in X or more countries, then interstate effects seems rather plausible. This nexus seems less stringent in the case of turnover thresholds, handing an advantage to competence allocation according to the X-plus rule. However, this advantage crucially depends on the taking up rules in the decentralised national competition policy regimes. If they allow for rather virtual market effects to constitute jurisdiction, misallocations become more frequent with the X-plus rule and the latter might become inferior to a two-tiered threshold.[87] In summary,

[86] As this jurisdiction may have deficient competition rules and antitrust proceedings, no welfare optimum is guaranteed. However, since there is no such thing as an unambiguously and ultimately 'right' antitrust policy derivable from an 'always-and-everywhere true', scientific competition theory, this residual imperfection is unavoidable in an indeterministic and imperfect world with (at best) subjectively rational and cognitively restricted human beings. See section 1.3.5 of Chapter 4.

[87] However, this effect applies to the stylised variant and may be healed rather easily by an harmonisation of standards for a sufficient nexus between a market effect and jurisdiction.

competence allocation according to turnover thresholds tends to produce more externalities on downward levels (through multiple reviews) than one according to the X-plus rule.

Different from the preceding three rules, the nondiscrimination rule and the mandatory lead jurisdiction model do not include an upward allocation of rule-making, rule-applying, and direct enforcement competences. Instead, the global level 'only' carries out a coordinating function. The nondiscrimination rule provides a limited coordination in terms of coordination objects ('discriminatory rule and practices only'), whereas the mandatory lead jurisdiction model implies an advanced coordination by appointing a fully competent and responsible lead jurisdiction. This advantage of the mandatory lead jurisdiction model, however, is compensated by the superior (though indirect) enforcement competence implied by the nondiscrimination rule. In the latter case, supervision and sanction competences are allocated upwards.

A competence allocation according to the mandatory lead jurisdiction model, instead, depends on the production of positive externalities in order to prevent negative external effects. From an economic perspective, this implies a considerable incentive problem (public goods problem, PD) and, consequently, raises severe doubts in terms of practicability and effectiveness. This is why the performance of competence allocation relying on positive spillover effects is assessed to represent a disadvantage in Table 5.1. The production of positive externalities is also expected from competent jurisdictions and agencies in competence allocations according to the location principle, best practice recommendations and peer pressure, and the advanced comity principle (lead jurisdiction model I). However, these competence rules differ regarding the rewards (also in terms of sanctions) provided for cooperating or defecting jurisdictions. The mandatory lead jurisdiction model includes a compulsory coordination of potentially competent jurisdiction. Competence allocations according to best practices and peer pressure as well as the advanced comity principle introduce voluntary and cooperative coordination. While the first is advantageous in regard to institutionalising superior informal compliance pressure, the latter is advantageous in terms of effectively reducing the number of jurisdictions that must be coordinated (case-by-case basis instead of all-including). Eventually, the location principle relies on an uncoordinated and unilateral production of positive externalities, thus, implying the lowest degree of compliance security. Additionally, anticompetitive arrangements between enterprises from different jurisdictions create completely uncoordinated concurrent competences, which may generate additional negative externalities.

The effects doctrine is more likely to produce additional negative externalities than contributing to internalisation. Since the number of affected markets is generally larger than the number of countries of enterprise origin, the performance of an effects doctrine-based competence allocation is significantly disadvantageous even if compared to a location principle-based one.

3.2 Cost Efficiencies

Regarding the efficiency criterion (one-stop-shop principle as well as static and dynamic economies of scale), the performance of competence allocations according to the mandatory lead jurisdiction model is superior. One single competition authority, selected and appointed by the international panel, provides a one-stop governance of a given anticompetitive arrangement or practice with cross-border effects. Since large shares of cross-border antitrust cases will have their primary effects in a small number of jurisdictions with large numbers of consumers, scale economies can also be reaped to a significant extent.

Also comparably efficient are competence allocations according to relatively simple, uncontroversial, and unambiguous quantitative criteria, like turnover thresholds or the X-plus rule. Both competence allocation rules induce a considerable process of centralisation, which offers an economisation on fixed costs as well as a comparably complete one-stop shop. Deficiencies arise in regard to multiple reviews on downward levels. Although their extent and inadequacy depends on the concrete design of the two rules, it seems impossible to exclude them completely. Yet, the X-plus rule more strictly reduces multiple reviews because multiple reviews themselves automatically induce an upward allocation of competences. In other words, competence allocation according to the X-plus rule effectively limits multiple reviews to X, whereas turnover thresholds do not implement a comparable safeguard.

A similar assessment (like the latter one) can be derived for voluntary lead jurisdiction-based competence allocation. To the extent of its smooth workability, the cooperative selection of a lead jurisdiction, with its authorities playing the role of a coordinating agency, allows for comparable efficiencies. Compared to turnover thresholds and the X-plus rule, the advanced comity principle offers the advantage of providing a one-stop shop for all cases but the disadvantage that this one-stop shop is an imperfect one, relying on voluntary compliance to the suggestions of the coordinating jurisdiction by the other ones involved. Furthermore, economies of scale might be reaped because of the best equipped rule for the identification of the appropriate lead jurisdiction, which implies that certain jurisdictions are likely to be much more often selected as lead jurisdiction than other ones.

The efficiency potentials of a competence allocation according to best practice recommendations and peer pressure must also be assessed positively. The induced voluntary 'best-rule harmonisation' process significantly reduces administration and transaction costs in particular concerning procompetitive or unproblematic arrangements and practices. However, the lack of both a true vertical structure (with a more than virtual upward level) and a lead jurisdiction cannot be compensated by harmonising procedural rules and practices in terms of scale economies and one-stop-shop principle.

Three other competence allocation rules – the effects doctrine, the nondiscrimination rule, and the location principle – offer very similar performances with regard to efficiency. None of them possesses considerable potentials concerning economies of scale and/or an approaching of the one-stop-shop principle. The better assessment of the location doctrine compared to the other two is due to its one-stop-shop character with regard to anticompetitive modes of behaviour by a market dominating enterprise. Such types of restraints to competition with cross-border effects fall exclusively under the jurisdiction of the misbehaving enterprise's country of origin – allowing for limited efficiency gains.

Eventually, the most negative assessment hits competence allocation according to the relevant markets rule. Rooting competence allocation and delimitation on such a complex, controversial, and ambiguous criterion, which represents an important and integral part of the competitive assessment of a given arrangement or practice itself, implies severe deficiencies. It is difficult to see how they might be solved to a significant extent.

3.3 Preference Conformity

No limitations of potential preference conformity appear in competence allocation according to best practice recommendations and peer pressure because participation and adoption is completely voluntary. Only if it complies with the preferences of its citizens, will a decentralised jurisdiction join the convergence process. Additionally, each participating jurisdiction can leave the process at any given time. Only small and maybe insignificant limitations occur if either the effects doctrine (regarding outbound arrangements) or the nondiscrimination rule (predominantly regarding strategic competition policies) governs competence allocation.

A comparably good performance can also be expected from the location doctrine. However, it is disadvantageous when compared to the preceding three competence allocation rules because – depending on its design – either problems regarding inbound arrangements or regarding outbound arrangements occur.[88] A comparable assessment results for the voluntary lead jurisdiction principle. Although theoretically almost no limitations are implied, effectiveness of the coordination efforts practically demands restrictions on the preferences of at least some of the participating jurisdictions except when all preferences are mutually compatible.

---

[88] See section 2.5.3 of this chapter.

All of the precedingly discussed competence allocation rules have an advantageous common feature. Limitations of preference conformity only originate from the (coordinated or not) interaction of the decentralised jurisdictions. There is no mandatory transfer of competition policy competences, neither horizontally from one jurisdiction to another, nor vertically to an upward, suprajurisdictional level. In other words, no real international level with forceful competences is introduced. This is different with the following competence allocation rules, which, therefore, depart from decentralised preferences.

A comparably modest type is represented by competence allocation according to the mandatory lead jurisdiction model. Here, the only competence allocated upwards to an international level is the competence to select the lead jurisdiction. The other competition policy competences (rule-making, enforcement) remain decentralised, although their application is limited.[89] In comparison, the relevant markets rule allocates comprehensive competition policy competences upwards if the extent of the relevant geographic market exceeds the territory of a downward jurisdiction. Although this jurisdiction on a decentralised level remains affected, it loses all competences to deal with this case according to its citizens' preferences. However, if competition on the relevant market is treated as an indivisible entirety, further sub-separations of preferences might be doubtful.

Eventually, turnover thresholds and the X-plus rule each limit preference conformity significantly because considerable processes of centralisation are likely to occur. During these dynamics, all kinds of competition policy competences are incrementally transferred to an international level while national and regional competition policy regimes become marginalised. An additional disadvantage of a turnover threshold-based competence allocation – when compared to the X-plus rule – occurs with the two-tiered threshold, which excludes some of the remaining decentralised competences. On the other hand, if the decentralised jurisdiction attempts to utilise this advantage (that is, claiming jurisdiction even if there is no sufficient nexus to a given anticompetitive arrangement or practice) in an X-plus rule-based competence allocation, centralising forces become strengthened and the continuous loss of competences accelerated. The assessment is further aggravated by the considerable probability with which both competence allocation rules induce and promote efforts to horizontal harmonisation on the downward level.[90] In the

[89] Concerning a given anticompetitive arrangement or practice, only the lead jurisdiction applies competition rules. However, it can also apply foreign ones. See section 2.9 of this chapter.

[90] The EU competition policy system offers a vital example. See section 2.2 of Chapter 4.

end, differences in the performance of these two competence allocation rules seem to be insignificant.

3.4 Minimisation of Lobbyism

The difficulty of assessing the potential of competence allocation rules to cope with the thread of distortionary influence from lobbyism relates to ambivalent results from economic theory.[91] There are arguments supporting the hypothesis that decentralisation restricts scope for lobbyism. There are contrary arguments, which promote the hypothesis that centralisation restricts scope for lobbyism. If the first hypothesis dominates, similar results to the preference conformity criterion follow. If the second one prevails, opposite assessments must be made. However, a decisively different issue is the ability and extent of lobbyism-induced home bias. In other words, the impact of lobbyism–bias on the overall competition policy system is assessed under the assumption that each country's antitrust authorities are similarly prone to capture.

In doing so, the nondiscrimination rule limits distortionary lobbyism most effectively through its internationally supervised ban of all discriminatory competition rules and antitrust practices. Competence allocations according to turnover thresholds, the relevant markets rule, or the X-plus rule might be assessed to perform as the second best – albeit by a considerable distance. The idea is that they balance competition policy competences between decentralised levels with authorities that are 'close to the markets' and more centralised levels with authorities that are less prone to local interests.

The other competence allocation rules are even less capable of dealing with distortionary influence through lobbyism. This particularly concerns competence allocation rules, which allow competent jurisdictions to exert power over foreign ones. For instance, the lead jurisdiction models entitle one jurisdiction to decide on behalf of other affected ones. Regarding the advanced comity principle, the incentive for lobbyism bias is slightly alleviated by the voluntary character of the coordinating agency's recommendations. In comparison, the case seems to be more serious for the mandatory lead jurisdiction model. The primarily affected jurisdiction becomes exclusively competent to deal with a given anticompetitive arrangement or practice. If it becomes captured by local interests, then it can force the resulting bias upon the also-affected jurisdictions. However, an alleviation is provided by the fact that 'most impacted' is measured according to the impact on consumers and, thus, a usually poorly organised group, which generally does not represent a strong lobby force.

---

[91] See section 1.3.4 of Chapter 4.

The latter line of argumentation hints to serious lobbyism problems for the overall competition policy system if the home authorities of powerful lobbyism forces like big enterprises and their associations are – more or less exclusively – competent to review this enterprises' outbound (anti-)competitive behaviour. However, this is the competence allocation resulting from the location doctrine. The effects doctrine encounters an only slightly milder assessment hit. It also provides incentives to engage in lobbyism-biased antitrust strategies. However, its inbound focus requires a more indirect stance towards those kinds of strategies and introduces a case for consumers' interests.

Eventually, the performance of competence allocation according to best practice recommendations and peer pressure regarding the lobbyism criterion is comparatively neutral. On the one hand, no explicit safeguard against distortions from lobbyism exist. On the other hand, the systematic interaction of antitrust authorities with its reciprocity effects should make individual antitrust authorities less prone to lobbyism-biased influences. An informal external pressure to abstain from such influences exists which, however, cannot guarantee their effective exclusion.

It must be emphasised, however, that decentralised safeguards against lobbyistic capture represent the most effective, efficient, and important instruments in this context. They can consist of an independence of competition policy authorities from vote-maximising governments, comprehensive competences for independent courts, or other institutional arrangements. If such decentralised safeguards were implemented, only insignificant differences between the analysed competence allocation rules in regard to the lobbyism criterion would prevail.

3.5 Adaptability

Regarding the evolutionary criterion of adaptability to changes in the market and business environment as well as with regard to scientific knowledge about competition and antitrust, the two lead jurisdiction models provide the most promising performance. Advantages include the changing lead jurisdiction and strong incentives for mutual learning. The latter would be further improved, however, if non-benevolent behaviour of an appointed lead jurisdiction was supervised or sanctioned in some way.

The nondiscrimination rule owes its slightly less positive assessment to the fact that it explicitly excludes a considerable number of competition policy strategies (rule designs, practices, and so on). However, as argued in section 2.3.5 of this chapter, it leaves open-ended, room for other competition policy options, including the creation of innovative ones. Additionally, competence allocation according to the nondiscrimination rule promotes mutual learning through interjurisdictional interaction via the supervision, complaint, and resolution mechanism – albeit incompletely because it is restricted to conflicts due to discrimination.

Principally, the effects doctrine and the location doctrine also offer a large variety of different competition policy designs and the implementation of antitrust innovations is also not restricted. However, the incentives for mutual learning are considerably weaker and, moreover, entail significant costs since jurisdictional conflicts represent a major driving force. Similarly, though for differing reasons, competence allocation according to the relevant markets rule principally provides sufficient scope for institutional diversity and innovation. Even in the face of ongoing market globalisation, the prevalence of regional and local markets is rather probable, securing a sustainable coexistence of different competition policy regimes on vertically interrelated levels of jurisdiction. Disturbance of adaptability occurs, however, as soon as the balance between centralism and decentralism of the vertical allocation of competences becomes eroded, for instance, in the course of top-down harmonisation efforts.

The danger of a dominance of centralising forces in the course of time, leading towards harmonisation, is stronger regarding such competence allocations that rely on proxies for geographically relevant markets. An X-plus rule based competence allocation requires some harmonisation on downward levels in order to prevent strong centralising dynamics. Turnover thresholds, which are nominally defined and static, also favour processes of centralisation. If the scope for decentralised competition policy competences on downward levels becomes incrementally omitted, however, incentives to learn from these regimes as well as incentives to implement innovative institutional solutions or incentives become eroded.

Best practice recommendations and peer pressure as a stylised competence allocation rule, receive the least favourable assessment. This might be subject to controversy since the prospects of considerable dynamics towards bottom-up harmonisation can be seriously doubted. However, harmonisation in the variant of 'best practice harmonisation' represents an important goal with all the major benefits of this competence allocation rule relying on cognitive, procedural, and eventually substantive convergence. The way it is stylised here, competence allocation according to best practice recommendations and peer pressure represent an innovative avenue towards comprehensive harmonisation, avoiding several shortcomings of the 'uniform worldwide competition policy regime' approach.[92] Nevertheless, it does represent an ambitious harmonisation approach.

---

[92] See section 2 of Chapter 3.

Table 5.1 Comparative evaluation of stylised competence allocation rules I

Stylised competence allocation rule	Externalities	Efficiency	Preference conformity	Lobbyism	Adaptability
Effects doctrine	- - -	- -	++	- -	+
Turnover thresholds	+(+)	+	- -	+	0
Nondiscrimination rule	+	- -	++	+++	++
Best practice recommendations and peer pressure	0	0	+++	0	- -
Location doctrine	-	-	+	- - -	+
Relevant markets rule	+++	- - -	0	+	+
X-plus rule	++	++	- -	+	0
Advanced comity principle	0	+	+	0	+++
Mandatory lead jurisdiction model	+	+++	0	0	+++

Note: {---; . . .; +++} ≈ {--- 3; . . .; 3}

Table 5.1 shows that the mandatory lead jurisdiction model represents the relatively best performing competence allocation rule with the nondiscrimination rule following closely. At the other end of the scale, the relatively disadvantageous performance of both effects doctrine-based and location doctrine-based competence location can be noticed, with the remaining competence rules somewhere in between.

For illustration only, Table 5.2 presents an average score for each competence allocation rule, whereby each criterion carries the same weight of 0.2. This illustration should not be interpreted as a serious quantification and serves only to enhance transparency. It would be very problematic to derive equal weights for each criterion from the analysis in this book. However, the same would be true for any other distribution of weights. It must be noted and emphasised that the value of the analysis in this chapter does not lie in creating a combined quantitative score. Instead, the differentiated insights on advantages and disadvantages as well as prospects and limits of stylised competence allocation rules represents the targeted scientific progress.

The analysis in this chapter provides important insights into the working mechanisms and inherent dynamics of multilevel systems of institutions. Against the background of its results, an international competition policy system as a multilevel system, which combines the advantages of centralism and decentralism, can now be described. Doing so, however, demands a departure from the stylisations and simplifications of the preceding analysis. Each stylised competence allocation rule that is subject to the preceding analysis may be modified, combined with elements from other ones, and comple-

Table 5.2 Comparative evaluation of stylised competence allocation rules II

Stylised competence allocation rule	Score (if each criterion deserves the weight 0.2)
Effects doctrine	– 0.8
Turnover thresholds	+ 0.3
Nondiscrimination rule	+ 1.2
Best practice recommendations and peer pressure	+ 0.2
Location doctrine	– 0.6
Relevant markets rule	+ 0.4
X-plus rule	+ 0.6
Advanced comity principle	+ 1.0
Mandatory lead jurisdiction model	+ 1.4

Note: {---; . . .; +++} ≈ {--- 3; . . .; 3}

mented in order to improve its performance. The resulting multitude of complex design options, however, would be too large to be analysed comprehensively. Therefore, it makes sense to focus on the competence allocation rules, which, comparatively, perform the best according to this analysis and allows them to serve as guiding principles. Consequently, the following discussion can focus exclusively on their improvement and can specifically address the remaining disadvantages. Obviously, this strategy is more promising than attempting to improve originally inferior competence allocation rules with a comparably disadvantageous performance in their stylised variants.[93]

---

93 Nevertheless, considerable scope for further research remains and complementary research programmes emerge. The analysis presented here is the first one, which systematically analyses competence allocation rules from an economic perspective. Therefore, it cannot comprehend all features and implications of the innovative research objective.

6. On the appropriate design of an international multilevel competition policy system

1. ELEMENTARY FEATURES OF AN INTERNATIONAL MULTILEVEL SYSTEM OF COMPETITION POLICIES

An international multilevel system of competition policies along the lines of section 1.2.1 of Chapter 4 represents a complex regime with a multitude of competition laws and agencies – interwoven with each other. Competition policy competences on different levels of the system imply a coexistence of horizontal and vertical interrelation between the elements of the systems. The mutual interrelation of the elements generates dynamics which jeopardise a sustainable balance of centralising forces – destroying the system by monocultivating and eroding diversity – and decentralising forces – destroying the system by causing decay and eroding coherence. As it is argued in this book, competence allocation is crucial in maintaining a sustainable balance between (radical) centralism and (radical) decentralism. Before the derived superior competence allocation rules are reformulated in the context of an international multilevel system of competition policies, the diversity of involved elements is explained in more detail.

Drawing on the current structure of antitrust in the world and in the leading jurisdictions, the following vertical structure of an international multilevel system of competition policies is assumed. The top level is global, thus paying tribute to the process of market globalisation. The second level, however, is also supranational. It consists of competition policy regimes that are international, albeit regionally limited. A natural example – and the most comprehensively developed one – is the competition policy of the EU.[1] However, there are a distinct number of additional free trade areas and economic integration projects, which either entail competition policy provisions or are likely to or possess potential to develop some in the future. The third level is the one of nationwide competition policy regimes, like the federal antitrust policy of

[1] See section 2.2 of Chapter 4.

the US,[2] or the antitrust policies of Japan or Germany. Eventually, a fourth level refers to subnational competition policy regimes, like the antitrust policy efforts of the US states or the state cartel offices in Germany. The delimitation of 'subnational', 'national', and 'supranational' follows the historically originated current structure of nations, their cooperations and confederations, and their internal institutional designs. As a consequence, competition policy regimes with significantly differing extent, power, or meaning can be located at the same level. However, every alternative vertical structure of levels would be subject to the disadvantage of being illusory.

In such a multilevel system, competition institutions are located in a multitude of jurisdictions (institutional diversity). For instance, on the national level, numerous countries each have their own competition policy regimes, which need to be sensibly integrated into the overall system. Next to such a horizontal institutional diversity there is a vertical multitude of competition institutions between the levels, demanding a smooth delimitation of the respective competences. Furthermore, there is an organisational diversity, represented by numerous antitrust authorities across the levels of the system. Again, their interrelation includes a horizontal and a vertical dimension. Even if the institutional framework of the overall multilevel system had been made uniform, the application of the monopolised rules by different competition agencies, courts, and other enforcement instances would have possessed the potential to produce incoherent outcomes to an extent, which could challenge the balance of centralising and decentralising forces.[3] However, the scenario of a completely harmonised institutional framework is neither promoted in this book, nor likely to emerge out of the contemporary antitrust world. Actually, its degree of centralisation would probably mean that diverging interpretations by decentralised enforcement authorities would be perceived as disturbances, accelerating already centralising dynamics.

Eventually, the structure of principles in local competition policy regimes matters in terms of centralism and decentralism. Basic regime types include the court system, the administration system, and the private litigation system. In the court system, final decisions are made by competition courts. A government attorney or a competent public agency files law suits against anticompetitive business arrangements and practices and is forced to prove its allegations. With respect to the US antitrust system, it is argued that the court system offers superior capabilities in terms of flexibility and innovation

---

2 See section 2.1 of Chapter 4.

3 For instance, the US–EU conflict over the defunct GE–Honeywell merger would most likely have emerged in similar dimensions if both jurisdictions had implemented the same standard for prohibiting mergers. See section 1.2.2 of Chapter 3. In other words, the wording of the law does not determine competition policy outcomes.

(Kovacic 1992, 1996, 2004). The reason is that plaintiffs have incentives to offer contrary evidence and theories against the government advocates with the judge weighing the different positions and, maybe, calling for additional and independent expertise.[4]

In an administration system, the competent competition authority both investigates and decides about anticompetitive business arrangements and practices. Courts become involved only if the respective enterprises file an appeal against the administrative decision. In such a scenario, it becomes important to distinguish between a government authority (like the European Commission) and agency independence.[5] The former is likely to experience difficulty withstanding distortionary influences from non-antitrust policy areas (and lobbyism), whereas the latter can focus exclusively on competition matters. Intra-regime diversity may be more limited in administration systems due to the strong position of the competent agency. However, regarding local regimes, this hardly represents a serious problem in the face of a multitude of local regimes.

In the system of private litigation, no public authority apart from 'ordinary' courts is involved. The private parties themselves enforce competition law through law suits filed by the injured party of an anticompetitive arrangement or practice (for example, vertically related parties like consumers, resellers, component suppliers, and so on, or horizontally related parties like competitors). Although this obviously entails a number of problems if the overall regime is based on private litigation, elements of private litigation are included in many antitrust regimes. Private litigation plays an important role within the US antitrust system and its meaning in the EU is increasing. Additionally, it has some regional importance in the enforcement of rules against unfair competition (for example, delusive and untrue advertising, defamatory actions against competitors, incorrect price marking, and so on).[6]

These basic regime types rarely occur in their pure variant in real-world antitrust regimes. Instead, local regimes usually represent specific mixtures of the described basic elements.

In summary, an international multilevel system of competition policies consists of:

---

4 However, the regime is asymmetric. If the government authorities decide not to challenge an arrangement or practice – on whatever grounds – no court supervision occurs.

5 A comprehensive example is represented by the European Central Bank. Within the antitrust world, the Federal Cartel Office of Germany possesses somewhat limited independence. See section 2.2 of Chapter 4.

6 See sections 2.1 and 2.2 of Chapter 4.

- a multitude of competition institutions, among many others global competition provisions, the EU competition rules, US statutes like the Sherman Act, the German Act against Restraints of Competition, Californian antitrust provisions, and so on;
- a multitude of antitrust authorities, among many others the US Federal Trade Commission, the Canadian Competition Bureau, state cartel offices in Germany, the European Commission, some global authority, and so on;
- a multitude of differently designed regimes across the levels, including court systems, government administration systems, independent administration systems, elements of private litigation, and all kinds of mixed types.

The workability of such a complex international multilevel system of competition policies demands intelligently designed competence allocation and delimitation rules based on the theoretical analysis in Chapter 5. The next two sections present an example of what adequate competence allocation rules for a coherent and federalist governance of global competition could look like. The emphasis is on example because the comparative approach of the analysis presented in this book does not allow for deriving a 'one-and-only' optimal solution.

2. THE FUNDAMENTAL PRINCIPLES OF COMPETENCE ALLOCATION

According to the preceding analysis, competence allocation in an international multilevel system of competition policies should be represented by a combination of the two comparatively best performing competence allocation rules. Thus, the mandatory lead jurisdiction model and the nondiscrimination rule serve as fundamental principles for competence allocation. More precisely, a thoughtful combination is targeted, which alleviates remaining weaknesses of each competence allocation rule. Fortunately, the stylised variants of the mandatory lead jurisdiction model and the nondiscrimination rule complement each other in the preceding assessment: the weaknesses of one are the strengths of the other one.[7] Perhaps, the only exception is represented by the

[7] According to Table 5.1 in section 3 of Chapter 5, relative weak points of the stylised mandatory lead jurisdiction model are the performances in regard to preference conformity and lobbyism, which, in turn, merely represent the relative best performances of the nondiscrimination rule. The latter, the other way around, possesses defi-

externalities criterion where each of the two rules only receives a modestly positive assessment. Therefore, modifications to the stylisations should pay tribute to an improved internalisation of externalities.

Both the nondiscrimination rule and the mandatory lead jurisdiction model imply that the top level neither prescribes concrete substantive provisions against cartels or abusive and predatory modes of enterprise behaviour, nor consists of a distinctive merger control. Instead, the upward allocation of competences is limited to the selection of competent jurisdictions as well as complaint and supervision competences. Therefore, these competence allocation rules predominantly address competence allocation between the top level and the nearest downward level(s). More distant downward levels, for instance subnational level(s), which face substantive competition policy regime on upward levels, require additional competence allocation rules.

On these downward levels, risks from overdecentralisation in the face of business internationalisation, causing welfare-decreasing cross-jurisdictional spillover effects, are more imminent than such from centralising forces. Therefore, simple rules, which safeguard that anticompetitive arrangements and practices with cross-jurisdictional effects (regarding the addressed level) are allocated upwards, are required. Their relatively centralising character – while dangerous on upward levels – seems less problematic on more local levels because the preceding upward levels themselves still consist of a considerably decentralised character.

With a diversity of substantive competition policy regimes existing on upward levels, an X-plus rule represents the superior choice, predominantly due to its simplicity and unambiguity when compared to turnover thresholds and the relevant markets rule. However, this is a conditional assessment with regard to required standards for notification rules and triggering events. They must ensure a sufficient nexus between claiming jurisdiction and the actual effects and (anti-)competitive impact of a given business arrangement or practice in order to alleviate the most severe disadvantages of X-plus rules through preventing negative effects and limiting centralising dynamics. Such safeguards against virtual effects constituting decentralised jurisdiction must systematically be incorporated in the overall system.

---

ciencies in regard to the efficiency criterion, an area of assessment in which the mandatory lead jurisdiction model receives a favourable assessment. Both competence allocation rules perform well regarding the evolutionary criterion of adaptability.

3. THE LEVELS AND THEIR INTERRELATIONS

3.1 The Global Level

The preceding analysis leads to the conclusion that a real 'global level' represents a precondition for a sound governance of worldwide competition. However, the differentiated analysis of the multilevel approach presented in this book allows for and requires a closer look at the competences that a global level inalienably needs in order to cope with its tasks. A combination of the two leading competence allocation rules (according to sections 2 and 3 of Chapter 5) implies that an international competition policy regime does not require substantive antitrust laws at the global level. A harmonisation or uniformisation of competition rules – either by concentrating these competences at the global level or by harmonising rules across the levels[8] – is even likely to produce harmful effects.

Nevertheless, the global level should be equipped with considerable competences, namely: (1) selection of competent jurisdictions (which incompletely represents a rule-application competence) according to the mandatory lead jurisdiction model; and (2) combat discriminatory rules and practices on other levels according to the nondiscrimination principle. The latter may be called a limited rule-making competence – limited to the ban of discriminatory antitrust. However, there is a difference that is important from an institutional-economic perspective. The global level is only entitled to prohibit discriminatory rules and practices. It cannot and must not prescribe what competition rules and antitrust practices on downward levels should look like. The most important aspect here is that:[9]

- a prohibition excludes only one specific option from the non-determined set of possible options,[10] whereas;
- a prescription effectively eliminates any scope of selection and de facto excludes all the other options by prescribing one of them.

---

[8] Strictly speaking, a mandatory harmonisation of national competition rules de facto transfers the rule-making competence to the level or authority, which designs the standard according to which the process of harmonisation converges. Consequently, this represents a variant of the 'concentration of competences at the global level' approach.

[9] See Hayek (1973, 1975) as well as, for example, Vanberg (1994), Kerber (1993, 1997), Wegner (1996, 1997, 2003), and Budzinski (2000, 2003c).

[10] The set of possible options is ex ante always indetermined because of the creative abilities of human agents to create formerly unknown – because non-existent – modes of behaviour and institutional arrangements. See, generally, Wegner (1997) and Budzinski (2003c).

In the first case, the downward levels maintain behavioural freedom, including the freedom to create innovative solutions. Each is effectively eroded in the second case.

Consequently, fundamental rule-making competences and the remaining scope of rule-application competences are not allocated to the top level. The same is true for direct enforcement competences. It is the lead jurisdiction, which applies its own or other competition rules to a given anticompetitive arrangement or practice and enforces the outcome of its proceedings. However, referring to the externality issue as the weakest point of both favoured competence allocation rules, the lead jurisdiction is expected to produce positive externalities (that is, protect competition also in regard to other jurisdictions' markets and consumers), which generates an incentive problem. Therefore, supervision competences must be additionally allocated to the global level.[11] One might call this a kind of indirect enforcement competence, but, again, upward competences only cover the ability to abolish deficient decisions of the lead jurisdiction regarding nondiscrimination and comity. The global level authorities are not competent to apply and enforce (whichever) competition law themselves.

In order to handle the outlined competences, which are specified below, an agency is needed at the global level. Allow me to call it the International Competition Panel (ICP).[12] According to the combination of the mandatory lead jurisdiction model and the nondiscrimination rule, its competences can be specified to include the following three elements:

- Selection of lead jurisdiction: the ICP appoints a lead jurisdiction, preferably from the second or third level. As a lead jurisdiction for a given anticompetitive arrangement or practice qualifies a jurisdiction that matches the following criteria to a large extent: (1) regional gravity of the aggregate turnover of the participating enterprises; (2) the absence of discriminatory provisions in the potentially competent competition policy regime; and (3) willingness and experience of the potentially competent antitrust authorities to employ a world welfare standard, that is, to safeguard comity to other jurisdictions' markets and consumers. The lead jurisdiction receives full competences to deal with the respective anticompetitive arrangement or practice under the oblig-

[11] The necessity of an external monitoring of activities of downward level jurisdictions in an otherwise federal or decentralised regime is also emphasised by Scott (2000: 187) and Figueiredo and Weingast (2005). While the first argues from a federalism perspective and in regard to Canadian environmental competences, the latter produce a game-theoretic model of federalism and constitutional rules.

[12] My intention was not focused on names. Any other denomination of this agency would also be fine as long as it is equipped with the described competences.

ation of nondiscrimination and pursuance of the common welfare of all affected consumers irrespective of their location.

- Supervision and sanctions: the ICP reviews the competition rules and codified practices of the downward levels' antitrust regimes regarding violations of the nondiscrimination principle. In cases of discriminatory rules or practices, it demands the modification of the respective provisions (however, without prescribing alternative designs[13]). If the respective competition policy regime refuses to adjust its rules and practices according to the requirements of the nondiscrimination principle, this regime is disqualified and suspended as lead jurisdiction. This procedure also applies a safeguard to a minimum necessary nexus of downward competition policy regimes with an anticompetitive arrangement or practice, to claim jurisdiction.[14] Additionally, the ICP supervises the review and decision process by the lead jurisdiction, but exclusively concerning violations of nondiscrimination and world welfare. Potential sanctions are similar to the general nondiscrimination review procedure.
- Complaints and conflict resolution: the ICP hears and reviews complaints from jurisdictions or enterprises: (1) about decisions of the lead jurisdiction, which disregard foreign consumers and/or nondiscrimination; and (2) about discriminatory rules or practices of downward level competition policy regimes (including insufficient nexus). Any complaints about wrong assessments by the competent antitrust authority or dissents regarding the facts of a case fall under the competency of the courts and appellation bodies of the lead jurisdiction. In this sense, the ICP provides a forum to deal with conflicts between downward level jurisdictions.

While the ICP represents the final instance regarding its supervision and conflict resolution tasks, an appellation body regarding its jurisdictional decisions (that is, appointment of the appropriate lead jurisdiction) is needed. An international court could be one suitable solution, a second chamber of the panel another. The latter may be preferable in order to keep the selection procedure compact. Otherwise, causing costs and the administrative burden on business would increase, causing institutional efficiency to deteriorate.

---

[13] It remains within the competencies of the decentralised competition policy regimes to develop an institutional solution, which solves the discrimination problem.

[14] Claiming jurisdiction without a sufficient nexus to the respective arrangement can be interpreted as representing an indirect kind of discrimination. It is necessary to include the nexus issue in the supervision and sanction mechanism with respect to competition policy competences on national and subnational–regional levels. See sections 3.3 and 3.4 of this chapter.

Anticompetitive arrangements and practices with more than negligible cross-jurisdictional effects concerning the downward levels fall under the described competences of the ICP. Regarding mergers and other interfirm alliances, the following procedure could prove to be compact and efficient. According to the self-assessment of the participating enterprises, these arrangements are pre-notified to the ICP.[15] A standardised notification procedure could minimise filing efforts while providing the necessary information to decide about the appropriate lead jurisdiction. If arrangements with considerable cross-border effects are only notified to a downward level jurisdiction, then the receiving agency must delegate the notification to the ICP.[16] Concerning illegal cartels, which are usually performed secretly, and abusive behaviour, a notification to the ICP occurs according to the assessment of the downward level antitrust authorities, which discover them. In such cases, the ICP's appointment of a lead jurisdiction must sometimes rely on provisional knowledge and hypotheses about the nature of the cartel or abuse. However, since – according to experience in anticartel interagency cooperation – overall cooperation between the affected regimes works rather well in such cases due to similar interests, the appointment of the second- or third-best appropriate jurisdiction does not represent a serious problem.

This leads towards the organisational design of the ICP. Actually, there are different ways to organise an agency with the competences outlined above. One obvious alternative would be to integrate the ICP within the WTO framework. This would complete the WTO as the primary organisation, which is responsible for the governance of global markets. With both public and private restraints of competition falling under the competence of the WTO, global competition would then be subject to coherent governance out of one single hand. The late completion of the postwar ITO vision[17] would be considerably welcomed. However, it can be useful to sacrifice this ideal paragon in favour of a more practicable or consensual solution. The major problem with a WTO

---

15 The self-assessment by the enterprises should not entail dangers of forum shopping because when assessing the cross-border effects, the respective enterprises are not choosing between different competition laws (since this decision is made by the ICP). Moreover, an ICP pre-notification of an anticompetitive arrangement or practice without considerable cross-border effects does not generate significant harm because the competence to deal substantially with the arrangement is allocated downwards anyhow. If only one downward level jurisdiction is really affected, the selection of a 'lead' jurisdiction is rather simple and indisputable.

16 Such cases are likely to occur only infrequently. If an arrangement affects more than one decentralised competition policy regime, the participating agencies are required to notify to more than one agency – and, at the same time, they experience the incentive to make use of the one-stop shop via an ICP pre-notification.

17 See section 2.3 of Chapter 4.

competition policy is the significant difference between the prevailing mechanisms of international trade policy and the demands of a decentralised international competition policy system. It represents an important practical difference whether one deals with state action restricting trade or with private business behaviour, which might produce anticompetitive effects – with respect to time frames, parties' rights, economic analysis, and so on. On the other hand, in the framework of an ICP, which is suggested here, the international authority only deals with public agencies – namely competition agencies – and their claims of jurisdiction and handling of assigned competences. Moreover, there are considerable overlaps, for instance, regarding discriminatory competition policy strategies (like selective non-enforcement of competition rules, promotion of outbound restrictions, and so on). Nevertheless, significant differences between the proposal in this study and the current WTO architecture are obvious and they might prove difficult to overcome.

Alternatively, the ICP could constitute a separate independent international agency. Such an agency must be designed to: (1) adequately represent the downward level jurisdictions; and (2) keep procedures compact and efficient. The first requirement facilitates the constitution and implementation of the ICP. In order to avoid an international political bargaining game,[18] the competition authorities of the existing national and supranational jurisdictions could serve as natural constituents and members of the ICP. To some extent, one of the constituting principles of the ICN serves as a paragon – namely aiming for a coordination among competition authorities instead of among governments. Furthermore, an obvious advantage of this strategy would be the possibility of developing the ICP out of the popular ICN – albeit, it would more likely entail the characteristics of a replacement.

Another organisational paragon for an international panel consisting of experts is represented by the European System of Central Banks or, more precisely, its major decision forum, the Governing Council.[19] Drawing on this, the ICP Governing Chamber could consist of a board of appointed ICP directors and the presidents, governors, and so on, of downward level antitrust authorities. However, in view of the second demand – compact and efficient procedures – the number of members of the Governing Chamber must not be excessive. Therefore, not every jurisdiction can be an acting member of the Governing Chamber at a given point of time. Along with, say, five directors,

---

18 The WTO ministerial conference in Cancún serves as a negative example. See Drexl (2004), Jenny (2004), Petersmann (2004), Stewart (2004), and section 2.3 of Chapter 4.

19 See, on the institutional aspects of European monetary governance and particularly on its decision bodies and processes, Budzinski et al. (1998), Baldwin (2001), Hefeker (2002), Budzinski et al. (2004), and European Central Bank (2004).

the chamber should consist of a maximum of 10 national or supranational-regional representatives. A rotation system must ensure that none of the participating jurisdictions is disadvantaged concerning its representation in the Governing Chamber. This rotation system could be designed to reflect the differing importance and meaning of the downward level jurisdictions in the world of antitrust. National or supranational-regional competition policy regimes with a large population and/or large economic weight should more often join the chamber than smaller ones. An indicator, which combines measures of population and economic activity, is not too difficult to develop. In fact, this mirrors the upcoming rotation system regarding participation of national central bank governors in the Governing Council of the European Central Bank, which became necessary in the face of the enlargement of the EU and enters into force if the new members qualify for and subsequently join the European Currency Unit.[20] Roughly, the organisational side mirrors the independent administration system.[21]

An additional precondition for compact and efficient procedures is the absence of veto rights or comprehensive consensus requirements. Instead of unanimity rules, a simple or qualified (for example, two-thirds of the votes) majority should suffice to generate a definite decision. This is especially true if the independence of both the ICP and the members of its chambers is secured. The independence of the ICP board of directors is served if it consists of antitrust experts, which are appointed by the leaders of the downward level competition agencies. Since comprehensive independence of national and supranational-regional competition authorities may be unrealistic[22] (though beneficial[23]), the design of the rotation system promotes the independence of the ICP if membership in the Governing Chamber is rather short (and, thus, rotation frequent) and overlapping (that is, the chamber does not frequently consist of representatives of the same antitrust authorities because the individual periods are not parallel).

If a second chamber (say Appellation Chamber) is employed in order to constitute an appellation body regarding jurisdictional decisions of the Governing Chamber (that is, selection of the lead jurisdiction according to the defined criteria), then an obvious choice would be to let it also consist of

---

[20] See, for critical analyses, for example, Baldwin (2001), Hefeker (2002), Belke (2003), Fendel and Frenkel (2003), Belke and Styczynska (2004), and Budzinski et al. (2004).

[21] See section 1 of this chapter.

[22] However, two decades ago the comprehensive independence of central banks in each EU member state would also have been deemed to be unrealistic.

[23] See, regarding the international coordination of competition policies, Worm (2004: 197–200).

representatives of national and supranational-regional competition authorities (second and third level) in a rotating way. Of course, jurisdictions must not fill a seat in both chambers at the same period of time. Again, a majority rule that prevents effective veto rights would be helpful.

The preceding description of how an ICP could be designed is only an exemplar for a number of alternative variants. In the context of this study, its main rationale is to demonstrate how a concrete operationalisation of a global level authority with the competences allocated and delimitated by the combination of mandatory lead jurisdiction model and nondiscrimination rule could look like. Therefore (and different from the competence allocation rules), the organisational questions are only outlined and not subject to a rigorous analysis.

3.2 The Supranational-Regional Level

The second level represents the first one, which disposes of substantive antitrust competences. It consists of joint competition policy regimes of confederations or associations of independent countries. Thus, competition policy competences are allocated to a supranational level, albeit with limited regional scope. The most natural and comprehensive example is represented by the EU competition policy system, which contains fully fledged competition rules and an experienced antitrust practice.[24] Additionally, there are antitrust provisions and agencies on a supranational level in the context of several other multicountry associations. For instance, both the Andean Community and the UEMOA (Union Economique et Monétaire Ouest Africaine) have implemented their own competition policy agencies, theoretically competent in enforcing specifically shaped community competition rules. Practically, however, the Andean regime is currently rather inactive. In contrast, competition policy competences within UEMOA are considerably centralised and the maturity of the common antitrust policy exceeds that of several member states (Bakhoum 2006). Comparatively elaborate competition policy competences are located at the EFTA (European Free Trade Association) Surveillance Authority, whereas free trade and economic integration associations, like NAFTA (North American Free Trade Agreement), ASEAN (Association of Southeast Asian Nations), Mercosur (Mercado Común del Conor Sur), CIS (Community of Independent [former soviet] States), CARICOM (Carribean Community and Common Market), FTAA (Free Trade Area of the Americas), SADC (South African Development Community), or CEN-SAD (Community of Sahel-Saharan States), currently

[24] See section 2.2 of Chapter 4.

only possess at best rudimental antitrust provisions. Meanwhile, COMESA (Common Market for Eastern and Southern Africa) is also reaching for implementing considerable supranational competition policy competences.[25]

Following the paragon of the EU, these associations and confederations might develop effective competition policy regimes with considerable competition policy competences in the course of time. Developed ones represent natural candidates for lead jurisdiction appointments as they jurisdictionally include a number of national markets and address consumers of different countries. Therefore, they automatically internalise parts of the externalities arising from cross-border business activities. Consequently, this level might become the major antitrust enforcement level in the long run – given that worldwide economic integration is proceeding.

Effective competition policy regimes at the supranational–regional level retain full rule-making, rule-application, and enforcement competences for cross-border anticompetitive arrangements and practices if the upward level appoints them to be lead jurisdiction in the respective case. Each regime autonomously shapes its own substantive competition rules, enforcement institutions, and agencies (including an individual composition of elements of the court system, government and independent administration system, and private litigation) minus discriminatory provisions and practices, which are excluded by the nondiscrimination rule and sanctioned by the global level. Against the background of these non-discriminatory institutions and practices, each regime is obliged to consider competitive effects outside its territory according to the common welfare of all affected consumers. Apart from that, the appointed lead jurisdiction is free to handle the referred case. Of course, it can seek the cooperation with and assistance by other – horizontally- or vertically-interrelated – antitrust regimes as far as it deems this to be necessary and/or helpful.

Regarding the vertical (and diagonal) delimitation of competences between the supranational–regional and the national level, a variant of the X-plus rule could provide an efficient and simple competence allocation rule. Moulding the X-plus rule in order to address downward allocation, one could call this an X-minus rule. Its content would be that any anticompetitive arrangement or practice, which is notified to or detected by a supranational–regional competition policy regime, must be allocated downwards if the effects of the respective arrangement or practice occur within X or less national antitrust regimes.

---

[25] See, for example, Tavares de Araujo and Tineo (1998), Lloyd and Vautier (1999), Vautier (2001), Rimoldi de Ladmann (2002), Jenny (2003b), Lloyd (2003), Drexl (2005), and Bakhoum (2006). See, regarding the seeds of a common Australian–New Zealand competition policy, Hutchins (2004).

3.3 The National Level

Since currently only one effective supranational–regional antitrust regime exists, the major level of substantive competition policy is likely to remain the national level for a considerable time. In particular, national competition policy regimes with large and important internal markets are likely to be frequently appointed as lead jurisdictions. Above all, this refers to the US antitrust system.[26] However, the competition policy regimes of countries like Canada, Australia, Brazil, Japan, Russia, China, India, and many more also represent frequent candidates if they qualify for a lead jurisdiction appointment.[27]

If national competition policy regimes are selected to serve as lead jurisdictions, their competences are identical with supranational–regional lead jurisdictions. Thus, they handle a referred case according to autonomously shaped, applied, and enforced competition rules, except of nondiscrimination and comity to extraterritorial markets and consumers, supervised by the global regime. Similarly, they are free to develop their individual composition of court system, government and independent administration system, and private litigation elements.

National competition policy regimes can be vertically interrelated to a supranational–regional level (as within the EU) and/or to a subnational-regional level (as in the US) – or lack any vertical interrelation concerning substantive competition policy. If a vertically interrelated supranational–regional level exists, an institutional arrangement rule for the upward allocation of competences is required. According to the preceding analysis in this chapter, an X-plus rule seems adequate. The more countries a supranational–regional level consists of, the more caution is required regarding the value of X because a very low X can promote (over-) centralising forces. In view of the EU discussion, this hints towards sustainable roles for national competition policy regimes within the EU, albeit with an efficient competence allocation, for instance, based on an X-plus/X-minus-rule.[28]

---

[26] See section 2.1 of Chapter 4.

[27] Next to inhabiting the main regional area of the aggregate turnover of the participating enterprises, a qualification to become appointed lead jurisdiction requires the absence of discriminatory provisions and practices as well as the proven willingness and experience to employ a world welfare standard. See section 3.1 of this chapter. This implies that some of the above mentioned countries might have a long way to go until they meet these criteria. Note, however, that the possibility to qualify as lead jurisdiction can entail important incentives to develop national competition policy regimes according to the modern international standards.

[28] Although the EU is currently the only viable example of a supranational–regional competition policy regime, the generalised treatment is justified because further such regimes can develop during the ongoing process of international (regional) economic integration. See section 3.2 of this chapter.

If a vertically interrelated subnational–regional level exists, downward allocation can be adequately designed against the background of an X-minus rule. In particular, large countries with big internal markets profit from internal decentralisation and, thus, from the existence of regional competition policy regimes. According to the economic analysis presented in this book, the maintenance of American antitrust federalism is beneficial as would be the creation of federalised competition policy structures in comparably sized countries (for example, Russia or China). However, the necessity of a reform of the competence allocation and delimitation rules within the US antitrust system can also be derived from this analysis in order to clarify and simplify competence allocation while reducing jurisdictional overlaps.

If no vertically interrelated subnational-regional level exists, a national competition policy regime needs adequate notification thresholds for mergers and interfirm cooperative arrangements in order to avoid jurisdiction being claimed if no sufficient nexus with the (anti-) competitive effects of a business arrangement or practice exists. Concerning prohibited cartels per se and abusive modes of behaviour, such thresholds are also necessary but naturally do not refer to notification. If a national antitrust regime detects such a cartel or mode of behaviour that does not meet the thresholds for a sufficient domestic nexus, it is obliged to notify a horizontally or vertically interrelated regime with a sufficient nexus (according to top level standards).

3.4 The Subnational–Regional Level

Subnational–regional competition policy regimes usually do not qualify as lead jurisdictions for cross-border antitrust cases. Their domains are local anticompetitive arrangements and practices because, in this respect, they can exploit their advantages of being very decentralised and very close to the locally affected markets. In such cases, however, they play an important role within a sound multilevel competition policy system. As discussed in the preceding section, particularly large countries with considerably segmented internal markets profit from downward level competition policy competences. Despite ongoing market globalisation, regional and local markets are unlikely to be completely eroded. Therefore, the scope for subnational competition policy regimes is a sustainable one.

However, it must be ensured that only anticompetitive arrangements and practices with purely local effects fall under the jurisdiction of the regimes at this decentralised level. Here, an imbalance of centralising and decentralising forces is more likely to tend towards overdecentralisation. Therefore, upward allocation should be based on a competence allocation rule, which effectively minimises multiple proceedings at this level. According to the preceding economic analysis, an X-plus rule with the value of X close to '2' represents an adequate institutional arrangement. Only if the subnational jurisdictions represent considerable numbers of consumers (because very large countries subdivide into comparatively large subunits), might a larger X be beneficial.

Obviously, competition policy regimes at this fourth level represent the most downward ones, wherefore the issue of a sufficient nexus between (anti-)competitive impact and the claiming of jurisdiction becomes rather sensitive. Therefore, the competition policy regimes at this level must implement triggering thresholds constituting jurisdiction and notification duties of private parties, which do not violate the safeguards for adequate jurisdiction according to top level standards.

4. CONCLUDING REMARKS

In the face of the ongoing process of market internationalisation and the accelerating globalisation of competition in goods and services, an adequate governance of this globalising competition becomes an increasingly urgent task. Consequently, a lively academic and political debate on this issue has emerged. In the course of this debate, both academic proposals and real-world developments towards the internationalisation of antitrust (in the context of the WTO and the ICN[29]) have occurred. My contribution innovates on this discussion in four ways:

- First, the major target of my analysis is to provide a theoretical framework for systematically analysing centralisation and decentralisation of competences. Competence allocation and delimitation are identified as being an important task of global governance in general, an insight which is predominantly neglected in the prevailing discussion. This theoretical framework, based on economic theory (economics of federalism, institutional economics, evolutionary economics), is principally applicable to numerous issues of global governance.
- Secondly, I derive elementary features of an international multilevel system of competition policies against the developed theoretical framework. Compared to other proposals of international antitrust, this entails the (methodological) advantage that the results are derived from transparent and science-based economic criteria.
- Thirdly, the resulting proposal consequently models the governance of global competition in the context of a multilevel system of institutions and authorities. Therefore, the proposal does not refer solely to the

29 See sections 2.3 and 2.4 of Chapter 4.

global level. Instead, it systematically and in an integrative approach spans competition policy regimes on supranational–regional, national, and subnational levels.

- Fourthly, and partly overlapping with the other aspects, even if one disagrees with the specific conclusions of this analysis, the study provides an analytical framework for further research and policy discussions in the context of antitrust. For instance, it represents a framework to analyse competence allocation rules or organising principles of international antitrust that have been neglected or ignored in this study as well as innovative ones that will be developed in the future.

Concerning the concrete proposal of this study, a number of differences and similarities in comparison to other proposals of international antitrust can be identified.[30] Contrary to many other proposals, this study abstains from allocating substantive rule-making competences to the global level. This particularly refers to the definition of mandatory minimum standards in regard to substantive cartel and merger policy. For instance, proposals somewhat related to the initial DIAC initiative[31] generally include comparatively ambitious minimum standards to which national competition rules must be adjusted. Examples are the prohibition of horizontal hardcore cartels, rule-of-reason provisions for all other cartels and cartel surrogates, a fully fledged merger control including mandatory regulation of anticompetitive mergers and acquisitions, and provisions regarding abusive and predatory business practices.[32] Since this initiative significantly influenced the European WTO approach in the 1990s, the respective development of international competition rules within the WTO framework shows considerable similarities.[33] More often than not, other WTO related proposals argue along comparable lines.[34] In

[30] In this section, I only refer to proposals which neither call for complete centralisation, nor argue against any kind of international antitrust. I dealt with these positions in Chapter 3 of this book.

[31] The DIAC was presented by the so-called Munich Group in 1995 as a fully fledged proposal for a comprehensive international competition order in the context of the WTO. Members of the Munich Group were the antitrust experts Wolfgang Fikentscher, Josef Drexl, Eleanor M. Fox, Andreas Fuchs, Andreas Heinemann, Ulrich Immenga, Hans Peter Kunz-Hallstein, Ernst-Ulrich Petersmann, Walter R. Schluep, Akira Shoda, Stanislaw J. Soltysinski, and Lawrence A. Sullivan. See for the original proposal, Fikentscher and Immenga (1995) as well as for applications, Fikentscher (1994, 1999), Drexl (1999, 2003), and Podszun (2003: 247–312).

[32] The 'modest minimum standards' proposed by Worm (2004: 215–219) deviate only slightly.

[33] See section 2.3 of Chapter 4 and the literature cited therein.

[34] See, for example, Scherer (1994), Wins (2000: 137–172), Dabbah (2003), Wilson (2003: 295–320), and Klodt (2005).

contrast to these proposals, my study assigns no rule-making and – at best – only indirect rule-application competences to the global level.

However, regarding enforcement competences these proposals also refer to national competition authorities (and more implicitly to supranational–regional as well).[35] Wilson (2003) explicitly introduces jurisdictional competences at the global level, although he limits his proposal to merger control. According to his proposal, the main task of the WTO Competition Office is to facilitate the consensual and cooperative selection of a lead jurisdiction by the affected member jurisdictions.[36] However, the binding decision of the lead jurisdiction must follow ambitious supranational minimum standards, which are moulded as a copy of US antitrust laws (Wilson 2003: 309, 314).

With regard to competence delimitation rules, most of the proposals remain silent or provide only vague information. A popular variant refers to interstate commerce clauses, however, in a more general way and without precision of the underlying institutional issues. The international rules shall become competent as soon as more than one member jurisdiction is somehow affected.[37] As I argued in section 1.1.2 of Chapter 5, this does not suffice in order to constitute an operational competence allocation rule. The DIAC additionally introduces turnover thresholds regarding competence allocation in merger control, a competence allocation rule, which is inferior according to the analysis in Chapter 5. Wins (2000: 145–147) builds his proposal upon the location doctrine, which he believes to be superior to the effects doctrine, whereas Worm (2004: 202–204) finds the opposite result and identifies the effects doctrine as a major element of her proposal. The comparative analysis in Chapter 5 demonstrates that both competence allocation rules are comparatively inferior in the theoretical framework of my analysis.

Finally, an important difference in the proposal presented in this study and other academic proposals is the role of institutional harmonisation. Virtually all proposals at least entail a perspective of harmonisation in the end,[38] that is, harmonised competition rules, practices, and policies are targeted in the long

---

[35] Maybe with the exception of Scherer (1994), whose proposal contains considerable enforcement competences of his International Competition Policy Office in the long run.

[36] See Wilson (2003: 312). He refers to the lead jurisdiction concepts by Campbell and Trebilcock (1993, 1997), which are also influential for the respective competence allocation rules in my analysis. See sections 1.2.4, 1.2.5, 2.8, and 2.9 of Chapter 5.

[37] See, for example, Wilson (2003: 312) and Worm (2004: 201–202). Interpreting this as an implicit 2-plus rule proposal would probably be over-interpreting in my opinion.

[38] See, for example, Scherer (1994), Dabbah (2003), Wilson (2003), and Klodt (2005).

run while institutional diversity and decentralised competences are viewed to be temporarily necessary but dispensable in the long run. Institutional diversity does not play a sustainable role. This is even true for Worm's (2004) 'decentralised system of international competition policy' in which the rejection of a top-down harmonisation is combined with a call for bottom-up harmonisation.[39] Contrary to such claims, I argue for a sustainable role of institutional diversity and the never-ending necessity of antitrust innovations, their injection into the system being facilitated by sustainable elements of decentralism.[40] Consequently, my proposal entails no (long-run) harmonisation targets – neither regarding top-down, nor regarding bottom-up harmonisation.

The analysis in this study and the derived proposal for an international multilevel system of competition policies contributes to the integration of the advantages of centralism with the advantages of decentralism. An adequate governance of global competition demands both coherence and diversity in order effectively to protect competition on markets extending jurisdictional borders while avoiding centralising dynamics. By focusing on competence allocation and delimitation rules as the decisive elements for the balance of centralising and decentralising forces within complex multilevel systems of institutions and authorities, the study disaggregates the discussion about adequate governance regimes. This allows for a more systematic approach that provides a comparative analysis of competence allocation rules based on economic criteria. The results of this analysis – the comparative economic superiority of the nondiscrimination rule and the mandatory lead jurisdiction model – enable the integrative design of an international multilevel system of competition policies that combines coherence and diversity as well as balances centralising and decentralising forces.

In this final chapter, an exemplary conceptualisation of the analytical results is provided. It assigns predominantly jurisdictional competences to the global level and allocates substantive antitrust competences to downward levels. The competition policy agency at the global level – tentatively labelled ICP – appoints (on a case-by-case basis) a lead jurisdiction from downward levels, which deals with a concrete antitrust case. Furthermore, it supervises the acting lead jurisdiction and ensures the nondiscriminatory character of its

[39] See Worm (2004: 211–214). Similarly, Wins (2000: 141–142) differentiates his approach from the DIAC by referring to bottom-up harmonisation instead of the – in his opinion – top-down harmonisation approach of the DIAC-related proposals. See, generally on top-down versus bottom-up harmonisation, First (1998) and Wegner (2003) as well as section 1.1.5 of Chapter 5.

[40] See, for the theoretical reasoning, section 1.3.5 of Chapter 4 and for an explicit discussion of different harmonisation strategies, section 2.4.5 of Chapter 5.

provisions, institutions, practices, and decisions. Apart from the nondiscrimination issue, downward jurisdictions are free to shape their competition policy regimes individually. However, for which cases they are competent or can claim to be competent is governed in a clearcut way, thus minimising both loopholes and conflicts. Such an international multilevel system of competition policies could represent more than a temporary solution and might constitute a sustainable framework for international competition governance.

This study represents the first attempt to analyse supranational governance against the background of an economic theory of competence allocation. Therefore, a voluminous field for further research emerges. First, subsequent studies may complement and scrutinise the results regarding international antitrust presented here. Secondly, the proposed framework can be applied to other fields of supranational governance, offering considerable potentials for new insights. Thirdly, the analytical framework itself can be developed and further scrutinised, leading to improved insights and policy recommendations.

References

Ackermann, Thomas (1998), 'Wettbewerb der Wettbewerbsordnungen im europäischen Binnenmarkt?', in Jahrbuch junger Zivilrechtswissenschaftler (ed.), *Europäisierung des Privatrechts – Zwischenbilanz und Perspektiven*, Stuttgart: Richard Boorberg Verlag, pp. 203–24.

Adam, Oliver (2002), *Die internationale Kontrolle von grenzüberschreitenden Unternehmenszusammenschlüssen*, Cologne: Institut für Wirtschaftspolitik.

Adkinson, William F. Jr. (2004), 'Multijurisdictional antitrust enforcement: a view from the Illinois brick road', in Richard A. Epstein and Michael S. Greve (eds), *Competition Laws in Conflict: Antitrust Jurisdiction in the Global Economy*, Washington, D.C.: AEI Press, pp. 288–315.

Ahlborn, Christian, Evans, David S. and Padilla, Jorge (2004), 'Competition policy in the new economy: is European competition law up to the challenge?', in David S. Evans and Jorge Padilla (eds), *Global Competition Policy: Economic Issues and Impacts*, Brussels: LECG, pp. 209–33.

Aiginger, Karl, Mueller, Dennis C. and Weiss, Christoph (1998), 'Objectives, topics and methods in industrial organization during the nineties: results from a survey', *International Journal of Industrial Organization*, **16** (6), 799–830.

Aiginger, Karl, McCabe, Mark, Mueller, Dennis C. and Weiss, Christopher (2001), 'Do American and European industrial organization economists differ?', *Review of Industrial Organization*, **19** (4), 383–405.

Aigner, Gisela (2004), *Transatlantic Cooperation in Competition Policy*, Siegen, Germany: University of Siegen.

Aigner, Gisela, Budzinski, Oliver and Christiansen, Arndt (2006), 'The analysis of coordinated effects in EU merger control: where do we stand after *Sony/BMG* and *Impala*?', *European Competition Journal*, **2** (2), 311–36.

Akbar, Yusaf (2002), 'Grabbing victory from the jaws of defeat: can the GE/Honeywell merger facilitate international antitrust policy co-operation?', *World Competition*, **25** (4), 403–22.

Amarasinha, Stefan (2004), 'East is east and west is west and the twain shall never meet – or shall they?', in Barry E. Hawk (ed.), *Annual Proceedings of the Fordham Corporate Law Institute Conference on International Antitrust Law & Policy*, New York: Juris, pp. 603–15.

Amato, Filippo (2001), 'International antitrust: what future?', *World Competition*, **24** (4), 451–73.

Anderson, Robert D. (2001), 'International cooperation in competition policy: approaches currently under consideration in the WTO', in Yang-Ching Chao, Gee San, Changfa Lo and Jiming Ho (eds), *International and Comparative Competition Law and Policies*, The Hague: Kluwer, pp. 217–33.

Anderson, Robert D. and Holmes, Peter (2002), 'Competition policy and the future of the multilateral trading system', *Journal of International Economic Law*, **5** (2), 531–63.

Andrade, Gregor, Mitchell, Mark and Stafford, Erik (2001), 'New evidence and perspectives on mergers', *Journal of Economic Perspectives*, **15** (2), 103–20.

Antitrust Division (1998), *Protocol for Coordination in Merger Investigations Between the Federal Enforcement Agencies and State Attorneys General*, Washington, D.C.: US Department of Justice, March 11, 1998, available at www.usdoj.gov/atr/public/guidelines/1773.htm.

Antitrust Division (2005), *Suggested Topics for Antitrust Modernization Commission Study*, Washington, D.C.: US Department of Justice, January 5, 2005, available at www.usdoj.gov/atr/public/comments/207122.htm (downloaded 20 March, 2005).

Antitrust Modernization Commission (2007), *Report and Recommendations*, available at www.amc.gov/report_recommendation/amc_final_report.pdf.

Audretsch, David B. (1988), 'Divergent views in antitrust economics', *Antitrust Bulletin*, **33** (1), 135–60.

Audretsch, David B., Baumol, William J. and Burke, Andrew E. (2001), 'Competition policy in dynamic markets', in *International Journal of Industrial Organization*, **19** (5), 613–34.

Baade, Hans W. (1980), 'Codes of conduct for multinational enterprises: an introductory survey', in Norbert Horn (ed.), *Legal Problems of Codes of Conduct for Multinational Enterprises*, Deventer, Netherlands: Kluwer, pp. 407–41.

Bakhoum, Mor (2006), 'Delimitation and exercise of competence between the West African Economic and Monetary Union and its member states in competition policy', *World Competition*, **29** (4), 653–81.

Baldwin, Richard E. (2001), 'Eastern enlargement and ECB reform', *Swedish Economic Policy Review*, **8** (1), 15–50.

Barnes, David W. (1988), 'Federal and state philosophies in the antitrust law of mergers', *George Washington Law Review*, **56** (2), 263–94.

Baron, David P. (1997), 'Integrated strategy and international trade disputes: the Kodak-Fujifilm case', *Journal of Economics and Management Strategy*, **6** (2), 291–346.

Barros, Pedro P. (2003), 'Looking behind the curtain: effects from the modernization of European Union competition policy', *European Economic Review*, **47** (4), 613–24.

Barros, Pedro P. and Cabral, Luís M. (1994), 'Merger policy in open economies', *European Economic Review*, **38** (5), 1041–55.

Basedow, Jürgen (1998), *Weltkartellrecht: Ausgangslage und Ziele, Methoden und Grenzen der internationalen Vereinheitlichung des Rechts der Wettbewerbsbeschränkungen*, Tübingen, Germany: Mohr Siebeck.

Basedow, Jürgen (2002, ed.), *Limits and Control of Competition with a View to International Harmonization*, The Hague: Kluwer.

Basedow, Jürgen (2004), 'Competition policy in a globalized economy: from extraterritorial application to harmonization', in Manfred Neumann and Jürgen Weigand (eds), *The International Handbook of Competition*, Cheltenham, UK and Northampton, MA, USA: Edward Elgar, pp. 321–38.

Baudenbacher, Carl and Behn, Karsten (2004), 'Back to "Betsy": Zur Empagran-Entscheidung des US Supreme Court', *Journal of Competition Law (Zeitschrift für Wettbewerbsrecht)*, **2** (4), 604–26.

BDI (2002), *Commentary on the Green Paper of the EU Commission of 11 December 2001*, Berlin: BDI, available at http://europa.eu.int/comm/competition/mergers/review/comments/ref047_bdi.pdf.

Becher, Klaus F. (2002), 'Globalisierung und Fusionskontrolle in der Unternehmenspraxis', in Jürgen Schwarze (ed.), *Europäisches Wettbewerbsrecht im Zeichen der Globalisierung*, Baden-Baden, Germany: Nomos, pp. 77–87.

Becker, Gary (1983), 'A theory of competition among pressure groups for political influence', *Quarterly Journal of Economics*, **143** (3), 371–400.

Beelders, Owen and Özden, Çaglar (2001), 'International dimensions of competition policies: European responses to American mergers', Emory University working paper, Atlanta, GA.

Behrens, Peter (1993), 'Merger control: conflicts between the E.E.C. and the U.S.A.', in Erhard Kantzenbach, Hans-Eckart Scharrer, and Leonard Waverman (eds), *Competition Policy in an Interdependent World Economy*, Baden-Baden, Germany: Nomos, pp. 165–84.

Belke, Ansgar (2003), 'The rotation system is not sustainable', *Intereconomics*, **38** (3), 119–24.

Belke, Ansgar and Styczynska, Barbara (2004), 'The allocation of power in the enlarged ECB governing council: an assessment of the ECB rotation model', CEPS research report in finance and banking 35, Brussels.

Belz, Dorothee (2005), 'Einblick aus der Praxis: Wettbewerbsrecht aus Sicht eines weltweit agierenden Unternehmens', Presentation to the workshop on Internationale Wettbewerbspolitik of the AG Wettbewerb, Verein für Socialpolitik, Marburg.

Bercero, Ignacio G. and Amarasinha, Stefan D. (2001), 'Moving the trade and competition debate forward', *Journal of International Economic Law*, **4** (3), 481–506.

Berg, Hartmut and Müller, Jens (1997), 'Advantage Boeing – Der Zusammenschluß Boeing/McDonnell Douglas und seine Konsequenzen für die Wettbewerbsposition von Airbus Industries', *List Forum für Wirtschafts- und Finanzpolitik*, **23** (1), 1–9.

Bergman, Mats A., Jakobsson, Maria and Razo, Carlos (2004), 'An econometric analysis of the European Commission's merger decisions', Uppsala University working paper 2003: 6, Uppsala, Sweden.

Bernheim, B. Douglas, Crawford, Vincent P., Hall, Robert E., Marshall, Robert C., Milgrom, Paul, Perloff, Jeffrey M. and White, Halbert L. (2004), *Brief as Amici Curiae in Support of Respondents, No. 03-724*, Washington, D.C.: Supreme Court of the United States.

Besley, Timothy and Coate, Stephen (2003), 'Centralized versus decentralized provision of local public goods: a political economic analysis', *Journal of Public Economics*, **87** (12), 2611–37.

Bhattacharjea, Aditya and Nanda, Nitya (forthcoming), 'Cross-border competition issues', in Pradeep S. Mehta (ed.), *Towards a Functional Competition Policy for India*, New Delhi: Academic Foundation.

Bird, Richard M. (2000), 'Fiscal decentralization and competitive governments', in Gianluigi Galeotti, Pierre Salmon and Ronald Wintrobe (eds), *Competition and Structure: The Political Economy of Collective Decisions*, Cambridge: Cambridge University Press, pp. 129–49.

Black, Bernard S. (2000), 'The first international merger wave', *University of Miami Law Review*, **54** (2), 799–818.

Bloom, Margaret (2005), 'The great reformer: Mario Monti's legacy in Article 81 and cartel policy', *Competition Policy International*, **1** (1), 55–78.

Bode, Mariana and Budzinski, Oliver (2006), 'Competing ways towards international antitrust: the WTO versus the ICN', in Patrick Morati (ed.), *Antitrust Policy Issues*, New York: Nova, pp. 85–107.

Boeder, Thomas L. (2000), 'The Boeing-McDonnell Douglas merger', in Simon J. Evenett, Alexander Lehmann and Benn Steil (eds), *Antitrust Goes Global – What Future for Transatlantic Cooperation?*, Washington, D.C.: Brookings Institution Press, pp. 139–44.

Böge, Ulf (2005a), 'The Commission's position within the network: the perspective of the NCAs', in Claus-Dieter Ehlermann and Isabela Atanasiu (eds), *Constructing the EU Network of Competition Authorities*, Oxford: Hart Publishing, pp. 247–54.

Böge, Ulf (2005b), 'Die Herausforderung einer internationalen Wettbewerbspolitik in Zeiten globalisierter Märkte', *Wirtschaft und Wettbewerb*, **55** (6), 590–99.

Böge, Ulf (2006), 'Das International Competition Network (ICN) als Ansatz einer internationalen Wettbewerbspolitik', in Peter Oberender (ed.), *Internationale Wettbewerbspolitik*, Berlin: Duncker & Humblot, pp. 73–86.

Bond, Eric W. (2005), 'Antitrust policy in open economies: price fixing and international cartels', in E. Kwan Choi and James Hartigan (eds), *Handbook of International Trade*, Vol. II, Oxford: Blackwell, pp. 333–57.

Breton, Albert (1996), *Competitive Governments: An Economic Theory of Politics and Public Finance*, Cambridge: Cambridge University Press.

Briggs, John DeQ. and Rosenblatt, Howard T. (2002), 'GE/Honeywell – live and let die', *George Mason Law Review*, **10** (3), 459–70.

Bright, Chris and Persson, Mikael (2003), 'Article 22 of EC merger regulation: an opportunity not to be missed?', *European Competition Law Review*, **24** (10), 490–97.

Brittan, Leon (1990), 'The law and policy of merger control in the EEC', *European Law Review*, **15** (5), 351–75.

Brittan, Leon and Miert, Karel van (1996), 'Towards an international framework of competition rules', *International Business Lawyer*, **24** (10), S. 454–7.

Broberg, Morten (2002), 'Muddying the clear waters: on the Commission's proposal for a new delimitation of jurisdiction in the field of merger control', *European Competition Law Review*, **23** (9), 429–33.

Brusick, Filippo (1983), 'UN control of restrictive business practices: a decisive first step', *Journal of World Trade*, **17** (4), 337–51.

Budzinski, Oliver (2000), *Wirtschaftspolitische Implikationen evolutorischer Ordnungsökonomik*, Marburg, Germany: Metropolis.

Budzinski, Oliver (2002a), 'Perspektiven einer internationalen Politik gegen Wettbewerbsbeschränkungen', *List Forum für Wirtschafts- und Finanzpolitik*, **28** (3), 233–52.

Budzinski, Oliver (2002b), 'Internationale Wettbewerbspolitik zwischen Zentralität und Dezentralität', in Alfred Schüller and H. Jörg Thieme (eds), *Ordnungsprobleme der Weltwirtschaft*, Stuttgart: Lucius & Lucius, pp. 469–93.

Budzinski, Oliver (2002c), 'Institutional aspects of complex international competition policy arrangements', in Clemens Esser and Michael H. Stierle (eds), *Current Issues in Competition Theory and Policy*, Berlin: VWF, pp. 109–32.

Budzinski, Oliver (2003a), 'Pluralism of competition policy paradigms and the call for regulatory diversity', *Marburg Papers on Economics*, **2003** (14), available at http://ssrn.com/abstract=452900.

Budzinski, Oliver (2003b), 'Towards an international governance of transborder mergers? Competition networks and institutions between centralism and decentralism', *NYU Journal of International Law and Politics*, **36** (1), 1–52.

Budzinski, Oliver (2003c), 'Cognitive rules, institutions, and competition', *Constitutional Political Economy*, **14** (3), 215–35.

Budzinski, Oliver (2004a), 'Die Evolution des internationalen Systems der Wettbewerbspolitiken', in Oliver Budzinski and Jörg Jasper (eds), *Wettbewerb, Wirtschaftsordnung und Umwelt*, Frankfurt: Lang, pp. 81–100.

Budzinski, Oliver (2004b), 'The international competition network as an international merger control institution', in John-ren Chen (ed.), *International Institutions and Multinational Enterprises*, Cheltenham, UK and Northampton, MA, USA: Edward Elgar, pp. 64–90.

Budzinski, Oliver (2004c), 'The international competition network: prospects and limits on the road towards international competition governance', *Competition and Change*, **8** (3), 223–42.

Budzinski, Oliver (2006), 'An economic perspective on the jurisdictional reform of the European merger control system', *European Competition Journal*, **2** (1), 119–40.

Budzinski, Oliver (forthcoming), 'Monoculture versus diversity of competition economics', *Cambridge Journal of Economics*.

Budzinski, Oliver and Aigner, Gisela (2005), 'Institutionelle Rahmenbedingungen für internationale Mergers & Acquisitions: Auf dem Weg zu einem globalen Fusionskontrollregime?', in Michael F. Strohmer (ed.), *Internationale Mergers & Acquisitions*, Frankfurt: Lang, pp. 189–232.

Budzinski, Oliver and Christiansen, Arndt (2005a), 'Aktuelle Reformen in der Europäischen Wettbewerbspolitik', *Wirtschaftswissenschaftliches Studium (WiSt)*, **34** (3), 165–9.

Budzinski, Oliver and Christiansen, Arndt (2005b), 'Competence allocation in the EU competition policy system as an interest-driven process', *Journal of Public Policy*, **25** (3), 313–37.

Budzinski, Oliver and Christiansen, Arndt (2007), 'The Oracle/PeopleSoft case: unilateral effects, simulation models and econometrics in contemporary merger control', *Legal Issues of Economic Integration*, **34** (2), 133–66.

Budzinski, Oliver and Kerber, Wolfgang (2003), *Megafusionen, Wettbewerb und Globalisierung*, Stuttgart: Lucius & Lucius.

Budzinski, Oliver, Jasper, Jörg and Kohler, Reinhard (1998), 'Die Bundesbank als Vorbild? Die Europäische Zentralbank und ihre stabilitätspolitische Effizienz', in Carsten Lange, Armin Rohde and Horst M. Westphal (eds), *Monetäre Aspekte der europäischen Integration*, Berlin: Duncker & Humblot, pp. 29–50.

Budzinski, Oliver, Jasper, Jörg and Tostmann, Ralf (2004), 'Geldpolitik im Europäischen System der Zentralbanken', Philipps-University of Marburg papers on economics 10-2004, Marburg.

Bulmer, Simon (1994), 'Institutions and policy change in the European

Communities: the case of merger control', *Public Administration*, **72** (3), 423–44.

Burnley, Richard (2002a), 'Interstate trade revisited: the jurisdictional criterion for Articles 81 and 82 E.C.', *European Competition Law Review*, **23** (2), 217–25.

Burnley, Richard (2002b), 'An appropriate jurisdictional trigger for the EC merger control regulation and the question of decentralisation', *World Competition*, **25** (3), 263–77.

Burns, Jean Wegman (2000), 'Embracing both faces of antitrust federalism', *Antitrust Law Journal*, **68** (1), 29–44.

Burton, John (1994), 'Competition over competition analysis: a guide to some contemporary economics disputes', in Julian Lonbay (ed.), *Frontiers of Competition Law*, London: Wiley, pp. 1–23.

Bush, Darren, Connor, John M., Flynn, John J., Gosh, Shubha, Grimes, Warren, Harrington, Joseph E., Hawker, Norman, Lande, Robert, Shepherd, William G. and Semeraro, Steven (2004), *Brief Amici Curiae in Support of Respondents, No. 03-724*, Washington, D.C.: Supreme Court of the United States.

Buxbaum, Hannah L. (2004), 'National courts, global cartels: F. Hoffman-LaRoche Ltd. v. Empagran, S.A.', *German Law Journal*, **5** (9), 1095–106.

Cabral, Luís M. (2003), 'International merger policy coordination', *Japan and the World Economy*, **15** (1), 21–30.

Cabral, Luís M. (2004), 'An equilibrium approach to international merger policy', Discussion Paper, New York: New York University.

Cadot, Olivier, Grether, Jean-Marie and De Melo, Jaime (2000), 'Trade and competition policy: where do we stand?', *Journal of World Trade*, **34** (3), 1–20.

Calbay, Yücel (2004), 'National systems of innovation in the context of industrial districts: historical roots and future prospects', in Oliver Budzinski and Jörg Jasper (eds), *Wettbewerb, Wirtschaftsordnung und Umwelt*, Frankfurt: Lang, pp. 243–58.

Calvani, Terry (2003), 'Devolution and convergence in competition enforcement', *European Competition Law Review*, **24** (9), 415–23.

Campbell, Neil and Trebilcock, Michael J. (1993), 'International merger review – problems of multi-jurisdictional conflict', in Erhard Kantzenbach, Hans-Eckart Scharrer and Leonard Waverman (eds), *Competition Policy in an Interdependent World Economy*, Baden-Baden, Germany: Nomos, pp. 129–63.

Campbell, Neil and Trebilcock, Michael J. (1997), 'Interjurisdictional conflict in merger review', in Leonard Waverman, William S. Comanor and Akira Goto (eds), *Competition Policy in the Global Economy*, London: Routledge, pp. 89–126.

Canenbley, Cornelis and Rosenthal, Michael (2005), 'Co-operation between antitrust authorities in- and outside the EU: what does it mean for multinational corporations?', *European Competition Law Review*, **26** (3), 178–87.

Carroll, Carolyn A. (2002), 'A century of mergers and acquisitions', in Benton E. Gup (ed.), *Megamergers in a Global Economy – Causes and Consequences*, Westport, CT: Quorum Books, pp. 19–43.

Cassel, Dieter (1996, ed.), *Entstehung und Wettbewerb von Systemen*, Berlin: Duncker & Humblot.

Castel, Jean-Gabriel (1984), 'The extraterritorial effects of antitrust laws', *Recueil des Cours*, **179** (1), 9–144.

Cengiz, Firat (2006), 'The role of state attorneys general in U.S. antitrust policy: public enforcement through private enforcement methods', CCP Working Paper No. 06-19, available at SSRN: http://ssrn.com/abstract=963992.

Chalmers, Alan F. (1990), *Science and its Fabrication*, Milton Keynes: Open University Press.

Chalmers, Alan F. (1995), 'Ultimate explanation in science', *Cogito*, **9**, 141–5.

Chang, Howard H., Evans, David S. and Schmalensee, Richard (2002), 'Has the consumer standard lost its teeth?', Brookings Joint Center working paper no. 4263-02, Washington, D.C.

Chenard, Pierre D. (2002), 'Transatlantic non-convergence – the cost of failing to change', in J. William Rowley (ed.), *International Merger Control: Prescriptions for Convergence*, London: International Bar Association, pp. 33–8.

Christiansen, Arndt (2006), 'The more-economic approach in EU merger control', *CESifo Forum*, **7** (1), 34–9.

Cimoli, Mario and Dosi, Giovanni (1995), 'Technological paradigms, patterns of learning and development', *Journal of Evolutionary Economics*, **5** (3), 243–68.

Clark, John W. (2000), 'Competition policy and regulatory reform in Brazil: a progress report', *OECD Journal of Competition Law and Policy*, **2** (3), 182–232.

Clarke, Julian L. and Evenett, Simon J. (2003), 'A multilateral framework for competition policy?', in State Secretariat of Economic Affairs and Simon J. Evenett (eds), *The Singapore Issues and the World Trading System: The Road to Cancún and Beyond*, Berne: State Secretariat of Economic Affairs, pp. 77–168.

Coase, Ronald H. (1960), 'The problem of social cost', *Journal of Law and Economics*, **3** (1), 1–44.

Coate, Malcolm B. (2000), 'Merger enforcement at the Federal Trade Commission in three presidential administrations', *Antitrust Bulletin*, **45** (2), 323–47.

Cocuzza, Claudio and Montini, Massimiliano (1998), 'International antitrust co-operation in a global economy', *European Competition Law Review*, **19** (3), 156–63.

Collie, David R. (2003), 'Mergers and trade policy under oligopoly', *Review of International Economics*, **11** (1), 55–71.

Connor, John M. (2004), 'Global antitrust prosecutions of modern international cartels', *Journal of Industry, Competition, and Trade*, **4** (3), 239–67.

Conrad, Christian A. (2005), *Improving International Competition Order – An Institutional Approach*, Basingstoke: Macmillan.

Cook, Paul (2002), 'Competition and its regulation: key issues', *Annals of Public and Cooperative Economics*, **73** (4), 541–58.

Correa, Carlos M. (1999), 'Competition law and development policies', in Roger Zäch (ed.), *Towards WTO Competition Rules*, Berne: Staempfli/Kluwer, pp. 361–93.

Cowie, Michael G. and Alves de Mattos, César C. (1999), 'Antitrust review of mergers, acquisitions, and joint ventures in Brazil', in *Antitrust Law Journal*, **67** (1), 113–57.

Da Costa, Carla T. and Bilreiro, Alexandra M. (2003), *The European Company Statute*, The Hague: Kluwer.

Dabbah, Maher M. (2003), *The Internationalisation of Antitrust Policy*, Cambridge: Cambridge University Press.

Damro, Chad (2004), 'Multilateral competition policy and transatlantic compromise', *European Foreign Affairs Review*, **9** (2), 269–87.

Davidow, Joel (1980), 'The UNCTAD restrictive business practices code', in Norbert Horn (ed.), *Legal Problems of Codes of Conduct for Multinational Enterprises*, Deventer, Netherlands: Kluwer, pp. 193–210.

Davidow, Joel (2002), 'International implications of US antitrust in the George W. Bush era', *World Competition*, **25** (4), 493–507.

Davidow, Joel (2004), 'Recent US antitrust developments of international relevance', *World Competition*, **27** (3), 407–17.

Davidow, Joel and Shapiro, Hal (2003), 'The feasibility and worth of a world trade organization competition agreement', *Journal of World Trade*, **37** (1), 49–68.

Davidow, William H. and Malone, Michael S. (1992), *The Virtual Corporation*, New York: HarperCollins.

Davison, Leigh and Johnson, Debra (2002), 'The EU's evolving stance on the international dimension of competition policy: a critical commentary', *Intereconomics*, **37** (5), 244–52.

De Bow, Michael (2004), 'State antitrust enforcement: empirical evidence and a modest reform proposal', in Richard A. Epstein and Michael S. Greve (eds), *Competition Laws in Conflict: Antitrust Jurisdiction in the Global Economy*, Washington, D.C.: AEI Press, pp. 267–87.

De León, Ignacio (1997), 'Should we promote antitrust in international trade?', *World Competition*, **21** (2), 35–63.

De Keyser, Kris and Laurila, Maija (2004), 'The new era of European antitrust enforcement: the main principles and mechanisms of the new regime for the enforcement of Articles 81 and 82 of the EC Treaty', *Kilpailuoikeudellinen Vuosikirja*, yearbook for 2003, pp. 11–20.

De Stefano, Martino and Rysman, Marc (2004), 'Competition policy as strategic trade', discussion paper, Boston.

Díaz, Francisco E. G. (2004), 'The reform of European merger control', *World Competition*, **27** (2), 177–99.

Doern, G. Bruce (1996a), 'Canadian competition policy institutions and decision processes', in G. Bruce Doern and Stephen Wilks (eds), *Comparative Competition Policy: National Institutions in a Global Market*, Oxford: Clarendon Press, pp. 68–101.

Doern, G. Bruce (1996b), 'The internationalization of competition policy', in G. Bruce Doern and Stephen Wilks (eds), *Comparative Competition Policy: National Institutions in a Global Market*, Oxford: Clarendon Press, pp. 302–26.

Dohmen, Frank (2005), *8000 Euro monatlich für den E.ON-Minister*, *Spiegel Online* 18 January, available at www.spiegel.de/wirtschaft/0,1518,druck-337319,00.html.

Domínguez Pérez, Dolores and Burnley, Richard (2003), 'The Article 9 referral back procedure: a solution to the jurisdictional dilemma of the European merger regulation', *European Competition Law Review*, **24** (8), 364–74.

Drauz, Götz (2002), 'Unbundling GE/Honeywell: the assessment of conglomerate mergers under EC competition law', in Barry E. Hawk (ed.), *Annual Proceedings of the Fordham Corporate Law Institute Conference on International Antitrust Law & Policy*, New York: Juris, pp. 183–201.

Drauz, Götz (2003), 'Merger review – jurisdictional issues', in Götz Drauz and Michael Reynolds (eds), *EC Merger Control: A Major Reform in Progress*, London: Richmond, pp. 17–27.

Drauz, Götz and Reynolds, Michael (2003, eds), *EC Merger Control: A Major Reform in Progress*, London: Richmond.

Drexl, Josef (1999), 'Trade-related restraints of competition', in Roger Zäch (ed.), *Towards WTO Competition Rules*, Berne: Staempfli/Kluwer, pp. 225–60.

Drexl, Josef (2003), 'Do we need "courage" for international antitrust law? Choosing between supranational and international law principles of enforcement', in Josef Drexl (ed.), *The Future of Transnational Antitrust: From Comparative to Common Competition Law*, Berne: Staempfli/Kluwer, pp. 311–41.

Drexl, Josef (2004), 'International competition policy after Cancún: placing a

Singapore issue on the WTO development agenda', *World Competition*, **27** (3), 419–57.

Drexl, Josef (2006), 'Gestaltungsansätze für eine internationale Wettbewerbspolitik', in Peter Oberender (ed.), *Internationale Wettbewerbspolitik*, Berlin: Duncker & Humblot, pp. 41–72.

Dunning, John H. (1997, ed.), *Governments, Globalization, and International Business*, Oxford: Oxford University Press.

Durand, Benoît, Galarza, Andrés F. and Mehta, Kirtikumar (2004), 'The interface between competition policy and international trade liberalisation – looking into the future: applying a new virtual anti-trust standard', *World Competition*, **27** (1), 3–12.

Easterbrook, Frank H. (1983), 'Antitrust and the economics of federalism', *Journal of Law and Economics*, **26** (1), 23–50.

Edquist, Charles (1997, ed.), *Systems of Innovation: Technologies, Organizations and Institutions*, London: Pinter.

Eguchi, Kiminori (2003), 'Cultural implications in the framework of basic issues of competition policy', in Josef Drexl (ed.), *The Future of Transnational Antitrust: From Comparative to Common Competition Law*, Berne: Staempfli/Kluwer, pp. 3–8.

Ehle, Dirk (1998), 'State regulation under the U.S. antitrust state action doctrine and under E.C. competition law: a comparative analysis', *European Competition Law Review*, **19** (6), 380–96.

Ehlermann, Claus-Dieter (1992), 'The contribution of EC competition policy to the single market', *Common Market Law Review*, **29** (2), 257–82.

Ehlermann, Claus Dieter (2000), 'The modernization of EC antitrust policy: a legal and cultural revolution', *Common Market Law Review*, **37** (3), 537–90.

Engel, Christoph (2004), 'Marktabgrenzung als soziale Konstruktion', in Andreas Fuchs, Hans-Peter Schwintowski and Daniel Zimmer (eds), *Wirtschafts- und Privatrecht im Spannungsfeld von Privatautonomie, Wettbewerb und Regulierung*, Munich: Beck, pp. 127–47.

Enriques, Luca (2003), 'Silence is golden: the European company statute as a catalyst for company law arbitrage', available at http://ssrn.com/abstract=384801.

Epstein, Richard A. and Greve, Michael S. (2004), 'In defense of small steps', in Richard A. Epstein and Michael S. Greve (eds), *Competition Laws in Conflict: Antitrust Jurisdiction in the Global Economy*, Washington, D.C.: AEI Press, pp. 333–52.

Erb, Thoralf, Jahraus, Jochen, Mummert, Uwe, Schulz, Axel and Voigt, Stefan (2000), *Konsequenzen der Globalisierung für die Wettbewerbspolitik*, Frankfurt: Lang.

European Central Bank (2004), *Statute of the ESCB and of the ECB Rules of Procedure*, Frankfurt: ECB.

European Commission (1996), Case No. IV/M.619 – Gencor/Lonrho, Regulation (EEC) No 4064/89 Merger Procedure, Brussels.
European Commission (1997), Case No IV/M.877 – Boeing/McDonnell Douglas, Regulation (EEC) No 4064/89 Merger Procedure, Brussels.
European Commission (2001a), Case NoComp/M.220 – General Electric/Honeywell, Regulation (EEC) No 4064/89 Merger Procedure, Brussels.
European Commission (2001b), Green Paper on the review of council regulation (EEC) No 4064/89, Brussels.
Evans, David S. and Salinger, Michael (2002), 'Competition thinking at the European Commission: lessons from the aborted GE/Honeywell merger', *George Mason Law Review*, **10** (3), 489–532.
Evans, David S., Nichols, Albert L. and Schmalensee, Richard (2005), 'US vs. Microsoft: did consumers win?' National Bureau of Economic Research working paper series 11727, Cambridge, MA.
Evenett, Simon J. (2002), 'How much have merger review laws reduced cross-border mergers and acquisitions?', in J. William Rowley (ed.), I*nternational Merger Control: Prescriptions for Convergence*, London: International Bar Association, pp. 39–55.
Evenett, Simon J. (2003), 'The cross border mergers and acquisitions wave of the late 1990s', National Bureau of Economic Research working paper no. w9655, London.
Evenett, Simon J., Levenstein, Margaret C. and Suslow, Valerie Y. (2001), 'International cartel enforcement: lessons from the 1990s', *World Economy*, **24** (9), 1221–45.
Falvey, Rod E. and Lloyd, Peter J. (1999), 'An economic analysis of extraterritoriality', GLM research paper 99/3, Nottingham.
Farrell, Joseph and Katz, Michael (2006), 'The economics of welfare standards in antitrust', *Competition Policy International*, **2** (2), 3–28.
Farrell, Joseph and Shapiro, Carl (1990), 'Horizontal mergers: an equilibrium analysis', *American Economic Review*, **80** (1), 107–26.
Fehr, Ernst and Gächter, Simon (2000), 'Fairness and retaliation – the economics of reciprocity', *Journal of Economic Perspectives*, **14** (3), 159–81.
Feinberg, Robert M. (1989), 'Imports as a threat to cartel stability', *International Journal of Industrial Organization*, **7** (2), 281–8.
Feinberg, Robert M. (1991), 'Antitrust policy and international trade liberalization', *World Competition*, **14** (4), 13–19.
Feld, Lars P., Zimmermann, Horst and Döring, Thomas (2004), *Federalism, Decentralization, and Economic Growth*, Philipps-University of Marburg papers on economics 30/2004, Marburg.
Fendel, Ralf and Frenkel, Michael (2003), 'Die Reform der

Abstimmungsregeln des EZB-Rates: eine kritische Analyse', *List Forum für Wirtschafts- und Finanzpolitik*, **29** (4), 407–22.
Figueiredo, Rui J. P. de and Weingast, Barry R. (2005), 'Self-enforcing federalism', *Journal of Law, Economics, and Organization*, **21** (1), 103–35.
Fikentscher, Wolfgang (1994), 'Competition rules for private agents in the GATT/WTO-system', *Aussenwirtschaft*, **49** (2–3), 281–325.
Fikentscher, Wolfgang (1998), 'Competition, culture, and economic (de-)regulation', in Hanns Ullrich (ed.), *Comparative Competition Law: Approaching an International System of Antitrust Law*, Baden-Baden, Germany: Nomos, pp. 77–91.
Fikentscher, Wolfgang (1999), 'Antitrust, market conceptualization and the World Trade Organization: the convention approach', in Roger Zäch (ed.), *Towards WTO Competition Rules*, Berne: Staempfli/Kluwer, pp. 73–94.
Fikentscher, Wolfgang (2003), 'Cultural implications in the framework of basic issues of competition law: comments', in Josef Drexl (ed.), *The Future of Transnational Antitrust: From Comparative to Common Competition Law*, Berne: Staempfli/Kluwer, pp. 9–19.
Fikentscher, Wolfgang and Immenga, Ulrich (1995, eds.), *Draft International Antitrust Code*, Baden-Baden, Germany: Nomos.
Finckenstein, Konrad von (2003), 'International antitrust policy and the international competition network', in Barry E. Hawk (ed.), *Annual Proceedings of the Fordham Corporate Law Institute Conference on International Antitrust Law & Policy*, New York: Juris, pp. 37–46.
Finger, Manuela and Schmieder, Sandra (2005), 'The new law against unfair competition: an assessment', *German Law Journal*, **6** (1), 201–16.
Fingleton, John (2005), 'The distribution and attribution of cases among the members of the network: the perspective of the Commission/NCAs', in Claus-Dieter Ehlermann and Isabela Atanasiu (eds), *Constructing the EU Network of Competition Authorities*, Oxford: Hart Publishing.
First, Harry (1998), 'Theories of harmonization: a cautionary tale', in Hanns Ullrich (ed.), *Comparative Competition Law: Approaching an International System of Antitrust Law*, Baden-Baden, Germany: Nomos, pp. 17–41.
First, Harry (1999), 'Towards an international common law of competition', in Roger Zäch (ed.), *Towards WTO Competition Rules*, Berne: Staempfli/Kluwer, pp. 95–126.
First, Harry (2000), 'Antitrust in Japan', *Pacific Rim Law & Policy Journal*, **9** (1) 1–71.
First, Harry (2001a), 'The vitamins case: cartel prosecutions and the coming of international competition law', in *Antitrust Law Journal*, **68** (3), 711–34.
First, Harry (2001b), 'Delivering remedies: the role of the states in antitrust enforcement', *George Washington Law Review*, **69** (5–6), 1701–37.

First, Harry (2003), 'Evolving toward what? – the development of international antitrust', in Josef Drexl (ed.), *The Future of Transnational Antitrust: From Comparative to Common Competition Law*, Berne: Staempfli/Kluwer, pp. 23–51.

First, Harry and Fox, Eleanor M. (2004), *Brief of Amici Curiae in Support of Respondents, No. 03-724*, Washington, D.C.: Supreme Court of the United States.

First, Harry and Shiraishi, Tadashi (2005), 'Concentrated power: the paradox of antitrust in Japan, law and economics', NYU School of Law working papers 11, New York.

Fisher, Franklin M. (1991), 'Organizing industrial organization: reflections of the handbook of industrial organization', *Brookings Papers on Economic Activity*, **1991** (1), 201–25.

Fisher, Franklin M. and Rubinfeld, Daniel L. (2001), 'U.S. v. Microsoft: an economic analysis', *Antitrust Bulletin*, **46** (1), 1–69.

Flexner, Donald L. and Racanelli, Mark A. (1994), 'State and federal antitrust enforcement in the United States: collision or harmony?', *Connecticut Journal of International Law*, **9** (3), 501–34.

Forrester, Ian (2004), 'Modernisation: an extension of the powers of the Commission?', in Damien Geradin (ed.), *Modernisation and Enlargement: Two Major Challenges for EC Competition Law*, Antwerp: Intersentia, pp. 83–97.

Forrester, Ian (2005), 'Diversity and consistency: can they cohabit?', in Claus-Dieter Ehlermann and Isabela Atanasiu (eds), *Constructing the EU Network of Competition Authorities*, Oxford: Hart Publishing.

Fox, Eleanor M. (1997), 'Toward world antitrust and market access', *American Journal of International Law*, **91** (1), 2–25.

Fox, Eleanor M. (1998a), 'International antitrust – against minimum rules; for cosmopolitan principles', *Antitrust Bulletin*, **43** (1), 5–13.

Fox, Eleanor M. (1998b), 'Antitrust regulation across national borders – the United States of Boeing versus the European Union of Airbus', *Brookings Review*, **16** (1), 30–32.

Fox, Eleanor M. (1999a), 'The merger regulation and its territorial reach: Gencor Ltd. v. Commission', *European Competition Law Review*, **20** (6), 334–6.

Fox, Eleanor M. (1999b), 'The problem of state action that blesses private action that harms "the foreigners"', in Roger Zäch (ed.), *Towards WTO Competition Rules*, Berne: Staempfli/Kluwer, pp. 325–40.

Fox, Eleanor M. (2000a), 'Antitrust and regulatory federalism: races up, down, and sideways', *New York University Law Review*, **75** (6), 1781–807.

Fox, Eleanor M. (2000b), 'National law, global markets, and Hartford: eyes wide shut', *Antitrust Law Journal*, **68** (1), 73–86.

Fox, Eleanor M. (2001), 'The kaleidoscope of antitrust and its significance in the world economy: respecting differences', in Barry E. Hawk (ed.), *Annual Proceedings of the Fordham Corporate Law Institute Conference on International Antitrust Law & Policy*, New York: Juris, pp. 597–603.

Fox, Eleanor M. (2002), 'U.S. and European merger policy – fault lines and bridges: mergers that creates incentives for exclusionary practices', *George Mason Law Review*, **10** (3), 471–88.

Fox, Eleanor M. (2003a), 'Can we solve the antitrust problems by extraterritoriality and cooperation? Sufficiency and legitimacy', *Antitrust Bulletin*, **48** (2), 355–76.

Fox, Eleanor M. (2003b), 'We protect competition, you protect competitors', *World Competition*, **26** (2), 149–65.

Fox, Eleanor M. (2003c), 'International antitrust and the Doha dome', *Virginia Journal of International Law*, **43** (4), 911–32.

Fox, Eleanor M. and Ordover, Janusz A. (1995), 'The harmonization of competition and trade law', *World Competition*, **19** (2), 5–34.

Fox, Eleanor M. and Sullivan, Lawrence A. (1987), 'Antitrust – retrospective and prospective', *New York University Law Review*, **62**, 936–68.

Freytag, Andreas and Zimmermann, Ralf (1998), 'Muß die internationale Handelsordnung um eine Wettbewerbsordnung erweitert werden?', in *Rabels Zeitschrift für ausländisches und internationales Privatrecht*, **62** (1), 38–58.

Friedman, James W. (1971), 'A noncooperative equilibrium for supergames', *Review of Economic Studies*, **38** (1), 1–12.

Fuchs, Doris A. (2004), 'Understanding business power in global governance', habilitation thesis, Munich: University of Munich.

Fullerton, Larry and Mazard, Camelia C. (2001), 'International antitrust cooperation agreements', *World Competition*, **24** (3), 405–23.

Gächter, Simon, Fehr, Ernst and Kment, Christiane (1996), 'Does social exchange increase voluntary cooperation?', *Kyklos*, **49** (4), 541–54.

García-Canal, Esteban, López Duarte, Cristina, Criado, Josep R. and Valdés Llaneza, Ana (2002), 'Accelerating international expansion through global alliances – a typology of cooperative strategies', *Journal of World Business*, **37** (2), 91–107.

Gaudet, Gérard and Kanouni, Rams (2004), 'Trade liberalization and the profitability of domestic mergers', *Review of International Economics*, **12** (3), 353–8.

Gerber, David J. (1998a), *Law and Competition in Twentieth Century Europe: Protecting Prometheus*, Oxford: Oxford University Press.

Gerber, David J. (1998b), 'Two models of competition law', in Hanns Ullrich (ed.), *Comparative Competition Law: Approaching an International System of Antitrust Law*, Baden-Baden, Germany: Nomos, pp. 105–16.

Gerber, David J. (1999), 'The U.S.–European conflict over the globalization of antitrust law: a legal experience perspective', *New England Law Review*, **34** (1), 123–42.

Gerber, David J. (2001), 'Modernising European competition law: a developmental perspective', *European Competition Law Review*, **22** (4), 122–30.

Gerber, David J. (2003), 'The European Commission's GE/Honeywell decision: US responses and their implications', *Journal of Competition Law (Zeitschrift für Wettbewerbsrecht)*, **1** (1), 87–95.

Gerber, David J. (2005), 'The evolution of a European competition law network', in Claus-Dieter Ehlermann and Isabela Atanasiu (eds), *Constructing the EU Network of Competition Authorities*, Oxford: Hart Publishing.

Gerken, Lüder (ed.) (1995), *Competition Among Institutions*, Basingstoke: Macmillan.

German Monopolies Commission (1999), *Kartellpolitische Wende in der Europäischen Union?*, *Sondergutachten 28*, Baden-Baden, Germany: Nomos.

German Monopolies Commission (2002a), *Zusammenschlussvorhaben der E.ON AG mit der Gelsenberg AG und der E.ON AG mit der Bergemann GmbH, Sondergutachten 34*, Baden-Baden, Germany: Nomos.

German Monopolies Commission (2002b), *Zusammenschlussvorhaben der E.ON AG mit der Gelsenberg AG und der E.ON AG mit der Bergemann GmbH, ergänzendes Sondergutachten 35*, Baden-Baden, Germany: Nomos.

Ghosal, Vivek and Gallo, Joseph (2001), 'The cyclical behavior of the Department of Justice's antitrust enforcement activity', *International Journal of Industrial Organization*, **19** (1–2), 27–54.

Gifford, Daniel J. (1997), 'The draft international antitrust code proposed at Munich: good intentions gone awry', *Minnesota Journal of Global Trade*, **6** (1), 1–66.

Gifford, Daniel J. and Kudrle, Robert T. (2003), 'European Union competition law and policy: how much latitude for convergence with the United States?', *Antitrust Bulletin*, **48** (3), 727–80.

Gifford, Daniel J. and Sullivan, Thomas (2000), 'Can international antitrust be saved for the post-Boeing-merger world?', *Antitrust Bulletin*, **45** (1), 55–118.

Gilbert, Richard J. and Katz, Michael (2001), 'An economist's guide to U.S. v. Microsoft', *Journal of Economic Perspectives*, **15** (2), 25–44.

Ginsburg, Douglas H. and Angstreich, Scott H. (2000), 'Multinational merger review: lessons from our federalism', *Antitrust Law Journal*, **68** (1), 219–37.

Giotakos, Dimitri (2002), 'GE/Honeywell: a theoretic bundle assessing conglomerate mergers across the Atlantic', *Journal of International Economic Law*, **23** (3), 469–511.

Giotakos, Dimitri, Petit, Laurent, Garnier, Gaelle, and De Luyck, Peter (2001), 'General Electric/Honeywell: an insight into the Commission's investigation and decision', *Competition Policy Newsletter*, **2001** (3), 5–13.

Goyder, Daniel G. (2003), *EC Competition Law*, 4th edn, Oxford: Oxford University Press.

Graham, Edward M. (2003), '"Internationalizing" competition policy: an assessment of the two main alternatives', *Antitrust Bulletin*, **48** (4), 947–72.

Graham, Edward M. and Richardson, J. David (eds) (1997), *Global Competition Policy*, Washington, D.C.: Institute for International Economics.

Greaney, Theresa M. (1999), 'Strategic trade and competition policies to assist distressed industries', *Canadian Journal of Economics*, **32** (3), 767–84.

Grewlich, Alexandre S. (2001), 'Globalisation and conflict in competition law: elements of possible solutions', *World Competition*, **24** (3), 367–404.

Griffin, Joseph P. (1999), 'Extraterritoriality in U.S. and EU antitrust enforcement', *Antitrust Law Journal*, **67** (1), 159–99.

Grimes, Warren S. (1998), 'International antitrust enforcement directed at restrictive practices and concentration: the United States' experience', in Hanns Ullrich (ed.), *Comparative Competition Law: Approaching an International System of Antitrust Law*, Baden-Baden, Germany: Nomos, pp. 219–39.

Grimes, Warren S. (2003), 'The Microsoft litigation and federalism in U.S. antitrust enforcement: implications for international competition law', in Josef Drexl (ed.), *The Future of Transnational Antitrust: From Comparative to Common Competition Law*, Berne: Staempfli/Kluwer, pp. 237–58.

Gröner, Helmut and Knorr, Andreas (1996), 'Internationalisierung der Wettbewerbspolitik', in Ulrich Immenga, Wernhard Möschel and Dieter Reuter (eds), *Festschrift für Ernst-Joachim Mestmäcker*, Baden-Baden, Germany: Nomos, pp. 579–91.

Grundmann, Stefan and Kerber, Wolfgang (2002), 'European system of contract laws: a map for combining the advantages of centralised and decentralised rule-making', in Stefan Grundmann and Jules Stuyck (eds), *An Academic Green Paper on European Contract Law*, Dordrecht, Netherlands: Kluwer, pp. 295–342.

Guersent, Olivier (2004), *The Fight Against International Cartels of the European Commission: 19 Decisions in 19 Months Between July 2001 and December 2003*, Brussels: EU.

Günther, Eberhard (1961), 'Die Problematik einer völkerrechtlichen Regelung internationaler Wettbewerbsbeschränkungen', in International Conference on Restraints of Competition (ed.), *Cartel and Monopoly in Modern Law*, Karlsruhe, Germany: Müller, pp. 551–602.

Güth, Werner and Kliemt, Hartmut (1994), 'Competition or co-operation: on the evolutionary economics of trust, exploitation and moral attitudes', *Metroeconomica*, **45** (2), 155–87.

Güth, Werner, Ockenfels, Peter and Wendel, Markus (1997), 'Cooperation based on trust: an experimental investigation', *Journal of Economic Psychology*, **18** (1), 15–43.

Guzman, Andrew T. (1998), 'Is international antitrust possible?', *New York University Law Review*, **73** (5), 1501–48.

Guzman, Andrew T. (2001), 'Antitrust and international regulatory federalism', *New York University Law Review*, **76** (4), 1142–63.

Guzman, Andrew T. (2004), 'The case for international antitrust', in Richard A. Epstein and Michael S. Greve (eds), *Competition Laws in Conflict: Antitrust Jurisdiction in the Global Economy*, Washington, D.C.: AEI Press, pp. 99–125.

Häckner, Jonas (2001), 'Market delineation and product differentiation', *Journal of Industry, Competition and Trade*, **1** (1), 81–99.

Hahn, Robert M. and Layne-Farrar, Anne (2003), 'Federalism in antitrust', *Harvard Journal of Law and Public Policy*, **26** (3), 877–921.

Haldrup, Niels (2003), *Empirical Analysis of Price Data in the Delineation of the Relevant Geographic Market in Competition Analysis*, Aarhus, Denmark: University of Aarhus.

Haley, John O. (1998), 'Culture, competition and deregulation: Japan's challenge to international harmonization of competition law', in Hanns Ullrich (ed.), *Comparative Competition Law: Approaching an International System of Antitrust Law*, Baden-Baden, Germany: Nomos, pp. 93–104.

Hamilton, Lynda S. and Flecher, Leslie B. (2004), 'A case study for international antitrust: Pepsi versus Coke', *Journal of Euromarketing*, **13** (2–3), 125–42.

Hamilton, Stephen F. and Stiegert, Kyle (2000), 'Vertical coordination, antitrust law, and international trade', *Journal of Law and Economics*, **43** (1), 143–56.

Hamlin, Alan P. (1991), 'Decentralization, competition and the efficiency of federalism', *Economic Record*, **67** (2), 193–204.

Hansen, Knud (2000, ed.), *Mega-mergers – a New Challenge for Antitrust Laws, Proceedings of the 9th International Conference on Competition*, Bonn: Bundeskartellamt.

Hanushek, Eric A. (2004), 'What if there are no "best practices"?', *Scottish Journal of Political Economy*, **51** (2), 156–72.

Haucap, Justus and Kruse, Jörn (2004), 'Ex-ante Regulierung oder Ex-post Aufsicht für netzgebundene Industrien?', in *Wirtschaft und Wettbewerb*, **54** (3), 266–75.

Haucap, Justus, Müller, Florian and Wey, Christian (2006), 'How to reduce conflicts over international antitrust', *Conferences on New Political Economy*, **23**, 307–43.

Hauser, Heinz and Schoene, Rainer E. (1994), 'Is there a need for international competition rules?', *Aussenwirtschaft*, **49** (2–3), 205–22.

Hayek, Friedrich August von (1937), 'Economics and knowledge', *Economica*, **4** (1), 33–54.

Hayek, Friedrich August von (1945), 'The use of knowledge in society', *American Economic Review*, **35** (4), 519–30.

Hayek, Friedrich August von (1973), *Law, Legislation and Liberty – 1: Rules and Order*, Chicago: University of Chicago Press.

Hayek, Friedrich August von (1975), 'The pretence of knowledge', *Swedish Journal of Economics*, **77** (4), 433–42.

Hazledine, Tim (1992), 'Trade policy as competition policy', in Shyam Khemani and William T. Stanbury (eds), *Canadian Competition Law and Policy at the Centenary*, Halifax: Institute for Research on Public Policy, pp. 45–60.

Head, Keith and Ries, John (1997), 'International mergers and welfare under decentralized competition policy', *Canadian Journal of Economics*, **30** (4), 1104–23.

Hefeker, Carsten (2002), 'Monetary policy in a union of 27: enlargement and reform options', *Intereconomics*, **37** (6), 315–20.

Heimler, Alberto (2003), 'The Green Paper on the review of Council Regulation 4064/89: some comments on the jurisdictional issues', in Götz Drauz and Michael Reynolds (eds), *EC Merger Control: A Major Reform in Progress*, London: Richmond, pp. 29–36.

Heine, Klaus (2003), *Regulierungswettbewerb im Gesellschaftsrecht: Zur Funktionsfähigkeit eines Wettbewerbs der Rechtsordnungen im europäischen Gesellschaftsrecht*, Berlin: Duncker & Humblot.

Heine, Klaus and Kerber, Wolfgang (2002), 'European corporate laws, regulatory competition and path dependence', *European Journal of Law and Economics*, **13** (1), 47–71.

Helfat, Constance E. and Lieberman, Marvin B. (2002), 'The birth of capabilities: market entry and the importance of pre-history', *Industrial and Corporate Change*, **11** (4), 725–60.

Hellmann, Wolfgang (2001), 'Global mergers and Australian merger control', *Wirtschaft und Wettbewerb*, **51** (11), 1055–64.

Héritier, Adrienne (2002, ed.), *Common Goods: Reinventing European and International Governance*, London: Rowman & Littlefield Publ.

Hewitt, Gary (1999), 'The relationship between competition and regulatory authorities', *OECD Journal of Competition Law and Policy*, **1** (3), 177–219.

Heyer, Ken (2005), 'A world of uncertainty: economics and the globalization of antitrust', *Antitrust Law Journal*, **72** (2), 375–422.

Heyer, Ken (2006), 'Welfare standards and merger analysis: why not the best?', *Competition Policy International*, **2** (2), 29–54.

Hirsbrunner, Simon (1999), 'Referral of mergers in E.C. merger control', *European Competition Law Review*, **20** (7), 372–8.

Hoekman, Bernard (1997), 'Competition policy and the global trading system', *World Economy*, **20** (4), 383–406.

Hoekman, Bernard and Mavroidis, Petros C. (1994), 'Competition, competition policy and the GATT', *World Economy*, **17** (2), 121–50.

Hoekman, Bernard and Mavroidis, Petros C. (2003), 'Economic development, competition policy and the WTO', *Journal of World Trade*, **37** (1), 1–28.

Hoekman, Bernard and Saggi, Kamal (2004), *International Cooperation on Domestic Policies: Lessons from the WTO Competition Policy Debate, DP4693*, London: Centre for Economic Policy Research.

Holmes, Peter (2002), 'Trade and competition in the new WTO round', in Chris Milner and Robert Read (eds), *Trade Liberalization, Competition and the WTO*, Cheltenham, UK and Northampton, MA, USA: Edward Elgar, pp. 147–75.

Hooghe, Liesbet and Marks, Gary (2001), *Multi-Level Governance and European Integration*, Lanham, MD: Rowman & Littlefield.

Hoppmann, Erich (1961), 'Wettbewerbspolitik und Exportkartelle', *Jahrbücher für Nationalökonomie und Statistik*, **173**, 343–82.

Horn, Henrik and Levinsohn, James (2001), 'Merger policies and trade liberalisation', *Economic Journal*, **111** (3), 244–76.

Hovenkamp, Herbert (1999), *Federal Antitrust Policy – The Law of Competition and its Practice*, 2nd edn, St. Paul, MN: West Group.

Hovenkamp, Herbert (2003), 'Antitrust as extraterritorial regulatory policy', *The Antitrust Bulletin*, **48** (3), 629–55.

Hovenkamp, Herbert (2005), *Federalism and Antitrust Reform*, University of Iowa Legal Studies research paper no. 05-24, available at SSRN: http://ssrn.com/abstract=819386.

Hudec, Robert E. (1999), 'A WTO perspective on private anti-competitive behavior in world markets', *New England Law Review*, **34** (1), 79–100.

Hüschelrath, Kai (2002), 'International cartels and competition policy – what's behind the recent success?', in Clemens Esser and Michael H. Stierle (eds), *Current Issues in Competition Theory and Policy*, Berlin: VWF, pp. 133–53.

Hüschelrath, Kai and Rommel, Kai (2004), 'Divergent views – the notional effects of the E.ON–Ruhrgas merger', in Michael Pickhardt and Kai Rommel (eds), *Competition Policy in Energy Markets*, Berlin: VWF, pp. 17–38.

Hussinger, Katrin (2005), 'Did concentration on core competencies drive merger and acquisition activities in the 1990s?', ZEW discussion paper 05-41, Mannheim.

Hutchins, Abbe (2004), *Moving Towards a Single Economic Market: Should Australia and New Zealand Further Co-ordinate their Competition Policy?*, Toronto: University of Toronto.

Iacobucci, Edward M. (1997), 'The interdependence of trade and competition policies', *World Competition*, **21** (2), 5–33.

ICN (2002), 'Report on the costs and burdens of multijurisdictional merger review, Napoli', available at www.internationalcompetitionnetwork.org/costburd.doc, downloaded in January 2004.

ICN (2003a), 'Analysis of merger guidelines', available at www.international-competitionnetwork.org/analysisofmerger.html, downloaded 10 March 2005.

ICN (2003b), 'Compendium of investigative tools', available at www.internationalcompetitionnetwork.org/ReportIT.pdf, downloaded 10 March 2005.

ICN (2004), 'Recommended practices for merger notification procedures', available at www.internationalcompetitionnetwork.org/mnprecpractices.pdf, downloaded 10 March 2005.

ICPAC (2000), *International Competition Policy Advisory Committee: Final Report*, Washington, D.C.: Department of Justice, Antitrust Division.

Immenga, Ulrich (1994), 'The failure of present institutions and rules to respond to the globalization of competition', *Aussenwirtschaft*, **49** (2–3), 201–04.

Immenga, Ulrich (2004), 'Internationalization of competition laws: levels of diversities', in Tzong-Leh Hwang and Chiyuan Chen (eds), *The Future Development of Competition Framework*, The Hague: Kluwer, pp. 3–10.

Inman, Robert P. and Rubinfeld, Daniel P. (1997), 'Rethinking federalism', *Journal of Economic Perspectives*, **11** (4), 43–64.

Irwin, Douglas A. and Pavcnik, Nina (2004), 'Airbus versus Boeing revisited: international competition in the aircraft market', *Journal of International Economics*, **64** (2), 223–45.

Isele, Kathrin (2003), 'Fusionskontrolle im Standortwettbewerb', University of Potsdam discussion paper, Potsdam.

Iyori, Hiroshi (1999), 'Competition culture and the aims of competition law', in Roger Zäch (ed.), *Towards WTO Competition Rules*, Berne: Staempfli/Kluwer, pp. 127–36.

Jacquemin, Alexis (1995), 'Towards an internationalisation of competition policy', *World Economy*, **18** (6), 781–9.

James, Charles A. (2001), 'Statement on the EU's decision regarding the GE/Honeywell acquisition', available at www.usdoj.gov/atr/public/press_releases/2001/8510.htm.

Janow, Merit E. (2000), 'Transatlantic cooperation on competition policy', in Simon J. Evenett, Alexander Lehmann and Benn Steil (eds), *Antitrust Goes Global – What Future for Transatlantic Cooperation?*, Washington, D.C.: Brookings Institution Press, pp. 29–56.

Janow, Merit E. (2003), 'Observations on two multilateral venues: the International Competition Network (ICN) and the WTO', in Barry E. Hawk (ed.), *Annual Proceedings of the Fordham Corporate Law Institute Conference on International Antitrust Law & Policy*, New York: Juris, pp. 47–68.

Janow, Merit E. and Lewis, Cynthia R. (2001), 'International antitrust and the global economy', *World Competition*, **24** (1), 3–21.

Jansen, Stephan A. and Müller-Stewens, Günter (2001), 'Pre- und Post Merger-Integration bei grenzüberschreitenden Zusammenschlüssen: Trends, Tools, Thesen und empirische Tests von Old und New Economy Deals', in Stephan A. Jansen, Gerhard Picot and Dirk Schiereck (eds), *Internationales Fusionsmanagement: Erfolgsfaktoren grenzüberschreitender Unternehmenskäufe*, Stuttgart: Schäffer-Poeschel, pp. 3–33.

Jarillo, J. Carlos (1993), *Strategic Networks: Creating the Borderless Organization*, Oxford: Butterworth-Heinemann.

Jenny, Frédéric (1995), 'Evolution of antitrust policies in France', in Giuliano Mussati (ed.), *Mergers, Markets and Public Policy*, Dordrecht, Netherlands: Kluwer, pp. 163–200.

Jenny, Frédéric (1999), 'Globalization, competition and trade policy: issues and challenges', in Roger Zäch (ed.), *Towards WTO Competition Rules*, Berne: Staempfli/Kluwer, pp. 3–41.

Jenny, Frédéric (2003a), 'Competition law and policy: global governance issues', *World Competition*, **26** (4), 609–24.

Jenny, Frédéric (2003b), 'International cooperation on competition: myth, reality and perspective', *Antitrust Bulletin*, **48** (4), 973–1003.

Jenny, Frédéric (2004), 'Competition, trade and development before and after Cancún', in Barry E. Hawk (ed.), *Annual Proceedings of the Fordham Corporate Law Institute Conference on International Antitrust Law & Policy*, New York: Juris, pp. 631–56.

Jin, Paul (2002), 'Turning competition on its head: economic analysis of the EC's decision to bar the GE–Honeywell merger', *Northwestern Journal of International Law & Business*, **23** (1), 187–212.

Jones, Clifford A. (2005), *Private Enforcement of Antitrust Law in the EU, UK and US*, Oxford: Oxford University Press.

Kaiser, Bruno and Vosgerau, Hans-Jürgen (2000), 'Global harmonisation of national competition policies', in Hans-Jürgen Vosgerau (ed.), *Institutional Arrangements for Global Economic Integration*, Basingstoke: Macmillan, pp. 35–59.

Karpoff, Jonathan M. and Wessels, David (2002), 'Large mergers during the 1990s', in Benton E. Gup (ed.), *Megamergers in a Global Economy – Causes and Consequences*, Westport, CT: Quorum Books, pp. 45–63.

Kaserman, David L. and Mayo, John W. (1995), *Government and Business:*

The Economics of Antitrust and Regulation, Fort Worth, TX: Dryden Press.

Kee, Hiau Looi and Hoekman, Bernard (2003), 'Imports, entry and competition law as market disciplines', World Bank policy research paper 3031, Washington, D.C.

Kemp, Murray C. and Shimomura, Koji (2002), 'Recent challenges to the classical gains-from-trade proposition', *German Economic Review*, **3** (4), 485–9.

Kennedy, Kevin C. (2001), *Competition Law and the World Trade Organisation: The Limits of Multilateralism*, London: Sweet & Maxwell.

Kenyon, Daphne A. and Kincaid, John (eds) (1991), *Competition Among States and Local Governments. Efficiency and Equity in American Federalism*, Washington, D.C.: Urban Institute Press.

Keohane, Robert O. (2002), 'Ironies of sovereignty: the European Union and the United States', *Journal of Common Market Studies*, **40** (4), 743–65.

Kerber, Wolfgang (1993), 'Rights, innovations and evolution: the distributional effects of different rights to innovate', *Review of Political Economy*, **5** (3), 427–52.

Kerber, Wolfgang (1997), 'Wettbewerb als Hypothesentest: Eine evolutorische Konzeption wissenschaffenden Wettbewerbs', in Karl von Delhaes and Ulrich Fehl (eds), *Dimensionen des Wettbewerbs: Seine Rolle in der Entstehung und Ausgestaltung von Wirtschaftsordnungen*, Stuttgart: Lucius & Lucius, pp. 29–78.

Kerber, Wolfgang (1998), 'Zum Problem einer Wettbewerbsordnung für den Systemwettbewerb', *Jahrbuch für Neue Politische Ökonomie*, **17**, 199–231.

Kerber, Wolfgang (1999), 'Wettbewerbspolitik als nationale und internationale Aufgabe', in Thomas Apolte, Rolf Caspers and Paul J. J. Welfens (eds), *Standortwettbewerb: Wirtschaftspolitische Rationalität und internationale Ordnungspolitik*, Baden-Baden, Germany: Nomos, pp. 241–69.

Kerber, Wolfgang (2000a), 'Rechtseinheitlichkeit und Rechtsvielfalt aus ökonomischer Sicht', in Stefan Grundmann (ed.), *Systembildung und Systemlücken in Kerngebieten des Europäischen Privatrechts. Gesellschafts-, Arbeits- und Schuldvertragsrecht*, Tübingen, Germany: Mohr Siebeck, pp. 67–97.

Kerber, Wolfgang (2000b), 'Interjurisdictional competition within the European Union', in *Fordham International Law Journal*, **23** (S), 217–49.

Kerber, Wolfgang (2002), 'German and European competition policy: perspectives for the 21st century', in Hiroyuki Ono (ed.), *Structural Changes in the Japanese and German Economies: What Can We Learn from Each Other?*, Tokyo: Toyo University, pp. 36–53.

Kerber, Wolfgang (2003), 'International multi-level system of competition laws: federalism in antitrust', in Josef Drexl (ed.), *The Future of Transnational Antitrust: From Comparative to Common Competition Law*, Berne: Staempfli/Kluwer, pp. 269–300.

Kerber, Wolfgang (2005), 'Applying evolutionary economics to economic policy: the example of competitive federalism', in Kurt Dopfer (ed.), *Economics, Evolution, and the State: The Complexity of Governance*, Cheltenham, UK and Northampton, MA, USA: Edward Elgar, pp. 296–324.

Kerber, Wolfgang and Budzinski, Oliver (2003), 'Towards a differentiated analysis of competition of competition laws', *Journal of Competition Law (Zeitschrift für Wettbewerbsrecht)*, **1** (4), 411–48.

Kerber, Wolfgang and Budzinski, Oliver (2004), 'Competition of competition laws: mission impossible?', in Richard A. Epstein and Michael S. Greve (eds), *Competition Laws in Conflict: Antitrust Jurisdiction in the Global Economy*, Washington, D.C.: AEI Press, pp. 31–65.

Kerber, Wolfgang and Eckardt, Martina (2005), 'Improving the international competitiveness of the EU by regulatory competition and the "open method of coordination" – the example of pension systems', in Cornelia Storz (ed.), *Germany and Japan in Competition for FDI: Tax Systems, Regulations and Business Strategies*, Marburg, Germany: Metropolis, pp. 96–118.

Kerber, Wolfgang and Eckardt, Martina (2007), 'Policy learning in Europe: the "open method of coordination" and laboratory federalism', *Journal of European Public Policy*, **14** (2), 227–47.

Kerber, Wolfgang and Heine, Klaus (2002), 'Zur Gestaltung von Mehr-Ebenen-Rechtssystemen aus ökonomischer Sicht', in Claus Ott and Hans-Bernd Schäfer (eds), *Vereinheitlichung und Diversität des Zivilrechts in transnationalen Wirtschaftsräumen*, Tübingen, Germany: Mohr Siebeck, pp. 167–94.

Kerber, Wolfgang and Schwalbe, Ulrich (2007), 'Economic foundations of competition law', in Franz-Jürgen Säcker, Günther Hirsch and Frank Montag (eds), *Competition Law: European Community Practice and Procedure – Article-by-article Commentary of the EC Competition Law*, London: Sweet & Maxwell, pp. 202–393.

Kingston, Suzanne (2001), 'A "new division of responsibilities" in the proposed regulation to modernise the rules implementing Articles 81 and 82 E.C.? A warning call', *European Competition Law Review*, **22** (8), 340–48.

Kiwit, Daniel and Voigt, Stefan (1998), 'Grenzen des institutionellen Wettbewerbs', *Jahrbuch für Neue Politische Ökonomie*, **17**, 313–37.

Klees, Andreas (2003), 'Der Vorschlag für eine neue EG-Fusionskontrollverordnung', *Europäische Zeitschrift für Wirtschaftsrecht*, **2003** (7), 197–202.

Klein, Joel I. (1996), 'A note of caution with respect to a WTO agenda on competition policy', available at www.usdoj.gov/atr/public/speeches/0998.pdf, downloaded July 2005.

Klein, Joel I. (2000), 'Time for a global competition initiative?', in International Bar Association (ed.), *EC Merger Control: Ten Years On*, New York: IBA, pp. 59–64.

Kleinert, Jörn and Klodt, Henning (2000a), *Megafusionen: Trends, Ursachen und Implikationen*, Tübingen, Germany: Mohr Siebeck.

Kleinert, Jörn and Klodt, Henning (2000b): 'Megafusionen: Auf dem Weg in die Unternehmensstrukturen der Zukunft?', *Zeitschrift für Wirtschaftspolitik*, **49** (2), 169–76.

Kleinert, Jörn and Klodt, Henning (2002), 'Causes and consequences of merger waves', Institute of World Economics working paper no. 1092, Kiel.

Klodt, Henning (2001), 'Conflict and conflict resolution in international antitrust: do we need international competition rules?', *The World Economy*, **24** (7), 877–88.

Klodt, Henning (2005), *Towards a Global Competition Order*, Berlin: Liberal.

Knorr, Andreas (1999), 'Wettbewerbsregeln statt Antidumpingregeln', *List Forum für Wirtschafts- und Finanzpolitik*, **25** (4), 414–31.

Kolasky, William J. (2002), 'Conglomerate mergers and range effects: it's a long way from Chicago to Brussels', *George Mason Law Review*, **10** (3), 533–50.

Komninos, Assimakis P. (2006), 'Public and private antitrust enforcement in Europe: Complement? Overlap?', *Competition Law Review*, **3** (1), 5–26.

Körber, Torsten (2004), 'Die Empagran-Entscheidung des US Supreme Court', *Journal of Competition Law (Zeitschrift für Wettbewerbsrecht)*, **2** (4), 591–603.

Kotsogiannis, Christos and Schwager, Robert (2006), 'On the incentives to experiment in federations', *Journal of Urban Economics*, **60** (3), 484–97.

Kovacic, William E. (1992), 'The influence of economics on antitrust law', *Economic Inquiry*, **30** (2), 294–306.

Kovacic, William E. (1996), 'Downsizing antitrust: is it time to end dual federal enforcement?', *Antitrust Bulletin*, **41** (3), 505–40.

Kovacic, William E. (2001), 'Transatlantic turbulence: the Boeing-McDonnell Douglas merger and international competition policy', *Antitrust Law Journal*, **69** (2), 805–74.

Kovacic, William E. (2003), 'The modern evolution of U.S. competition policy enforcement norms', *Antitrust Law Journal*, **71** (2), 377–478.

Kovacic, William E. (2004), 'Toward a domestic competition network', in Richard A. Epstein and Michael S. Greve (eds), *Competition Laws in Conflict: Antitrust Jurisdiction in the Global Economy*, Washington, D.C.: AEI Press, pp. 316–32.

Kovacic, William E. and Shapiro, Carl (2000), 'Antitrust policy: a century of economic and legal thinking', *Journal of Economic Perspectives*, **14** (1), 43–60.

Krattenmaker, Thomas G. and Pitofsky, Robert (1988), 'Antitrust merger policy and the Reagan administration', *Antitrust Bulletin*, **33** (2), 211–32.

Kroes, Neelie (2005), 'Editorial', *Competition Policy Newsletter*, **2005** (1), 1–2.

Krugman, Paul (1987), 'Is free trade passé?', *Journal of Economic Perspectives*, **1** (2), 131–44.

Kühn, Kai-Uwe (1997), 'Germany', in Edward M. Graham and J. David Richardson (eds), *Global Competition Policy*, Washington, D.C.: Institute for International Economics, pp. 115–49.

Kuhn, Thomas S. (1962), *The Structure of Scientific Revolutions*, Chicago: Chicago University Press.

Ladeur, Karl-Heinz (1997), 'Towards a legal theory of supranationality – the viability of the network concept', *European Law Journal*, **3** (1), 33–54.

Lakatos, Imre (1970), 'Falsification and the methodology of scientific research programmes', in Imre Lakatos and Alan Musgrave (eds), *Criticism and the Growth of Knowledge*, Cambridge: Cambridge University Press, pp. 91–196.

Lakatos, Imre (1978), *The Methodology of Scientific Research Programmes*, Cambridge: Cambridge University Press.

Lamoureaux, Naomi R. (1985), *The Great Merger Movement in American Business 1895–1904*, Cambridge: Cambridge University Press.

Lampert, Thomas (1999), 'International co-operation among competition authorities', *European Competition Law Review*, **20** (4), 214–24.

Lande, Robert H. (1990), 'When should states challenge mergers: a proposed federal/state balance', *New York Law School Law Review*, **35**, 1047–62.

Leary, Thomas B. (2001), 'The significance of variety in antitrust analysis', *Antitrust Law Journal*, **68** (3), 1007–22.

Leary, Thomas B. (2002), 'The essential stability of merger policy in the United States', *Antitrust Law Journal*, **70** (1), 105–42.

Lee, Hwang (2002), 'Influencing a global agenda: implications of the modernization of European competition law for the WTO', *Erasmus Law & Economics Review*, **1** (2), 111–41.

Lee, Nam-Kee (2002), *Toward a Mature Market Economy: Competition Law and Policy in Korea*, Seoul: Korea Fair Trade Commission.

Lenaerts, Koen and Gerard, Damien (2004), 'Decentralisation of EC competition law enforcement: judges in the frontline', *World Competition*, **27** (3), 313–49.

Letin, Alexander B. (2004), 'Globalization and development of competition policy in the Russian Federation', in Tzong-Leh Hwang and Chiyuan Chen (eds), *The Future Development of Competition Framework*, The Hague: Kluwer, pp. 89–92.

Levenstein, Margaret C. and Suslow, Valerie Y. (2002), 'What determines cartel success?', University of Michigan working paper 02-001, Ann Arbor, MI.

Levenstein, Margaret C. and Suslow, Valerie Y. (2004), 'Contemporary international cartels and developing countries: economic effects and implications for competition policy', *Antitrust Law Journal*, **71** (2), 801–52.

Lever, Jeremy (2002), 'The German Monopolies Commission's report on the problems consequent upon the reform of the European cartel procedures', *European Competition Law Review*, **23** (7), 321–25.

Levy, Nicholas (2005), 'Mario Monti's legacy in EC merger control', *Competition Policy International*, **1** (1), 99–132.

Lin, Ping, Raj, Baldev, Sandfort, Michael and Slottje, Daniel (2000), 'The US antitrust system and recent trends in antitrust enforcement', *Journal of Economic Surveys*, **14** (3), 255–306.

Lindsay, Alistair, Lecchi, Emanuela and Williams, Geoffrey (2003), 'Econometrics study into commission merger decisions since 2000', *European Competition Law Review*, **24** (12), 673–82.

Lipstein, Robert A. (1997), 'Using antitrust principles to reform antidumping law', in Edward M. Graham and J. David Richardson (eds), *Global Competition Policy*, Washington, D.C.: Institute for International Economics, 405–38.

Litan, Robert E. and Shapiro, Carl (2001), 'Antitrust policy during the Clinton administration', Competition Policy Center paper CPC 01-022, Berkeley, CA.

Lloyd, Peter J. (2003), 'Competition policy in APEC, ASEAN and the WTO', in Tran Van Hoa (ed.), *Competition Policy and Global Competitiveness in Major Asian Economies*, Cheltenham, UK and Northampton, MA, USA: Edward Elgar, pp. 15–28.

Lloyd, Peter J. and Vautier, Kerrin M. (1999), *Promoting Competition in Global Markets*, Cheltenham, UK and Northampton, MA, USA: Edward Elgar.

Lo, Changfa (2004), 'Refreshed approaches to the development of global competition framework', in Tzong-Leh Hwang and Chiyuan Chen (eds), *The Future Development of Competition Framework*, The Hague: Kluwer, pp. 93–106.

Lundvall, Bengt-Åke (1992, ed.), *National Systems of Innovation: Towards a Theory of Innovation and Interactive Learning*, London: Pinter.

Lundvall, Bengt-Åke and Borrás, Susana (2005), 'Science, technology, and innovation policy', in Jan Fagerberg, David C. Mowery, and Richard R.

Nelson (eds), *The Oxford Handbook of Innovation*, Oxford: Oxford University Press, pp. 599–631.

Lyons, Bruce R. (2003), 'Could politicians be more right than economists? A theory of merger standards', European University Institute working papers RSC 2003/14, San Domenico di Fiesole, Italy.

Lyons, Bruce R. (2004), 'Reform of European merger policy', *Review of International Economics*, **12** (2), 246–61.

Maher, Imelda (2002), 'Competition law in the international domain: networks as a new form of governance', *Journal of Law and Society*, **29** (1), 111–36.

Marin, Bernd and Mayntz, Renate (eds) (1991), *Policy Networks – Empirical Evidence and Theoretical Considerations*, Frankfurt: Campus.

Markl, Rainer and Meissner, Werner (2000), 'Strategic trade and international competition policy', in Wolfram Elsner and John Groenewegen (eds), *Industrial Policies after 2000*, Dordrecht, Netherlands: Kluwer, pp. 175–98.

Marks, Gary (1996), 'An actor-centred approach to multi-level governance', *Regional and Federal Studies*, **6** (2), 20–38.

Martin, Stephen (1998, ed.), *Competition Policies in Europe*, Amsterdam: North-Holland.

Massey, Patrick (2000), 'Market definition and market power in competition analysis: some practical issues', *Economic and Social Review*, **31** (4), 309–28.

Masson, Paul (2001), 'Globalization: facts and figures', IMF policy discussion paper 01/4, Washington, D.C.

Mavroidis, Petros C. and Neven, Damien J. (2001), 'From the White Paper to the proposal for a council regulation: how to treat the new kids on the block', *Legal Issues of Economic Integration*, **28** (2), 151–71.

McCurdy, Gregory (2004), 'The impact of modernisation of the EU competition law system on the courts and private enforcement of the competition laws: a comparative perspective', *European Competition Law Review*, **25** (8), 509–17.

McGinnis, John O. (2004), 'The political economy of international antitrust harmonization', in Richard A. Epstein and Michael S. Greve (eds), *Competition Laws in Conflict: Antitrust Jurisdiction in the Global Economy*, Washington, D.C.: AEI Press, pp. 126–51.

Meessen, Karl M. (1989), 'Competition of competition laws', *Northwestern Journal of International Law & Business*, **10** (1), 17–30.

Meessen, Karl M. (2000), 'Das Für und Wider eines Weltkartellrechts', *Wirtschaft und Wettbewerb*, **50** (1), 5–16.

Meiklejohn, Roderick (1999), 'An international competition policy: do we need it? Is it feasible?', *World Economy*, **22** (9), 1233–49.

Melamed, A. Douglas (1997), 'International antitrust in an age of international

deregulation', available at www.usdoj.gov/atr/public/speeches/1234.pdf, downloaded July 2005.
Messerlin, Patrick A. (1995), 'Should antidumping rules be replaced by national or international competition rules?', *World Competition*, **18** (3), 37–54.
Messner, Dirk (1997), *The Network Society*, London: Frank Cass.
Miller, Charles (2002), 'U.K. competition policy reform: impact of the latest proposals on process and influences', *European Competition Law Review*, **23** (2), 68–71.
Mitchell, Andrew D. (2001), 'Broadening the vision of trade liberalisation: international competition law and the WTO', *World Competition*, **24** (3), 343–65.
Monti, Mario (2004a), 'EU competition policy after May 2004', in Barry E. Hawk (ed.), *Annual Proceedings of the Fordham Corporate Law Institute Conference on International Antitrust Law & Policy*, New York: Juris, pp. 403–13.
Monti, Mario (2004b), 'Competition policy in a global economy', *International Finance*, **7** (3), 495–504.
Morgan, Eleanor J. (2001), 'A decade of EC merger control', *International Journal of the Economics of Business*, **8** (3), 451–73.
Morgan, Eleanor J. and McGuire, Steven (2004), 'Transatlantic divergence: GE-Honeywell and the EU's merger policy', *Journal of European Public Policy*, **11** (1), 39–56.
Möschel, Wernhard (2005), 'Wettbewerb der Wettbewerbsordnungen', *Wirtschaft und Wettbewerb*, **55** (6), 599–605.
Möschel, Wernhard (2006), 'Wettbewerbspolitik im Systemwettbewerb', in Wolf Schäfer (ed.), *Wirtschaftspolitik im Systemwettbewerb*, Berlin: Duncker & Humblot.
Mueller, Dennis C. (1996), 'Antimerger policy in the United States – history and lessons', *Empirica*, **23** (3), 229–53.
Müller, Margrit (1998), 'Fusionen und Übernahmen aus historischer Sicht', in Hans Siegwart and Gregory Neugebauer (eds), *Mega-Fusionen: Analysen, Kontroversen, Perspektiven*, Berne: Haupt, 63–81.
Müller, Markus (2005), 'The European Commission's decision against Microsoft: a violation of the antitrust agreements between the United States and the European Union?', *European Competition Law Review*, **26** (6), 309–15.
Nader, Ralph (1997), 'FTC approval of the Boeing–McDonnell merger: the collapse of antitrust enforcement', *Antitrust Law & Economics Review*, **27** (4), 105–10.
Nalebuff, Barry (2002), 'Bundling and the GE–Honeywell merger', Yale School of Management working paper 22.

Nelson, Richard R. and Rosenberg, Nathan (1993), 'Technical innovation and national systems', in Richard R. Nelson (ed.), *National Innovation Systems: A Comparative Analysis*, Oxford: Oxford University Press, pp. 1–18.

Neugebauer, Andrea (2004), *Internationale Wettbewerbspolitik: Eine Problemanalyse anhand der Theorie des institutionellen Wandels mit dem Schwerpunkt EU–USA*, Aachen, Germany: Shaker.

Neven, Damien J. (2006), 'Competition economics and antitrust in Europe', *Economic Policy*, **21** (48), 742–91.

Neven, Damien J. and Röller, Lars-Hendrik (2000), 'The allocation of jurisdiction in international antitrust', *European Economic Review*, **44** (4–6), 845–55.

Neven, Damien J. and Röller, Lars-Hendrik (2003), 'On the scope of conflict in international merger control', *Journal of Industry, Competition and Trade*, **3** (4), 235–49.

Neven, Damien J. and Röller, Lars-Hendrik (2005), 'Consumer surplus versus welfare standard in a political economy model of merger control', *International Journal of Industrial Organization*, **23** (9–10), 829–44.

Neven, Damien J. and Seabright, Paul (1997), 'Trade liberalization and the coordination of competition policy', in Leonard Waverman, William S. Comanor and Akira Goto (eds), *Competition Policy in the Global Economy*, London: Routledge, pp. 381–406.

Neyer, Jürgen (2003), 'Discourse and order in the EU: a deliberative approach to multi-level governance', *Journal of Common Market Studies*, **41** (4), 687–706.

Nicolaides, Phedon (1992), 'Competition among rules', *World Competition*, **16** (2), 113–21.

Nicolaides, Phedon (1994), 'Towards multilateral rules on competition', *World Competition*, **17** (3), 5–48.

Nicolaides, Phedon (1996), 'For a world competition authority', *Journal of World Trade*, **30** (4), 131–45.

Nicolaides, Phedon (2002), 'Development of a system for decentralised enforcement of EC competition policy', *Intereconomics*, **37** (1), 41–51.

Niosi, Jorge and Bellon, Bertrand (1996), 'The globalization of national innovation systems', in John de la Mothe and Gilles Paquet (eds), *Evolutionary Economics and the New International Political Economy*, London: Pinter, pp. 138–59.

Nörr, Knut W. and Waibel, Dieter (2001), 'Die Genfer Weltwirtschaftskonferenz von 1927 und die Frage der internationalen Kartelle', in Claus D. Classen et al. (eds), *In einem vereinten Europa dem Frieden der Welt dienen: Liber amicorum Thomas Oppermann*, Berlin: Duncker & Humblot, pp. 345–65.

North, Douglass C. (1990), *Institutions, Institutional Change and Economic Performance*, Cambridge: Cambridge University Press.

Nourry, Alex and Jung, Nelson (2006), 'EU state measures against foreign takeovers: "economic patriotism" in all but name', *Competition Policy International*, **2** (2), 98–127.

Oates, Wallace E. (1999), 'An essay on fiscal federalism', *Journal of Economic Literature*, **37** (3), 1120–49.

O'Brien, Anthony Patrick (1988), 'Factory size, economies of scale, and the great merger wave of 1898–1902', *Journal of Economic History*, **48** (3), 639–49.

O'Connor, Kevin J. (2002), 'Federalist lessons for international antitrust convergence', *Antitrust Law Journal*, **70** (2), 413–41.

Organisation for Economic Co-operation and Development (OECD) (2002), *Report on the Nature and Impact of Hard Core Cartels and Sanctions against Cartels under National Competition Law*, Paris: OECD.

Ogawa, Hikaru (2001), 'Allocation of authority under central grants', *Economics of Governance*, **2** (2), 159–72.

Olson, Mancur (1965), *The Logic of Collective Action*, Boston, MA: Harvard University Press.

Ordover, Janusz and Baumol, William J. (1988), 'Antitrust policy and high-technology industries', *Oxford Review of Economic Policy*, **4** (4), 13–34.

Ostrom, Vincent, Tiebout, Charles M. and Warren, Robert (1961), 'The organization of government in metropolitan areas: a theoretical inquiry', *American Political Science Review*, **55** (4), 831–42.

Owen, Bruce M. (2004), 'Imported antitrust', Stanford University Olin working paper no. 281, Stanford, CA.

Owen, Bruce M., Sun, Su and Zheng, Wentong (2005), 'Antitrust in China: the problem of incentive compatibility', *Journal of Competition Law and Economics*, **1** (1), 123–48.

Palim, Mark R. A. (1998), 'The worldwide growth of competition law: an empirical analysis', *Antitrust Bulletin*, **41** (3), 105–45.

Pangestu, Mari, Aswicahyono, Haryo, Anas, Titak and Ardyanto, Dionisius (2002), 'The evolution of competition policy in Indonesia', *Review of Industrial Organization*, **21** (2), 205–24.

Parisi, John J. (1999), 'Enforcement co-operation among antitrust authorities', *European Competition Law Review*, **20** (3), 133–42.

Parmentier, Lucie C. (2002), 'Reform of French competition law: adoption of a mandatory pre-merger control regime', *European Competition Law Review*, **23** (2), 99–106.

Patterson, Donna E. and Shapiro, Carl (2001), 'Transatlantic divergence in GE/Honeywell: causes and lessons', *Antitrust Magazine*, **16** (Fall), 18–22.

Pavic, Vladimir (2001), *Extraterritoriality in the Matters of Antitrust*, Fucecchio, Italy: European Press Academic Publishing.

Peiró, Francisco (2002), 'The vitamin cartels', *Competition Policy Newsletter*, **2002** (1), 30–4.

Peritz, Rudolph J. R. (2000), *Competition Policy in America: History, Rhetoric, Law*, Oxford: Oxford University Press.

Peters, Guy (1994), 'Agenda-setting in the European Community', *Journal of European Public Policy*, **1** (1), 9–26.

Petersmann, Ernst-Ulrich (1996), 'International competition rules for governments and for private business', *Journal of World Trade*, **30** (3), 5–35.

Petersmann, Ernst-Ulrich (1999), 'Competition-oriented reforms of the WTO world trade system: proposals and policy options', in Roger Zäch (ed.), *Towards WTO Competition Rules*, Berne: Staempfli/Kluwer, pp. 43–71.

Petersmann, Ernst-Ulrich (2004), 'WTO core principles and trade/competition roundtable', in Barry E. Hawk (ed.), *Annual Proceedings of the Fordham Corporate Law Institute Conference on International Antitrust Law & Policy*, New York: Juris, pp. 669–84.

Pflanz, Matthias and Caffarra, Christina (2002), 'The economics of GE/Honeywell', *European Competition Law Review*, **23** (3), 115–21.

Phillips, Bernard J. (1994), 'Comments on the draft international antitrust code', *Aussenwirtschaft*, 49 (2–3), 327–48.

Phillips, Bernard J. (2004), 'A competition framework for developing economies and technical assistance', in Tzong-Leh Hwang and Chiyuan Chen (eds), *The Future Development of Competition Framework*, The Hague: Kluwer, pp. 241–60.

Picot, Arnold, Ripperger, Tanja and Wolff, Birgitta (1996), 'The fading boundaries of the firm – the role of information and communication technology', *Journal of Institutional and Theoretical Economics*, **152** (1), 65–79.

Pierce, Richard J., Jr (2000), 'Antidumping law as a means of facilitating cartelization', *Antitrust Law Journal*, **67** (3), 725–44.

Pigou, Arthur Cecile (1920), *The Economics of Welfare*, London: Macmillan.

Piilola, Anu (2003), 'Assessing theories of global governance: a case study of international antitrust regulation', *Stanford Journal of International Law*, **39** (2), 207–51.

Pleatsikas, Christopher and Teece, David (2001), 'The analysis of market definition and market power in the context of rapid innovation', *International Journal of Industrial Organization*, **19** (5), 665–93.

Poapongsakorn, Nipon (2002), 'The new competition law in Thailand: lessons for institution building', *Review of Industrial Organization*, **21** (2), 185–204.

Podszun, Rupprecht (2003), *Internationales Kartellverfahrensrecht*, Berne: Staempfli.

Pons, Jean-François (1999), 'International co-operation in competition matters', in Roger Zäch (ed.), *Towards WTO Competition Rules*, Berne: Staempfli/Kluwer, pp. 195–204.

Popper, Karl R. (1959), *The Logic of Scientific Discovery*, New York: Basic Books.

Popper, Karl R. (1962), *Conjectures and Refutations: The Growth of Scientific Knowledge*, New York: Basic Books.

Popper, Karl R. (1972), *Objective Knowledge: An Evolutionary Approach*, London: Clarendon Press.

Posner, Richard A. (2001), 'Antitrust in the new economy', *Antitrust Law Journal* **68** (3), 925–43.

Posner, Richard A. (2004), 'Federalism and the enforcement of antitrust laws by state attorneys general', in Richard A. Epstein and Michael S. Greve (eds), *Competition Laws in Conflict: Antitrust Jurisdiction in the Global Economy*, Washington, D.C.: AEI Press, pp. 252–66.

Prahalad, Carl K. and Hamel, Gary (1990), 'The core competence of the corporation', *Harvard Business Review*, **68** (3), 79–91.

Pryor, Frederic L. (2001a), 'The worldwide merger wave, the new economy, and competition', in Lars-Hendrik Röller and Christian Wey (eds), *Die Soziale Marktwirtschaft in der neuen Weltwirtschaft*, Berlin: WZB, pp. 195–218.

Pryor, Frederic L. (2001b), 'Dimensions of the worldwide merger boom', *Journal of Economic Issues*, **35** (4), 825–40.

Qian, Yingyi and Weingast, Barry R. (1997), 'Federalism as a commitment to preserving market incentives', *Journal of Economic Perspectives*, **11** (4), 83–92.

Rahl, James A. (1970), *Common Market and American Antitrust: Overlap and Conflict*, New York: McGraw-Hill.

Raustiala, Kal (2002), 'The architecture of international cooperation: transgovernmental networks and the future of international law', *Virginia Journal of International Law*, **43** (1), 1–92.

Régent, Sabrina (2002), *The Open Method of Co-ordination: A Supranational Form of Governance?*, DP/137/2002, Geneva: International Institute for Labour Studies.

Reynolds, Robert J. and Ordover, Janusz A. (2002), 'Archimedean leveraging and the GE/Honeywell transaction', *Antitrust Law Journal*, **70** (1), 171–98.

Reynolds, Sarah J. (2004), 'Competition law and policy in Russia', *OECD Journal of Competition Law and Policy*, **6** (3), 7–86.

Ridyard, Derek (2004), *The Commission's New Horizontal Merger Guidelines – an Economic Commentary*, RBB Economics discussion paper, Brussels.

Riley, Alan (2003), 'EC antitrust modernisation: the Commission does very nicely – thank you! Part one: Regulation 1 and the notification burden, Part two: between the idea and the reality: decentralisation under Regulation 1', *European Competition Law Review*, **24** (11–12), 604–615, 657–72.

Rill, James F. and Wilson, Christine C. (2000), 'The A. C. Nielsen case', in Simon J. Evenett, Alexander Lehmann and Benn Steil (eds), *Antitrust Goes Global – What Future for Transatlantic Cooperation?*, Washington, D.C.: Brookings Institution Press, pp. 192–4.

Rill, James F., Wilson, Christine C. and Bauers, Sarah E. (2000), 'The Amadeus Global Travel Distribution case', in Simon J. Evenett, Alexander Lehmann and Benn Steil (eds), *Antitrust Goes Global – What Future for Transatlantic Cooperation?*, Washington, D.C.: Brookings Institution Press, pp. 195–8.

Rimoldi de Ladman, Eve (2002), 'MERCOSUR', in Jürgen Basedow (ed.), *Limits and Control of Competition with a View to International Harmonization*, The Hague: Kluwer, pp. 273–93.

Rishikesh, Deepa (1991), 'Extraterritoriality versus sovereignty in international antitrust jurisdiction', *World Competition*, **14** (3), 33–66.

Rodriguez, A. E. and Williams, Mark D. (1998), 'Recent decisions by the Venezuelan and Peruvian agencies: lessons for the export of antitrust', *Antitrust Bulletin*, **41** (3), 147–78.

Röller, Lars-Hendrik and De La Mano, Miguel (2006), 'The impact of the new substantive test in European merger control', *European Competition Journal*, **2** (1), 9–28.

Röller, Lars-Hendrik and Wey, Christian (2003), 'Merger control in the new economy', *Netnomics*, **5** (1), 5–20.

Romano, Roberta (1985), 'Law as a product', *Journal of Law, Economics, and Organization*, **1** (2), 225–83.

Rose, Jonathan (1994), 'State antitrust enforcement, mergers, and politics', *Wayne Law Review*, **41** (1), 71–134.

Rosenau, James and Czempiel, Ernst-Otto (eds) (1992), *Governance without Government: Order and Change in World Politics*, Cambridge: Cambridge University Press.

Rosenthal, Douglas E. and Nicolaides, Phedon (1997), 'Harmonizing antitrust: the less effective way to promote international competition', in Edward M. Graham and J. David Richardson (eds), *Global Competition Policy*, Washington, D.C.: Institute for International Economics, 355–83.

Ross, Thomas W. (1988), 'On the price effects of mergers with freer trade', in *International Journal of Industrial Organization*, **6** (2), 233–46.

Roth, Steffen and Voigtländer, Michael (2002), 'Die Ministererlaubnis für den Zusammenschluss von Unternehmen: ein Konflikt mit der Wettbewerbsordnung', *Zeitschrift für Wirtschaftspolitik*, **51** (2), 231–51.

Rowley, J. William, Wakil, Omar K. and Campbell, A. Neil (2000), 'Streamlining international merger control', in International Bar Association (ed.), *EC Merger Control: Ten Years On*, New York: IBA, pp. 15–37.

Safarian, A. Edward (1997), 'Trends in the forms of international business organization', in Leonard Waverman, William S. Comanor and Akira Goto (eds), *Competition Policy in the Global Economy*, London: Routledge, 40–65.

Sagers, Chris (2006), 'A critical introduction to the US Antitrust Modernization Comission', *Journal of Competition Law (Zeitschrift für Wettbewerbsrecht)*, **4** (3), 278–93.

Salmon, Pierre (1987), 'Decentralisation as an incentive scheme', *Oxford Review of Economic Policy*, **3** (2), 24–43.

Salmon, Pierre (2000), 'Vertical competition in a unitary state', in Gianluigi Galeotti, Pierre Salmon and Ronald Wintrobe (eds), *Competition and Structure: The Political Economy of Collective Decisions*, Cambridge: Cambridge University Press, 239–56.

Salop, Steven C. (2005), *What is the Real and Proper Antitrust Welfare Standard? The True Consumer Welfare Standard*, available at www.amc.gov/public_studies_fr28902/exclus_conduct_pdf/051104_Salop_Mergers.pdf.

Sanekata, Kenji and Wilks, Stephen (1996), 'The Fair Trade Commission and the enforcement of competition policy in Japan', in G. Bruce Doern and Stephen Wilks (eds), *Comparative Competition Policy: National Institutions in a Global Market*, Oxford: Clarendon Press, pp. 102–38.

Schaub, Alexander (2001), 'Konvergenz kartellrechtlicher Normen und deren Anwendung auf globale Sachverhalte', *Wirtschaft und Wettbewerb*, **51** (10), 928–33.

Schaub, Alexander (2002), 'Continued focus on reform: recent developments in EC Commission policy', in Barry E. Hawk (ed.), *International Antitrust and Policy: 28th Annual Proceedings of the Fordham Corporate Law Institute*, New York: Juris Publishing, pp. 31–51.

Schaub, Alexander (2005), 'The Commission's position within the network: the perspective of the Commission', in Claus-Dieter Ehlermann and Isabela Atanasiu (eds), *Constructing the EU Network of Competition Authorities*, Oxford: Hart Publishing.

Scherer, Frederic M. (1994), *Competition Policies for an Integrated World Economy*, Washington, D.C.: The Brookings Institution.

Schinkel, Maarten Pieter, Carree, Martin and Günster, Andrea (2004), 'European antitrust policy: an empirical analysis of Commission decisions and their appeal histories 1964–2001', EARIE conference paper, Berlin.

Schmidt, André (2001), 'Non-competition factors in the European competition policy: the necessity of institutional reforms', CeGe discussion paper 13, Göttingen.

Schmidt, Jessica (2004), 'The new ECMR: "significant impediment" or "significant improvement"?', *Common Market Law Review*, **41** (6), 1555–82.

Schmitz, Stefan (2002), 'How dare they? European merger control and the European Commission's blocking of the General Electric-Honeywell merger', *Journal of International Economic Law*, **23** (2), 325–83.

Schoenbaum, Thomas J. (1994), 'The international trade laws and the new protectionism – the need for a synthesis with antitrust', *North Carolina Journal of International Law and Commercial Regulation*, **19** (3), 393–436.

Schröter, Harm G. (1996), 'Cartelization and decartelization in Europe, 1870–1995: rise and decline of an economic institution', *Journal of European Economic History*, **25** (1), 129–53.

Schultz, Christian (2002), 'Export cartels and domestic markets', *Journal of Industry, Competition, and Trade*, **2** (3), 233–46.

Schwalbe, Ulrich (2005), 'Die Berücksichtigung von Effizienzgewinnen in der Fusionskontrolle: Ökonomische Aspekte', in Peter Oberender (ed.), *Effizienz und Wettbewerb*, Berlin: Duncker & Humblot, pp. 63–94.

Scott, Andrew (2006), 'National champions and the two-thirds rule in EC merger control', University of East Anglia Centre for Competition Policy working paper 06-6, Norwich.

Scott, Anthony (2000), 'Assigning powers over the Canadian environment', in Gianluigi Galeotti, Pierre Salmon and Ronald Wintrobe (eds), *Competition and Structure: The Political Economy of Collective Decisions*, Cambridge: Cambridge University Press, pp. 174–219.

Selten, Reinhard (1978), 'The chain-store paradox', *Theory and Decision*, **9** (2), 127–59.

Shapiro, Carl (2002), 'Competition policy and innovation', OECD STI working paper 2002/11, Paris.

Shenefield, John H. (2004), 'Coherence or confusion: the future of the global antitrust conversation', *Antitrust Bulletin*, **49** (2), 385–434.

Singh, Shrawan Kumar (2003), 'Competition policy in India', in Raj Kumar Jen (ed.), *Economic Reforms and Development*, New Delhi: Deep & Deep, pp. 297–312.

Sinn, Hans-Werner (1990), 'The limits to competition between economic regimes', *Empirica*, **17** (1), 3–14.

Sinn, Hans-Werner (1999), 'The competition between competition rules', CESifo working paper no. 192, Munich.

Sinn, Stefan (1992), 'The taming of Leviathan: competition among governments', *Constitutional Political Economy*, **3** (2), 177–96.

Slaughter, Anne-Marie (2000), 'Governing the global economy through government networks', in Michael Byers (ed.), *The Role of Law in International Politics: Essays in International Relations and International Law*, Oxford: Oxford University Press, pp. 177–205.

Slot, Piet Jan (2002), 'Is decentralization of competition law enforcement dangerous? Drawing lessons from the US experience', in Barry E. Hawk (ed.), *Annual Proceedings of the Fordham Corporate Law Institute Conference on International Antitrust Law & Policy*, New York: Juris, pp. 101–14.

Soames, Trevor and Maudhuit, Sylvie (2005), 'Changes in EU merger control', *European Competition Law Review*, **26** (1), 57–64.

Smets, Hilde and Van Cayseele, Patrick (1995), 'Competing merger policies in a common agency framework', *International Review of Law and Economics*, **15** (4), 425–41.

Smits, René (2005), 'The European competition network: selected aspects', *Legal Issues of European Integration*, **32** (6), 175–92.

Stephan, Paul B. (2000), 'Regulatory cooperation and competition: the search for virtue', in George A. Bermann, Matthias Herdegen and Peter L. Lindseth (eds), *Transatlantic Regulatory Cooperation: Legal Problems and Political Prospects*, Oxford: Oxford University Press, pp. 167–202.

Stephan, Paul B. (2004), 'Against international cooperation', in Richard A. Epstein and Michael S. Greve (eds), *Competition Laws in Conflict: Antitrust Jurisdiction in the Global Economy*, Washington, D.C.: AEI Press, pp. 66–98.

Stevenson, Cliff and Filippi, Ilaria (2004), 'How does the European Commission's new chief economist think?', *European Competition Law Review*, **25** (2), 122–5.

Stewart, Taimoon (2004), 'The fate of competition policy in Cancun: politics or substance?', *Legal Issues of Economic Integration*, **31** (1), 7–11.

Stierle, Michael H. (1999, ed.), *Globalisation: Effects on Enterprises, Employment and Government*, Berlin: VWF.

Stiglitz, Joseph E. (2002), *Globalization and Its Discontents*, New York: Norton.

Stiglitz, Joseph E. and Orszag, Peter R. (2004), *Brief of Amici Curiae in Support of Respondents, No. 03-724*, Washington, D.C.: Supreme Court of the United States.

Stockmann, Kurt (2001), 'Principles of German competition law under the 6th Act to Amend the Act Against Restraints of Competition (ARC)', in Yang-Ching Chao, Gee San, Changfa Lo and Jiming Ho (eds), *International and Comparative Competition Law and Policies*, The Hague: Kluwer, pp. 143–62.

Stockmann, Kurt (2003), 'Optimising case allocation in the European Union and dealing with multijurisdictional filings', in Götz Drauz and Michael Reynolds (eds), *EC Merger Control: A Major Reform in Progress*, London: Richmond, pp. 37–42.

Straw, Robert F. (1997), *International Competition Rules? An Economic Analysis*, Bamberg, Germany: Difo.

Streit, Manfred E. and Wohlgemuth, Michael (1999, eds.), *Systemwettbewerb als Herausforderung an Politik und Theorie*, Baden-Baden, Germany: Nomos.

Sullivan, Lawrence A. and Grimes, Warren S. (2000), *The Law of Antitrust: An Integrated Handbook*, St. Paul, MN: West Group.

Suzuki, Kenji (2002), *Competition Law Reform in Britain and Japan: Comparative Analysis of Policy Networks*, London: Routledge.

Swaine, Edward T. (2001), 'The local law of global antitrust', *William and Mary Law Review*, **43** (2), 627–774.

Swaine, Edward T. (2003), 'Against principled antitrust', *Virginia Journal of International Law*, **43** (4), 959–1002.

Sykes, Alan O. (1999), 'Externalities in open economy antitrust and their implications for international competition policy', *Harvard Journal of Law & Public Policy*, **23** (1), 89–96.

Tacke, Alfred (2002), 'Statement on the E.ON/Ruhrgas merger', in *Financial Times Deutschland Online*, 19 September 2002, available at www.ftd.de/ub/di/1032245712795.html?nv=s.

Tarullo, Daniel K. (2000), 'Norms and institutions in global competition policy', *American Journal of International Law*, **94** (3), 478–504.

Tavares de Araujo, José and Tineo, Luis (1998), 'Harmonization of competition policies among Mercosur countries', *Antitrust Bulletin*, **41** (3), 45–70.

Tay, Abigail and Willmann, Gerald (2005), 'Why (no) global competition policy is a tough choice', *Quarterly Review of Economics and Finance*, **45** (2–3), 312–24.

Temple Lang, John (1999), 'Decentralised application of community competition law', *World Competition*, **22** (4), 3–20.

Tharakan, P.K.M., Vermulst, Edwin and Tharakan, Joe (1998), 'Interface between anti-dumping policy and competition policy', *World Economy*, **21** (8), 1035–60.

Timberg, Sigmund (1973), 'An international antitrust convention: a proposal to harmonize conflicting national policies toward the multi-national corporation', *Journal of International Law and Economics*, **8** (2), 157–84.

Tirole, Jean (1994), 'The internal organization of government', *Oxford Economic Papers*, **46** (1), 1–29.

Todino, Mario (2003), 'International competition network: the state of play after Naples', *World Competition*, **26** (2), 283–302.

Torremans, Paul (1996), 'Extraterritorial application of E.C. and U.S. competition law', *European Law Review*, **21**, 280–93.

Trebilcock, Michael J. and Howse, Robert (1998), 'Trade liberalization and regulatory diversity: reconciling competitive markets with competitive politics', *European Journal of Law and Economics*, **6** (1), 5–37.

Trebilcock, Michael J. and Iacobucci, Edward (2002), 'Designing competition law institutions', *World Competition*, **25** (3), 361–94.
Trebilcock, Michael J. and Iacobucci, Edward (2004), 'National treatment and extraterritoriality: defining the domains of trade and antitrust policy', in Richard A. Epstein and Michael S. Greve (eds), *Competition Laws in Conflict: Antitrust Jurisdiction in the Global Economy*, Washington, D.C.: AEI Press, pp. 152–76.
Ullrich, Hanns (1998), 'International harmonisation of competition law: making diversity a workable concept', in Hanns Ullrich (ed.), *Comparative Competition Law: Approaching an International System of Antitrust Law*, Baden-Baden, Germany: Nomos, pp. 43–74.
Van den Bergh, Roger (1996), 'Economic criteria for applying the subsidiarity principle in the European community: the case of competition policy', *International Review of Law and Economics*, **16** (3), 363–83.
Van den Bergh, Roger (2000), 'Towards an institutional legal framework for regulatory competition in Europe', *Kyklos*, **53** (4), 435–66.
Van den Bergh, Roger and Camesasca, Peter D. (2001), *European Competition Law and Economics: A Comparative Perspective*, Antwerp: Insertia.
Van Gerven, Walter (2005), 'Private enforcement of EC competition rules', paper presented at the IBA Conference on Antitrust Reform in Europe: A Year in Practice, 10-11 March, Brussels.
Van Gerwen, Gerwin (2003), 'Optimising case allocation in the European Union and dealing with multijurisdictional filings', in Götz Drauz and Michael Reynolds (eds), *EC Merger Control: A Major Reform in Progress*, London: Richmond, pp. 49–67.
Vanberg, Viktor (1994), *Rules and Choice in Economics*, London: Routledge.
Vanberg, Viktor (2000), 'Economic constitutions, protectionism, and competition among jurisdictions', in Gianluigi Galeotti, Pierre Salmon and Ronald Wintrobe (eds), *Competition and Structure: The Political Economy of Collective Decisions*, Cambridge: Cambridge University Press, pp. 364–85.
Vanberg, Viktor (2001), 'Constitutional order and economic evolution: competitive and protectionist interests in democratic society', in Ram Mudambi, Pietro Navarra and Giuseppe Sobbrio (eds), *Rules and Reason*, Cambridge: Cambridge University Press, pp. 33–55.
Vanberg, Viktor and Kerber, Wolfgang (1994), 'Institutional cCompetition among jurisdictions: an evolutionary approach', *Constitutional Political Economy*, **5** (2), 193–219.
Vautier, Kerrin M. (2001), 'International approaches to competition laws: government cooperation for business competition', in Yang-Ching Chao, Gee San, Changfa Lo and Jiming Ho (eds), *International and Comparative Competition Law and Policies*, The Hague: Kluwer, pp. 187–216.
Vedder, Hans (2004), 'Spontaneous harmonisation of national (competition)

laws in the wake of the modernisation of EC competition law', *Competition Law Review*, **1** (1), 5–21.
Veljanovski, Cento G. (2004), 'EC merger policy after GE/Honeywell and Airtours', in *Antitrust Bulletin*, **49** (1), 153–93.
Venit, James S. (2003), 'Brave new world: the modernization and decentralization of enforcement under Articles 81 and 82 of the EC Treaty', *Common Market Law Review*, **40** (3), 545–80.
Victor, Paul A. (1992), 'Export cartels – an idea whose time has passed', *Antitrust Law Journal*, **60** (2), 571–81.
Vihanto, Martti (1992), 'Competition between local governments as a discovery procedure', *Journal of Institutional and Theoretical Economics*, **148** (3), 411–36.
Virtanen, Martti (2004), 'Perspectives on the modernized implementation of the rules on competition laid down in Articles 81 and 82 of the EC Treaty', paper presented at the Conference on Competition, Law and Economics, August 2004, Tartu, Estonia.
Vogelaar, Theo W. (1980), 'The OECD guidelines', in Norbert Horn (ed.), *Legal Problems of Codes of Conduct for Multinational Enterprises*, Deventer, Netherlands: Kluwer, pp. 127–39.
Voigt, Stefan and Schmidt, André (2004a), 'Switching to substantial impediments of competition (SIC) can have substantial costs', *European Competition Law Review*, **25** (9), 580–86.
Voigt, Stefan and Schmidt, André (2004b), 'The Commission's guidelines on horizontal mergers: improvement or deterioration?', *Common Market Law Review*, **41** (6), 1583–94.
Voigt, Stefan and Schmidt, André (2005), *Making European Merger Policy More Predictable*, Berlin: Springer.
Von Bogdandy, Armin and Bast, Jürgen (2002), 'The European Union's vertical order of competences: the current law and proposals for its reform', *Common Market Law Review*, **39** (2), 227–68.
Weber Waller, Spencer (2003), 'Public choice theory and the international harmonization of antitrust law', *Antitrust Bulletin*, **48** (2), 427–38.
Wegner, Gerhard (1996), *Wirtschaftspolitik zwischen Selbst- und Fremdsteuerung*, Baden-Baden, Germany: Nomos.
Wegner, Gerhard (1997), 'Economic policy from an evolutionary perspective – a new approach', *Journal of Institutional and Theoretical Economics*, **153** (3), 485–509.
Wegner, Gerhard (2003), 'Evolutionary markets and the design of institutional policy', in Pavel Pelikan and Gerhard Wegner (eds), *The Evolutionary Analysis of Economic Policy*, Cheltenham, UK and Northampton, MA, USA: Edward Elgar, pp. 46–66.
Weingast, Barry R. (1995), 'The economic role of political institutions:

market-preserving federalism and economic development', *Journal of Law, Economics, and Organization*, **11** (1), 1–31.

Weinrauch, Roland (2004), *Competition Law in the WTO*, Graz, Austria: NWV.

Weinstein, Michael M. (2005, ed.), *Globalization: What's New?*, New York: Columbia University Press.

Weizsäcker, Carl Christian von (1998), 'Transnationale Fusionen aus der Sicht des Wettbewerbspolitikers', *Wirtschaftsdienst*, **78** (7), 386–89.

Wells, Wyatt (2002), *Antitrust and the Formation of the Postwar World*, New York: Columbia University Press.

Werden, Gregory J. (2004), 'Economic evidence on the existence of collusion: Reconciling antitrust law with oligopoly theory', *Antitrust Law Journal*, **71** (2), 719–800.

Werden, Gregory J. and Froeb, Luke M. (1993), 'Correlation, causality, and all that jazz: the inherent shortcomings of price tests for antitrust market delineation', *Review of Industrial Organization*, **8** (3), 329–53.

Whish, Richard and Wood, Diane P. (1994), *Merger Cases in the Real World: A Study of Merger Control Procedures*, Paris: OECD.

Wigger, Angela (2004a), 'The European Commission, a norm entrepreneur in global competition governance?', ECPR Joint Sessions discussion paper, Uppsala, Sweden.

Wigger, Angela (2004b), 'Revisiting the European competition reform: the toll of private self-enforcement', Free University of Amsterdam working papers political science no. 2004/07, Amsterdam.

Wigger, Angela (2006), 'Towards a market-based approach: the privatization and micro-economization of EU antitrust law enforcement', Amsterdam Research Centre for Corporate Governance Regulation working paper.

Wilber, Charles K. (2003), 'Ethics in economic theory', *Post-Autistic Economics Review*, **20** (1), available at www.paecon.net/PAEReview/issue20/wilber20.htm.

Wilks, Stephen (2005), 'Agency escape: decentralisation or dominance of the European Commission in the modernization of competition policy?', *Governance*, **18** (3), 431–52.

Williams, Mark (2004), 'Competition law in Thailand: seeds of success or fated to fail?', *World Competition*, **27** (3), 459–94.

Williams, Mark (2005), *Competition Policy and Law in China, Hong Kong and Taiwan*, Cambridge: Cambridge University Press.

Wils, Wouter P. J. (2002), *The Optimal Enforcement of EC Antitrust Law*, Dordrecht, Netherlands: Kluwer.

Wils, Wouter P. J. (2003a), 'The principle of *Ne Bis in Idem* in EC antitrust enforcement: a legal and economic analysis', *World Competition*, **26** (2), 131–48.

Wils, Wouter P. J. (2003b), 'Should private enforcement be encouraged in Europe?', *World Competition*, **26** (3), 473–88.
Wils, Wouter P. J. (2004), 'European competition law and policy: the reform of competition law enforcement – will it work?', in Dermot Cahill (ed.), *The Modernisation of EU Competition Law Enforcement in the European Union*, Cambridge: Cambridge University Press, pp. 661–736.
Wilson, Joseph (2003), *Globalization and the Limits of National Merger Control Laws*, The Hague: Kluwer.
Wins, Henning (2000), *Eine internationale Wettbewerbsordnung als Ergänzung zum GATT*, Baden-Baden, Germany: Nomos.
Winslow, Walter T. (2001), 'OECD programmes for international responses to global competition issues', in Yang-Ching Chao, Gee San, Changfa Lo and Jiming Ho (eds), *International and Comparative Competition Law and Policies*, The Hague: Kluwer, pp. 235–48.
Wood, Diane P. (1992), 'The impossible dream: real international antitrust', *University of Chicago Legal Forum*, **1992** (1), 277–97.
Wood, Diane P. (2003a), 'Soft harmonization among competition laws: track record and prospects', *Antitrust Bulletin*, **48** (2), 305–18.
Wood, Diane P. (2003b), 'International law and federalism: what is the reach of regulation', *Harvard Journal of Law & Public Policy*, **23** (1), 97–110.
Wood, Diane P. (2004), 'Cooperation and convergence in international antitrust: why the light is still yellow', in Richard A. Epstein and Michael S. Greve (eds), *Competition Laws in Conflict: Antitrust Jurisdiction in the Global Economy*, Washington, D.C.: AEI Press, pp. 177–88.
Woolcock, Stephen (2003), 'The Singapore issues in Cancún: a failed negotiation ploy or a litmus test for global governance?', *Intereconomics*, **38** (5), 249–55.
Worm, Heike (2004), *Grundlagen eines dezentralen Systems internationaler Wettbewerbspolitik*, Hamburg: Kovač.
WTO (2004a), 'Doha development agenda: Doha work programme: the July 2004 package', available at www.wto.org/english/tratop_e/dda_e/dda_package_july04_e.htm.
WTO (2004b), 'Doha work programme: decision adopted by the General Council on 1 August 2004', available at www.wto.org/english/tratop_e/dda_e/ddadraft_31jul04_e.pdf.
Wurmnest, Wolfgang (2005), 'Wettbewerbspolitik, Industriepolitik und der "more economic approach"', *Journal of Competition Law (Zeitschrift für Wettbewerbsrecht)*, **3** (1), 111–20.
Young, Oran R. (1999), *Governance in World Affairs*, Ithaca, NY: Cornell University Press.
Zäch, Roger (1998), 'International cooperation between antitrust enforcement agencies: a view from a small country', in Hanns Ullrich (ed.),

Comparative Competition Law: Approaching an International System of Antitrust Law, Baden-Baden, Germany: Nomos, pp. 257–65.

Zahariadis, Nikolaos (2004), 'European markets and national regulation: conflict and cooperation in British competition policy', *Journal of Public Policy*, **24** (1), 49–73.

Zanettin, Bruno (2002), *Cooperation Between Antitrust Agencies at the International Level*, Oxford: Hart Publishing.

Zimmer, Daniel (2004), 'Significant impediment to effective competition', *Journal of Competition Law (Zeitschrift für Wettbewerbsrecht)*, **2** (2), 250–67.

Zimmerman, David A. (1999), 'Why state attorneys general should have a limited role in enforcing the federal antitrust law of mergers', *Emory Law Journal*, **48** (2), 337–66.

Index